VOYAGES IN ENGLISH

VOYAGES in English

Carolyn Marie Dimick

General Editor

Maria Byers
Carolyn Marie Dimick
Joan I. Rychalsky

Authors

Loyola University Press ★ Chicago

CONTRIBUTORS   Elaine Lauble
                Midge Stocker

PROJECT EDITORS Deborah Astudillo
                Janet Battiste

DESIGNER   William A. Seabright

ISBN 0-8294-0561-5 Teacher's Edition

ISBN 0-8294-0560-7

©1987 Loyola University Press
3441 N. Ashland Ave.   Chicago, IL 60657

Preface

In every grade, language development challenges teachers and students to explore their world through the spoken and the written word. Language in all its aspects is essential to the development of the individual on a personal as well as a social level. Language is a vehicle for expressing wonder and delight, a tool for exchanging ideas, a medium for transmitting information, and a resource for bridging the differences among peoples of other cultures. These are the ultimate goals of language and the underlying philosophy of *Voyages in English*.

The revised *Voyages in English* is designed to include the major areas of the language arts curriculum: writing, grammar, correct usage, mechanics, dictionary and library skills, speaking and listening skills, and literature. These areas should not be considered separate and distinct from one another. For purposes of instruction, the skills are often taught in isolation, but the challenge of the teacher is to see that the areas are integrated and that the students begin to perceive the parts of the language arts curriculum as a whole. Finally, students should view the entire language arts program as an essential tool for building competency and success in other curriculum areas.

Before teaching the material contained in *Voyages in English,* the teacher should become acquainted with the format of the book. There are two distinct sections in the textbook: writing and grammar. Neither section is meant to be taught in its entirety at one time. Familiarity with the chapters in both areas will enable the teacher to move with ease between the two sections. For example, when working with the students in the proofreading stage of the writing process, the teacher will discover areas of weakness in correct usage and mechanics. At this point, it is recommended that the teacher turn to the lesson in the grammar section that corresponds to that particular area of weakness and teach the concept within the context of the writing activity. When teaching an area of grammar such as adjectives, the lessons on word substitution, sentence expansion, or descriptive writing provide an effective way of integrating grammar and writing. The correlations are many, and at all times the instructional goal should be integration, not isolation.

Developing good writing skills is essential at every grade level. The teacher should read the section entitled "The Writing Process" and become familiar with the components of the writing process. Students enjoy writing and should be engaged in the process as frequently as possible. **MORE TO EXPLORE** (grades 7–8) and **WRITE AWAY!** (grades 3–6) are an extension of the activities in each writing lesson. They may or may not be completed depending upon student ability to handle the extra material. Some students will need the challenge, others will not.

SHARPENING YOUR SKILLS (grades 7–8) and **PRACTICE POWER** (grades 3–6) provide a writing or skill-extension activity following each grammar lesson. In some cases, it is simply writing sentences or completing a review exercise; in others, it involves writing a brief paragraph or poem. With teacher assistance, the students should be led to realize the importance of integrating grammar, correct usage, and mechanics with writing skills.

The **CHAPTER CHALLENGE** at the end of each grammar chapter is a paragraph designed to incorporate all the skills the students have learned in the chapter. Identification of various grammatical structures is more difficult in paragraph form than in isolated sentences. In most cases, it should be teacher directed and not used as a testing tool.

The full page **ILLUSTRATION** that opens each chapter has a lead question that is designed to be a springboard for class discussion. Many of the illustrations have a connection with the chapter that follows, but some may be more appropriately used with other text material. The ideas explored through the illustrations can often become the subject of a poem or composition; therefore, having an overview of all the illustrations in the text is helpful so that at *anytime* throughout the year *any* photograph or art reproduction can be used as a basis for a writing activity. Although poems and compositions are encouraged, in simpler ways students can write different kinds of sentences about the picture: declarative, interrogative, etc. A simple sentence about the illustration can be expanded by words, phrases, or clauses, all of which could include various types of figurative language or, in the upper grades, the use of verbals.

WRITING CORNER (grades 6–7) provides more activities in the area of writing. It moves away from the structure presented in the writing chapters, and permits the students to explore other creative writing styles. In a few instances, these activities deal with research skills and with techniques helpful in practical classroom writing.

The selections from literature in **CREATIVE SPACE** are meant to be enjoyed first and then analyzed. For most students, they open up new writing possibilities; therefore, using literature as a model for students' original work is to be encouraged. Likewise, teachers creating original pieces of writing along with the students is a way of helping them see the challenge, effort, and satisfaction involved in the writing process.

The **TEACHER'S GUIDE** sets the objectives and presents directives for initiating each lesson. The teacher's guide in part 1 (grades 5–8) includes an **ENRICHMENT** section that provides a challenge for the better students. This should be used at the discretion of the teacher. The teacher's guide in part 2 contains an extended application for many of the exercises. This will aid the teacher in making as thorough use of the exercises as possible. The lessons within the chapters are not necessarily meant to be taught in one day. Many will require two or three days of instruction. The pacing of this instruction depends upon class as well as individual needs.

It is hoped that *Voyages in English* will provide students with a thorough knowledge of the English language and lead them to a greater appreciation for the gift that language is. A textbook can only accomplish so much, but coupled with a teacher's own love of language and attentiveness to its many nuances and subtleties, it can be a vehicle for growth and development in all areas of the curriculum.

The Writing Process

Exploring and discovering meaning through written language should be a part of every child's educational experience. Schools should place a high priority on developing writing skills, allowing teachers and students the freedom and time to foster the writing process within the curriculum. When the process is begun in the early school years, children have no fear or anxiety about writing. Instead, they often find it an exhilarating and happy experience. There is a sense of satisfaction in knowing a piece is well-written and has expressed exactly what the author intended to say.

Although much research is yet to be done regarding the composing or writing process, most authorities would agree that the process can be separated into four major divisions: prewriting, writing or drafting, revision, and editing. No division is isolated from the other. Writing is a cyclic process and thus implies that all divisions overlap, allowing the writer to wander in and out of all stages during the writing process.

The **PREWRITING** stage is the preliminary activity that goes on before the writer begins an actual draft. Observing, discussing, note-taking, reading, journaling, interviewing, brainstorming, imagining, and remembering are a few of the pre-draft experiences. In this stage, the writer zeros in on a subject, narrows it, and makes decisions about audience and purpose. For whom is the composition being written? Why is it being written? What form should the writing take? This stage is where a great deal of enthusiasm is generated. Interaction between student and teacher helps attest to the value of what the student is going to write. Students should be encouraged to share their ideas so that they can hear their thoughts, which ultimately lead them to be selective about their choice of material, make associations, and evaluate their information.

The student writer next moves into the **WRITING** stage, which is the creation of a first draft. Getting the information down on paper is the essential part of this stage. The writer should be encouraged to keep the ideas flowing without worrying about sentence structure or correct usage. There should be an effort to complete the piece from beginning to end at one sitting. Keeping up the momentum is important so that all ideas are on paper. The first draft is the visible form of what went on in the prewriting stage. It allows the writer to see what shape the work is taking. Students in this stage should be encouraged to write without making corrections, and to write on every other line so as to provide room for revision.

One of the most difficult, yet most vital areas, is **REVISION**. Here the student takes time to look at the work again and again. First drafts are rarely well-organized or cohesive. Vocabulary needs development, sentences need variety, and ideas need clarification. All this takes more than one revision, and students should be encouraged to write as many drafts as necessary.

It is at this stage of the writing process that teacher/student interaction is paramount. When trust has been built up, students will readily share their work. The teacher can act as a guide by asking essential questions: What are you writing about? Is there more you can say about your subject? Have you said it the best way you can? What is the part you like best? least? Deleting, adding, and rearranging ideas are essential to the revision process.

Students should be taught to look for specific things in examining their own work: Is the beginning sentence effective? clever? Is there a sentence that states the topic? Is there enough sentence variety? Are strong action verbs used? Does the ending sentence draw everything to a close? Since peer response is important, students should ask these questions when critiquing one another's work as well. The more feedback from students and teacher, the better the revision will be. Language at this point can be exciting and challenging. Trying to get the right word in the right place at the right time is the challenge of revision.

EDITING is the final stage before publication. It is here that students must look to the correctness of their piece. Punctuation, spelling, capitalization, and correct usage are important if the audience is to believe what the author is saying. All students should be taught the importance of proofreading and should be encouraged to do much of it on their own. But frequently the author gets caught up in content (which is not the domain of editing) instead of being attentive to mechanical details. To avoid this, it is often helpful to have another student edit the work. Some expert editors can be assigned in the classroom to help students who have difficulty in this area. The teacher can also control the editing process by naming the specific areas to be edited, making certain that all students are checking out four or five areas of concern.

It is important to note again that writers wander in and out of the various stages. Many times, one begins to revise even while writing a first draft. Frequently, it is necessary to return to a prewriting stage in order to gather more information or to think through an idea. Bits of editing are done while revising. No student should be locked into writing stage by stage.

Finally, students are ready to publish their work. All work should be as perfect as possible for publication. The audience has the right to demand that finished pieces be comprehensible and stylistically correct. But all publication is not meant for the teacher. Parents, principals, other students, and the community are all appropriate audiences. If the audience receives the work well, then the student has learned much from becoming totally involved in the process of writing. Student joy is teacher joy. The satisfaction that comes from a good piece of writing is immeasurable. The hard work is well worth the effort!

Contents

Part II   Grammar, Correct Usage, Mechanics

Exploring Our Language

Part I

Written and Oral Communication

Chapter 1

Building the Paragraph

Lesson 1 Selecting and Narrowing a Topic

A topic is the idea about which a composition or paragraph is written.

Sometimes when you are asked to write for a class, you are given a topic. Other times you have to choose one yourself. In either case, you must think about what you are going to write before you begin writing.

Suppose you have been assigned "winter sports" as a topic. You know that is too big a topic to write about in a paragraph, so you need to narrow it down. The first thing you should do is brainstorm for as many ideas as you can think of that are related to winter sports. Your thoughts on paper might look like this:

It takes talent, desire, and discipline to become a proficient skater. How would these same qualities help you become a proficient writer?

Next, consider your audience. For whom are you writing? Your teacher? Other students? Your friends? Your parents? What kind of topics would appeal to your audience? Would these topics also appeal to you? Remember that you write best when you write about things that interest you. Sometimes these are things you read about and sometimes they are part of your life: people you know, places you have been, things you have done. Your own life experience is often your best source.

After looking over the ideas you jotted down in relation to winter sports, you might decide that skating would interest you and your audience the most. "Skating," therefore, becomes your *narrowed topic*. Now you have to decide what you would like to say about skating. You remember how many funny things happened when you first learned to skate, and you decide to tell about those. How you learned to skate becomes the *specific idea* about which you will write.

Your thinking process as you narrowed your topic to one specific idea is shown below.

> *Topic*: Winter sports
> *Narrowed topic*: Skating
> *Specific idea*: How I learned to skate

Activity A

Consider the following list of topics. Suggest a narrowed topic and a specific idea for each blank space.

Topic	Narrowed Topic	Specific Idea
Collecting	Baseball cards	A rare baseball card
Vacations	Drama camp	_____
Television	_____	_____
Wild animals	_____	_____
Board games	_____	_____
France	_____	_____
Mysteries	_____	_____
Anger	_____	_____
Saturdays	_____	_____
Music	_____	_____

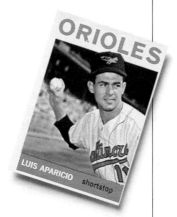

Activity B

Think about the levels of topics again. This time suggest ideas to fit under the headings where there are blank spaces.

Topic	Narrowed Topic	Specific Idea
Parks	Central Park	Our Sundays in Central Park
Spring	April rain	An unexpected drenching
Carnivals	Rides	Why I'll never ride the Thriller again
Basketball	Boston Celtics	Why I'm a Celtics fan
Summer sports	Sailing	My first sailboat ride
Birds	Robins	Watching our baby robins grow
Airplanes	Overseas flights	Our long flight to Peru
Outdoor sports	Fishing trips	How Mom caught the bass
Tall buildings	Sears Tower	Going to the top of the Sears Tower
Transportation	Subways	Rush hour on the subway

Activity C

This is a list of broad topics. Take them through the stages of narrowing to reach an idea limited enough for a paragraph.

reading   weather
space   politics
love   family
school   food
cars   plants

More to Explore

Choose three topics of your own. Narrow them to specific ideas.

ACTIVITY B: This activity continues to help the students understand the narrowing process. They should begin to realize that it is possible to go from the topic to the specific idea without giving a narrowed topic. The narrowing process is often done automatically. The answers given are suggestions only. Accept any appropriate responses.

ACTIVITY C: Have the students give three steps in the narrowing of each topic. Compare at least two students' narrowing processes for each topic. Note the similarities and differences.

MORE TO EXPLORE: Suggest that the students brainstorm for a list of relevant topics. Narrow down one or two at the chalkboard and then have them choose three (the same as or different from those on the chalkboard) to narrow on their own. These topics might be kept in a notebook for future development.

ENRICHMENT
Put the following specific ideas on the chalkboard. See if the students can reverse the narrowing process in three or four steps.

How to study for a test

Why the TV show _____ is so popular

How to overcome the fear of snakes

My first glimpse of the moon from outer space

A long-remembered Saturday

THE STUDENTS SHOULD LEARN
—the purpose of a topic sentence
—how to write a topic sentence

Lesson 2 Writing a Topic Sentence

A topic sentence states the main idea of a paragraph.

TEACHING THE LESSON
Explain that topic sentences are road maps to the paragraph—telling where the paragraph is actually headed. Have the students read the opening paragraph and determine which sentence is the topic sentence. The students would be correct in identifying sentence 1, sentence 2, or both as the topic sentences. Sentence 2, however, is a better choice since it is more specific. Have them explain the reason for their choice. Next, they should read the three topic sentences provided. There should be little difficulty determining the possible content of each paragraph.

The topic sentence is the most important sentence in the paragraph. It identifies the topic and tells the reader what kind of information to expect. The topic sentence tells the reader what the paragraph is about. Read the following paragraph and tell what you think is the topic sentence.

What would the indoors be like without windows? Whether they are oblong, square, or circular, as in the porthole variety on ships, to me windows seem indispensable. Windows join the outdoors with the indoors. For students working slavishly in classrooms, windows are reminders that life after school does exist. For children home sick in bed, windows work healing miracles. They simply point invitingly to sunshine or snowflakes. For older people confined to homes or apartments, windows provide a daily morale-building view of seasonal beauty or busy neighborhood activity. Some modern architects and engineers think that buildings without windows would have more efficient air-conditioning and heating. In the name of all the window-watchers in the world, I protest!

Now read the following topic sentences and tell what you think will be in each paragraph.
1. Running in the track meet was the greatest moment of my life.
2. My carelessness in leaving my gerbils' cage open had disastrous results!
3. Karen and Dom enthusiastically planned an exciting end-of-the-year party.

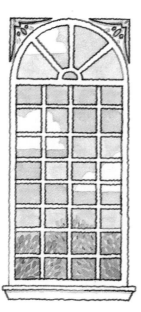

Activity A

Read the following topic sentences. Identify the topic and specific idea of each. The first one is done for you.

1. A number of weather conditions result in the formation of fog—a "cloud" near the ground.

   Topic: Fog

   Specific idea: The causes of fog

2. When I baked my first pie, it was a disaster.
3. Good composition requires original thought.
4. The harbor was alive with ships from every part of the world.
5. The center of activity in our home is the small but cheerful kitchen.

ACTIVITY A: Carefully study the example. Make sure the students understand how the *topic* and *specific idea* were drawn from the topic sentence. Do the second sentence with the class and then have them work independently on the remaining ones. All answers from the students should be similar.

Activity B

Write a topic sentence for each specific idea.

Topic	Specific Idea
Moving	Moving to this town
Swimming	Swimming at the YMCA
Trees	The old oak tree in front of the school
Boats	Barges on the Mississippi
Fashion	Popular fashion trends among teenagers

ACTIVITY B: Compare as many sentences as possible. The students should be able to tell some ideas that the paragraph would contain.

ACTIVITY C: This activity provides additional practice in analyzing the relationship between topics, specific ideas, and topic sentences. Discuss student responses to all four paragraphs.

ANSWERS

The following are suggestions only. Accept any appropriate answers.

1. *Topic sentence*: You may escape the icy clutches of winter if you become experienced in building a furnace fire.

   Topic: Ways of keeping warm in winter

   Specific idea: How to build a furnace fire

Activity C

Find the topic sentence in paragraphs 1 and 2. Based on that sentence, name the topic and the specific idea of the paragraph.

1

You may escape the icy clutches of winter if you become experienced in building a furnace fire. After the grates have been cleaned, crumple two or three sheets of newspaper, lay them in the center of the firebox, and add a few pieces of kindling or light wood. Cover with a few pieces of coal. All these articles must be dry, since the least bit of moisture will dampen and kill your fire. Make sure the draft is open, so that oxygen will reach the flames. Then light a match, carefully ignite at least two corners of the paper, and close the furnace door. After a short time, the wood and coal should be blazing. When this happens, add more coal and give it a chance to ignite. Then close the draft so that the coal will not burn too rapidly. If you follow these instructions, you will be assured of a fire that will successfully heat your cottage.

2

Pecos Bill is a cowboy in American legend. Did you know that before Bill there were no lassos? Cowboys would catch steers by laying a rope on the ground, hiding behind a bush, and waiting for the steer to step into the rope. Then one day Bill stretched a snake into a twenty-foot rope and made it into a loop. Riding on a mountain lion, he tossed the rope over an armadillo, thus originating the art of lassoing. Bill once roped a cyclone, rode it, and made it pour rain on the dry Southwest. When he fell off the cyclone, the dent he made formed Death Valley. Another thing Bill originated was the set of spurs on cowboy boots. Would you be surprised to hear that he taught cowboys to sing cowboy songs? Legends often tell about the origins of things, and many of the customs of cowboys are traced directly to Pecos Bill.

Paragraphs 3 and 4 lack a topic sentence. See if you can name the topic and the specific idea of each paragraph. Then write a topic sentence for each.

3

Sometimes we fight about who has to take her. This happens when it is very cold or when it is raining. Usually, though, she has no shortage of offers. Goldie's upbeat personality and affectionate nature make her a valued companion. Often we all go for a long walk with her together, and she seems to like this the best. She runs back and forth among the five of us, never sure who will play with her, chase her, and pet her. Walking our dog, Goldie, is really a pleasure for the entire family.

4

Copernicus's theory about the universe startled the people of his time. They thought the earth was the center of the universe and that it never moved. In the sixteenth century, when Copernicus announced that he thought differently, his ideas were met with much resistance from the scientific community and other areas of society. He dared to suggest that the earth is not the center of the universe, but that the sun is. The earth rotates around the sun. Furthermore, he said that not only is the earth not still, but it is actually racing rapidly through space. People are not aware of this motion because they are traveling with the earth. It was many years before the theories of Copernicus were generally accepted.

2. *Topic sentence*: Legends often tell about the origins of things, and many of the customs of cowboys are traced directly to Pecos Bill.
   Topic: The legendary character of Pecos Bill
   Specific idea: How many cowboy customs originated with Pecos Bill
3. *Topic*: Our dog
   Specific idea: Our dog is fun to walk.
4. *Topic*: Theories about the universe
   Specific idea: Copernicus's revolutionary theory about the universe

Nicolaus Copernicus, the founder of modern astronomy

More to Explore

Think about these broad topics. Narrow them to specific ideas and then write a topic sentence for each one.

Outer space
Computers
Oceans
Art
Work

Lesson 3 Writing Beginning Sentences

A beginning sentence is always the first sentence in a paragraph and introduces the topic of the paragraph in some way. It may be, but is not always, the topic sentence.

As the first sentence in a paragraph, the beginning sentence must

arouse a reader's interest
encourage him or her to keep reading
hint at the topic of the paragraph

When the beginning sentence is also the topic sentence, it must give the main idea of the paragraph. It should also attract a reader's attention and make him or her want to read further. "This paragraph is about the playful tricks of my cat" fulfills its role as both a beginning and a topic sentence, but "Once upon a time, in a small house in Lee Park, there lived a playful cat named Flipper" attracts more attention.

When the beginning sentence is *not* the topic sentence, it is often a question related to the topic or an exclamation specifically designed to catch the reader's eye. The beginning sentence acts like a hook (and the reader a fish!).

Activity A

Examine the following beginning sentences. How well do they fulfill the requirements of a beginning sentence? How much do they tell you about each paragraph?

1. An interesting book can be a smooth highway to enchanting lands.
2. Have you ever seen an elephant in a bathing suit?
3. What feelings of dismay engulfed me on the occasion of my teacher's first visit to our home!
4. The third time Kiki stuffed a wad of snow down the back of my coat, I decided to do something about it.
5. Sitting on the peak of Mount Evans, I felt as if I were the only living person in the world.
6. Gretchen was not pleased about her brother's gift.
7. "Watch out for the hole in the road!" shouted Philip.
8. How many times in your life will you see a real shooting star?
9. The rapids foamed white as our canoe approached.
10. A loud crash broke the silence of the cozy little room.

The morning quiet was suddenly shattered by the deafening sound of four motorcycles.

Without a worry in the world, Sara Golden sat quietly under the maple tree reading her assigned book.

Why can't I learn not to leave things until the last minute?

Swiiish! The limousine zoomed by at an unbelievable speed.

"Get your popcorn here!" bellowed the street vendor.

Which sentences tell what the paragraph may be about? Which do not? Topic sentences are easier to write in expository writing than in narrative or descriptive writing.

ACTIVITY A: Analyze each beginning sentence carefully. Some sentences tell more about the paragraph than others. There should be a variety of student responses as to what might be the content of the paragraphs.

ACTIVITY B: The sentences provided are only suggestions. Suggest that the students try to write dialogue, interrogative, and exclamatory sentences in order to create a variety of beginnings.

Activity B

Write a good beginning sentence for each paragraph.

Dolphins have interested and enchanted people from the very earliest times.

Artists over the ages have captured them riding the bows of ships and performing their graceful, joyous leaps. They are intelligent, playful, and friendly mammals, with built-in smiles and merry-looking eyes. While humans have not always been kind to dolphins, dolphins have been well-disposed toward us. There is no record of a dolphin attacking a person, even while being mistreated, and there are many reports of dolphins rescuing people from drowning. A dolphin's brain is comparable in size to that of a human, and it has been demonstrated that they can convey instructions to one another, solve complex problems, and perform elaborate tasks. They are also able to converse with one another, using a language made up of an enormous variety of sounds. Computer-aided efforts are being made to understand their language and to teach them human speech. If this succeeds, we may find they have some valuable lessons to teach us.

An ancient Greek portrait of a dolphin

<u>"Come on! It's easy and much faster," claimed my brother.</u> When in a moment of weakness I accepted his foolish suggestion, the journey homeward resulted in a cross-country race. Streets were taboo. Only the wide-open spaces and the narrow wooded trails were considered. Hurdling fences, crawling beneath bridges, groping through fields thick with weeds, on and on my brother traveled, followed closely by breathless me. Finally, on reaching our destination, I sank exhausted to the ground, vowing that never, never again would I permit my brother to entice me into taking a short-cut home.

<u>The disks called Frisbees have floated through the air in large numbers in this century.</u>

The first Frisbees apparently were ten-inch-wide pie tins made by the Frisbee Pie Company in Connecticut. According to tradition, in the early 1900s, students in college found that the pie tins could be made to "fly." They began the game of throwing the tins back and forth. It wasn't until the 1940s and 1950s that Frisbees were made of plastic and manufactured in large numbers. By the 1960s, the sales of Frisbees began to soar. The fad became a sport, with players doing elaborate tricks with the flying disks. There is even an international Frisbee competition in Pasadena, California.

Activity C

Write creative beginning sentences for the following paragraph topics. Use a variety of declarative, exclamatory, and interrogatory sentences.

1. A hot-air balloon ride
2. Roller skating for the first time
3. Buying a new tropical fish
4. Working at an ice-cream parlor
5. Watching a building burn down

ACTIVITY C: Some students should be able to write two different beginning sentences for each topic. Encourage the creation of unique and clever beginnings. Put as many beginning sentences on the chalkboard as possible so that the students can analyze the effectiveness of each one.

Topic Sentence vs. Beginning Sentence

A *topic sentence* often comes at the beginning of a paragraph, but it can also come in the middle or at the end. A topic sentence tells exactly what the paragraph is about. It states the main idea.

A *beginning sentence* is always the first sentence of a paragraph. It does not have to state the specific idea of the paragraph, but it should give a hint of what the paragraph is about. It is often used to arouse the curiosity of the reader.

Activity

ACTIVITY: Have the students do this activity independently. Discuss why the one sentence is the topic and the other is not. From the sentences not selected, discuss whether any of them would make effective beginning sentences.

One sentence in each of the following pairs is a topic sentence. The other is either a beginning sentence or one of the sentences that develop the topic. Identify the topic sentences.

1. a. Many parents take pride in the accomplishments of their children, and Warren's father is no exception.
    b. No one leaves Mr. Harmon's office without hearing about some of Warren's awards.

2. a. With the end of summer and the beginning of fall arrive many changes—some pleasant, some not.
    b. The steamy heat has faded.

3. a. Have you ever played at sailing the skies without an airplane?
    b. One ride on an old rope swing dangling from a huge maple tree convinced me that this could become one of my favorite pastimes.

4. a. Gone are the days of strong men and women pushing plows through the earth behind a straining horse or mule.
    b. Farming techniques have improved remarkably during the past one hundred years.

5. a. The words "consider all the avenues of life" echo in my ears as a panorama of careers passes before my eyes.
    b. I see a researcher in a laboratory coat seeking a cure for cancer.

6. a. Collecting stamps always seemed a childish hobby to me until I met Benjamin.
   b. He showed me why it is really a valuable way of recording history.

7. a. "How could you say such a thing!" declared Lou, stomping from the room.
   b. My brother did not understand my comment about his new boots.

8. a. Taking proper care of diskettes is essential to the successful and happy use of your computer.
   b. If they get bent or dirty, you can lose all of the programs or data stored on them.

9. a. "If I had known you needed a ride, I would have waited for you," Henry explained, too late.
   b. I walked four adventure-filled miles in the pouring rain.

10. a. Reading science fiction keeps Julia very busy.
    b. Last week she read three books by Ray Bradbury.

More to Explore

Sentences 1, 2, and 3 are topic sentences; for each of them, create a beginning sentence. Sentences 4, 5, and 6 are beginning sentences; for each of them, create a topic sentence.

1. Creating exotic sandwiches was Roberta's specialty.
2. Word processing makes revising your writing easier than ever.
3. Sometimes Leonard sits for hours just staring out the window.
4. How can a person think with all of the noise in this room!
5. What a foolish thing I have done!
6. The boat slipped through the water, whisked along by the wind.

Lesson 4 Writing the Middle Sentences

The middle sentences develop the central thought of the paragraph.

Middle sentences present the supporting evidence for the topic of a paragraph. They tell the facts one by one, give details, explain a process step by step, or relate specific actions and events of a story.

A sentence that introduces some outside thought or idea and does not relate to the topic of the paragraph is called a *misfit*. Do not permit misfit sentences to creep into your paragraphs.

One way to keep yourself on target is to map your sentences before writing the paragraph. This will help organize your thoughts, so that your sentences relate naturally to one another as well as to the topic.

Word Mapping

Suppose you chose the topic "music" and narrowed it to "how a rock band gets started." Let's use the word mapping technique to list the details related to your specific idea or topic.

1. Write your topic and draw a ring around it.

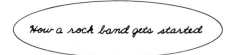

2. Around the ring, name things that are related to your topic. These ideas are called *subtopics*. Draw lines connecting each subtopic to the topic in the center.

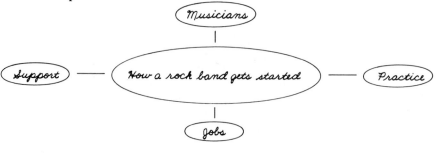

14

3. Around each subtopic, write any *details* relating to that particular subtopic. These details may be things you already know, or you may need to learn more about your topic by reading or talking to knowledgeable people in the field.

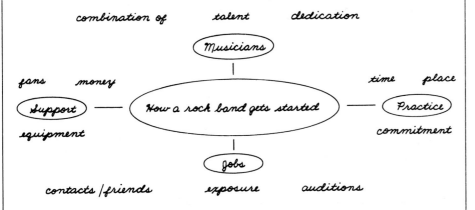

combination of   talent   dedication

(Musicians)

fans   money   time   place

(Support) — (How a rock band gets started) — (Practice)

equipment   commitment

(Jobs)

contacts/friends   exposure   auditions

4. Look at your word map. Do you have too much information for one paragraph? If you do, draw lines through some details (in the clusters around your subtopics) that seem less important than others.

5. Think about your subtopics in relation to your topic. Is there any particular order or arrangement that the subtopics should have? Do the subtopics relate to one another in a particular way?

For the sample topic, the subtopics do relate in a kind of logical order. To form a rock band, you first need musicians. Once you get the musicians together, they have to practice and develop some support (fans, money, etc.). Finally, if they are good (and lucky) they will get jobs.

6. You already know how to write a good topic/beginning sentence based on your topic. Now you need to write one sentence for each of your subtopics. These will be your middle sentences.

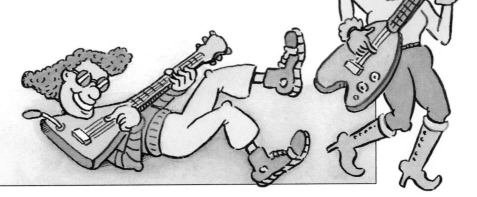

How a rock band gets started	Hard work plays a key role in starting a successful rock band.
Musicians ──────────────▶	It takes just the right combination of talented musicians dedicated to their own music but working together to create a great band.
Practice ──────────────▶	Group practice requires three things: time, a place to get together, and commitment on the part of each band member.
Support ──────────────▶	Most people think of support for rock bands in terms of fans, but money for such things as the proper equipment and costumes counts too.
Jobs──────────────▶	Auditions, contacts, and generally getting as much exposure as possible enables the band to achieve its goal—getting jobs.

The sentences may need to be altered in order to fit together as a good paragraph. You may need to change or add words to make the sentences flow. Remember to watch for repeated words, replacing them where possible with synonyms for variety.

After several revisions the paragraph might read this way:

<u>Hard work plays a key role in starting a successful rock band.</u>

[It takes just the right combination of talented musicians dedicated to their craft and working together to create a great band. Group practice is essential and requires three things: time, a place to get together, and commitment. Most people think of support for rock bands in terms of fans, but money for proper equipment and costumes is equally important. Auditions, contacts, and generally getting as much exposure as possible enables the band to achieve its goal—being offered gigs.] <u>ending sentence.</u>

Activity A

Turn back to lesson 2, activity C, and create a word map of paragraph 1.

Activity B

Make a word map for each of the following paragraph topics:

How to prepare dinner
How weather affects people's lives
How driving a car can make a difference in one's life

More to Explore

Create sentences based on one of the word maps you made for activity B. Then put the sentences together to form a paragraph.

Lesson 5 Writing Ending Sentences

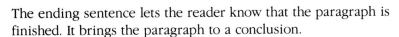

The ending sentence draws the paragraph to a conclusion.

The ending sentence lets the reader know that the paragraph is finished. It brings the paragraph to a conclusion.

An ending sentence often does one of the following:

1. It gives a last fact or detail.
2. It gives a summary of details or makes a statement that draws together the information in the paragraph.
3. It makes a personal comment. In a personal comment, the writer often states his or her reactions or feelings toward what is described in the paragraph.

ACTIVITY A: This paragraph is about building a furnace fire. Have the students work independently and then put some word maps on the chalkboard. Word maps should be somewhat similar.

ACTIVITY B: Let the students work in pairs to create these word maps. Then have them form larger groups of four or six to compare their results. They should choose one from the group to put the most accurate word map on the chalkboard. Make sure all topics are represented.

MORE TO EXPLORE: Choose one word map from activity B and form a class paragraph. The time spent developing each sentence and then the paragraph should make it easier for students to attempt one on their own. To help the students start their own paragraphs, work as a class developing a topic sentence for the remaining two topics.

ENRICHMENT
The students should be able to supply real or imaginary details for each of the subtopics shown below. Have them draw a word map of the topic and subtopics, write one or two sentences for each subtopic (including details), and then form a paragraph.
Topic:
A day I shall never forget
Subtopics:
place
people involved
special happenings
feelings at the end of day

THE STUDENTS SHOULD LEARN
—the function of an ending sentence
—how to write effective ending sentences

An ending sentence makes the reader know the paragraph is ending and often forces him or her to think about what the writer has said. Sometimes emotional endings, personal comments, etc., are given.

James Naismith

Read the following paragraph and study the difference between the three possible ending sentences.

Did you know that basketball is the only major sport that is a completely American invention? It was begun by a teacher named James Naismith in Springfield, Massachusetts, in the 1880s. Naismith developed the sport to fill the needs of his students. They wanted an exciting, competitive sport that could be played indoors during the winter. First, Naismith decided that the sport would use a ball. He rejected the idea of using a bat or stick for hitting the ball as too dangerous. The ball, he decided, would be bounced and passed. Players would make points by putting the ball in baskets at either end of the gym. One problem remained. The players from one team could stand in front of their opponents' basket and block any points. That's when Naismith got the final, essential idea of raising the basket.

Possible ending sentences

Last detail To honor Naismith for his ideas, the Basketball Hall of Fame is named for him and located in Massachusetts.

Summary Naismith, then, had put together all the elements that make up today's sport: the ball, the bounce, and the high basket.

Personal comment Thousands of players and spectators owe thanks to Naismith for producing the active, exciting sport of basketball.

Activity A

Read the following ending sentences carefully. What kind of ending does each sentence represent: a last detail, a summary, or a personal comment?

1. I can't believe that this happened to me, but I was glad it did!
2. Now that you know what to look for, you can check your houseplants for signs of these pests.
3. Within ten years after these first appearances, comic strips were included in most newspapers in the country.
4. All those qualities—intelligence, energy, and sense of humor— would make Nick a good president.
5. This first experience made me determined to try again and to overcome stage fright.
6. With qualities such as these, no wonder Helen Keller was one of the most admired people of her time.
7. Then refrigerate the cake for four hours before serving.
8. No doubt about it, this was the sport for me.
9. The disappearance of the crew of the *Mary Celeste* will probably never be explained.
10. Ironically, Harry Houdini died from a blow to the stomach, not from a failure in an escape attempt.

Activity B

The following ending sentences each express an emotion or feeling (such as pride, relief, or fear). Read each sentence and write the feeling you think it expresses. Then write what you think might be the topic of the paragraph in which the sentence appears.

1. Unfortunately, dreams do sometimes come true.
2. I was so pleased to be playing in the final round of the tennis tournament, I almost didn't care if I won or lost.
3. Her first-place finish in the contest surprised everyone— especially Rita herself.
4. I know I will have another dog some day, but I will never forget old Mongrel Sam.
5. When I am as old as she is, I hope to be as full of joy.

Write an ending sentence that effectively expresses each of the following emotions: fear, hope, pride, relief, gratitude.

ACTIVITY C: Discuss the kinds of emotions that might be appropriate for the ending sentence of each paragraph. Give special note to the personification of the jar of mustard in paragraph 1. The endings provided are only suggestions.

MORE TO EXPLORE: It is best that the students look at endings to stories they have already read. This will give them a sense of how the last lines fit in with the paragraph. Remind the students that sometimes an ending in a story may be more than one sentence. An entire paragraph is often the concluding remark.

ENRICHMENT
Display a series of posters or art prints in the classroom. Have the students make up an ending sentence for the story the picture might be telling. They should put their endings on strips of paper and then place them in an envelope. Have another student pick one and try to match it with the appropriate poster or print.

Activity C

Write an effective ending sentence for each paragraph.

The Mustard Passes On

Life is short—very, very short if you happen to be the only jar of mustard at a barbecue. Before that horrible truth became clear, I was passed politely from one set of hands to the next. I could feel my contents growing smaller and smaller, but the loss was so gradual that I barely noticed. The hands that were waiting for me, however, began to suspect. Anxious fingers grasped me tightly, and only reluctantly handed me on. They began frantically scraping my insides with knives. Finally, they realized that the end had come. <u>Faces drooped as I gave my last gasp.</u>

A Green Centerpiece

Rush hour is a dangerous time for carrying something as delicate as a bouquet of flowers on the subway. I learned this lesson the painful way the evening I was to bring home a centerpiece for my mother's bridge party. The first problem was that by the time I finally made it onto a crowded train my huge bouquet had shed its wrappings. The aisle was packed. As people squeezed by me, getting on and off the train, my colorful bundle gradually lost its brightness. Flowers took root in umbrella spokes, shopping bags were transformed into floral baskets, and suited executives acquired decorations in their lapels. When the train finally reached my stop, and I emerged into the open spaces, my hands clutched a bunch of blossomless stems. <u>I wondered if my mother would like to invest in some artificial flowers.</u>

More to Explore

Look at the ending sentences of some short stories that you have read. Find three examples of final sentences that you particularly like, and tell what they do for the story. For example, do they give the story a twist? Express a final emotion? Summarize the theme of the story?

Lesson 6 Creating a Title

The title is the name of a written work.

The title, like the beginning sentence, must attract the reader's attention. A good title is usually short and creative. It expresses the main idea of a composition by naming a central figure (person, place, or event) in the composition or by indicating its theme.

Would these titles capture your attention? Do they make you want to read the composition or paragraph?

Topic	Title
The circus	Canvas City
A photograph	Framed Memories
Riding an escalator	Experiencing the Ups and Downs

How the words sound in a title is important. Clever titles sometimes use literary devices like these:

alliteration	My Curious Culinary Concoction
personification	Our Moody Family Car
play on words	Cubs Bear Twin Losses
allusion	As the Stomach Growls

Follow these suggestions to create a good title:
1. Focus on the main idea.
2. Use your imagination.
3. Keep it short.

Activity A

Read each paragraph topic and the possible titles after it. Choose the best title for each example. Explain your choice.

1. Being an identical twin
   a. Mirror Image
   b. There Are Two
2. A collector of old coins
   a. Old Money
   b. A Modern Midas
3. A canoeing accident
   a. How I Lost My Glasses
   b. Tippycanoe and Trouble for Two
4. Cleaning out the attic
   a. Hidden Treasures
   b. Dusty Old Stuff
5. Being very cold
   a. The Human Popsicle
   b. How Cold Was It?

ACTIVITY B: See how many different ideas the students think each title suggests. *Winged Adventure*, for example, might refer to an airplane ride or a fledgling learning to fly.

ACTIVITY C: Of the two titles, suggest that the students write one using a literary device. Have them ask another student which title seems more effective. Write five or six student titles for each paragraph on the chalkboard. Have the students vote for the best one.

Activity B

Read the following paragraph titles. Tell what you think each paragraph might be about.

1. Spring's Herald
2. Winged Adventure
3. A Fishing Line
4. Computer Thief
5. All Sewn Up

Activity C

Suggest two possible titles for each paragraph.

1

Fear and excitement clashed in my stomach when I stepped into the riotously colored roller coaster. As the little car chugged confidently up the first steep incline, my timidity faded. I peeped over the edge of the miniature train to look down upon the park growing rapidly smaller before my eyes. Suddenly, I realized that we had reached the top. With mounting terror, I prepared to fly into space. Down rushed the car, to the accompaniment of my frantic but delighted screams. Hardly had I regained my breath when the chariot again ascended, intent on dropping me once more into the yawning abyss. Whoosh! Abruptly, the ride ended. Smiling bravely, I assured my waiting friends that this was the most exciting thing I'd ever experienced.

2

Have you ever heard the expression "A Trojan Horse"? It refers to a trick that leads to defeat. Actually, the horse could be called "a Greek horse." The reason will be clear once you know the story in mythology in which the horse appears. The Greeks and Trojans were fighting a war. For nine years, the Greeks attacked the city of Troy, and the citizens defended themselves behind their city walls. The Greeks finally won the war by means of a trick. They left a huge wooden horse and then pretended to depart. The Trojans, thinking the horse a gift, took it within their walls. There were, however, Greek warriors hiding in the horse. They opened the gates to the Greek army, and thus Troy was defeated.

3

Open the heavy door of Klein's bakery and find yourself in an old-fashioned wonderland. The sweet aroma of ginger, molasses, and chocolate pervades the air. On top of the showcase is a huge cake, its pink-and-white frosting dancing with the word "Welcome." Sugar and currant cookies look happily at one another from their decorative flowered boxes inside this sparkling display cabinet. From a prominent place on the trim, orderly shelf, little peppermint-stick ladies and gentlemen sedately bow in candy greeting. Hidden deep in delicious pastry closets are enough treasures to tempt any boy or girl. Not the least of all the treasures is Mrs. Klein herself, whose beaming smile and quaint stories of long ago induce you to return again and again.

More to Explore

Suggest a creative title for each of these paragraph topics.
1. Staying overnight in the hospital
2. Feeding the neighbors' ducks
3. Taking a week-long bike trip
4. My first singing solo
5. How to wash a dog

MORE TO EXPLORE: To generate more ideas, have the students work in pairs or small groups. Have one from each group print the titles on oaktag or cardboard. Cut them out and post them around the classroom.

ENRICHMENT
Using the same posters or art prints from the previous lesson, have the students create a title for each picture. Call on a volunteer to give a title and have another student match it with the correct poster or print.

Writing Corner 1

Personification

Writing Corner is a special section, occurring after each writing chapter, that provides the students with writing opportunities beyond those suggested in the lessons.

The writing experiences explore the use of *alliteration, writer's viewpoint, characterization*, and *comparison and contrast*. These activities are designed to develop and enhance the creative skills of the students.

Those Writing Corners on *note taking, bibliography*, and *Readers' Guide* relate to tools needed for more formal writing experiences. They could be taught in conjunction with report writing and research skills (covered in chapters 5 and 8).

Has it ever seemed to you that a book was "talking" to you? Has a fire engine ever sounded to you as if it was "screaming" on its way down the street? In these examples, the book and the fire engine are doing something that humans do. Books do not really talk and fire engines do not really scream.

When a writer gives human qualities or characteristics to inanimate objects or ideas, the result is *personification*. Personification is often used in descriptive writing and in poetry. It gives life and action to the world of nature—or to any object or idea.

Study the following sentences and tell which word is being personified. Then explain what it is doing that makes it humanlike.
1. The worn-out shoes ached and groaned for one more mile.
2. The tree, mourning the loss of summer, shed leaf tears.
3. The windmill nodded in encouragement at the light breeze.
4. The wipers played a repetitive song on the windshield.
5. Winter could boast of another whitewash.

You are right if you noticed that—
1. shoes ached and groaned
2. the tree mourned and shed tears
3. the windmill nodded
4. wipers played a song
5. winter could boast

★ Write a sentence about each of the inanimate objects below. Use personification to describe the actions of the objects or to give them feelings.

rain pounded	**sunlight** danced	**stomach** growled
pebbles skipped	**pain** grabbed	**chair** groaned
cloud wandered	**waves** swallowed	**car** coughed

Sometimes a town or city can take on the qualities of a person. Think about any interesting city. Do you visualize this city as a man or a woman? How would this city be dressed? What are the things that make this city so outstanding? Here is how one student described the city of Philadelphia.

Sauntering down the street in a designer business suit and with a briefcase clutched to his side, Mr. Philadelphia heads toward the downtown historic area. He remembers the colonial days as he passes the Betsy Ross House, Constitution Hall, and Franklin Square. He struts proudly past the Liberty Bell, symbol of our nation's freedom. Stepping out of the past and into the present, Mr. Philadelphia admires the fine stores, factories, and ports that provide work for his many friends. He makes frequent visits to the Academy of Music to hear a performance from his renowned orchestra. Even during a busy day, he takes time to enjoy a famous soft pretzel with mustard. As night falls, Mr. Philadelphia strolls through the theater and restaurant district. A night on the town is the perfect ending to a perfect day.

★ Which city has a personality all its own? Paris? New York? London? Los Angeles? Write a paragraph personifying it as a man or a woman. Have your city act and feel the way a person would. Share the personality you have created with your class.

Prefixes

A prefix is a syllable or syllables added to the beginning of a word that changes the meaning of the word.

Below are some common prefixes and their meanings.

anti-	against
mis-	badly, poorly
post-	after
pre-	before
sub- (also *sup-* and *sus-*)	under

The word to which a prefix is added is called a *root word*. The meaning of the new word is based on the root.

Activity A

Copy and complete the chart below. Use the example as a model.

Prefix	Root	Word	Meaning	Other Words
anti	war	antiwar	against war	antismoking
				antitheft
mis	shapen	misshapen	shaped badly	Answers will vary.
post	election	postelection	after an election	
pre	paid	prepaid	paid before	
sub	zero	subzero	below zero	

Activity B

Find a word that would complete each sentence. Use a word that begins with the prefix that is at the top of each set.

anti-

1. Every winter my dad puts ___antifreeze___ in our car.
2. A person who never associates with others is considered ___antisocial___.

mis-

3. I ___miscounted___ the number of students in our field trip group, and I thought one of us was lost!
4. Francis ___misplaced___ the instructions for caring for the begonia, and so he had to spend ten minutes looking for them.

pre-

5. Ellen's six brothers and sisters always gather in the living room on Sunday for the football ___pregame___ show.
6. The triceratops, like all dinosaurs, is a ___prehistoric___ animal.

post-

7. When we have completed a chapter, we take a ___posttest___.
8. I added a ___postscript___ to the letter to Anita because I had forgotten to mention that I had a new kitten.

sub-

9. Washington, D.C., has a very modern ___subway___ system.
10. Under each topic in my outline, there are three ___subtopics___.

Activity C

Add an appropriate prefix from this Word Study to each of the following words. Then give the meaning of the new word, and use it in a sentence.

teen	behave
total	slavery
flight	committee
trust	judge
inform	standard

ACTIVITY C: Put as many sentences as possible on the chalkboard. Check to see that the new words are used accurately in each sentence.

ANSWERS

preteen	misbehave
subtotal	antislavery
post(pre) flight	subcommittee
mis(anti) trust	mis(pre) judge
misinform	substandard

ADDITIONAL ACTIVITY

Scientists have recently isolated a very unusual strain of bacteria. What is this bacteria like? What is the reaction of the scientists? Challenge the students to write a short paragraph using words from this Word Study. All five prefixes should be included.

Chapter 2

Developing Your Writing Skills

Lesson 1 Unity

A paragraph has unity when all sentences relate to the topic or main idea.

When you write the middle sentences of a paragraph, you must make sure that every sentence not only contributes important information but also relates to the topic of the paragraph. Any sentence with information not directly related to the topic is a *misfit* sentence.

To find misfit ideas, identify the topic sentence and examine the middle sentences. Find the misfit sentence in this paragraph:

A Special Glow

Think of the downtown area of a big city at night, and the picture in your mind probably includes the glow of neon lights. How do neon lights produce their special glow? The answer lies in the unusual qualities of the element neon. Neon is a colorless gas, like helium. While neon is used in lights, helium is used in all types of balloons. Neon reacts in a special way when it comes into contact with electricity. If neon is put in a tube and an electric current flows through the tube, the neon gives off a bright red glow. Put a little mercury in the tube with the neon and the light becomes blue. Use various combinations of elements, and signs of all colors can be produced—giving the city its rainbow glow.

In this case, the topic sentence is "How do neon lights produce their special glow?" One middle sentence does not relate to the topic ("While neon is used in lights, helium is used in all types of balloons."). It gives the reader information about helium, but no additional information about neon. Without that misfit sentence, the paragraph would be unified.

THE STUDENTS SHOULD LEARN
—how to identify sentences that do not relate to a paragraph
—how to write a unified paragraph

TEACHING THE LESSON
Discuss what is meant by things, ideas, or persons that are related. Apply this concept to paragraph writing: all sentences should be related. Sentences that do not fit the topic should be noted during revision and then either omitted or replaced with related sentences. Have the paragraph in the introduction read aloud at least twice. Discuss where the topic sentence is located and why it is the topic. It is important that the topic sentence be identified so that the writer can determine which sentences are related and which are not. Since the paragraph is about how neon lights produce a glow, the sentence on helium balloons is a misfit sentence.

Neon lights draw attention. Words also attract attention. What are some ways the media use words to attract attention and sell products?

ACTIVITY A: After the students have identified the misfit sentence, discuss how this non-related sentence might be used as a beginning rather than a middle sentence. For example: Although Grandpa likes other sports, baseball will always rank number one.

Have the students try this with the misfit sentences from groups 2 and 3. For extension, have them create an ending sentence for each group.

Activity A

Read each group of middle sentences and tell which is the misfit sentence.

Group 1

1. Every afternoon he sits with rapt attention behind home plate.
2. Grandpa likes other sports, too.
3. From the first batter to the last, Grandpa's full attention is on the field.
4. If the opposing batter pops a foul tip, Grandpa shouts encouragement to the catcher.

Group 2

1. First, put the oil into the pan.
2. When it starts to sizzle, put in the tortilla.
3. Have the other ingredients ready.
4. This is Pete's favorite treat.

Group 3

1. Mom detected a slight film of smoke in the basement of our house.
2. Immediately, she called the fire department.
3. I had just been talking to my friend on the telephone.
4. Luckily, the firefighters came just in time.
5. Some electric wires had started to burn.

Activity B

Use the following set of sentences to write a unified paragraph. Eliminate those sentences that do not relate to the topic. Be sure to include a topic sentence. You may want to add good beginning and ending sentences.

Topic: Kinds of signs used by the hearing-impaired to communicate
1. The language widely used by the hearing-impaired was developed by a French priest in the eighteenth century.
2. It was introduced into the United States by T. H. Gallaudet.
3. I have visited Gallaudet College in Washington, D.C.
4. The sign language uses gestures of the hands and arms.
5. Often the sign is related to the thought it expresses.
6. A finger rubbed across the lips means "You are not telling the truth."
7. Sometimes the sign is not directly related to what it means.
8. A tap on the chin with three fingers means "my uncle."
9. Native Americans used similar kinds of sign language to communicate with tribes speaking different languages.
10. The sign language is supplemented by a manual alphabet.
11. In the manual alphabet, a specific sign stands for each letter in the alphabet.
12. A closed fist with the thumb outside the fingers stands for the letter *e*.

Activity C

Choose three paragraph topics from the following list. For each of the topics you choose, give three or four supporting details that relate to the topic. Also give one misfit detail.
1. Planning a class trip
2. How to care for a new puppy (or kitten)
3. Redecorating your bedroom
4. How to be a successful student
5. Taking your little brother or sister to the zoo

More to Explore

Use one of the sets of details you gathered for activity C and write a unified paragraph. Remember to write a clear topic sentence and a good ending sentence. (Do not use your misfit detail!)

ACTIVITY B: The sentences that are misfit are 3 and 9. As the students write their paragraphs, encourage them to add a good beginning sentence and to have a clear topic sentence. Suggest that they add transition words to make the paragraph read smoothly.

ACTIVITY C: Choose one topic to work on as a class, and then have the other topics completed independently. Some topics will require an imaginative approach. Have the students exchange papers and locate the misfit sentences.

MORE TO EXPLORE: Remind the students of the need for a topic sentence when writing their paragraph. They should try to incorporate the misfit sentence as a beginning idea; if not, it should be omitted. Stress the need for the students to proofread their completed paragraph.

ENRICHMENT
Have the students examine social studies and science textbooks to obtain a well-written paragraph with a topic sentence. Tell them to rewrite the paragraph inserting a misfit sentence. Each paragraph could then be read aloud while the other students listen attentively for the misfit sentence.

Lesson 2 Coherence

A paragraph has coherence when it is in logical and natural order. *Coherence* **means "sticking together."**

THE STUDENTS SHOULD LEARN
—how to write a paragraph using sequential and spatial order
—to connect one sentence to the other by means of transition words

TEACHING THE LESSON

Elicit from the students the meaning of sequential and spatial relationships. Have them give examples of things that have a time order or a sequence about them: stories, how to make things, relating an incident, etc. Have them then give examples of things that have a spatial order: describing a building, any nature scene, a specific room, etc. The students should be able to supply various transition words that are used with each type. List the words on the chalkboard and then consult the introduction to the lesson for signal words the students may have missed.

The ideas in a paragraph must be presented in an orderly fashion so that one sentence will flow naturally into the next. This order of ideas is usually based on a *sequential* (time) or a *spatial* (space) relationship between things. If you were writing about a baseball game, you would never write about the fifth inning and *then* the third. Nor would you describe the batter who had just hit a home run shaking hands with his or her teammates and *then* running around the bases. Many kinds of topics have a similar order: *first* this happened, *then* this, *then* that, and *finally*, the last thing. This order is based on time—*when* things happened. It is *sequential* order.

Certain transition words help to make a paragraph written in sequential order flow smoothly. These words connect the sentences and show the relationship between them. Listed below are some of the most commonly used transition, or signal, words for sequential order.

after	in conclusion	now
afterward	later	soon
as soon as	meantime	then
finally	meanwhile	to begin with
first, second, etc.	next	

Sometimes the details in a paragraph are presented in *spatial* order. This means they are arranged from left to right, down to up, near to far, etc. The arrangement depends on the position of the observer. If you write a paragraph describing a room you entered by a back door, for instance, you might use a different spatial order from the one you would use if you had entered by a front door. Some of the transition words used for spatial order are given below.

above	between	opposite to
across	farther	to the left
before	here	to the right
behind	in front of	under
below	next to	underneath

Activity A

Explain the kind of order (sequential or spatial) used in the following paragraphs. Tell what signal words acted as clues for you.

Sleeping In

Some days getting out of bed is a mistake. Yesterday was that kind of day for me. To start the day wrong, my alarm clock did not go off. Fortunately, my cat woke me before I missed the bus; unfortunately, she did this by knocking over my water glass. The day continued with one problem after another: first, the milk was sour; then, I left my homework at home; next, I did not have enough money to buy lunch (of course I had not had time to bring lunch from home!); and, finally, I forgot the combination to my gym locker. I think that I will stay in bed the next time my alarm fails to wake me.

Sleeping Room

When I moved into my older brother's empty room, I had to decide how to arrange my furniture. I had never had so much room before, and filling the space was a challenge. I put the bed in the center of the room, with its head between the windows. On each side of the bed I put an empty milk crate, the plastic kind. The new chest of drawers, with a small mirror hanging over it, went by the wall at the foot of the bed, between the closet and the door. To the right of the bed went the old rocking chair I found in the alley. Then I had just enough space in which to make a mess, so my parents would never forget that they were in my room, not my brother's.

ACTIVITY A: "Sleeping In" is written in sequential order. Have the students note how smoothly the paragraph reads because of the transition words. "Sleeping Room" is written in spatial order. The transition words help the reader to see clearly the position of objects within the room.

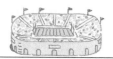

Activity B

For each of the topics listed, tell how the paragraph should be ordered, sequentially or spatially. Some paragraphs may be ordered in either way.

1. How to train for a marathon *sq*
2. How a computer works *sq*
3. Finding your seat in the stadium *sp and sq*
4. Describing the antics of a rock star on stage *sq or sp*
5. How to make an overseas phone call *sq*
6. How to write a check *sp and sq*
7. How to draw a sketch of your house *sp and sq*
8. Directions to the tigers' habitat at the zoo *sq or sp*
9. How to make pancakes *sq*
10. An explanation of the life cycle of a butterfly *sq*

More to Explore

Choose one of the topics from activity B and write a paragraph using either sequential or spatial order to organize your details.

Lesson 3 Choosing the Best Word

Choosing the best word involves working with precise words and *synonyms* (words that have similar meanings).

Precise words make interesting sentences. They also help to convey the exact idea you have in mind. As you write, you need to think of different words that mean what you want to say until you hit upon the one that is closest to your thought.

Start with a simple sentence:

The boat came toward us.

If you are talking about a motorboat, better word choices might be these:

The speedboat roared right at us.

If you are talking about a rowboat, you might mean this:

The launch drifted toward us.

If you are talking about a sailboat in a good wind, these words might do:

The scull tacked in our direction.

Each of the sentences means something quite different, yet they all mean "The boat came toward us." The changed words make the thought more vivid. Consider how the use of specific words makes the second sentence in each of the pairs below more vivid.

A group of excited birds chirped uneasily as the cat walked toward their tree.
A flock of excited sparrows twittered anxiously as the tomcat crept toward their tree.

A loud noise was heard through the house.
A thundering crash resounded through the house.

THE STUDENTS SHOULD LEARN
—to recognize the slight shades of meaning among similar words
—to choose the word that expresses the precise meaning

TEACHING THE LESSON
After noting the differences among the sample sentences, suggest that the students try to create one more about a yacht or luxury liner. Other vivid sentences can be created about the birds and the loud noise. Be sure to discuss the various meanings of *old* in the paragraph. Write the meaning of each word on the chalkboard. To illustrate the fact that synonyms do not have identical meanings, have the students try to substitute one synonym for another. Many are not interchangeable.

Synonyms are words that have the same general meaning. They are not identical in meaning, however. Notice how the shades of meaning can change even though all the words have the same general meaning.

The Pirates *beat* the Mets.
The Pirates *edged* the Mets.
The Pirates *trounced* the Mets.

Each of a series of similar words has a shade of meaning not expressed specifically by another. What is the exact meaning of each synonym for *old* in this paragraph?

In a remote section of our town stands a little *antique* shop, ready to transport you to the Land of Long Ago. As you enter its musty interior, the *venerable* shopkeeper squints a welcoming glance over his *antiquated* square-rimmed spectacles. Among the many relics of bygone days that he is proud to exhibit is a rare book, bearing an *ancient* publication date. Also numbered among the curiosities of the shop are many articles that have now become *obsolete*.

Activity A

List the words that make these sentences vivid. Some of the words may be unfamiliar to you; if so, look them up in the dictionary.
1. The battered warship limped into the harbor.
2. Rose-tinted clouds piled high in the sunset sky.
3. Spring announces its advent with the blossoming of the fruit trees.
4. The roar of the waves crashing on the beach roused the baby.
5. The silvery water cascaded majestically down the mountain.
6. Night descended like a heavy blanket on the weary travelers trudging homeward.
7. Accompanied by a doleful Scottie, the newcomer stood hesitatingly on the porch.
8. The lazy stream meandered through a cool, verdant forest.
9. The quaint village inn invited wayfarers to sample its hospitality.
10. Fascinated by the hooting of the owl, we stood transfixed beneath the gnarled elm.

ACTIVITY A: Have the students change each sentence by omitting the adjectives and simplifying the verbs. Discuss with them how this changes the meaning.

The warship came into the harbor.

Clouds rose high in the sky.

Spring comes when blossoms are on the fruit trees.

ANSWERS
The following words are the ones the students should list as making the sentences vivid.
1. battered, limped
2. Rose-tinted, piled, sunset
3. announces, advent, blossoming, fruit
4. roar, crashing, roused
5. silvery, cascaded, majestically
6. descended, heavy, weary, trudging
7. doleful, hesitatingly
8. lazy, meandered, cool, verdant
9. quaint, village, wayfarers, sample
10. Fascinated, hooting, transfixed, gnarled

Activity B

From the group of words after each sentence, select the one that is closest in meaning to the italicized word and that can replace it. The sentence will give you a clue to the exact meaning of the italicized word. Notice that each italicized word is more difficult and more formal than the word that can replace it.

1. My sister becomes *enraged* when I tease her about her boyfriend.
   happy   quiet   angry   friendly   sad
2. Medical science has almost *eradicated* several diseases that were common a century ago.
   extended   eliminated   advanced   suppressed
3. The castle was considered to be *impregnable*, safe from any enemy.
   unconquerable   large   steady   old
4. The price charged for the repair was *exorbitant*, much more than I expected.
   low   high   just   free   small
5. The principal *lauded* the students' efforts in raising money for the victims of the earthquake.
   noticed   caused   praised   encouraged
6. The new law was *promulgated* yesterday, and it will go into effect next month.
   revised   studied   rejected   proclaimed
7. The girls' basketball team received a *cordial* invitation to visit their sister team in Japan.
   personal   neat   attractive   printed   friendly
8. The wealthy man will long be remembered for his generous *benefactions* to charity.
   donations   will   words   kindness   orations
9. Hanging over the cliff with one hand on its edge, the hero was in a *precarious* situation.
   odd   exciting   annoying   dangerous
10. *Ample* time was given for the speech to be thoroughly prepared.
    little   free   meager   enough   extended

ACTIVITY B: This activity should be completed independently. For extension, have the students think of another synonym, besides the one given, that can be an appropriate substitute for the italicized word.

ANSWERS
1. angry
2. eliminated
3. unconquerable
4. high
5. praised
6. proclaimed
7. friendly
8. donations
9. dangerous
10. enough

Activity C

Rewrite the following sentences, replacing each italicized word with a synonym.

1. If you *discharge* each of your duties well, you will succeed.
2. He made it a *custom* to feed the pigeons every afternoon.
3. The nurse displayed *efficiency* in caring for the wounded stranger.
4. The hot, moist lowlands of Queensland produce an *abundant* supply of sugar cane.
5. Lucia enjoyed reading to Mrs. Melendez in her *charming* sitting room.
6. An *investigation* is being made to determine the cause of the fire.
7. The mayor issued a *candid* statement.
8. They *ceded* to the parks a vast expanse of land.
9. I *contemplated* how I could earn money to buy the guitar.
10. The chimpanzees *copied* everything he did.

Activity D

Improve each sentence by changing the italicized words to more descriptive words.

1. The *thin* woman *walked slowly* and *sadly* into her home.
2. A *worn-out* automobile *broke down* at the foot of the hill.
3. *Different* ways of solving the problem were *talked over* by the class.
4. Gretchen *stood* on the edge of the pool, took a deep breath, and *went* into the *clear* water.
5. A *real* desire to *gain* knowledge made Luis study *hard*.
6. The canyon was *cut* out of solid rock by a *small* but *wild* stream.
7. A flag, *tied* to a high pole, *was waving* in the breeze.
8. *Groups* of robins, *singing* loudly, gathered to get ready for their *long* journey.
9. A *small house* stood among the trees.
10. The *clapping* of the spectators *was heard* throughout the building.

More to Explore

Select the best synonym to complete each sentence. Use your dictionary to check the meaning of each word.

1. Once the money was paid, the small child was (<u>ransomed</u>, emancipated).
2. The tornado that swept through the town was a (hardship, <u>disaster</u>).
3. As the rivers rose, more people (deserted, <u>vacated</u>) their homes.
4. Manny tried to (<u>impersonate</u>, duplicate) the comedian.
5. (<u>Anticipating</u>, predicting) snow, I decided to wear my shoe boots.

Write original sentences for each set of synonyms. Make sure your sentences show the difference in meaning between the words.

1. fracture/shatter
2. debate/quarrel
3. startle/astonish
4. toss/hurl
5. brittle/frail

MORE TO EXPLORE: See if the students can explain the meaning of each word in parentheses without using a dictionary. Then have them check the dictionary to verify their answers. Discuss how the synonyms in each set differ in meaning. Follow the same procedure for the second part of the activity. Have sentences put on the chalkboard and check that they reflect the correct meaning of the word.

Lesson 4 Revision

Revision is "the act of seeing again." To revise a piece of writing means to take a second look at it and decide whether you should *Change* sentences around, *Add* or *Remove* words, or *Substitute* new ones (CARS).

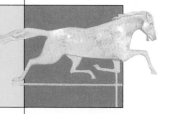

Through revision, you add sparkle and interest to your writing and express your ideas in the clearest fashion.

When you write, you begin by putting down all the ideas you have about your subject. This step is called a *first draft*. Then you decide what you can add, take out, or change to make your meaning clearer. You may write several drafts before you are satisfied with the final version.

THE STUDENTS SHOULD LEARN
—that revision is a necessary part of the writing process
—that revision is a matter of *changing* sentences around, *adding* words, *removing* words, *substituting* new words

ENRICHMENT
Have the students locate three or four sentences from short stories, novels, or poems that contain descriptive words. Tell them to rewrite the sentences or lines substituting synonyms for the descriptive words. The students should be attentive to the changes in meaning.

Lead a class discussion about the revision of the sample paragraph. Using the revision questions as a guide, note all the changes that were made between the original and the revised version of the paragraph. Have the students suggest other kinds of changes they might make. Encourage the students to think of the word *CARS* when revising: *Changing* sentences around, *Adding* words, *Removing* words, *Substituting* new words.

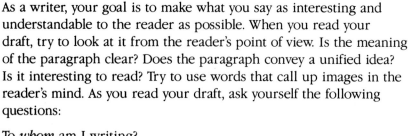

As a writer, your goal is to make what you say as interesting and understandable to the reader as possible. When you read your draft, try to look at it from the reader's point of view. Is the meaning of the paragraph clear? Does the paragraph convey a unified idea? Is it interesting to read? Try to use words that call up images in the reader's mind. As you read your draft, ask yourself the following questions:

To *whom* am I writing?
—myself
—my teacher
—other students
—the community

What is the subject of my writing?

Why am I writing?
—to describe
—to inform
—to tell a story
—to persuade

Then, rewrite your work so that the message you give your readers is clear and exactly what you want to say.

The following paragraph needs revision. Read it over and decide how you would rewrite it to make it smoother and more coherent. Use the Checkpoints for Revision below as a guide.

First-Draft Paragraph

   Leonardo da Vinci was a famous painter. He lived during the Renaissance era. Many people don't know that he was also an inventor and scientist. His paintings, such as the *Mona Lisa* and the *Last Supper*, are among the greatest works of art in history. He drew the first design for an airplane and a car. He also studied anatomy, geology, and mathematics. He was a man of many talents. The term "Renaissance man" seems to have been coined for him.

**A self-portrait
by Leonardo da Vinci**

Checkpoints for Revision

—Is there a topic sentence that clearly states the main idea of the paragraph?
—Are there enough supporting details?
—Do all of the details fit the topic?
—Are the details in the correct order?
—Are effective transitions used?
—Are there different kinds of sentences?
—Are the words precise and accurate?
—Is there a strong ending sentence?

Now read a revised version of the paragraph about Leonardo da Vinci. How did the writer improve the paragraph? What has been changed, added, or removed?

Revised Paragraph

Leonardo da Vinci was a famous artist and scientist of the Renaissance era. His best-known paintings, the *Mona Lisa* and the *Last Supper*, are among the greatest works of art in history. Many people, however, don't realize that his genius extended to science as well. Leonardo was an inventor who drew the first designs of an airplane and a car. He also studied anatomy, geology, and mathematics. The term "Renaissance man" perfectly describes Leonardo da Vinci—a man of many diverse talents.

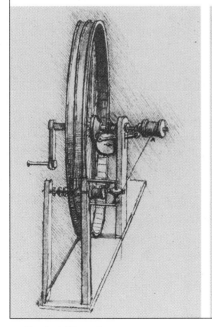

Sketches of inventions
by da Vinci

Mona Lisa by da Vinci

Activity A

Combine the following sentences to create a paragraph. Then revise and rewrite the paragraph. Add, remove, and change whatever is necessary to make a smooth paragraph.

ACTIVITY A: Have two or three students read their revised paragraphs aloud. If possible, write one version on the board or on the overhead projector. Discuss why certain revisions were made and how they improved the paragraph.

Topic sentence When you have many things to do, one way to get everything done is to make a list.

Supporting details
1. Make a list of everything you have to do, in any order.
2. Think about which things are most important.
3. Also think about which things you can do immediately (without waiting for permission or for someone else to do something).
4. When you have made some decisions, put numbers next to the items on your list to indicate those decisions.
5. Rewrite the list in the order of the numbers.

Ending sentence When you have your list in order, start completing the tasks on it.

Activity B

Revise the following paragraph, using the Checkpoints for Revision as a guide. Ask: To *whom* am I writing? *What* is my subject? *Why* am I writing? Make the paragraph as smooth, precise, and logical as possible.

ACTIVITY B: Group the students in pairs. Have them exchange and read each other's papers. Then instruct each pair to write one final copy based on a combination of each member's original revision. Remind the students that sentences need to be removed for the sake of logic, and short sentences should be combined.

Most people have their own methods for forecasting the weather. These methods were used long before scientific methods existed. Many people, particularly people with arthritis, say that they feel it in their bones when it is going to rain. Many people say that they can smell rain in the air before it comes. Many people just watch the clouds. Clouds with certain shapes indicate rain. Radar can be used to track where rain is falling. Nature has its ways of telling, too. Horses settle in with their backs in the direction of a storm. Cows also settle with their backs in the same way. Trees turn over their leaves. The white side of the leaf is up. The shiny side is down. I mostly listen to the radio.

More to Explore

Write a paragraph about a place you know well (your street, back yard, a city park, etc.). Then take the point of view of the reader. Think how you would make the reader *see* the place about which you are writing. What kinds of words would you use? What details would you include to create a vivid image in the reader's mind? Revise the paragraph so that it will lead others to see the place the way you do.

MORE TO EXPLORE: The students should incorporate into the revision process what they have learned about unity, coherence, and word choice. During the second and possibly third drafts, the Checkpoints for Revision should be consulted frequently. Have the students share their revised paragraphs.

Ansonia, a painting by Richard Estes

ENRICHMENT
Select two or three short feature articles from the newspaper. Make copies for the students and have them choose one to revise. They should be instructed to *add* one word, *delete* one, *change* sentence structure, and *find synonyms* for overused words. Have them glue the original article to a piece of paper and write their revision next to it. Share student revisions.

Lesson 5 Proofreading

Proofreading is reading a piece of writing and marking the errors in it.

When you are preparing a composition for someone else to read, you want it to be perfect. That is why you proofread.

When you proofread a piece of writing, look for mistakes in spelling, punctuation, and capitalization. Mark them and then correct them. Also look for subjects and verbs that don't agree (in tense, person, or number) and for any other words you might want to change.

Read the following paragraph and notice how the mistakes are marked:

> My father reads the newspaper every evening. He always reads it the same way. First, he reads the comics, which are on the back page. Then he goes to the beginning, reads the front page, and goes through the first two sections of news. Sometimes he reads the letters-to-the-editor out loud. When he finishes the reguler news, dad glances at the business page for articles about computers or telephones. He never looks at the Sports, and he saves the ads for last. By the time Dad is ready to read the ads, the rest of us are ready to eat dinner, so we make him stop reading. He sometimes spends the entire rest of the evening reading the ads and asking us if we want to buy this or that on sale. Reading the newspaper provides real entertainment for my father.

What symbol marks the misspelled word? What symbol means to make a capital letter? How do you know that you should begin a new paragraph? What other symbols are used? What do they mean?

Here are the proofreading symbols that are used most often.

Symbol	Meaning	Example
¶	begin a new paragraph	over. ¶ Begin a new
⌒	close up space	close u⌒p space
∧	insert	the ∧students think
ℓ	delete, omit	that the the book
/	lowercase letter	/Mathematics
∼	letters are reversed	letters are reversⱰed
≡	capital letter	≡washington

Activity A

Rewrite the paragraph, making the changes indicated by the proofreading marks.

All living tissue, both plant and anmial, contains protein. Over half the body, excluding its water, is Protein. Proteins are essential for tissue maintenence and growth, and provide the frame work of many body structures: mucsle and connective tissue, plasma and hemoglobin circulating in the blood, Keratin in the skin, nails and hair. enzymes, hormones, and antibodies, which regulate many of the body's most important functions, are mostly protein. DNA and Rna, the substances in every cell that caryy the genetic code which cells need to reproduce their proteins in the processes of growth and repair, themselves reqire protein enzymes for their formation. We need portein in our diet to maintin all these body proteins, and young people need much more to provide the raw material for growth.

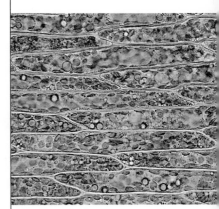

An enlarged picture of a plant cell

ACTIVITY B: After the students have completed this activity independently, call on volunteers to put each sentence on the chalkboard, using the correct proofreading symbols to indicate the errors.

ANSWERS
The part where the error occurred is indicated by an underline.
1. pe<u>o</u>ple; meat
2. veg<u>a</u>tarians; <u>e</u>at
3. ch<u>i</u>ken; . . . and fish<u>,</u>
4. eat<u>-</u> (no comma); bu<u>t</u>ter
5. vegetarians<u> </u>(no apostrophe); because <u>re</u>ligious (word should be inserted)
6. th<u>e</u>ir; h<u>ea</u>lth
7. care<u>f</u>ully; <u>n</u>utrients
8. <u>P</u>rot<u>e</u>in; nutri<u>en</u>t
9. se<u>v</u>eral; ki<u>n</u>ds
10. <u>S</u>oybeans; prot<u>e</u>n
11. in<u> </u>them; amino<u>-</u>
12. b<u>e</u>ans; conta<u>i</u>n
13. By mixing th<u>e</u>; they eat (changed word order)
14. av<u>a</u>ilable; f<u>o</u>od
15. <u>v</u>egetarians; <u>S</u>tates

Activity B

Each of the following sentences contains two errors. Copy the sentences exactly as they are and use proofreading symbols to indicate the corrections that are needed.

1. Vegetarians are poeple who do not eat meeat.
2. Some vegatarians do not Eat any meat at all.
3. Others eat some chiken and fish but they do not eat beef or pork.
4. Some do not eat, butte, eggs, or milk.
5. Some people are vegetarians' because religious beliefs.
6. Some people do not eat meat because they believe it is bad for thier heath.
7. Vegetarians plan their diets care fully to get a good balance of Nutrients.
8. protein is an important nutriant that most people get from meat.
9. Proteins are made of sev eral kins of amino acids.
10. soybeans contain whole proten.
11. This means that they have inbthem the three most essential Amino acids.
12. Other types of beens and vegetables contaiin some protein.
13. By mixing teh grains and vegetables eat they, vegetarians stay well fed.
14. Many products high in protein are avalable in health fod stores.
15. The number of Vegetarians in the United states has increased in recent years.

More to Explore

Following are ten sentences with errors in them. Copy each sentence exactly as it is and mark the errors with the correct proofreading symbols. Then rewrite the sentence, making the corrections.

1. That's eether a spider o r a very large speck of duts.
2. maria likes to phootograph Flowers.
3. Birdwatchin g was mch more fun than we expectedd.
4. Sandy swa a red-head ed wooodpecker.
5. Mrs. garcia was sweeping her porch stps.
6. The smells from the Kitchen tuld me we weer havin lasagna.
7. Steve turned no his knew ster eo, and alll the lights went out.
8. My grandfather once triveled down the amazon River.
9. Sofia rites some of her journal netries in Code.
10. i think there's a racco on in the alley bhind our building.

MORE TO EXPLORE: It would be helpful to have this page duplicated so that the students could mark the symbols on the page. On the chalkboard, have them write the sentence with the symbols and then the correctly written sentence underneath it.

ANSWERS
The part of the word where the error occurred is indicated by an underline.
1. either; or; dust
2. Maria; photograph; flowers
3. Birdwatching; much; expected
4. saw; red-headed; woodpecker
5. Garcia; steps
6. kitchen; told; were; having
7. on; new; stereo; all
8. traveled; Amazon
9. writes; entries; code
10. I; raccoon; behind

ENRICHMENT

Direct the students to create eight sentences with two or three errors in each and then exchange papers with another student. They should use proofreading symbols to identify the errors. The students could also find errors in newspaper articles and mark those with appropriate proofreading symbols.

Writing Corner 2

Writer's Viewpoint

People often have different attitudes toward the same situation. These attitudes are reflected in what they write about the situation.

A famous rock duo, Jelly and Roll, is performing in your town. Reporters from three different newspapers are preparing articles for tomorrow's papers. Study the different attitudes of the three reporters.

Reporter 1

The famous rock duo Jelly and Roll performed last evening at the Horse Castle to about 15,000 fans. The first two hours were devoted to songs from the early days of their career. After the intermission, fans were treated to dance routines and hits from Jelly and Roll's recent albums. Because of the large number of fans, exits were jammed for as long as two hours.

Reporter 2

The world's most popular rock duo, Jelly and Roll, performed spectacularly last evening at the Horse Castle to a sell-out crowd of 15,000. Fans jammed the entrances and aisles in what was standing room only for the last 3,000 that entered the Castle. For the first two hours, the performers entranced and delighted the audience with their old classic songs. After intermission, the high-spirited Jelly and Roll pulled out all the stops. Under the strobe lighting, they stunned the crowd with their unique dance routines and hits from their recent albums. Fans lingered long afterwards just to recover from four hours of thrill and excitement.

Reporter 3

Last evening's performance by rock stars Jelly and Roll not only caused innumerable problems, but did little to promote their popularity. With the Horse Castle's maximum seating capacity of 12,000, the extra 3,000 people had to be jammed into every available space. As a result, entrances and aisles were blocked, causing serious concern about exiting in case of fire. The first two hours of entertainment proved uninteresting—a repeat of old, stale material. After an overlong intermission, Jelly and Roll attempted to arouse the spirit of the crowd by offering trite dance routines interspersed with hits from their recent albums. The two hours it took to exit just added to the already boring evening experienced by disappointed supporters.

You are right if you noticed that Reporter 1 has a neutral attitude. He or she simply states the facts. Reporter 2 has a positive attitude toward the evening's performance. Can you find words in his or her article that support this attitude? Reporter 3 is quite negative. Find words that support this negative impression.

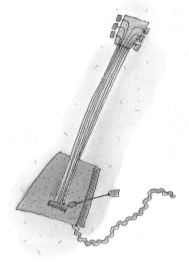

★ Now try reflecting people's attitudes through writing. Use one of the situations below or one of your own. Share your completed work with the class.
1. You are thinking about getting a personal computer. There is much discussion in your home about its benefits as well as its expense. What is your attitude? Your parents? What about the attitude of your grandparents, who aren't sure about this "newfangled" piece of equipment? What are the feelings of your sister, who wants a VCR?
2. This is the last chance for your team to win the game. You are their only hope. You come to bat and strike out. What is your attitude? Your teammates'? Your coach's? Your opponents'? The other team's pitcher?

Prefixes

A prefix is a syllable or syllables added to the beginning of a word that changes the meaning of the word.

The prefixes given in Word Study 1 are just a few of the prefixes that are commonly used. Here are some others.

extra-	beyond
in- (also *im-, il-, ir-*)	not
inter-	between
super-	above, over
trans-	across

Activity A

Copy and complete the chart below. Use the example as a model.

Prefix	Root	Word	Meaning	Other Words
extra	ordinary	extraordinary	beyond the ordinary	extrasensory extracurricular
in	ability	inability	lack of ability	Answers will vary.
inter	galactic	intergalactic	between galaxies	
super	human	superhuman	greater than human	
trans	port	transport	to carry across	

Activity B

Below are definitions of words that begin with the prefixes *extra, in* (*im, il, ir*), *inter, super,* and *trans*. Name each word that is being defined. Use your dictionary if you need help.

1. not yet arrived at full development or growth   immature
2. unfinished   incomplete
3. to plant in another place   transplant
4. between continents   intercontinental
5. not lawful   illegal
6. a high-speed road   superhighway
7. to send a message across a distance, such as by telegraph   transmit
8. relating to a sound that is above what humans hear; vehicles that move faster than the speed of sound are called this   supersonic
9. something from beyond this planet   extraterrestrial
10. across the ocean   transoceanic

ACTIVITY B: After the students have correctly identified the new words, instruct them to choose eight words from the exercise and write an original sentence to illustrate the correct use of each word.

Activity C

Identify the words in the following paragraph that have prefixes you have studied in this Word Study, as well as any from Word Study 1 on pages 26 and 27. Then give a definition for each.

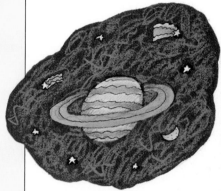

It was the first interplanetary trip for the new supership Helix. The purpose of the flight was to transport people to start a new colony on a distant planet. Nothing had misfunctioned until suddenly all the power went out. It was impossible for the ship to transmit signals! The preflight training paid off—no one panicked. The chief engineer, showing extraordinary control, went to work with a flashlight and soon found the source of the problem. It was incredible, but a mouse had gotten into the main power source. With the mouse now in a place of honor on the control panel, the ship continued on its journey.

ACTIVITY C: List on the chalkboard the words that the students identify. Have volunteers come to the chalkboard and underline the prefix in each word and give its meaning.

ANSWERS
Answers are underlined in the paragraph.

ADDITIONAL ACTIVITY
Have the students refer to the completed chart in activity A. Direct them to write one sentence for each prefix and to use *both* of their other words in the same sentence:

It was difficult for the astronaut to *interpret* the *interplanetary* message.

Chapter 3

Refining Your Writing Skills

Lesson 1 Combining Independent Clauses

Combining independent clauses helps to avoid choppy sentences and provides variety in sentence length.

A paragraph is composed of a group of sentences. Independent clauses are sentences, but they are usually short. If you have a number of independent clauses in a row, your paragraph will seem choppy. The short sentences might also confuse a reader, since the connection between one sentence and the next will not be clear.

In revising your writing, you should check to see if you have written series of short sentences, each with only one independent clause. If you have, you should try to combine ideas that go together. In this chapter, you will study several ways to combine ideas to improve the flow of your writing and to make your ideas easier for your reader to follow.

THE STUDENTS SHOULD LEARN
—the reasons for combining independent clauses
—how to select a coordinator that indicates the appropriate relationship between clauses

TEACHING THE LESSON
This lesson should be presented in combination with pages 386–387 (grammar chapter 6, section on coordinate conjunctions) and pages 424–426 (grammar chapter 7, section on compound sentences). This lesson stresses the relationship that each coordinate conjunction creates between the independent clauses. Use the examples in the introduction to illustrate just how each coordinator works. Have the students note that the coordinator *nor* is used with the negative adverb *not*.

Like paintings, paragraphs create moods. What mood is created by this painting?

One way to combine independent clauses is to create a *compound sentence*. Most of the time, you will do this by using the coordinate conjunctions *and, but, nor, or,* and *yet.* It is important to choose a coordinator based on the relationship between the clauses you are combining.

Coordinator	Relationship of Clauses	Example
and	ideas of equal importance	Paula is going swimming, and Jim is going, too.
but	opposite or contrasting ideas	Paula is going swimming, but Jim is not.
yet	opposite or contrasting ideas	Paula is going swimming, yet she is afraid of the water.
or	alternative ideas (options)	Jim may go swimming, or he may just fish from the dock.
nor	ideas of equal importance	Paula is not going swimming, nor is Jim.

When you use these coordinators between independent clauses, put a comma at the end of the first independent clause (as in the above examples).

Activity A

Combine the two sentences in each of the following pairs. Be sure to use a comma and an appropriate coordinator.
1. Bats have furry bodies. Their wings are smooth and flexible.
2. The weather may be sunny tomorrow. It may rain.
3. Lem cannot go to the movies. Lem cannot go to the game.
4. Patsie cannot go to the movies. Patsie does not want to go.
5. Raul cannot go to the movies. Raul really wants to go.
6. I oppose Pam's views. We remain friends.
7. Beethoven had great musical talent. The violin and piano were his special instruments.
8. Brian lost five dollars. He can't find it anywhere.
9. With the introduction of television, many people thought radio would disappear. Radio remains a source of entertainment and information.
10. Lynn makes paper flowers with special colored paper. Lynn gives the flowers to her friends as gifts.

Activity B

The coordinators in the following compound sentences are used incorrectly. Replace them with appropriate coordinators.

1. I know I should drink milk, and it makes me sick.
2. Ava ran to the train station, or the train was late anyway.
3. My mother works for the city, yet my father runs a business of his own.
4. I do not put butter on pancakes, but do I put it on French toast.
5. Dan was itchy when he had the chickenpox, or the doctor told him not to scratch.
6. We will go camping this weekend, but we will go to the zoo.
7. Andy will go to Memphis State University, and he will go to the University of Tennessee.
8. Henrietta will not tell us what she wants for her birthday, but her birthday is the day after tomorrow.
9. Do you want to go to the symphony, yet do you want to go to the theater?
10. The Harrises eat spaghetti every Thursday, yet the Smiths eat spaghetti every Friday.

More to Explore

Write five compound sentences using coordinators correctly. Remember to include a subject and verb in each clause, and to use a comma before the coordinator.

ACTIVITY B: Direct the students to tell why the original coordinate conjunction is inappropriate. What change does the new coordinator make in the sentence?

ANSWERS
1. but   6. or
2. but   7. or
3. and   8. and
4. nor   9. or
5. but   10. and (or but)

MORE TO EXPLORE: Suggest that the students use information from their classes to create the compound sentences, and that they use a different coordinator for each sentence. Put a sufficient number of sentences on the chalkboard to ensure that the proper relationship exists between the clauses.

ENRICHMENT

The students should be able to locate a number of compound sentences in magazines and newspapers. Have them cut out paragraphs that contain the compound sentences, highlight the sentences, and then glue the examples (eight to ten) on a piece of cardboard. They should try to locate sentences using the different coordinators.

Lesson 2 Using Adjectival Clauses to Combine Sentences

In a complex sentence, the adjectival clause (dependent clause) contains the idea of lesser importance. The principal clause contains the more important idea.

When you combine two sentences with a coordinator to make a compound sentence (as in lesson 1), they remain independent clauses. When you make one of the sentences a *dependent* clause, creating a *complex sentence*, you indicate something different about the relationship between the original sentences. You emphasize the idea of the independent clause and make the idea of the dependent clause seem less important. *An adjectival clause is always a dependent clause.*

Using adjectival clauses to combine sentences requires careful thought about the relationship between the ideas of the sentences. Consider the relationship between these two sentences:

> Maya Angelou is a modern black writer and performer.
> Maya Angelou has written about growing up in the South in the 1930s.

To make one sentence into an adjectival clause, use a relative pronoun (*who* in the following example). The adjectival clause (in brackets) is a dependent or subordinate clause. The other sentence (underlined) remains an independent clause—the principal clause of the new sentence.

> Maya Angelou, [who has written about growing up in the South in the 1930s], is a modern black writer and performer.

The adjectival clause, beginning with the pronoun *who*, states the idea of lesser importance. The writer wanted to emphasize who Maya Angelou is. The fact that Angelou has written about growing up in the South is interesting, but not essential to the sentence. The writer could have left the adjectival clause out to give greater emphasis to the fact that Angelou is a black writer and performer.

Suppose the writer wanted to make a different point. Then the sentence might read this way:

Maya Angelou, [who is a modern black writer and performer], has written about growing up in the South in the 1930s.

What is the most important idea in the sentence above?
What is the idea of lesser importance? Why?

Relative pronouns that can be used to combine sentences in this way include the following: *who, whom, which, that.*

Activity A

Underline
ad

Name the <u>principal clause</u> in each of the following complex sentences with <u>adjectival clauses</u>.

1. The car that had sped by us on the highway <u>was stopped by the police.</u>
2. The man who waved to me <u>normally operates the Ferris wheel.</u>
3. <u>Puffins,</u> which are Lucy's favorite birds, <u>live on sea cliffs in the wild.</u>
4. <u>Penguins,</u> which are aquatic birds like puffins, <u>cannot fly.</u>
5. <u>The horse</u> that is neighing <u>is an Appaloosa.</u>
6. <u>Her instrument,</u> which is made of brass, <u>is a French horn.</u>
7. <u>The painting</u> that the student is copying <u>was painted by van Gogh.</u>
8. <u>Chameleons,</u> which are a type of lizard, <u>are noted for their ability to change color.</u>
9. <u>Greenland,</u> which is on the Arctic Circle, <u>is not green but mostly ice covered.</u>
10. <u>The scissors</u> that are in the cabinet <u>do not cut paper well.</u>

Activity B

For each of the sentences in activity A, identify the dependent clause. Then reverse the two clauses of each sentence to change the emphasis. (Example: The car that was stopped by the police had sped by us on the highway.)

Activity C

Combine each pair of sentences to form a complex sentence with an adjectival clause. Let the first sentence of each pair be the main idea of the new sentence.

1. Kyle read *Brave New World*. The book gives a nightmarish view of future society.
2. Playing tennis is Barb's favorite activity. Playing tennis requires great concentration.
3. That computer is on sale this week. Jack likes that computer best.
4. The llama does not have a hump. The llama is in the camel family.
5. Mainframe computers are used by many large companies. Mainframe computers are much more powerful than microcomputers.

6. The football team began practice in early August. The football team has just been organized.
7. Athena was a Greek goddess. Athena sprang from the head of her father.
8. Tickets for the rock concert are sold out. Tickets went on sale yesterday.
9. My great-grandmother rides her bicycle every day. My great-grandmother is eighty-three years old.
10. Meercats inhabit the Kalahari Desert in southern Africa. Meercats are distant relatives of the mongoose.

More to Explore

Rewrite the following two paragraphs by combining some of the sentences with adjectival clauses. When you finish, paragraph 1 should be just three sentences long. Paragraph 2 might be as short as seven sentences.

1

In the cave we heard echoes. The echoes were unlike any we had heard before. They had a mysterious ringing. The ringing was long and sharp. Many people were very frightened by the sound. They were not used to being underground.

2

Some products may no longer be readily available. These products were once easy to buy. For example, when Mom was little, she ate a product called a push-up. This was ice cream in a tube. At the bottom of the tube was a stick. You pushed the stick to raise the ice cream. Another product was a kind of sugar candy. This product can no longer be bought in all places. The candy consisted of small, multicolored gobs of sugar. The gobs were hard and sweet. The gobs were glued onto a narrow sheet of white paper. The paper was a little like the tape from a cash register. Can you buy these products where you live?

Lesson 3 Using Adverbial Clauses to Combine Sentences

Combining sentences with adverbial clauses lengthens sentences and creates sentence variety. A special relationship exists between the principal clause and the adverbial clause.

THE STUDENTS SHOULD LEARN

—to recognize adverbial clauses as dependent clauses in sentences

—that a subordinate conjunction establishes a specific relationship between the principal clause and the adverbial clause

—that the placement of the adverbial clause, at the beginning or end of the sentence, helps provide sentence variety

TEACHING THE LESSON

Parallel this lesson with pages 392–393 (grammar chapter 6, section on subordinate conjunctions) and pages 411–414 (grammar chapter 7, section on adverbial clauses). Continue to remind the students that a clause must contain a subject and a predicate. Put this sentence on the chalkboard: After World War I, the United States welcomed an age of prosperity. Explain that *After World War I* is a *phrase*, not a clause. To have a clause, the sentence would have to read *After World War I had ended*, the United States....This lesson particularly stresses the relationship that subordinate conjunctions create between clauses. The sample sentence shows how a sentence changes in meaning simply by the use of a different conjunction. The students should study carefully the list of the various relationships and the sentences that illustrate them.

An adverbial clause is a type of dependent clause. When you combine two sentences by making one an adverbial clause, you create a complex sentence, just as you do when you combine sentences using adjectival clauses. To form an adverbial clause, use a subordinate conjunction. Choose a conjunction based on the relationship between the sentences you are combining. One word can change the whole meaning of a sentence.

```
                    after
                   /     \
The game ended—before—Pat scored again.
                   \     /
                    because
```

Some common subordinate conjunctions used to form adverbial clauses are shown below according to the relationships they indicate.

Time	Cause and Effect	Conditional	Comparative	Contrast
after	because	if	than	
as	since	provided		
before	so that	unless		
when				
while				

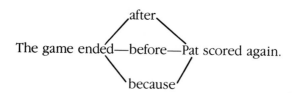

60

Here are some examples of adverbial clauses and the relationships they express.

> *After the concert was over*, we went to the café. (Time)

> Kim was angry *because her kitten had been stolen*. (Cause and effect)

> *If you want to make her happy*, you will have to behave differently. (Conditional)

> Ben ran faster *than he thought he could*. (Comparative)

Adverbial clauses may be placed either at the beginning of a sentence or at the end of a sentence. When they come at the beginning, they are always followed by a comma. When they come at the end, they are usually not marked by a comma. In the preceding examples, the adverbial clauses are used both ways.

Activity A

Complete each sentence with an appropriate subordinate conjunction.

1. _____ the storm hit our town, warning was given.
2. My family and I went to a local shelter _____ we would be safe from the storm.
3. _____ the storm hit, we were all a bit frightened.
4. _____ the storm was over, people tried to return to their homes.
5. _____ many trees had been blown down, many roads were blocked.
6. The Red Cross sent rescue teams to provide emergency shelter and food _____ many people had to leave their homes.
7. _____ we finally got back to our house, we found that part of the roof had caved in.
8. Our house had less damage _____ many other houses in our neighborhood did.
9. _____ the storm had struck nearer, our entire house could have been destroyed.
10. Dad said that we would have to move into an apartment _____ the damage is fixed.

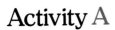

ACTIVITIES A AND B: The appropriate subordinate conjunction for each sentence is easy to determine. If the students choose conjunctions other than those specified, make sure they can support their answers.

ANSWERS
Answers may vary.
1. Before
2. so that
3. When
4. After
5. Because
6. since
7. When
8. than
9. If
10. until

Activity B

Choose an appropriate subordinate conjunction from the following list to combine each pair of sentences. Make the italicized sentence the dependent clause. Tell what kind of relationship you have made between the clauses.

since	because	if	when
before	after	unless	
until	while	so that	

1. Women in the United States could vote only after 1920. *The Nineteenth Amendment gave them the right to vote.*
2. Skyscrapers were not practical. *The elevator was invented.*
3. *All people will be fairly represented.* We hope to change the rules of the convention.
4. This carpet is in good condition. *It is fairly new.*
5. *The game was over.* Everyone cheered.
6. *You decide to enter the craft show.* Let me know.
7. I did my homework after school. *I had basketball practice in the evening.*
8. You will not get into the concert. *You bought tickets in advance.*
9. *Silent movies were shown.* An organist would play appropriate music.
10. Polio is now under control. *Jonas Salk developed an effective vaccine.*

Activity C

Move the adverbial clause in each sentence. If it is at the beginning, put it at the end; if it is at the end, put it at the beginning. (Remember to use a comma where needed.)

1. Although he is remembered primarily as an inventor, Benjamin Franklin also wrote interesting publications.
2. We had to get ready for school in the dark since the electric power was out in our neighborhood.
3. Helen always wears shorts when she runs.
4. Before you make your decision, consider all the facts.
5. If we have enough money, we can eat out tonight.

More to Explore

Use an adverbial clause to combine each pair of sentences.
1. Fran got her new car. Fran walked to school every day.
2. She worked after school and on weekends for two years. She could save enough money.
3. She had finally saved the money. Her parents were still uneasy.
4. She learned to change the oil and tires on her car. They would not approve her purchase.
5. They finally agreed. She began to drive a shiny blue car to school.

Lesson 4 Expanding Sentences

Expanding sentences involves adding descriptive words, phrases, or clauses to make the sentences more interesting.

You can use different parts of speech to expand sentences. Adjectives, adverbs, and prepositional phrases are especially good. Notice how the addition of different parts of speech expands the following sentence and makes it more interesting.

> The horse trotted home. (*Plain sentence*)
> The well-groomed horse trotted home. (*Adjective added*)
> The well-groomed horse trotted briskly home. (*Adverb added*)
> The well-groomed horse trotted briskly home across the snowy field. (*Prepositional phrase added*)

Be selective in expanding sentences. In writing compositions, never use sentence expansion just to make longer sentences. Always have a reason for adding that extra detail.

Activity A

Expand each sentence by adding extra words, phrases, or clauses where the arrows indicate.

1. The streetlamps cast∧light∧.
2. We have many∧trees∧.
3. The∧rabbits hopped∧off∧.
4. Judy's∧turtle lives here∧.
5. The∧cat∧jumped∧.

Activity B

Expand these sentences as you choose. Use your imagination.

1. That building leans.
2. The baby slept.
3. The flag waved.
4. The bridge fell.
5. Ginger baked a cake.
6. Harvey made brownies.
7. The boat rocked.
8. The cat stared.
9. Pamela's goat gives milk.
10. James practices.

Activity C

Expand the following sentences, using details that you observe in the picture at the top of the next page.

1. The storm approaches.
2. The clouds gather.
3. The sails fill.
4. The waves heighten.
5. The boats race.

More to Explore

Expand and combine sentences in the following paragraph to make it more interesting.

A tree is an indicator of the seasons. In spring, it is good to see buds appear. The colors of green blend together. The leaves covering the tree in summer provide shade. The colors of the autumn leaves are beautiful. A paintbrush moves from limb to limb. A tree in winter battles against wind and snow. It will struggle to have new growth again in the spring.

MORE TO EXPLORE: The students can do much to expand this paragraph. Adjectives, adverbs, phrases, and clauses will give life to each sentence and will provide a rich picture of the seasons. Allow the students to be as imaginative as possible. Explain that this is a process of revision and should be employed in all types of writing.

ENRICHMENT

Select a paragraph from any piece of literature. Rewrite it in simple sentences, leaving out adjectives, adverbs, and prepositional phrases. The students can rewrite it, using the skills learned in this chapter. Then show the students the original paragraph. Discuss the differences.

Lesson 5 Dividing and Trimming Sentences

Divide and trim sentences for clear, simple expression.

Madame Curie

Dividing Sentences

Just as you should combine and expand sentences that are too short, so should you divide and trim sentences that are too long. Sometimes sentences are *rambling* or *stringy*. Stringing many short sentences together makes for monotonous reading. Connectives such as *and* and *but* are often overused. Here is an example of a *rambling sentence*:

> A number of beautiful spruce trees adorn the lawn outside Tom's home, and last Tuesday a swarm of bees selected one of these trees and they built a hive in it, but Tom had to have the troublemakers removed.

To avoid rambling sentences, create shorter sentences and combine ideas where possible.

> A number of beautiful spruce trees adorn the lawn outside Tom's house. Last Tuesday a swarm of bees selected one of these trees for their new hive, but Tom had to have the troublemakers removed.

Sometimes sentences are too long because two or more sentences *run* together without the proper punctuation or no punctuation between them. They should actually be two or three separate sentences. Here are examples of *run-on sentences*.

> The Polish-born Marie Curie was one of the most respected modern scientists she discovered the elements of polonium and radium.

> Tigers inhabit the forests of Asia, some kinds of tigers are actually larger than their cousins, the lions.

To avoid run-on sentences, decide where each complete thought should stop. Put a period at the end, and begin the next word with a capital letter.

The Polish-born Marie Curie was one of the most respected modern scientists. She discovered the elements of polonium and radium.

Tigers inhabit the forests of Asia. Some kinds of tigers are actually larger than their cousins, the lions.

Rambling sentences are not grammatically incorrect, but are stylistically poor. They are simply a series of too many ideas connected by conjunctions. Run-on sentences are grammatically incorrect since there are two or more sentences joined together with either an incorrect mark of punctuation or no punctuation at all.

Activity A

Divide these rambling sentences into shorter ones. You may want to create two or more new sentences. Make sure that you include all the information from the original sentence.

1. Last night as we were having dinner the fire alarm sounded and we ran to the window and saw the house across the street on fire.
2. There were many fashionable models on display and Bianca found it difficult to choose a spring outfit from among them, but she finally selected an attractive tan suit and selected brown accessories.
3. After you go through the park, then you go across Main Street and then you walk along it for five blocks to 2933 where we live.
4. The bus came up the hill and it was packed to capacity and it was going very fast and when it reached the top it came to a sudden stop.
5. Arrange your paper neatly and keep a one-inch margin to the left and a narrower one to the right and be very sure to center your title on the first line and indent the first word of each paragraph one inch from the margin.

ACTIVITY A: Remind the students that not every *and* needs to be deleted. For each sentence, they should create at least two separate sentences, yet still combine ideas where possible.

ANSWERS
The following are suggested answers.
1. Last night as we were having dinner, the fire alarm sounded. We...
2. Bianca found it difficult to choose a spring outfit from the many fashionable models on display. She finally...
3. After you go through the park, you go across Main Street. Then you walk along Main Street five blocks. We live at 2933.
4. The bus, packed to capacity, raced up the hill. When it...
5. Arrange your paper neatly by keeping a one-inch margin to the left and a narrower one to the right. Be sure to center...

ACTIVITY B: The sentences need to be properly punctuated. The students should notice where their voice drops to complete a thought. This is an indication that a period is needed. Make sure that the students understand that the sentences are grammatically incorrect. They should look for and correct such sentences as they proofread their writing. Mention that run-on sentences may also be corrected by adding a coordinating conjunction preceded by a comma.

TEACHING THE LESSON

Redundancy is common in student writing. In their efforts to expand sentences, students may tend to repeat ideas. Write the following sentences on the chalkboard and see if the students can identify the repeated idea in each.

John began to *repeat* his sentence *over and over again*.

Her appointment was scheduled for *4:30 p.m.* Thursday *afternoon*.

A *huge*, *gigantic* building was constructed on the Parkway.

Help the students understand that to *repeat* means to do something *over and over again*; *p.m.* implies the *afternoon*; and *huge* means the same thing as *gigantic*.

Activity B

Correct the following run-on sentences. Consider where each complete thought ends and place a period after it. Then begin the next word with a capital letter.

1. The East Indies lie between southern Asia and Australia this chain of beautiful green islands is rich in natural resources.
2. Ice skating is no longer a sport limited to colder climates, indoor rinks with artificial ice have made this winter sport popular even in southern climates.
3. The dappled horses were hitched to a new carriage, they wore shining harnesses and attracted the attention of all.
4. We organized a club and called it Northeastern Athletic Society its purposes are to uphold the ideals of honorable sports conduct and to arrange games between schools.
5. Iris and I practiced our duet every day after school for a whole semester, her suggestions helped me to improve my part.

Trimming Sentences

When you trim sentences, you shorten them by removing unnecessary words. Unnecessary words repeat ideas that are already stated. They simply add to the length of a sentence, but not to its meaning. As you revise your writing, you should remove unneeded words. Study the following example. What can be eliminated?

> The travelers were impressed by the blue, azure water of the Mediterranean.

The words *blue* and *azure* have similar meanings. One of those words can be eliminated. In revising the sentence, you might substitute a word that describes another quality of the water, such as *mirrorlike*. Here is another example.

> The movie's unique spaceship, which was unlike any I had ever seen before, had the shape of a giant oil well.

The entire adjectival clause *which was unlike any I had ever seen before* is not needed. The word *unique* suggests that the spaceship was "one of a kind." It is not necessary to state that fact again. The revised sentence can simply read "The movie's unique spaceship had the shape of a giant oil well."

Activity

Trim the following sentences by removing unnecessary words. Be ready to give a reason for your answers.

1. The construction workers built the tall fifty-story skyscraper in less than two years.
2. Our Scrabble team has actually won ten consecutive tournaments in a row.
3. The huge, enormous submarine sandwich was shared by the whole family.
4. Everyone was pleased by the total, complete change in Nicole's attitude.
5. Ivan's victory in the essay contest was astonishing news that surprised everyone.
6. That was the most dull and boring program I've seen all year!
7. Nina lay and reclined on the sandy beach, watching the children build sand castles.
8. The biography about the life of the baseball player Roberto Clemente had many action-filled photographs in it.
9. After Janna read the chapter for history class once, she reread it again.
10. Emmett Kelly always played the sad, mournful clown.

More to Explore

The following paragraph contains unnecessary words and rambling sentences. Rewrite the paragraph, dividing and trimming sentences as necessary.

> With the first spring thunderstorm of rain the water made the grass begin to spring up from under the ground. The earth felt soft, mushy, and wet underfoot as we walked across the swampy baseball diamond toward the neon lights of the all-night convenience store. Before too long the blaring bright light of the sun would be beating down on the desolate earth and we would hear the sound of bats and balls and tramping feet on solid, hard, dry, dusty ground but for a while, a few months anyway, we and the birds and mosquitoes would have this lagoon to ourselves.

Emmett Kelly

Writing Corner 3

Characterization

As you know, characters in a story are the *persons* involved in the story. However, the word *character* also refers to the *inner qualities* of people. Some people in literature and in life have good inner qualities, such as kindness or honesty. Some, unfortunately, have inner qualities such as unkindness or dishonesty. In many people, there is a mixture of qualities, but usually a few predominate. As you get to know people, you learn that they are *usually* kind, *usually* energetic, or *usually* undependable. These qualities make up their character.

As a writer, you want the reader to "get to know" the people in your story. The methods writers use to let the reader understand the inner person are called *characterization*.

Read this characterization paragraph about a teacher.

> Maybe because she always stood so erectly in the front of the room, Miss Linaldi seemed tall to us. We knew that she wasn't really young, but somehow she seemed young. There were clear brushes of authentic gray in her wavy dark hair. Today, her blue pleated skirt and pale green blouse seemed just right. I guess it was because they reflected, in a way, the in-between shades of her blue-green eyes. Her eyes, I realized, were the youthful part! They were clear and strong, too. She looked at us with respect, yet she challenged us. Sometimes we noticed an almost hidden twinkle. Her eyes *were* the young part.

What method of characterization does the writer use? You are right if you noticed that the writer stresses the *physical appearance* of the teacher. However, the writer chose only those physical traits that help you see what kind of person Miss Linaldi is. What are some of the inner qualities of this teacher expressed in the paragraph?

Read this characterization paragraph about the same teacher.

As the class worked hard on their final exam, Miss Linaldi stood at the lectern in the front of the room. Unobserved, she took this quiet time to look at each student. She knew that soon summer would scatter the energies that now were directed toward their exam. Those energies would run in a hundred different directions. She would miss that energy. Even as she, too, looked forward to the calmer cadence of summer, she smiled as she thought of the "new" insights into English literature that this class had provided her. Literature and life, she thought. They really need each other. Each person here had added to that *life*.

What method of characterization is used here? You are right if you noticed that the writer focuses on the *inner thoughts* of Miss Linaldi. However, the writer selected only those thoughts which emphasize that specific inner quality that makes the teacher a special person. How does this paragraph help you to get to know Miss Linaldi better? Which of the teacher's qualities are made clear?

Here are some ways you can help your reader understand what a person is really like.

1. You can write about the *physical traits* of a person. Choose only those traits that reflect important inner qualities.
2. You can describe the *inner thoughts* of a person. Select those that focus on the special inner qualities of the person.

★ Think of a person you really know—for example, a friend, a teacher, a parent, a brother, or sister. List a few important inner qualities of that person. Decide which of the methods described above would best help your reader know the person as you do.

Write a paragraph focusing on *one* of the methods of characterization. When you have finished, write about the same person using the other method of characterization. Have another person read your two paragraphs. Ask about the reader's impressions of the person you described. Are the reader's impressions the ones you had hoped to convey?

Root Words

A root word is a base word from which other words are built.

Many root words come from the Latin and Greek languages. Some can stand alone; others are used only with other word parts added to them. Below are some common root words and their meanings.

dict	to say or speak
graph	to write
pend	to hang
port	to carry
spect	to see

Activity A

Copy and complete the chart below. Use the example as a model.

Word Part	Root	Word	Meaning	Other Words
e	dict	edict	speech from an authority	dictionary dictator
tele	graph	telegraph	to send words by wire	Answers will vary.
de	pend	depend	to rely on	
im	port	import	to carry into	
circum	spect	circumspect	seeing all factors, cautious	

Activity B

Complete each of the following sentences with a word based on the root shown in parentheses.

1. One basic (port) of the United States to other countries is technology and scientific knowledge.
2. That famous movie star, who likes to keep her privacy, seldom signs her (graph) for fans.
3. The mover was able to (port) all the furniture in one truckload.
4. The police (spect) sent to investigate the robbery interviewed everyone who worked in the bank.
5. Look up words you don't know in the (dict).
6. With the clouds becoming so dark overhead, we had a sense of the (pend) storm.
7. Nikki takes that new (port) radio everywhere.
8. Susan can make beautiful, handwritten signs because she studied the art of (graph).
9. The two witnesses began to (dict) each other about what happened during the robbery.
10. The Colosseum in Rome held fifty thousand (spect).
11. The ability to speak clearly and well is called (dict).
12. Around her neck, Evelyn wore a golden (pend), which had been given to her by her grandmother.
13. In a surprise reversal of roles, the secretary (dict) a letter to the executive.
14. Wanda can draw pictures on her computer, which are called computer (graph).
15. The swinging (pend) on the grandfather clock puts me to sleep.

FOTY

Chapter 4

Types of Paragraphs

Lesson 1 Writing Expository Paragraphs

An expository paragraph explains something to the reader or gives the reader information.

Expository writing does not tell a story (a narrative paragraph does that). It does not use sense words to create a vivid picture (a descriptive paragraph does that). The purpose of expository writing is simple—to give information. You encounter expository writing around you constantly, at home and at school. You find it in how-to books, cookbooks, encyclopedias, and science textbooks. It is the kind of writing that you are doing when you explain how to do a craft project or explain what something, such as a hurricane, is.

It is important that expository writing be *clear*. As a reader, you need to understand all the steps that the writer is presenting. If the steps are not clear, you may not be able to complete the project or follow the explanation. Doing expository writing, you should constantly ask yourself, "Have I given my reader all the information he or she needs?"

How-to Paragraphs

One kind of expository writing provides instructions for performing an action or explaining how objects work. The information is given in logical order. Often the order of the paragraph follows the order in which the events occur. Transition words tie the ideas together. Some of the commonly used transition words are *first, second, after, next, then,* and *finally*.

Some people stretch to achieve excellence. Others stretch their talents. What makes the difference?

Here is an example of an expository paragraph that tells how to make a Christmas ornament. Note how the first sentence states what is being made. The second sentence lists the materials needed, while the sentences that follow give the procedure. The ending sentence states the value and pleasure derived from creating the object.

Making Christmas ornaments can be both fun and easy. You will need a small Styrofoam ball, wooden cocktail toothpicks, liquid starch or tempera spray paint, and powdered tinsel. First, stick the toothpicks into the Styrofoam close together so that the toothpicks seem to radiate from the ball. Next, dip the ornament into the liquid starch, or spray it with tempera paint. Then while the starch or paint is still wet, sprinkle the ornament with powdered tinsel. Finally, suspend the ball from string or ribbon if you want to use it as a Christmas tree ornament. Or you can place the ball among boughs of evergreens on a mantel. This home-made decoration will provide years of holiday beauty.

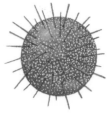

Paragraphs That Define

Another kind of expository writing provides definition of things or ideas. When you are required to define a word, first tell the general class to which the term belongs. Then give specific characteristics about that term.

Pretend you are writing for someone who has never seen such a thing and has no idea what it is like. You will find it helpful to begin by brainstorming for the characteristics of the item. Write down all the characteristics you can think of in the form of a list. Here is a sample list for a *parrot*, followed by an expository paragraph based on the list.

Term to be defined: parrot
General classification: large bird
Specific characteristics:
    imitates the human voice
    brightly colored
    lives in tropical climates
    eats seeds and fruits
    popular as a cage pet
    lives as long as seventy-five years

A parrot is a large bird that can imitate the human voice. Usually brightly colored, these birds are tree creatures and live in tropical climates. Their diet consists mainly of seeds and fruits. Parrots are popular as cage pets, often becoming very friendly and affectionate. These interesting animals have been known to live as long as seventy-five years.

Paragraphs That Explain

Another kind of expository writing gives facts and details that support or explain a topic. Below is an example of this kind of paragraph. The paragraph explains why it is necessary to be careful when riding a bicycle in the city. Notice most of the middle sentences in the paragraph give *reasons* to support that idea.

When bicycle riding in the city, you have to be very careful. You must follow the rules of the road, stopping at red lights and stop signs and keeping to the right. If you don't watch the roadway carefully, you may hit a bump that will fling you into the path of oncoming cars. You also have to watch the cars in the traffic around you, particularly a car that is about to make a right turn in front of you. Sometimes people, adults and children, step out into the street, and you have to avoid hitting them. These are only a few of the hazards of bicycling in the city!

Activity A

Put the following directions in the proper order, and then write the ideas as one paragraph. Add transition words where needed.

1. Get out a big mixing bowl for the ingredients you have just gathered. 4
2. Gather all the ingredients: the cake mix, one cup of water, one-third cup of vegetable oil, and three eggs. 3
3. First, preheat the oven to 350 degrees. 2
4. Use an electric mixer or a hand egg beater to blend the ingredients together. 6
5. Pour all of the ingredients carefully into the bowl. 5
6. To make a box cake, all you have to do is follow the directions. 1
7. In thirty minutes, you will have a hot cake fresh from the oven. 8
8. When the batter is smooth, pour it into a baking pan, and put the pan into the oven. 7

Activity B

Try writing a paragraph defining any two of the items listed below. Pretend you are writing for someone who has never seen such a thing and has no idea what it is like. You will find it helpful to begin by brainstorming for all the characteristics of the item you can think of and writing them in a list. For example:

Snail
small animal, is a kind of shellfish
lives both in and out of water
moves slowly
moves in a spiral-type hard shell
considered a gourmet delicacy
served as escargot in expensive restaurants

1. apple tree
2. cat
3. book
4. clock
5. trumpet

ACTIVITY A: Accept any logical sentence order other than that indicated. The paragraph should be written and then read aloud so that the students can *see* and *hear* the logical order. Continue to stress the need for transition words to help make smooth connections between sentences.

ACTIVITY B: Study the example on how to define a snail. Point out the progression from the general to the specific, and then have the students develop a paragraph using this information. After they have chosen two objects to be defined, remind them to brainstorm for as many specific characteristics as possible and then list them before beginning to write. They do not need to do research but should simply list what they know about each item. Have them consult the checklist at the end of this lesson. Have an oral sharing of paragraphs.

Activity C

Choose two of the following topics. Make a list of details to support the topics of your choice. Choose one of those lists of details and use it to create a paragraph. Be sure to use transition words to make your paragraph clear. (For the last two topics, you may have to look in an encyclopedia.)

1. How to ride a skateboard
2. Why people need exercise
3. How to plant a garden
4. Why newspapers are important
5. How to make scrambled eggs
6. How to find your way to my house
7. Why a computer is useful to have at home
8. Why a hobby is important to have
9. What an armadillo is
10. What a coral reef is

More to Explore

Choose one of the following suggestions and write an expository paragraph as directed.

1. You live in the city, and you want to take the bus and/or train to the zoo. You call the bus company for directions. Write a paragraph that includes the directions they give you.
2. You have developed a sure-fire strategy of making record high scores on a popular computer game. Write a paragraph explaining your strategy.
3. You have organized a group of friends to go on a bike trip. Tell how many are in your group and the route you plan to take.
4. You want to make your favorite food for dinner, and so you look up a recipe, shop for the ingredients, and are finally ready to start preparing the food. Describe what you do.
5. Look up "chameleon" in an encyclopedia and write a paragraph in which you try to define what it is. Be sure to include its general classification and its interesting characteristics.
6. In a paragraph, explain what a "fast food" restaurant is. The trick is that you are writing the paragraph for someone who comes from another country that does not have such places.

ACTIVITY C: Have the students exchange paragraphs to revise one another's work. Tell them to check for items in logical order and the effective use of transition words. Share student writing.

MORE TO EXPLORE: Have the students discuss what would be entailed in each one of the suggestions. Share as many student paragraphs as possible.

ENRICHMENT
Suggest that the students write directions for a science experiment or directions for doing an art project. One student might give directions to the class for the art project and then have the class attempt to complete it. This is a good way to check for clarity and preciseness of directions.

Revising an Expository Paragraph

As you reread your paragraph, ask yourself the following questions:

—Are all the details in the correct order?

—Was I able to use transition words to connect sentences? (Try to use at least two.)

—Does my beginning or ending sentence state what I am explaining or defining?

—Have I used a blend of simple, compound, and complex sentences?

—Are my sentences clear and precise? Have I used specific vocabulary?

—Does my paragraph make sense? *Now* is the time to add, delete, or rearrange your ideas. Talk over these changes with another student or your teacher. Rewrite the paragraph and go on to proofreading.

Proofreading an Expository Paragraph

As you look over your paragraph, ask yourself these questions:

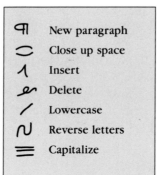

¶	New paragraph
⌒	Close up space
⋏	Insert
℘	Delete
/	Lowercase
∿	Reverse letters
≡	Capitalize

—Have I used the correct marks of punctuation at the ends of my sentences?

—Can I explain all other marks of punctuation?

—Are all appropriate words capitalized?

Start at the last word of the paragraph and check for correct spelling. Rewrite the paragraph if necessary.

Lesson 2 Writing Descriptive Paragraphs

A descriptive paragraph uses words to portray a person, place, or thing vividly.

When you write a descriptive paragraph, you are *describing* a person, place, or thing. You want the reader to know what you saw, smelled, tasted, heard, or felt. To do this effectively, you must think carefully about your subject. You must give details.

Picture your experience in your mind. Try to relive it. Then use precise language to describe it to the reader. If you were to write about a day at the beach, for example, you would probably want to describe how the water looked. Think about it. If it was blue, what kind of blue was it? Sky blue? Blue-green? Blue as if someone had dropped in hundreds of blue dye tablets? Be specific, and use words creatively!

Read the following description of a scene from *The Red Pony* by John Steinbeck.

> The afternoon was green and gold with spring. Underneath the spread branches of the oaks the plants grew pale and tall, and on the hills the feed was smooth and thick. The sagebrushes shone with new silver leaves and the oaks wore hoods of golden green. Over the hills there hung such a green odor that the horses on the flats galloped madly, and then stopped, wondering; lambs, and even old sheep, jumped in the air unexpectedly and landed on stiff legs, and went on eating; young clumsy calves butted their heads together and drew back and butted again.

Did you notice how Steinbeck uses many descriptive words, particularly color words—green, gold, and silver? For example, the oaks wore "hoods of golden green." He even uses the word *green* to describe the fresh odor of the hills in spring.

THE STUDENTS SHOULD LEARN
—how to employ sense impressions in the writing of a descriptive paragraph

TEACHING THE LESSON
Sense impressions are extremely important to the writing of a good descriptive paragraph. Spend sufficient time on the paragraphs in the introduction. Have the students point out words that particularly help to give a clear description of the spring and the old man. The students should realize that most of the description is visual, but that the senses of hearing, smell, taste, and touch are just as effective in a descriptive paragraph. Perhaps the "class artist" could actually draw a sketch of the spring hills and man approaching the ranch.

The checklist at the end of this lesson will help the students give direction to their writing.

Now read the following description of a person from the same story by Steinbeck. In the passage, the ten-year-old main character, Jody, is watching someone approach the ranch on which he lives.

…In a few moments he had trudged close enough so that his face could be seen. And his face was as dark as dried beef. A mustache, blue-white against the dark skin, hovered over his mouth, and his hair was white, too, where it showed at his neck. The skin of his face had shrunk back against the skull until it defined bone, not flesh, and made the nose and chin seem sharp and fragile. The eyes were large and deep and dark, with eyelids stretched tightly over them. Irises and pupils were one, and very black, but the eyeballs were brown. There were no wrinkles in the face at all. This old man wore a blue denim coat buttoned to the throat with brass buttons, as all men do who wear no shirts. Out of the sleeves came strong bony wrists and hands gnarled and knotted and hard as peach branches. The nails were flat and blunt and shiny.

Notice how the paragraph gives a great deal of detail so that a picture can form in your mind.

Activity A

ACTIVITY A: Discuss the imagery in the sample sentence under each sense impression. Have an oral discussion about each of the suggestions listed before the students actually begin writing a descriptive sentence. Share as many student sentences as possible.

Using your senses is vital to writing a good descriptive paragraph. Below are sample sentences that use the senses of sight, sound, taste, touch, and smell. After reading each sentence, choose two of the suggestions below it and write descriptive sentences of your own.

SIGHT

The fireworks sprinkled sequins of color across the sky.
Try describing: an abandoned house
      a race horse
      a sunrise

SOUND

The old train chugged, coughed, and choked up the steep hill.
Try describing: a music station on your radio
      the school cafeteria
      a traffic accident

TOUCH

The damp, cold night penetrated my aching body.
Try describing: the veins on a leaf
a piece of sandpaper
a snake

TASTE

The sour grapes left a bitter taste in my mouth.
Try describing: chocolate ice cream
an apple
pizza

SMELL

The fragrance of the honeysuckle filled the meadow with its heavy sweetness.
Try describing: a bakery
a new car
a farm

Activity B

The following sentences lack detailed description. By using as many sense impressions as possible, make each sentence come alive. (You may want to change the structure of the sentence.)

1. It rained.
2. The meatballs were hot.
3. The trashcan fell.
4. The rose garden smells good.
5. Downtown is busy.
6. Tight shoes bother me.
7. The radio was loud.
8. The weather was hot.
9. The room was painted brightly.
10. Thad ate some potato chips.

ACTIVITY B: Words create different effects. Discuss the different imagery that each student uses and how one sentence differs from the other.

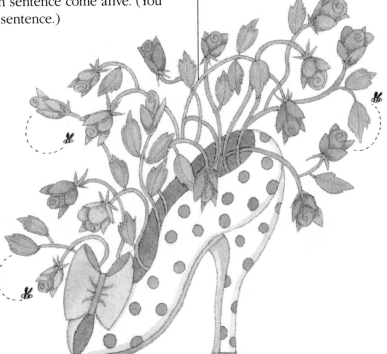

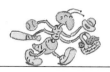

Activity C

Rewrite the following paragraph, adding details. Be sure to use all senses: sight, sound, taste, touch, and smell.

> The park is full on Saturdays. People play baseball. Some have picnics. Others sleep in the sun. I like to swim. Mikki windsurfs. Reynaldo listens to the radio. Everyone goes home at night.

More to Explore

Choose two of the following ideas and develop them into descriptive paragraphs.

1. It is a hot summer day, and you are spending it at the city pool with some friends. Explain how you feel when you are in the water, and describe the sights and sounds around you.
2. You have both a backyard and a dog. You are unaware that the neighbor's cat is in the backyard. You let out the dog. Describe the scene that follows.
3. You have as much money as you want to decorate and furnish your own bedroom. Describe what it will look like.
4. You are riding down a country road in the car. You pass a small farmhouse. There are a man, woman, and child in the yard. Describe the scene in detail.
5. It is Saturday night in an apartment building. People of different nationalities live here, and it seems as if they are all cooking. You are climbing the stairs to the top floor. Describe the sights, sounds, and smells you encounter on the way.
6. Your family moved, and you had to change schools. This is your first day in the new school. Describe how you feel and what the scene is like around you.
7. You are at a family picnic with an outdoor grill. People are involved in various activities, and lots of good food is being prepared. Describe it all.

Revising a Descriptive Paragraph

Reread the paragraph and underline all the sensory details. Ask yourself the following questions:

—Which senses predominate in my piece of writing?

—Can I picture the characters or scenes in my mind? Could they be drawn on a piece of paper?

—Did I use a creative beginning sentence?

—Does my title attract attention?

—Did I use strong action verbs? Did I avoid verbs of being?

—Is there a blend of simple, compound, and complex sentences?

—Does my paragraph make sense?

Now is the time to add, delete, or rearrange ideas. Discuss these changes with another student or your teacher. Rewrite the paragraph and then go on to proofreading.

Proofreading a Descriptive Paragraph

As you look over your paragraph, ask yourself these questions:

¶	New paragraph
⌒	Close up space
⋏	Insert
℘	Delete
/	Lowercase
𝇎	Reverse letters
=	Capitalize

—Is the correct mark of punctuation used at the end of each sentence?

—Have I used commas after introductory phrases and clauses? Can I explain the other marks of punctuation?

—Did I capitalize the important words in the title?

Start at the last word of the paragraph and check for correct spelling. Rewrite the paragraph if necessary.

Lesson 3 Writing Narrative Paragraphs

A narrative paragraph tells a story.

THE STUDENTS SHOULD LEARN

—that a narrative paragraph contains a logical order of events

—that different kinds of narrators can tell a story

—that appropriate transitions should be used in narrative writing

TEACHING THE LESSON

Initiate a class discussion about the narrative paragraph in the introduction. Focus on the transitions that show the order of events. This concept was presented on pages 32–35 (sequential order). The students should also propose other things that they might want to know about the story, and why these things might have been omitted. Explain that in this paragraph the *first person narrator* is used because the narrator is part of the story. The *third person narrator* is used when the narrator is an observer and outside the story. Thoroughly discuss the questions at the end of the paragraph. The transition words are *by the time, by that time, then, eventually.*

The checklist at the end of this lesson will help the students give direction to their writing.

A narrative paragraph tells what events occurred, where they happened, who was involved, and, usually, how the story ended. The paragraph is written from the point of view of the speaker, or *narrator*, who may be a person in the story or a person observing the story.

Every story involves some kind of action, and the events take place in a particular order. Transition words are important in a narrative paragraph because they show how events are related to one another.

Read the following paragraph and notice how the events happen one after another.

> Some days working at the Burger Bay are just amazing! Last Saturday I went in at 11:30 to work the lunch shift. Everything was a mess. The people who worked breakfast had been too busy to get the place cleaned up. By the time the lunch crowd hit, all five of us workers were in a frenzy. We could not find anything. A customer came up and ordered a medium drink, and we were out of cups. It took ten minutes for the manager to bring the new cups up from the basement. By that time, the customer had finished yelling at me—but a line seven customers long had formed behind him. They were all upset because they had to wait so long for service. Then the grill caught fire. One of the customers jumped over the counter, knocking over Penny, who was spraying the grill with a fire extinguisher, and started waving a coat at the flames, which only made things worse. Eventually, the fire department arrived—after we had put out the fire, but just in time to eat the leftover hamburgers. The customers had decided that trying to get food at Burger Bay was too much work.

Answer these questions about the paragraph.

Where does the story take place?

Who is involved?

What happens?

Does the narrator take part in the story or observe the action?

Is the story interesting?

How would you feel if you were there?

Name some transition words that connect the different events.

Activity A

Below and on the next page are two groups of sentences that are out of order. For each group, list the sentences in the correct order and then write them as a logical narrative.

Group 1

1. Dan had forgotten to replace the bolt to plug the drain hole. 8
2. Eventually, the bolt loosened and fell onto the ground. 3
3. Dan was changing the oil in his father's car for the first time. 1
4. When he was all finished, his father walked out and asked, "Did you remember to change the oil filter while you had the oil all drained out?" 11
5. Dan pushed a pan under the spouting oil. 5
6. Then he added four more quarts. 10
7. When all the oil had drained out, Dan poured a quart of fresh oil into the engine. 6
8. Splash! The new oil rushed through the engine and sprayed into the pan under the car. 7
9. Oil poured out. 4
10. He scrambled under the car to put the bolt in before all the new oil drained out. 9
11. He couldn't find a wrench the right size to loosen the bolt at the bottom of the oil pan, so he used a pair of vise grips and nearly flattened the edges of the bolt. 2

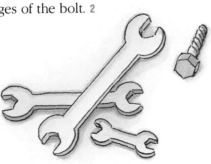

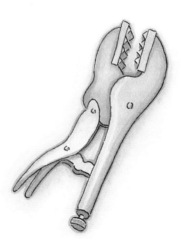

ACTIVITY A: Accept sentence orders other than those indicated if they are logical. For most students, it will be helpful to write both groups of sentences as complete paragraphs. Stress the need to use transition words to connect ideas smoothly. Have volunteers read their paragraphs aloud so that they and the other students can *hear* the sequence of events and the transition words.

Group 2

1. She wanted to keep herself loose for the game in the afternoon. 3
2. She was pitching. 4
3. The morning dragged on and on. 6
4. By 3:15, it was over, and Marcia had pitched the best game of her career, a 7–0 no hitter! 12
5. She thought the noon bell would never ring. 7
6. After the morning run, shower, and breakfast, she rode her bike to school. 5
7. The game started at 1:00 p.m. 11
8. Finally, it did. 8
9. Marcia was off to the locker room. 9
10. Marcia jumped out of bed, eager to get out of the house for an easy run. 2
11. She quickly changed into her uniform, grabbed her glove, and strode toward the playing fields. 10
12. The day dawned clear and bright. 1

Activity B

Choose one of the following topic sentences and list three or four specific details that relate to it. Then write a narrative paragraph, using the topic sentence and your details. Be sure to use appropriate transitions.

1. There was a strange incident in our neighborhood.
2. My sister (brother) bothers me all of the time.
3. Practicing _____ is hard work.
4. Going to the dentist is no fun.
5. I'm glad dreams aren't for real.

More to Explore

Write a narrative paragraph of your own, using one of the following topics (or a topic of your choice):

1. The most interesting trip I've taken
2. A most unusual camp experience
3. A retelling of a well-known fairy tale
4. The funniest movie I've seen
5. The bravest thing I've done

ACTIVITY B: As a class, have the students suggest details appropriate for each topic. This will help the students decide which paragraph they wish to develop. Going through the process of listing details, putting them in order, and forming them into a paragraph is good practice in logic. Review the difference between first and third person point of view. Be sure the students have a chance to draft/revise their work. They should consult the checklist at the end of this lesson during revision and proofreading.

MORE TO EXPLORE: Discussion of each topic will help with student choice. The students should begin by arranging the details of the story in logical order, and then decide whether they wish to tell the story from the first or third person point of view. The checklist should be consulted frequently and the students should continually exchange ideas.

ENRICHMENT
Assign a short story for the entire class to read. Discuss the point of view and order of events. Consider how the story would change if written from a different point of view.

Revising a Narrative Paragraph

In your mind, list the events of the story as they happened. Check that they are *written* in the same order.

Ask yourself the following questions:

—Have I used effective transition words to connect sentences?

—Are my characters well described? Can the setting (if one was used) be pictured in my mind?

—Do I have an effective beginning and ending?

—Does my title attract attention?

—Have I used a blend of simple, compound, and complex sentences?

—Did I use strong action verbs? Did I avoid verbs of being?

—Does my paragraph make sense?

Now is the time to add, delete, or rearrange ideas. Discuss these changes with another student or your teacher. Rewrite the paragraph and go on to proofreading.

Proofreading a Narrative Paragraph

As you look over your paragraph, ask yourself these questions:

¶	New paragraph
⌒	Close up space
⋏	Insert
℘	Delete
/	Lowercase
∿	Reverse letters
≡	Capitalize

—Is the correct mark of punctuation used at the end of each sentence?

—Have I used commas after introductory phrases and clauses? Can I explain the other marks of punctuation?

—Did I capitalize the important words in the title?

Start at the last word of the paragraph and check for correct spelling. Rewrite the paragraph if necessary.

Lesson 4 Writing with Dialogue

Dialogue is written conversation between people.

Sometimes, having people speak in dialogue tells a story more clearly and effectively than a simple narrative. If you are writing something that has dialogue in it, you must follow the rules for using quotation marks.

Consider the following pieces of writing. The first is a narrative paragraph telling a story; the second uses dialogue to tell the same story.

Narrative Version

Karen and Jake went down to the river to swim. On the way, they passed Susan and asked her to join them. She went along to watch, because she couldn't swim very well. When they all got to the river, some other people were already swimming. Karen and Jake stripped down to their swimsuits and waded in. Susan took off her shoes, sat on the bank, and dangled her feet in the water. She laughed and waved at Karen and Jake. Suddenly she realized her bracelet had slipped from her arm and fallen into the water. Without thinking, she bent over to grab it before it sank, and immediately fell head first into the river. She became panicky and started bobbing up and down. Karen, calling Susan's name, quickly swam toward her and pulled her to safety. Karen and Jake decided that Susan's swimming lessons should begin the very next day!

Dialogue Version

Karen and Jake went down to the river to swim. "Would you like to join us, Susan?" asked Karen as they walked by her on the street.

"I can't swim very well," said Susan, "but I'd like to come watch, anyway." So they all walked together to the river.

"Look!" called Jake, "Lots of people are already swimming. Let's get in there, Karen!" He and Karen stripped to their suits and waded in.

Susan took off her shoes and stuck her feet in the water from the bank. "Don't get wet," she called, laughing and waving at Jake and Karen.

No sooner had Susan said this than her bracelet slipped from her arm and fell into the water. Without thinking, she bent over to grab it before it sank, and immediately fell head first into the river. "Help! I . . . can't swim," cried Susan. In water over her head, she panicked and started bobbing up and down.

Karen swam quickly toward her, calling "Susan, Susan!" and pulled her to safety.

Jake helped them both out of the water and said, "Susan, your swimming lessons begin tomorrow."

"You're right," Karen chimed in. "The sooner the better."

What are some of the differences between the first piece of writing and the second? Which do you prefer? Why? Why is there so much indentation in the second piece? Can you tell when to indent?

When you write with dialogue, try to make it sound real. Imagine people talking and saying the things you are writing. Act it out with a friend. Use words that make sense to describe the voices. Words like *said, cried, screamed, yelled, murmured, exclaimed,* and *called* can all be used at different times. When you choose one of those words, make sure it fits the action. If your characters are having a quiet conversation, for example, probably one of them is not going to suddenly yell.

Observe the following rules when using dialogue:

1. Start a new paragraph every time you change speakers. If your characters are trading one-line comments, your paragraphs may be very short. That's fine.
2. Put quotation marks around anything that is being spoken.
3. Use commas to set the quoted words apart from the speaker of the words, as in the example.
4. Make use of other punctuation as needed.

Activity A

ACTIVITY A: Provide a copy of the correct punctuation for each student through duplication, on a transparency, or opaque projector. Give special attention to the proper places for indentation. The students should be able to explain why they indented the paragraph at a specific point.

The following dialogue is written incorrectly. On a separate sheet of paper, correct it by adding quotation marks, other punctuation, and paragraph indentations where needed.

On a spring day like this said Nan my favorite thing is taking a long walk. Really? said Margarita I like to sit on the back porch and read. Priscilla laughed at them. How can you even think of doing anything as quiet as sitting on the porch or taking a walk? I want to have a huge party, with music and dancing! Michael responded I guess everybody just likes different things. If I had my choice, I would go for a long bike ride.

Activity B

Take the action from the following narrative paragraph and turn it into dialogue. Keep checking on the rules for writing dialogue.

Ruby and Thad go hiking in the park. They have been hiking for an hour when they find an injured squirrel on the path. It is a baby squirrel and seems to have fallen from a tree. They try to decide what to do. Ruby isn't sure whether they should touch it; she has heard that baby animals who have been touched by humans will be abandoned by their parents. Thad agrees but doesn't think that the little squirrel will live if they don't help it. It is hardly moving. They make a sling out of Thad's shirt, roll the squirrel into it, and carry it carefully to the closest telephone. They call the park ranger, who comes to take care of the animal.

Activity C

Select two of the following situations. Write a brief dialogue to show what you think might happen between the people involved.

1. An ice-cream truck goes slowly down the street ringing its bell. Peter and Julio hear it and then run after it to buy ice-cream sandwiches.
2. It is time for math class, and the teacher is walking around the room collecting the assignments. Jane has not done her homework. The teacher reaches Jane's desk.
3. Oliver was listening to the radio on his way to school when the announcer said that the station would give a free baseball cap to everyone who came by the station before 5:00 that afternoon. Oliver is supposed to go straight home after school. He calls home to see if he can get permission to go to the radio station.
4. Ned just finished reading a good book and is telling Ginny about it. Ginny asks Ned questions in response to his comments.
5. A friend asks you to go to the movies on Saturday afternoon. You want to go, but you are playing in a softball game.

More to Explore

Make up a situation for a story. Write it on paper as a narrative paragraph. Then exchange papers with someone in the class. Now, write a dialogue to fit the narrative paragraph of your partner.

Writing Corner 4

Comparison and Contrast

Many times in social studies, science, or literature classes, you are asked to compare or contrast two persons, events, things, or ideas. When you write a paragraph that shows *similarities*, you are using a method of writing called *comparison*. When you write a paragraph that shows *differences*, you are using a method of writing called *contrast*.

Comparison

In science class, Ken was asked to write a paragraph comparing ants and bees. To help organize his work, he developed a chart like this:

Ants	Bees
live in colonies	live in colonies
queens, males, workers	queens, males, workers
store nectar and honeydew in abdomens	store nectar and pollen in cells of honeycomb
fight to defend homes	fight to defend homes

Study the paragraph below. The *signal* or *transition* words that help to express comparison are italicized.

Both the ant and the bee have more in common than most people realize. *Just as* the ant lives in a colony that supports hundreds and even thousands of ants in one nest, *so too*, the bee is a colony dweller and thousands of bees will claim one hive as their home. *Similarly*, the ant and the bee have queens to bear the young, males for mating, and workers for labor. Some ants store nectar and honeydew in their abdomens for the times when food is scarce. *Likewise*, bees store nectar and pollen, but they store it in the cells of the honeycomb. *Finally*, did you realize that both insects will protect their homes even to the point of death? Without a doubt, these fascinating insects must be first cousins.

Contrast

Emily's class was assigned a paragraph contrasting home videos with movie theaters. Emily felt that home videos had more advantages than movie theaters. To help organize her writing, she developed a chart like this:

Home Videos	Movie Theater
watch film when convenient	definite showings
inexpensive	expensive
see show several times	see show once
pause/rewind	see complete film
unlimited choices	limited choices

Study the paragraph below. The *signal* or *transition* words that help to express contrast are italicized.

Watching films on videocassette has far more advantages than going to the movie theater. With videos, you are free to watch the film at your convenience, *whereas* at the theater, movies are scheduled at definite times. *Unlike* the movie theater, where admission can be expensive and a movie can be seen only once, home videos are inexpensive and can be viewed as many times as you wish. With videos, you can push the pause button if you want to run to the kitchen for a bite to eat, or you can rewind them if you wish to see a segment over again. *By contrast*, at the theater you are almost forced to purchase your food before the film starts, and once a scene is over, it is over forever. *Finally*, with videos, there are thousands of choices of films, *but* at the theater, you are limited to what is most current or popular. No wonder videocassettes are making movie theaters an outdated form of entertainment.

★ Try writing one paragraph of comparison and one of contrast. Develop a chart to organize your information. Use the topics below or create original ones.

Compare	Contrast
a snake, a lizard	a tent, a cabin
a motel, a hotel	traveling by car, by plane
roller skates, ice skates	your bedroom, your
yogurt, ice cream	sister's/brother's
	typewriter, word processor

Word Study 4

Suffixes (Adjective Endings)

A suffix is a syllable or syllables added to the end of a word that changes the function (use) of the word.

Some suffixes create adjectives, some create nouns, and some create adverbs. The suffixes below all create adjectives when added to words.

Suffix	Meaning	Example
-able (also *-ible*)	capable of being	readable, divisible
-al	relating to	fictional
-ant (also *-ent*)	having the quality of	pleasant, obedient
-ive	having the quality of	attentive
-less	without	useless
-ous	full of	joyous

For example, if the suffix *-ous* is added to the word *poison*, the adjective *poisonous* results. The adjective means "full of poison": People once thought tomatoes were *poisonous*.

Activity A

Copy the following chart onto a sheet of paper. To each word, add an adjective suffix from the list above to create a new word. Be careful to spell the new word correctly.

Word	New Word	Word	New Word
courtesy	courteous	access	accessible
manage	manageable	cranium	cranial
speech	speechless	harmony	harmonious
attract	attractive	agriculture	agricultural
excel	excellent	effect	effective

Activity B

Supply a suffix from this Word Study section to complete each sentence.

1. Nocturnal animals are act<u>ive</u> at night.
2. It seems quite point<u>less</u> to argue about which river is longest—let's look the answer up in the encyclopedia.
3. The apartment, which was advertised as spac<u>ious</u>, was actually the size of a large closet.
4. The clay pot was too por<u>ous</u> to hold water.
5. We visited the center for psychologic<u>al</u> testing at the university.
6. Tania's gull<u>ible</u> nature sometimes gets her into trouble.
7. The fabric of the couch is treated with a water-resist<u>ant</u> chemical.
8. That the butler was guilty seemed quite evid<u>ent</u>.
9. Jeans are very dur<u>able</u> and do not wear out easily.
10. The deer sat motion<u>less</u> at the edge of the forest.
11. The hundredth anniversary of the Statue of Liberty in 1986 was a marvel<u>ous</u> celebration.
12. Allison has trouble with spat<u>ial</u> relations—she puts square pegs into round holes.
13. Prevent<u>ive</u> medicine's goal is to stop illness before it occurs.
14. Farmland in Nebraska is very product<u>ive</u>.
15. In pantomine, gestures and fac<u>ial</u> expressions tell the story.

Folk art tray from the 1920s of the Statue of Liberty

Activity C

Complete each sentence with a word you formed in activity A.

1. The use of a computer makes many jobs more __manageable__.
2. The manager's __courteous__ attention to our problem impressed us.
3. The United States and Canada have long had __harmonious__ relations.
4. The cottage was __accessible__ by only one narrow path.
5. When everyone yelled "Surprise," I was __speechless__.

ACTIVITY B: Most students will have no difficulty in determining the correct suffix. Have them spell the word while you put it on the chalkboard. Make certain the students understand the meaning of each word as it is used in that specific context.

ACTIVITY C: If the students have difficulty with this activity, review the meaning of the words in activity A. In each sentence, the students should be able to identify the word that each adjective modifies.

ADDITIONAL ACTIVITY

See how many other words the students can create using the suffixes in this lesson. Make lists of new words on the chalkboard. The students should be able to define each word. Select a representative number to use in sentences.

Chapter 5

Writing Reports and Articles

Lesson 1 Creating an Outline

An outline is a plan, or way of organizing ideas, for a long composition.

An outline is a tool to help you build orderly paragraphs and longer compositions. The outline puts the topic, subtopics, and details for a composition into a logical order.

In chapter 1, you studied how to build a word map to organize ideas in writing a paragraph. A word map is a flexible way to develop ideas about a topic. In word mapping, you put your main topic in the center of a page. Then you freely jot down ideas around the main topic. You put subtopics and related details together. You then decide which ideas you will include in your writing. An outline, however, has a specific form and follows certain rules.

An outline follows this form:

   I.   Topic
       A. Subtopic
          1. Detail
          2. Detail
          3. Detail
       B. Subtopic
          1. Detail
          2. Detail
          3. Detail

In writing compositions, you may find it useful to combine the two techniques of organizing ideas:

1. Begin by making a word map. Write down topics and subtopics.
2. Decide on a logical organization for the composition.
3. Prepare a formal outline, using the form studied in this lesson.

THE STUDENTS SHOULD LEARN
—the format of an outline
—how to create an outline from a word map
—how to use an outline as the basis for a composition

TEACHING THE LESSON
The students should understand that outlines are not generally used for one-paragraph compositions. They are used to plan and organize material for compositions or reports of two or more paragraphs. An outline keeps the writer on track, helping to maintain unity and coherence.

Have the students study the outline with the explanation that accompanies it. Then compare the outline on "how a rock band gets started" with the word map and paragraph on pages 14–16. The students should be attentive to the format of the outline and especially to the fact that there should be two or more subtopics under each paragraph topic, and two or more details under each subtopic.

Our knowledge expands when we ask questions and seek answers about our world. What questions could you ask about the birds in this painting?

An outline must follow the rules listed below. Notice how the outline on rock bands is correctly set up according to the rules.

1. Use a roman numeral followed by a period for the topic of each paragraph. When several paragraphs are outlined as part of the same composition, there will be several roman numerals. The periods after them must form a column.
2. Use a capital letter followed by a period for each subtopic within the paragraph. Indent each capital letter so that it is directly below the first letter of the first word of the topic.
3. Use an arabic numeral followed by a period for each detail of a subtopic. Indent each arabic numeral so that it is directly below the first letter of the first word of the subtopic.
4. Be sure there are at least two subtopics under each topic and two details under each subtopic.
5. Begin the first word of each topic, subtopic, and detail with a capital letter. Do not use capital letters for other words in the outline unless they are proper nouns or proper adjectives.
6. Use the same structure for each line of the outline: a sentence, a clause, a phrase, or a word. If one subtopic is a sentence, all subtopics should be sentences. If one detail is a prepositional phrase, all details should be prepositional phrases.

An outline for the paragraph developed in the word mapping section (pages 14 to 16) looks like this:

I. How a rock band gets started (*Topic*)
   A. Musicians (*Subtopic*)
      1. Talent (*Detail*)
      2. Dedication (*Detail*)
      3. Combination (*Detail*)
   B. Practice
      1. Time
      2. Place
      3. Commitment
   C. Support
      1. Fans
      2. Money
      3. Equipment
   D. Jobs
      1. Auditions
      2. Contacts/Friends
      3. Exposure

Activity A

Study the outline below and then answer the questions.

Subject: Camping

Narrowed topic: Ways people go camping

I. Recreational vehicles
  A. Kinds
    1. Van
    2. Pickup camper
    3. Camper-trailer
  B. Features
    1. Built-in gas stove
    2. Plumbing

II. Tents
  A. Kinds
    1. Family-sized
    2. Two-person
  B. Sleeping
    1. Cot
    2. Air Mattress
    3. Ground
  C. Cooking
    1. Portable gas stove
    2. Campground grill
    3. Wood fire

III. Backpacking
  A. Places
    1. Woods
    2. Mountains
  B. Sleeping
    1. Foam mat
    2. Ground
  C. Cooking
    1. Wood fire
    2. Dehydrated food

1. Name the three paragraph topics indicated on the outline.
2. Explain why the paragraphs might be put in that order.
3. After each lettered subtopic, what occurs?
4. What two things do all the lines of the outline have in common?
5. How many subtopics does the outline have altogether?
6. What indicates a detail on the outline?

ACTIVITY B: Direct the students to compare the first paragraph with roman numeral I in the outline. Have them note how the subtopics plus details are all included within the one paragraph. Complete the second paragraph as a class, making certain that everything under roman numeral II is included. The students should attempt the third paragraph on their own. Review the material under roman numeral III and work with the students on an individual basis. Have volunteers share their writing. Work with the class in creating an ending sentence.

Activity B

Following is the first paragraph of a composition based on the outline in activity A. Topic sentences are provided for the two other paragraphs. Complete the paragraphs, based on the outline.

People go camping in many different ways. For some, it's as if they've hardly left home. They bring all the comforts of home with them in their recreational vehicles (RVs): vans, pickup campers, or camper-trailers. All of these RVs have beds in them, and most have additional features such as built-in gas stoves and plumbing. Many even have televisions and air conditioning!

Topic sentence (paragraph 2): Other people like to be a little more rustic, and so they camp in tents.

Topic sentence (paragraph 3): People who really like to get away from civilization when they camp go backpacking.

Activity C

Make an outline of a composition based on this word map.

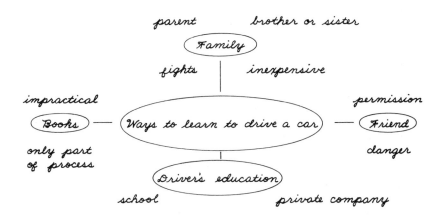

More to Explore

Create an outline, using information found in your social studies or science textbook. Make the outline for a two-paragraph composition with two subtopics in each paragraph and as many details as you need under each subtopic.

ACTIVITY C: The students should be able to complete the outline on their own, but should consult the guidelines for creating an outline if necessary. For extension, the students could write their own paragraph based on their outline.

MORE TO EXPLORE: Material for outlines abound in social studies and science textbooks. Allow the students to search out their own information, so that the outlines will vary.

ENRICHMENT
Ask each student to choose a subject of interest and read about it in an encyclopedia. From this information, each student can create an outline and then use it as a basis for an oral report.

Lesson 2 Writing a Report

A report is a composition of at least several paragraphs that provides specific information about its topic and follows a specific outline form.

THE STUDENTS SHOULD LEARN
—how to develop a report from an outline

TEACHING THE LESSON
This lesson takes the students through the development of a report without their having to do much research. Having the information provided helps them concentrate on the format of a report. Also, writing the middle (body) paragraphs first, they should find it easier to write the introductory and concluding paragraphs. Since most students have written very few, if any, lengthy reports, this lesson should be taken slowly with as much individual attention given to each student as possible.

A report is a composition about a particular topic. To write a report you must gather information from encyclopedias, books, magazines, or other sources. Once you have collected the information you need, you should construct an outline to organize your facts.

The organization of a report, and that of any longer composition, is similar to that of a paragraph. A report has a beginning (the *introductory paragraph*), a middle (*body paragraphs*), and an ending (the *concluding paragraph*).

A roman numeral is used in a report outline to indicate each paragraph topic. All of the information under a particular numeral goes into that paragraph when it is written. Both the introductory paragraph and the concluding paragraph can be fairly short—two or three sentences. The introductory paragraph, based on the first roman numeral, must indicate clearly what the report is going to be about. It should also arouse the readers' interest so that they continue reading.

The concluding paragraph, based on the last roman numeral, must let the reader know that the report is finished. It usually contains a summary of details, gives one last detail, or refers specifically to something said in the introductory paragraph.

The body paragraphs start with the second roman numeral (II.) in the outline. It is important that these paragraphs clearly relate to the main subject of the report. A reference to the subject at the beginning of each paragraph will help to give the report unity.

In the activities for this lesson, you will actually be taken through the steps of writing a report. You will be given an outline to use as the basis for a report. When you write reports on your own, you may find it helpful to use the following techniques:

1. Begin by reading some books and articles about your topic and start taking notes.

2. Make a word map about the topic you have read about. Ask yourself what you want to include in your report, based on your reading.
3. Decide which topics in the word map that you want to use in your report.
4. Prepare a formal outline that includes topics, subtopics, and details arranged in a logical order.
5. Continue reading and take notes that relate to each topic and subtopic.
6. Write your report, using the outline and notes you have prepared. In some cases, you may decide to make changes in your original outline.

ACTIVITY A: The students should be encouraged to read more information about cave dwellers, but it is not absolutely necessary since the paragraph can be written from the material provided. Have the students first copy the topic sentence. Then as they write sentences that include the information under each capital letter, have some of those sentences put on the chalkboard and discussed. This will give slower students a chance to see how the report is developing.

Activity A

Here is a sentence outline and a topic sentence for the first middle (body) paragraph of a report on creatures that live in caves. Complete the paragraph. Use the encyclopedia or other books for more information if you need it.

II. Cave visitors, called *trogloxenes*, are animals of various kinds who spend some of their time in caves but who must return to the surface regularly.
   A. Some cave visitors are occasional visitors.
     1. Bears hibernate in caves.
     2. Weasels, raccoons, and small rodents sometimes build nests in caves.
   B. Some cave visitors are regular visitors.
     1. Bats are the most popular example.
     2. Oilbirds are rather like bats in their cave habits.
     3. Cave crickets, moths, and mosquitoes are insects that fall into this category.
     4. Eyed salamanders are very common.
   C. Cave visitors share certain characteristics.
     1. They must live near a cave entrance.
     2. They leave guano (waste) for cave dwellers.
     3. They need food from outside the cave.

Topic sentence: Cave visitors, called trogloxenes, spend some of their time in caves but must return to the surface regularly.

ACTIVITY B: Follow the same procedure as for activity A. Draw the students' attention to the transition phrase in the topic sentence, *Unlike cave visitors*..., which helps to make a smooth connection between paragraphs.

Activity B

Here is a sentence outline and a topic sentence for the second middle (body) paragraph of a report on creatures that live in caves.

Complete this paragraph, remembering that it follows the paragraph you wrote in activity A and that it is part of a report on creatures that live in caves.

   III. Cave guests, called *troglophiles*, can live in a cave during their entire life cycle, but they can also go outside.

      A. Many cave guests are insects.

         1. Spiders, pseudoscorpions, and millipedes are insects that live as cave guests.

         2. Daddy longlegs, spiderlike animals often mistaken for insects, also live as cave guests.

      B. Cave guests have certain things in common.

         1. They live near the entrance, as do cave visitors, in the twilight zone.

         2. They have not physically adapted to total darkness.

         3. They generally feed on dead insects or other organic matter.

Topic sentence: Unlike cave visitors, cave guests are able to complete their entire life cycle within a cave; like cave visitors, they can also go outside.

Activity C

This is an outline of the third middle (body) paragraph of a report on creatures that live in caves. Write a topic sentence to begin the paragraph, and then complete the paragraph. After writing your topic sentence, decide which transition word best connects the second middle paragraph to the third: *like, similar to, unlike, also, by contrast.*

IV. Cave dwellers, called *troglobites*, live their entire lives inside caves.
  A. The animals that live in caves require a damp or wet environment.
    1. Thirty-two kinds of blind fish are troglobites.
    2. Many kinds of blind crustaceans, including white crayfish, cave shrimp, copepods, amphipods, and isopods, live near cave waters.
    3. Blind flatworms float on the surface of cave streams, ponds, and lakes.
    4. Blind salamanders also stay near the water.
  B. Troglobites share certain characteristics.
    1. They live deep within the cave, in total darkness.
    2. All are sightless; many have no eyes.
    3. They have reduced pigmentation and are therefore white or pinkish.
    4. They have thin skins or shells.
    5. They maintain some constant activity at a very low basic metabolism.

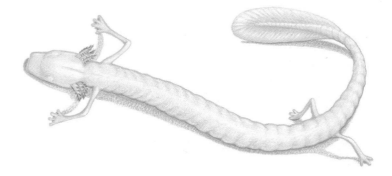

More to Explore

To finish the report on creatures that live in caves, compose three things: an introductory paragraph, a concluding paragraph, and a title.

ACTIVITY C: The topic sentence for this paragraph includes the information next to roman numeral IV. Since cave dwellers are not like cave guests or visitors, a transition phrase might be *In contrast to cave guests and cave visitors*...or *Cave dwellers, unlike cave guests or cave visitors*....

MORE TO EXPLORE: Work with the class on developing introductory and concluding paragraphs and title. The information for the introductory paragraph should include ideas from each of the topic sentences of the three middle paragraphs.

Many interesting creatures inhabit the caves of our world. Some are merely visitors, some are guests, and some make their homes permanently in the recesses of these dark caverns. (This would be roman numeral I in the outline.)

A possible concluding paragraph might be:

No doubt, caves are homes to a great variety of creatures. They would be most interesting places to explore in order to learn more about the many inhabitants of the darker corners of our world. (This would be roman numeral V in the outline.)

ENRICHMENT

The outline created for the "Enrichment" section of lesson 1 could be developed into a full length report. Paragraphs do not have to be lengthy, but should be long enough to show a change in topic.

Lesson 3 Writing a News Article

A news article reports the facts of an important event that actually occurred, usually in the recent past.

THE STUDENTS SHOULD LEARN

—that a news article presents facts about an event

—that a news article begins with a lead paragraph

—how to structure a news article

—how to write headlines

TEACHING THE LESSON

Have a news article duplicated for each student. After the students review the introductory material to this lesson, have them identify the different parts of a news article in the one provided. Explain that the inverted pyramid philosophy is essential to a news writer because he or she knows that the reader may want to learn the important information without reading the whole article. Most of the time the lead paragraph will answer the Five W's. Sometimes the *why* may not be included until a later paragraph.

A news article follows the basic rules of any report, but it has some special features, too. For example, a news article has something called a *lead* (pronounced *leed*). The lead comes in the first paragraph; it leads the reader into the article. In this way it is much like a topic sentence. However, the lead may be more than one sentence. It may be the whole paragraph.

The lead does a specific job: it tells *what* happened, *who* was involved, *when* and *where* it happened, and often *why* it happened. The five things that the lead tells—who, what, when, where, and why—are called the Five W's of newswriting.

Another feature of the news article is the order in which the facts are presented. The most important facts are presented first (in the lead), the less important facts come next, and the unimportant facts come last. When a news article is published, the newspaper editor sometimes has to make it shorter to fit the space available. Since the editor needs to make the change quickly, it is easiest if the end of the article can simply be chopped off. That is why news articles are written with the most important facts at the top. Journalists call this an *inverted pyramid* structure.

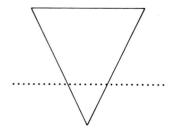

If you cut off the bottom of an inverted pyramid, most of the mass of the shape is left, and the structure does not fall over.

Activity A

Read the following news article, noticing the decreasing importance of the facts as you near the end. Identify the Five W's of this article, giving the information exactly as it is written in the article.

Residents of the Lincoln Square area will be inconvenienced this summer by the loud noise and muddy mess of City Department of Streets and Sanitation crews digging up the streets to bury new water mains. The construction will start at the east end of Jefferson Lane, proceed west, and then move north on Western Avenue. William O'Reilly, director of the Department of Streets and Sanitation, reports that all repairs should be completed by the middle of September.

Car owners are asked to park off the streets under repair. A temporary parking facility is available on Prescott Avenue, but it requires a special parking sticker. These stickers will be given only to those residents immediately affected by the construction.

The new water mains, made of a special fiber, replace rusting metal ones that were laid 53 years ago. The project was to have started a year ago, but due to financial problems and lack of support within the department, the much-needed repairs were indefinitely delayed. Pressure from local residents finally prompted the City Department of Streets and Sanitation to take the necessary action.

Activity B

Arrange the following information to create a lead paragraph containing the Five W's.

The three people who live in the house at 8238 Dogwood Road are George, Lois, and Andy Packer. 5

The house at 8238 Dogwood Road has an emergency generator. 4

On Thursday, April 14, a tornado destroyed many of the homes on Dogwood Road. 1

The tornado also tore down power lines for most of the Germantown area. 2

Germantown residents were without electricity for three days after the storm. 3

The Packers prepared food for the many workers and residents trying to repair their homes in the aftermath. 6

Activity C

One final feature that distinguishes news articles from other kinds of reports is how they are labeled. While most reports have *titles*, news articles have *headlines*. A headline summarizes the main idea of an article. It is short and to the point, and often it contains just a subject and a verb. Short words such as *a, an, the,* and *is* almost never appear in headlines.

Read the following sample headlines and see if you can tell what the stories would be about.

Spring Baby Boom at Zoo
Fireworks Fizzle
Tigers Win, 6-2
Students Save the Day
UFO Sighted in Area
Ocean Oversteps Bounds
Cow Captures Prize

Now create two headlines for the stories in activities A and B.

More to Explore

Choose any headline from activity C and write the lead paragraph. Exchange your paragraph with a partner and check each other's newswriting for the Five W's.

Lesson 4   Writing an Editorial

An editorial expresses the writer's opinion about a subject.

Unlike a news article, which can only present the facts about a subject, an editorial gives the writer the freedom to express opinions. Most editorials appear on a special editorial page, but some are scattered throughout the entire paper.

The purpose of an editorial is to convince the reader to think the way the writer does. When you are writing an editorial, it is important to support opinions with facts. *Facts* can be proven; *opinions* can be questioned. Decide which of the following statements are facts and which are opinions. Be ready to support your choices.

Walnut Street has one streetlight for every seven houses. **F**

Walnut Street must have more streetlights in order for the people who live there to feel safe. **O**

Computers are powerful tools. **F**

Everyone wants to be able to use a computer these days. **O**

The Pagoda serves Chinese food. **F**

Knife and Fork is the best restaurant in town. **O**

More aides are needed to assist the president. **O**

The president is a busy person. **F**

Activity A

Locate the facts and the opinions in the following editorial. Give reasons for your choices.

Should the wearing of seat belts be made mandatory? Already, some states have passed laws requiring that everyone—adults, teens, and children—wear seat belts in moving automobiles. Such laws are an invasion of privacy.

The trend toward this invasion started with child safety laws. These seemed reasonable enough—at first glance. Since children (aged four and under) cannot decide for themselves whether or not to use a seat belt, someone must make the choice for them. Lawmakers decided to take that choice away from the parents and place it in the hands of the law. Requiring that children be in safety seats will save many innocent lives.

Adults and teens, however, are old enough to decide for themselves whether they will or won't use a seat belt. Unlike the case of parents and four-year-olds, their choice is personal. It affects no one's safety but their own. If a teen or an adult dies as a result of not using a seat belt, that is tragic—but it is still the individual's right to make that choice. It is not the role of government to protect the people from themselves, only to protect them from one another. Seat-belt wearing should not be made mandatory because to do so would be to violate individual freedom.

111

ACTIVITY B: Again, have a class discussion concerning this issue. As the discussion ensues, suggest that the students begin to write down their own feelings/opinions. The students should begin writing their response by stating some of the facts from the list and then going on to express their opinion and/or countering with other facts. Remind them that their argument should be persuasive and convincing. Have volunteers read their editorials to the class and have the class identify the fact and opinion sentences.

Activity B

Review the following *facts* about the issue of a closed campus. Make a list of your *opinions* (pro and con) about the issue. Then write an editorial that reveals the side about which you feel strongest.

Facts about the Closed Campus at Middleborough School

1. Middleborough School has a closed campus. The following school rule has been in effect for six years: "No student shall leave the school grounds before the end of the school day without written permission from a parent or guardian, and such permission shall be accepted by the school only on a limited basis and for exceptional reasons (e.g., that the student has become ill during the school day, that the student must otherwise see a physician, that there has been a death in the student's immediate family, etc.)."
2. Students at Middleborough School range in age from five to thirteen, grades one through eight.
3. Seventh and eighth grade students feel that they are more responsible for their own safety than younger students might be.
4. Some students have older brothers and sisters who attended Middleborough before the closed campus rule was in effect, and they went home for lunch regularly.
5. The year before the closed campus rule was imposed, a female seventh grade student was kidnapped at lunchtime when she was walking back to the school from the hamburger stand three blocks away.

More to Explore

MORE TO EXPLORE: Since editorials are a type of persuasive writing, the students should try to have their most convincing arguments at the end of the editorial—the last thing for the reader to see. After some have been read aloud in class, discuss how effective each editorial was.

Write an editorial opposing the opinion given in the editorial in activity A or one opposing the opinion given by another student in activity B.

ENRICHMENT

Consider some of the controversial issues that are currently present in your classroom, school, or community. Have one student (or yourself) write an editorial regarding a specific issue. Have the students respond in writing to the presentation.

Lesson 5 Writing about Books

Book Reports

A book report summarizes the information contained in a book and usually follows a specific format.

You might remember that when Ali Baba of the *Arabian Nights* wanted to enter the magic cave, he had to say "Open Sesame" as a kind of password. Books are the passwords that admit us to a far more wonderful place than the one Ali Baba enjoyed. Books give us access to a whole world of treasures. They allow us to take part in the adventures of men and women of all times and of all nations. Books can be our guides to the beauties of the great physical world about us. Through literature, we learn to appreciate the wisdom of great men and women who have lived in years gone by.

Have you enjoyed reading a good book recently? Talking or writing about favorite books in class makes others eager to read the stories you have enjoyed, and it helps you discover interesting books that you might like to read.

Keeping a record of books you have read will help you to remember them. A book report does not have to be long, just long enough to summarize the story. When you finish reading a book, you should first write a rough draft that includes the main ideas in the story. Then write down the information that is needed to complete the following basic format:
1. Title
2. Author
3. Publisher and date of publication
4. Type of book (fiction, science fiction, historical fiction, fantasy, nonfiction, biography, play, etc.)
5. Principal characters
6. Brief summary
7. Personal reaction

THE STUDENTS SHOULD LEARN
—how to write a book report
—how to write a book character report

TEACHING THE LESSON
Have a class discussion about some of the books the students have read recently. What made the book particularly interesting and worthwhile reading? Did they like the characters in the book? Could they relate to the charac- ters' thoughts and feelings? Read and analyze the book report in the introduction. Notice that with- out giving every incident in the story, the summary includes the setting, explains who the main characters are, then, in just a few sentences tells the highlights of the plot. The personal reaction should be more than "I liked the book because it was interesting."

MODEL: A Book Report

TITLE: *The Island of the Blue Dolphins*

AUTHOR: Scott O'Dell

PUBLISHER: Houghton Mifflin Company, 1960

TYPE: Historical fiction

CHARACTERS: Karana, an Indian girl; Ramo, her brother; Rontu, leader of the wild dogs

SUMMARY: In his novel, *The Island of the Blue Dolphins,* Scott O'Dell weaves the tale of Karana, an Indian girl, and Ramo, her younger brother. Alone on their deserted island home, they battle starvation, wild dogs, and their own fear as they anxiously await the return of the "big ship." When Ramo is killed by the dog pack, Karana swears revenge. Her resolute anger begins a lifestyle of determination and resourcefulness. For eighteen years, this remarkable girl leads an almost solitary existence, her only friends the creatures she manages to tame.

Karana learns that life's lessons are often ironic when she befriends the target of her hatred, the leader of the dog pack. The dog then enriches her lonely exile. Her understanding of herself deepens each time she experiences nature's protection or treachery.

In an attempt to reconstruct the details of the girl's almost incredible island life, O'Dell creates a story that captivates with a sense of daring adventure. At the same time, the story demonstrates to the reader the great strength of the human spirit. Readers will not soon forget the island or the girl who conquered it.

MY REACTION: I kept thinking about the tremendous power of human beings to survive and to accept life's hardships. Karana's mastery of the wilderness inspired me and made me admire her courage and determination.

Activity

Write a book report based on a novel you have read recently. Be sure that your report follows the format used in the example.

More to Explore

Choose and read a book different from the type you usually read. For example, if you usually prefer science fiction, try biography. As you write your report, add to the standard form one paragraph especially suited to this type of book. A report on biography, for instance, could have an extra paragraph called "ways I hope to be like this person."

Book Character Reports

A *book character report* describes and analyzes one or two of the book's major characters.

In almost every story you read, one or two characters stand out more than any of the others. Sometimes a book becomes popular because the characters are so vividly portrayed, or because so many people have experienced emotions similar to a particular character.

To write a book character report, use items 1 to 4 (title, author, publisher, and type of book) of the basic book report form. Then follow this format for the rest of the book character report:

5. Character or characters about whom you've chosen to write
6. Why these characters are so memorable (things they did, personality traits they have)
7. How these characters have influenced you personally

ACTIVITY: Time might be given for the students to read a new book. When they begin to write the report, have them follow the format provided and remind them to underline the title. Point out to the students that the publisher and date of publication are usually found on the title page of the book and the page that follows it.

MORE TO EXPLORE: All students have a favorite type of book that they like to read, but they should be encouraged to read various types in order to experience the diversity that literature has to offer. Have the students decide what extra paragraph they might add for science fiction (Will this ever happen in real life?) or fantasy (What is the moral or lesson to be taught?).

TEACHING THE LESSON
Characters in books are interesting to analyze. Sometimes they are very much like ourselves. Other times they are people we admire and would like to imitate in some way. Have the students talk about characters that have impressed them and tell why. Ask the students: In the story *Julie of the Wolves*, why was Julie such a unique young girl? What makes her different from other girls her age? Would Julie have an influence on how someone might handle a situation?

MODEL: A Book Character Report

TITLE:	*Julie of the Wolves*
AUTHOR:	Jean Craighead George
PUBLISHER:	Harper and Row, 1972
TYPE:	Fiction
CHARACTER:	Julie, a young Eskimo girl. She is also called *Miyax.*

WHY JULIE IS MEMORABLE: After Julie runs away from her bad home situation, she finds herself lost on the bleak Arctic tundra. She has no food. She has little shelter. She is all alone. In spite of these incredible difficulties, Julie/Miyax doesn't give up. She survives by remembering and using all the skills her Eskimo father taught her. She makes herself tools and shelter. She hunts and gathers to get herself food. As terrifying as it is, she befriends a pack of Arctic wolves and learns their ways. In the end, she also discovers she must adapt to the ways of the human pack and go back to civilization.

PERSONAL INFLUENCE: Julie/Miyax of *Julie of the Wolves* is an example to me of strength and courage. No matter how impossible things look, she doesn't despair. She uses her fear to motivate her to try new ways of doing things. "Change your ways when fear seizes" is Julie's motto which she learned from her father. It has become my motto, too.

Activity

Write about a character who has made an impression on you. Follow the format used in the example.

More to Explore

Write a book character report in which you compare and contrast two characters in one report. Follow the book character report format, telling under headings 5, 6, and 7 how the two characters are similar and how they are different. Describe their impact on you.

ACTIVITY: The same book that was used for the book report at the beginning of the lesson might also be used for a book character report. The students should follow the format in the introduction.

MORE TO EXPLORE: The students should compare and contrast characters that are somewhat similar, especially in their struggles, fears, and anxieties. The students could also try writing about characters from short stories that the class has read. Having a class discussion about the characters, listing similarities and differences, is a needed preliminary to writing a book character report.

ENRICHMENT

Suggest that the students write another chapter to the story, or have them write a letter to their book character telling what they admire in the person and why or how they would have acted had they been in his or her place.

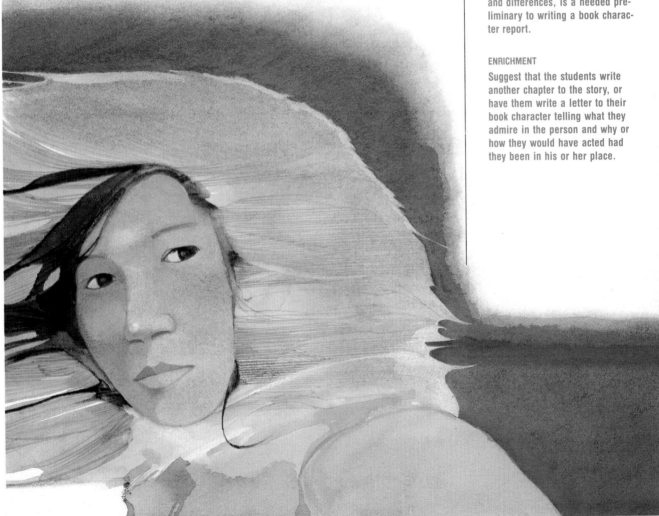

Writing Corner 5

Note Taking

Having students do this Writing Corner in connection with lesson 2 in chapter 5 will help them with the note-taking skills they need to do reports on their own. Writing Corners 6 and 8, on bibliography and the *Readers' Guide* respectively, will also be useful in conjunction with report writing.

Kelly is working on her history assignment. She has been assigned to research information on the topic "The Japanese-American People." Kelly has in front of her three groups of index cards with notes on them. As she reads, she writes some ideas on another index card and adds it to one of the groups. Shown below are the three index cards from the *top* of each group on her desk. Study these three cards carefully.

Japanese-Americans : First Contact with the West

Marco Polo, a Venetian traveler, first told Europeans about the wonders of Japan. With awe, he described this country as "the land where the sun rises."

Universal Encyclopedia, p. 54

Japanese-Americans: First Immigration

214,000 Japanese immigrants arrived in the United States in the first two decades of the 20th century. Researchers said that at first they had no intentions of staying. "They were sojourners—birds of passage…"

Geographic Monthly, p. 42

> *Japanese-Americans : Contributions*
>
> *The cultural contributions of the Japanese-Americans are beautifully reflected in much of the architecture and landscaping of the city of Los Angeles.*
>
> *One Nation, Many Cultures* p. 237

Answer these questions about the note cards.
  A. What three types of books has Kelly used to find information?
  B. Into what *three topics* has she divided her information?
  C. If Kelly wants to indicate where she found the information on her cards, how will she be able to locate it quickly?
  D. How has she shown when she used the *exact* words of the book?

You are right if you noticed the following:
  A. Kelly used an *encyclopedia, textbook,* and *magazine article.*
  B. The topics are "First Contact with the West," "Immigration to the United States," and "Contributions to Our Culture."
  C. The *book* and *page number* locate the information.
  D. The exact words of the book are in *quotation marks.*

For part 1 of her report, Kelly will refer to the group of cards labeled "Japanese-Americans: First Contact with the West." She will write parts 2 and 3 by referring to groups 2 and 3 of her cards.

Here is the process for note taking on separate cards:
  1. Write the *topic* at the top of the card.
  2. Write the information *in your own words.* (If you use the exact words of the book, show this in quotation marks.)
  3. Note, in a brief way on each card, the *book* and the *page.*
  4. Keep cards with the *same topic* together.
  5. Refer to each group of cards as you write your report.

★ Use this method of note taking for the next report you do.

Word Study 5

Suffixes (Noun Endings)

A suffix is a syllable or syllables added to the end of a word that changes the function (use) of the word.

THE STUDENTS SHOULD LEARN
—that specific suffixes added to words create nouns
—how to use suffixes to form new words

TEACHING THE LESSON
Review the adjective-forming suffixes taught in Word Study 4 on pages 96 and 97. Explain to the students that other suffixes added to words can create nouns or variations on other nouns (as in the case of *companionship* and *readership*).

ACTIVITY A: Work through this activity with the students, making sure the new words are spelled correctly. If the activity is completed independently, suggest that the students consult their dictionaries for the correct spelling. For each suffix, have the students create at least one word not already listed in this activity: *active—activity, invent—invention, advance—advancement, lord—lordship, ruthless—ruthlessness*.

Some suffixes create adjectives, some create nouns, and some create adverbs. The suffixes below all create nouns when added to words.

Suffix	Example
-ion	convention
-ity	generosity
-ment	assignment
-ness	kindness
-ship	leadership

All these noun suffixes have the general meaning of "the state of being" or "the act of." For example, the word *popularity* means "the state of being popular."

Activity A

Copy the following chart onto a sheet of paper. To each word, add a noun suffix from the list above to create a new word. Be careful to spell the new word correctly.

Word	New Word	Word	New Word
agile	agility	reader	readership
omit	omission	postpone	postponement
grave	gravity	keen	keenness
companion	companionship	fulfill	fulfillment
happy	happiness	recess	recession

120

Activity B

Supply a suffix from this Word Study section to complete each sentence.

1. The teacher granted everyone permiss<u>ion</u> to spend five more minutes outside.
2. In fables, the fox is famous for its clever<u>ness</u>.
3. My brother got a promo<u>tion</u> and a raise in salary.
4. Pete's cooking abi<u>lity</u> always wins him praise—and many guests.
5. The rapid<u>ity</u> with which the storm came up took us by surprise.
6. To gain citizen<u>ship</u>, a foreigner must live in the United States five years.
7. The develop<u>ment</u> of motion pictures was a gradual process in the late nineteenth century, involving the work of many people.
8. Our dog seems to have a compuls<u>ion</u> to chew on our shoes.
9. The domin<u>ion</u> of Emperor Charles V in the sixteenth century included much of Europe and of the New World.
10. What sort of floral arrange<u>ment</u> do you want for the wedding chapel?
11. When she writes poems, Marge's creativ<u>ity</u> really comes through.
12. The bike-a-thon was under the sponsor<u>ship</u> of several local businesses.
13. A major tourist attract<u>ion</u> of London is Madame Tussaud's museum, with its wax figures of famous people.
14. At Plymouth, Massachusetts, there is a re-creation of the original Pilgrim settle<u>ment</u>.
15. The cute<u>ness</u> of the panda makes it a popular zoo animal.

ACTIVITY B: After the students have completed this activity, direct them to name the root word and its part of speech:

1. permit (verb)
2. clever (adj.)
3. promote (verb)
4. able (adj.)
5. rapid (adj.)
6. citizen (noun)
7. develop (verb)
8. compel (verb)
9. dominate (verb)
10. arrange (verb)
11. create (verb)
12. sponsor (verb/noun)
13. attract (verb)
14. settle (verb)
15. cute (adj.)

ADDITIONAL ACTIVITY
See how many new words the students can create using the suffixes in this lesson. Make lists of new words on the chalkboard. The students should be able to define each word. Select a representative number to be used in sentences.

Chapter 6

Letter Writing

Lesson 1 The Parts of a Social Letter

A social letter has five parts: heading, salutation, body, complimentary close, and signature.

Can you think of some occasions in which you have needed to write letters? You may have written to thank your grandmother for letting you spend the weekend with her. You may have written to a business to obtain a catalog with items you were thinking of ordering. You will probably find that in the future you will have more and more occasions to write letters. Your letter-writing skills will become more important to you. In this chapter, you will study the two kinds of letters: social letters and business letters.

Social letters are ones that you write to friends and relatives. You may need to write social letters to mark special occasions. You may want to thank a relative for sending you the very gift you wanted for your birthday. You may want to invite a new friend to join you in a family outing. Or you may want to write a letter simply to share news with someone who lives far away from you.

Many social letters are really like conversations in writing. Your letters should sound natural, as if you were speaking to the person to whom you are writing. In your social letters, you share your feelings, ideas, and experiences. You write about topics that will interest the person receiving the letter.

Even though social letters are personal, they follow a standard form. Each social letter has five parts. Study the model letter on the next page. Then read about what is included in each part.

THE STUDENTS SHOULD LEARN
—the five parts of a social letter
—the marks of punctuation used in the heading, salutation, and complimentary close

TEACHING THE LESSON
The students have been taught the format of a social letter since third grade. Most will be able to name the parts of the social letter and their specific functions. However, review each part as it is presented in the introduction. As each is reviewed, have the students relate it to the model letter.

How many kinds of mail does your family receive? Do they feel differently about receiving different kinds? Explain.

123

MODEL: Social Letter

Heading

101 Monticello Road
Columbus, Ohio 43219
October 2, 19—

Dear Jeremy,   Salutation

 I was really glad to get your letter in the mail yesterday! I've missed you a lot since you moved away. We always had fun together — playing ball after school, studying together at the library, riding bikes through town.

 I'm glad to hear you're making friends at your new school. Have you found some kids to play ball with? I've heard there are good bike paths through some of the parks in New York City. Is that true?   Body

 We're getting ready for the soccer season here now, as you know. The team is really going to miss you as fullback. Kyle and Jennifer asked me to say "hi."

 Please write again soon.

Complimentary close   Your friend,
Signature   Andrea

1. Heading

When you write a letter, put your address and the date in the upper right corner of the page. This is the heading. On the first line of the heading, write your street address (or PO number); on the second, write your city, state, and zip code; on the third, write the date.

Use commas to separate elements. For example, if your address includes an apartment number, use a comma after the street address:

101 Monticello Road, Apt. 3

The city and state should always be separated by a comma, as should the date and the year. There is no comma between the state and the zip code. The heading should be about an inch from the top of the page and slightly to the right of center. Each line should be written directly under the one above it. If the letter is very short, start the heading farther down the page (maybe two inches). For some social letters, especially those written to friends, you may use only the date for the heading.

2. Salutation

The salutation is a greeting at the beginning of the letter, consisting of only one line. It is written on the line below the heading and starts at the left margin. The first word and any proper nouns are capitalized. In a social letter, the salutation is followed by a comma.

What you say in the greeting depends on your relationship to the person to whom you are writing. *Dear* _____ is a standard greeting that you can use to write to anyone. Here are some other greetings:

Hello Mom and Dad,   *Hi Lisa,*

My dearest grandson,   *Greetings friend,*

3. Body

In the body of the letter, say whatever you want to say to the person to whom you are writing. In the model, Andrea is writing to a friend who has moved away. Telling the person about what you are doing and asking about what he or she is doing is a good way of showing your interest. Notice how Andrea talks about things that she and Jeremy have done together and about people they both know.

4. Complimentary Close

The complimentary close ends the letter. It consists of a concluding word or group of words. It is written on a line by itself at the bottom of the body of the letter and starts just to the right of the center of the page (so that it is even with the heading). The complimentary close is followed by a comma, and only its first word is capitalized.

The way you word the complimentary close depends on your relationship with the person to whom you are writing. Here are some examples:

Your friend, *Your loving daughter,*

Affectionately, *Love,*

5. Signature

Sign your name; do not print. When you're writing to friends and relatives, you only need to use your first name (unless there might be some question about whom you are). If the person to whom you are writing does not know you well, use your full name. The signature goes directly below the complimentary close.

Activity A

Arrange each of the following lists of addresses and dates in the proper form for the heading of a letter.

1. [2]St. Louis, Missouri 63139, [1]2750 South King Street, [3]May 10, 19___
2. [3]December 7, 19___, [1]1830 Broadway, Apartment 4, [2]Cincinnati, Ohio 45210
3. [1]8122 Michner Avenue, [2]Philadelphia, Pennsylvania 19150, [3]March 12, 19___
4. [1]PO Box 87, [3]June 14, 19___, [2]Detroit, Michigan 48024
5. [2]July 31, 19___, [1]Fort Collins, Colorado 80521
6. your own address, today's date

Activity B

Write a salutation for a letter to each of the people listed.

1. your grandparents
2. your uncle George
3. a classmate
4. a friend
5. your father
6. your teacher
7. your favorite basketball player
8. a cousin
9. a friend's mother
10. your sister or brother

Write the complimentary close for a letter to each person listed.

1. your brother or sister
2. your teacher
3. the captain of your school football team
4. your parents
5. a close friend
6. a former neighbor

Activity C

Find the complimentary close in the second column that matches each salutation in the first column. Rewrite them in pairs, punctuating each correctly.

1. Dearest Mom and Dad
2. Dear Teacher
3. My dearest Grandmother
4. Dear Rita
5. Dear Mr Jackson

Sincerely yours
Your student
Your friend
Your devoted grandchild
Your loving daughter

Lesson 2 Special Types of Social Letters

A social letter is an informal way of writing to friends, acquaintances, or relatives.

THE STUDENTS SHOULD LEARN

—how to write a friendly letter, thank-you letter, and letter of congratulations

—to fold a letter properly

—to address an envelope correctly

TEACHING THE LESSON

Discuss with the students any advantages of writing a letter over receiving a phone call. (Letters can be kept, read and re-read, referred to.) Ask them what types of letters they write most frequently. What is included in most of their letters? (thoughts, interests, feelings, experiences, etc.) Remind the students that letters to their friends should be conversational in tone.

Most of the time you write a friendly letter just to exchange news. Chatting by mail with your friends can be an exciting experience. Think of the last time you received a letter from a friend. Remember your excitement? Letters are both fun to write and fun to receive.

Certain occasions, however, require that you write special types of social letters. Besides the usual friendly letters, you may want to write a thank-you letter or a letter of congratulations. Carefully study the different types of letters in this lesson.

Friendly Letters

The letter on the next page is a casual letter in which the writer chats with her friend about plans for an upcoming visit. It is an example of a friendly letter.

649 Satinwood Drive
Memphis, Tennessee 38193
February 15, 19—

Dear Erin,

    I'm excited that you're coming to visit next week. I can hardly wait to see you again! It's been nearly two years since our families got together.

    David and I hope you still like ice skating. We are planning to go skating at Lane Pond if the weather stays the way it's been. Is there anything special you'd like to do while you're here? If so, just let me know, and I'll make arrangements to do it.

    Be sure to bring your running shoes. I know you've been training with the track team there, and you'll get no vacation here. I'm running, too, and am looking forward to having a running partner for a few days. See you soon.

                Your cousin,
                Holly

Activity

Write a friendly letter. You may choose one of the ideas given below or write to someone you actually know.

1. Write to your best friend, who is visiting grandparents in another state. Tell about how you are spending your summer.
2. Write to a friend who is in the hospital. Cheer him or her up.
3. You are on vacation with your cousin. Write to your parents, telling them about what you are doing.
4. Write to a former teacher of yours, telling about your work in school now.
5. Write to your brother or sister who is away at college. Tell how much you miss him or her, and give some family news.
6. Write a letter to a friend in which you talk about a new hobby you have started. Also ask about a hobby in which your friend is interested.
7. Write a letter to a pen pal in another country. Describe what your typical school day is like.
8. While visiting your grandparents, you made the acquaintance of a person your age. Write a letter to that new friend, going over the good times you had together.
9. Write a letter to a friend in which you describe and recommend some good books that you have recently read.
10. Write a letter to a cousin of your own age who is coming from out of town to visit you. Tell your cousin about some of the things you might do together during the visit.

Thank-You Letters

A thank-you letter is an expression of appreciation for a gift or a thoughtful act. It is important to make the person receiving the letter feel that what he or she did was special. If you are thanking someone for a party or another occasion, you should always mention some of the things that happened that you particularly enjoyed. If you are thanking someone for a gift, you should mention the gift by name and tell why you particularly like it. The letter on the next page is an example of a thank-you letter.

MODEL: Thank-You Letter

398 West 89th Street
Pittsburgh, Pennsylvania 19903
July 7, 19—

Dear Grandma,

Thank you so much for the beautiful afghan you sent for my birthday. The colors go perfectly with my bedroom walls and rug, and I'm sure I will spend many cool fall and winter days wrapped in it while I'm reading. You are very thoughtful to remember me and to spend all that time making such a lovely gift.

I look forward to seeing you at the family reunion in September.

Your loving granddaughter,
Katy

ACTIVITIES: Have the students read the sample for a thank-you letter and a letter of congratulations. What occasions would prompt them to write each type of letter? The students should note that these letters are short, casual, and right to the point. The topics for each type of letter are only suggestions. The students will write a better letter if they write about familiar topics to someone they know.

Most stationery has matching envelopes so that the paper is simply folded in half and inserted into the envelope with the crease at the bottom. For practice with other sizes, make sure that each student has two or three large pieces of paper (8½″ by 11″) to practice folding for both a small and a legal size envelope. Have the students follow you as you fold the paper, and then have them try it by following the directions and illustrations in the text.

Draw the outline of an envelope on the chalkboard. Write in an address, showing the students the proper spacing and positioning. Then direct the students to either draw envelopes on a plain piece of paper or use real envelopes to practice writing an address. Write in a return address on the model envelope on the chalkboard and instruct the students to do the same on their envelopes. Point out the list of state abbreviations given in the text.

Activity

Write a thank-you letter. Use one of the ideas given below or write an actual thank-you letter to someone you know.

1. Your friend's parents took you along with their family to the symphony concert on Sunday afternoon. Write to thank them for taking you.
2. A boy who lives in the house down the street took care of your dog while your family was on vacation. Write to thank him for keeping your dog happy.
3. Write a letter to a former teacher, thanking him or her for getting you interested in a particular subject.
4. Write a letter to your aunt and uncle who let you live with them on their farm over the summer.
5. Write a letter to your cousin who taught you how to swim.
6. Write a letter to thank a friend for visiting you while you were in the hospital.
7. Write a letter to thank your teacher for extra tutoring that he or she gave you after class.
8. Write a letter to thank a friend for lending you a book that you particularly wanted to read.
9. Write a letter to thank a cousin for including you on a camping trip. Let your cousin know why you enjoyed the experience.
10. Write a letter to thank a friend for the gift that he or she gave you for your birthday.

Letters of Congratulations

Letters of congratulations are joyous letters. They are written when a friend or relative has achieved something special. Your letter should show how pleased you are for the person, and it should make him or her feel happy. The letter on the next page is a sample letter of congratulations.

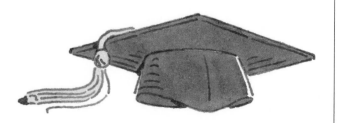

MODEL: Congratulatory Letter

56983 Las Flores Boulevard
Los Angeles, California 93029
May 16, 19—

Dear Raoul,

I extend to you my sincere congratulations on your graduation day. You should certainly feel proud of your achievements at Highland School! I have no doubt that you will take Circle High by storm when you continue your education there in the fall.

I wish you the very best of luck in the future.

Your friend,
Rich

Activity

Write a letter of congratulations. Use one of the ideas given below or write an actual letter to someone you know.

1. Write a letter to the coach of the track team, congratulating him or her on the team's successful season.
2. A member of your class has been elected to the student council. Write a letter of congratulations from the class.
3. Write a letter to a former teacher of yours who is getting married.
4. Write a letter to your friend congratulating him or her for making the cheerleading squad.
5. Write a letter to your friend congratulating him or her for making the basketball team.

Finishing Touches for Letters

The appearance of your letter is very important. A neatly written letter reflects your own high standards. You should use a good quality of stationery and black or blue ink. The letter should be written legibly, clearly, and neatly. Leave a margin on every edge of the paper—top, bottom, left, and right.

Always read over a letter when you finish writing it and correct any misspelled words or grammatical errors. Rewrite the letter if the original gets too messy.

Folding the Letter

Social letters are usually mailed in small envelopes. If you use a small piece of paper, you fold it in half (horizontally) and place it in the envelope. The crease should be at the bottom of the envelope.

If you use a larger piece of paper and need to put it into a small envelope, you have to fold it differently. First, fold it in half (as you did the small paper). Then with the crease at the bottom, fold the right side in toward the middle, and fold the left side on top of the right side. As with the small paper, place this letter in the envelope with the last crease at the bottom of the envelope.

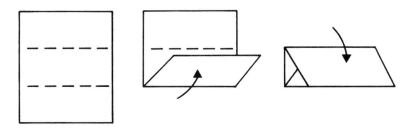

If you have a long (business-sized) envelope and a large piece of paper, the folding is a little different. For a large piece of paper, fold the bottom half a third of the way up the letter. Then fold the top half down until it comes to within a quarter of an inch from the bottom crease. Put the letter in the envelope with the last crease at the bottom. This is how all business letters are folded.

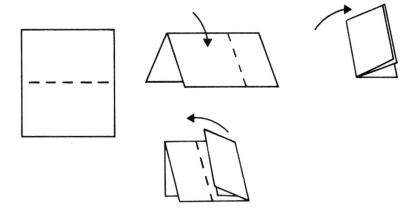

Addressing the Envelope

The envelope should have two addresses when you mail it: your address and the address of the person to whom you are sending the letter. The form and punctuation for the addresses should be similar to that of the heading of the letter. On the envelope, however, abbreviate the state to the two letters used by the post office.

AL	Alabama	KY	Kentucky	OH	Ohio
AK	Alaska	LA	Louisiana	OK	Oklahoma
AZ	Arizona	ME	Maine	OR	Oregon
AR	Arkansas	MD	Maryland	PA	Pennsylvania
CA	California	MA	Massachusetts	RI	Rhode Island
CO	Colorado	MI	Michigan	SC	South Carolina
CT	Connecticut	MN	Minnesota	SD	South Dakota
DE	Delaware	MS	Mississippi	TN	Tennessee
DC	District of	MO	Missouri	TX	Texas
	Columbia	MT	Montana	UT	Utah
FL	Florida	NE	Nebraska	VT	Vermont
GA	Georgia	NV	Nevada	VA	Virginia
HI	Hawaii	NH	New Hampshire	WA	Washington
ID	Idaho	NJ	New Jersey	WV	West Virginia
IL	Illinois	NM	New Mexico	WI	Wisconsin
IN	Indiana	NY	New York	WY	Wyoming
IA	Iowa	NC	North Carolina		
KS	Kansas	ND	North Dakota		
GU	Guam	VI	Virgin Islands	PR	Puerto Rico

Write the address to which the letter is being sent slightly to the left of center on the front of the envelope.

Robert Paul
Oswego Avenue
Houston, TX 77095

Your address on the envelope is called the *return address*. It consists of your name, street address, city, state, and zip code. If you put the wrong mailing address on the envelope by mistake, the post office will return the letter to the return address. Your address goes in the upper left corner of the envelope, and the stamp goes in the upper right corner. Reduce the size of your handwriting so that all information fits neatly in the left-hand corner.

Dorothy Saunders
Lance Drive
Sarasota, FL 33581

56

Marcia Roscoe
Lincoln Avenue
New Haven, CT 06511

Activity

Trace outlines of small envelopes on a plain piece of paper. Write the following names and addresses as they should be written on an envelope. Use your own return address. Be sure to use the two-letter state abbreviations.

1. John Kaplan, PO Box 340, El Paso, Texas 76101
2. Margaret Hansem, PO Box 242, Nantucket, Massachusetts 02554
3. Jennie Peters, 1998 Cherry Street, Toledo, Ohio 43608
4. Felice Jones, 550 South Third Street, St. Paul, Minnesota 55110
5. Thomas Dunn, 1039 Linden Avenue, Oak Park, Illinois 60302

More to Explore

Using a piece of typing paper, draw a colorful border along the left side and at the bottom of the paper. Write a social letter, fold the paper correctly, address the envelope, and mail if possible.

ACTIVITY: Draw outlines of envelopes on the chalkboard and have the students fill in the addresses from this activity. Remind them to refer to the list of state abbreviations. Check to see that the format is correct and that return addresses have been included. The students should draw light lines on the envelope if they have difficulty keeping their handwriting straight.

MORE TO EXPLORE: Before the students decorate their paper, have them decide to whom they are writing. This might help determine what kind of border they use: sports design, flowers, music, etc. If they are writing to an imaginary person, have them create a clever address for the envelope.

Lesson 3 Parts of a Business Letter

A business letter has six parts: heading, inside address, salutation, body, complimentary close, and signature.

A business letter has a special part that is not included in a social letter. This is the *inside address*. Study the model letter below. Pay special attention to where you will include the inside address, and notice that the mark of punctuation after the salutation is different from that used in a social letter.

MODEL: Business Letter

101 Treetop Lane
Seattle, Washington 43219
May 12, 19—

XYZ Company
9238 Redwood Road
Portland, Oregon 57681

Dear Sir or Madam:
    I am interested in the bicycle accessories made by your company. Please send me a copy of your catalog.
    I look forward to doing business with you.

                    Sincerely,
                    Barbara Hemmer
                    Barbara Hemmer

138

1. Heading

The heading in a business letter is exactly the same as the heading in a social letter. It contains your street address, city, state, zip code, and date. Remember that there is no comma between the state and the zip code. Here is an example:

1540 Cottman Avenue
Philadelphia, Pennsylvania 19149
August 14, 19___

2. Inside Address

This part of a business letter is not used in a social letter. The inside address is exactly the same as the mailing address that goes on the envelope. It includes the complete name and address of the person, company, or organization to whom the letter is written. The inside address is written at the left side of the page, under the heading and above the salutation.

Loyola University Press
3441 North Ashland Avenue
Chicago, Illinois 60657

3. Salutation

The salutation (or greeting) in a business letter is more formal than in a social letter. It is always followed by a colon. If you do not know the name of the person who will be reading the letter, be very general:

Dear Sir or Madam: To Whom It May Concern:

If you know something about the person to whom you are writing, that can be indicated in the greeting:

Dear Customer Service Representative: Dear Editor:
Dear Order Department: Dear Manager:

If you have the name of a specific person, use that in the greeting:

Dear Mr. Hughes: Dear Ms. Silverstein:

4. Body

The body of the letter contains the message. State clearly and briefly why you are writing to the person or company. Be accurate. If you are ordering something, give the exact name of the item, the order number (if there is one), the size or color, the quantity, and the price. If you refer to another letter between you and the company, give the date of the letter. If you are requesting information, state clearly what you want to know.

5. Complimentary Close

The complimentary close, like the salutation, is more formal in a business letter than in a social letter. It is followed by a comma.

Yours truly,   Respectfully,   Sincerely,
Yours very truly,   Respectfully yours,   Very truly yours,

6. Signature

For a business letter, sign your full name and then print it below your signature. Printing your name makes it easier for the company to respond to your letter correctly.

Activity A

Use your own address to write a heading, and use each of the following sets of information for the inside address of a letter. Put the information in the correct order, using the proper form and spacing.

1. [3]6095 Washburn Avenue; [2]Masters Computer Company; [1]James Ferguson; [4]Wichita, Kansas 57693
2. [2]Chicago Area Runners' Association; [3]708 North Dearborn; [1]Sam Gutterman; [4]Chicago, Illinois 60610
3. [3]Atlanta, Georgia 30326; [1]Southern Skateboard Company; [2]5098 Peachtree Road
4. [2]PO Box 65892; [3]Portland, Maine 10265; [1]Olde Maine Syrup Industries
5. [1]Glenna Taylor; [4]Dallas, Texas 78940; [3]203 West Jonquil; [2]J. T. Hat Company

Activity B

Match the salutation on the left with the correct person on the right.

1. Dear Mr. Cruz: your dentist
2. Dear Sir or Madam: Linda Lakewood
3. Dear Personnel Manager: Julio Cruz
4. Dear Ms. Lakewood: Smithsonian Institution
5. Dear Dr. Thomas: the person who hires people

ACTIVITY A: This activity gives the students practice in writing just the heading and the inside address. Have them refer to the list of state abbreviations on page 136. Check carefully that the students are using the proper format. For extension, suggest that they write an appropriate salutation for each letter, varying the type of greeting.

ACTIVITY B: Discuss other types of salutations that the students may have seen in business letters: *Dear Customer:, Dear Resident:, Dear Colleague:*. To extend this activity, instruct the students to create an inside address for each person. Remind them that when a person's name is known, it should be the first line of the inside address:

Ms. Linda Lakewood
World Pen-Pal Associates
3309 Katherine Boulevard
Lincoln, Nebraska 68506

ANSWERS
1. Dear Mr. Cruz:
   Julio Cruz
2. Dear Sir or Madam:
   The Smithsonian Institution
3. Dear Personnel Manager:
   the person who hires people
4. Dear Ms. Lakewood:
   Linda Lakewood
5. Dear Dr. Thomas:
   your dentist

Lesson 4 Types of Business Letters

A business letter is a formal letter with a specific purpose.

People often have to write letters to companies or other organizations requesting information, placing orders, making complaints, or seeking help. Business letters should be clear, simple, and brief. Use the polite, formal tone that you would use in speaking to a business person.

It is acceptable for you to send hand-written business letters. However, if it is possible for you to type a business letter do so since typed letters are easier to read.

A Letter Placing an Order

Business letters are often written to place orders. When you write a letter to order merchandise, state the quantity needed, the name of the item, the order number (if any), the size and color (if appropriate), and the cost. It is also a good idea to tell how you want the merchandise sent. If you are enclosing a check or money order, say so. If you are charging the merchandise to a credit card, give the credit card name, number, and expiration date, and have the person whose name is on the credit card sign the letter.

235 Windermere Avenue
Wayne, Pennsylvania 19087
November 19, 19__

Mountain Ski Company
P.O. Box 93452
Pottsville, PA 19173

Dear Order Department:
    Kindly send by parcel post, as soon as possible, the following items:

2 boys' cotton shirts (1 red, 1 brown), #104, size 20	$20.00
1 shorts (green), #243, size 28	8.00
1 hat (tan), #98	5.00
	33.00

    I have enclosed a money order for $33.00 in payment for these items.

                    Yours truly,
                    Mary E. Laskowski
                    Mary E. Laskowski

ACTIVITY: Have the students study the introduction and the model letter for placing an order. Discuss the specific characteristics of this type of letter: order number, size, color, cost, method of delivery, method of payment. Have the students follow the same format as the model letter, making their information appropriate to the items being purchased.

Activity

Write a letter to a business in your community to order one of the groups of items listed.
1. camera, film, photo album
2. backpack, flashlight, binoculars
3. notebook, pencils, ink, stationery
4. ice skates, wool socks, sweater
5. three books (give the titles and authors)

A Letter Reporting an Error

Sometimes after you have ordered a product, it takes much too long for the item to arrive. If you have not received the item ordered or any letter from the company within a reasonable time, then you need to write a letter reporting the delay.

MODEL: Reporting a Delay

351 Main Street
Baltimore, Maryland 21222
December 15, 19—

Linda Cooper
New Volume Book Store
Westminster, Maryland 21157

Dear Ms. Cooper:

On November 29, I placed an order at your shop for <u>The Hawk That Dared Not Fly by Day</u> by Scott O'Dell. The clerk, Ronald Pilot, promised to have it sent to me within ten days. I have not yet received that book.

Since I intend to give this book as a holiday gift, it is important that I receive it immediately. Please notify me if you cannot fill my order.

Very truly yours,
Teresa Ambrogi
Teresa Ambrogi

Activity

Choose one of the following situations and write an appropriate business letter.

1. The costumes ordered by the Dramatic Club for the school play have been received by the committee in charge. There is a grave error in the sizes of two costumes. Report the error to the New York Costume Company, 563 E. 9th Street, New York, NY 10032. Make arrangements to have the correct sizes substituted.

2. You returned a shirt that you ordered from the Outdoor Clothing Company, PO Box 9784, Gainesville, FL 78934. You asked the company to send you the same shirt in a different size. Six weeks have passed, and you haven't heard from the company. Write to the company asking if it has received the shirt you returned and requesting that it take action soon.

3. The watch that you ordered from Fashion Accessories, 349 Maple Street, Fanwood, NJ 21467, loses five minutes every hour. Write a letter to enclose with the watch when you send it back.

A Letter Requesting a Response

Sometimes you need a response of some kind from a business or other organization. You may be asking for a favor (perhaps permission to take a tour of the company), an application for a job or program, or some definite piece of information. Be as specific as you can in your request so that you will get the response you need.

When you write such a letter, it is a good idea to enclose a stamped envelope with your address on it to make it easier for the person who receives your letter to respond. After you receive the response, whatever it is, write a letter of gratitude.

MODEL: Letter of Request

Henry W. Longfellow School
Salem, Oregon 97301
April 6, 19__

Salem Police Department
Twenty-third Precinct
402 Long Park Street
Salem, Oregon 97301

Dear Officer:

Our class of twenty-five students would like to visit the police station. We have been studying people who work in the helping professions, and we want to get a better idea of how the police department actually works.

We have heard that you regularly give tours on Wednesday afternoons, and that is a good time for us. Please let us know what specific date would be best for us to come.

Respectfully,

Jean Madden

Jean Madden (Secretary)

Activity A

Rewrite the following in letter form. Paragraph the letter and use the correct punctuation and capitalization.

354 green street, nashville, tennessee 37202, march 25, 19__, Nashville Youth Baseball, 216 quartz avenue, nashville, tennessee 37206, dear sir or madam our baseball team would like to enter the baseball tournament sponsored by your organization. Please send us an application blank gerry reynolds coaches our team and has given us permission to enter the tournament. very truly yours john vermuth (captain)

MODEL: Letter of Gratitude

Henry W. Longfellow School
Salem, Oregon 97301
May 2, 19__

Salem Police Department
Twenty-third Precinct
402 Long Park Street
Salem, Oregon 97301

Dear Sergeant Till:

On behalf of the members of my class, I wish to express our sincere gratitude to you, not only for your attention to us during our visit to the police station, but also for the work you do in the community.

The class is most grateful for the posters, which are already on display in our classroom.

Sincerely,

Jean Madden

Jean Madden (Secretary)

Activity B

Write a letter of thanks in response to the application forms received for the baseball tournament (activity A).

More to Explore

Find the name and address of an actual company that offers a product of interest to you. You can find the product and company through magazine ads or the yellow pages. Write a letter requesting more information on the product. Follow the correct format for a business letter.

Lesson 5 Completing Forms

Forms are specially designed papers that request specific information.

Businesses and other organizations use forms frequently as efficient means of obtaining information and fulfilling requests. Forms have blank spaces for people to fill in with specific bits of information. By having everyone fill in the same form for the same request, an organization ensures that it will receive all of the information it needs. The person processing the form can tell at a glance if any information is missing because there will be blank spaces.

Organizations that use forms usually have to deal with large numbers of people or with people who are not known to representatives of the organization. Many governmental units use forms: the Internal Revenue Service, the police, the libraries. The most common forms you might see are order forms and employment application forms.

When you are asked to complete a form, be sure to read and follow the directions printed on that particular form. *Print* (or type) all of the information the form requests as neatly as you can in the space allowed. Fill in every space where you are asked for information. Some forms have places on them that will be filled in by the organization itself. Do not mark in those places.

THE STUDENTS SHOULD LEARN
—why organizations use forms
—how to complete specific types of forms

TEACHING THE LESSON
Before reading the introductory material, discuss with the class why so many companies use forms. What advantage might a form have over a letter? Ask the students what specific kind of information they should have memorized: parents' places of employment, addresses, and telephone numbers; mother's maiden name; social security number; etc. What are some of the differences they have noticed in forms? (Some can be filled in by writing; others require printing. On some, the information requested is written above the line; on some, it is below the line.) Ask the students to mention the different types of forms they have already completed.

Activity A

Here is a sample of a completed form. Study the form, and then answer the questions below.

TICKET ORDER FORM

Karen   S.   Johnson
FIRST NAME (please print)   INITIAL   LAST NAME
947 N. Hayes St.   386-6102
NUMBER AND STREET   DAYTIME TELEPHONE
Oak Park   IL   60302
CITY   STATE   ZIP CODE

(Please refer to pages 4–6 for concert information.)

Date	No. of Seats	Price	Total
July 21	2	$14.00	$28.00
August 9	4	$6.00	$24.00
August 16	1	$5.00	$5.00
		Total amount of order	$57.00

If the price category for a particular performance is SOLD OUT, please:
(Check one box) ☐ Substitute available ticket prices
                 ☐ Return payment

Please enclose self-addressed, stamped business-size envelope along with your check or money order.

---

1. In what order is the ticket buyer's name to appear?
2. Where does the ticket buyer get the information about dates and prices of tickets?
3. What two mathematical functions is the ticket buyer expected to do?
4. How does the ticket buyer indicate what the office is to do in the event a particular category is sold out?
5. What three things will be in the envelope the ticket buyer sends in to order the tickets?

Activity B

Copy and complete the following application form for a library card. Print neatly and give all the required information. Then answer the questions that follow.

Date Issued_____ Expires_____

Do not write above this line. Please print on the lines below.

_____
NAME   BIRTHDATE

_____
ADDRESS (include street, city, state, and zip code)

_____
PLACE OF EMPLOYMENT AND ADDRESS

_____
HOME PHONE   BUSINESS PHONE

I apply for the right to use the library and will abide by its rules. I agree to pay fines charged to me.

_____
SIGNATURE

---

1. What type of writing is the applicant to use in filling out the application?
2. What information on the form is the applicant definitely not supposed to complete?
3. What information on the form might the applicant not be able to complete and why?
4. How many times will the applicant's name appear on the form?
5. By signing the form, to what two things does the applicant agree?

ACTIVITIES B AND C: If possible, photocopy these forms. Explain to the students that before completing any form, it is wise to read it through first, just to be familiar with what is being asked, and the method of filling in the form. After the students have completed each one, and the questions have been answered, discuss some of the similarities and differences between the forms. Which form is the easiest to fill in? Which requires the most information?

ANSWERS
1. printing
2. date issued, expires
3. place of employment and address, business phone — if the applicant is not employed
4. two
5. to abide by the library rules and to pay fines charged

Activity C

Copy and complete the following form to order these items: 2 blue beach balls (#103), at $2.50 each; 1 jade shirt, size 32 (#562), at $14.00; 1 pair buckle sandals, size 5 (#41), at $12.00.

ENCLOSE THIS FORM WITH YOUR ORDER BLANK

DATE

1. Complete this section if you wish to charge your order to your account.

ACCOUNT NUMBER

SIGNATURE

2. Print one number or letter per box. Skip one box between words.

AREA CODE   HOME PHONE NUMBER   BUSINESS PHONE NUMBER

NAME (first, middle initial, last) USE THE SAME NAME FOR ALL ORDERS from your household.

ADDRESS

CITY/STATE   ZIP CODE

3. Please list here the information about your order.

Item	How many	Catalog #	Size	Price	Total
beach balls	2	103		2.50	5.00
jade shirt	1	562	32	14.00	14.00
buckle sandals	1	41	5	12.00	12.00

Total amount of order   31.00

1. What special instructions for filling in the boxes is the buyer given in section 2?
2. In what order does the form ask the buyer to write his or her name?
3. Which people are required to sign the form?
4. What information does the form ask about each item in section 3?
5. In what section should the buyer write the date?

More to Explore

Find a magazine subscription form or a record club application form in a newspaper or magazine. Bring it to class for discussion and comparison with other forms. Then complete the form.

Bibliography

This Writing Corner could be used, together with Writing Corner 8, in conjunction with chapter 5, lesson 2, on report writing.

Look at the note cards on page 118. At the bottom of each card, Kelly recorded the *sources* of her information in a way that was clear to *her*, so that she could refer to these sources as she developed her report. In her final report, she has to give the sources of her information in a formal, more complete way, so that anyone who reads her report might easily find the same sources she used. This formal listing of sources is called a *bibliography*. Study the bibliography below to learn the format and punctuation required.

Magazine Article

Sims, Natalie A. "Japanese-Americans: New Ways and Old." *Geographic Monthly,* April, 1987, pp. 42-51.

Encyclopedia Article

Taylor, George. "Japanese-Americans." *Universal Encyclopedia*, Vol. 2, 1982 ed., pp. 54-61.

Book

McNiff, Estelle R. *One Nation, Many Cultures.* New York: Horn Publications, 1980.

Answers these questions about a bibliography.
A. What three types of sources are listed here?
B. In each entry, where is the name of the author placed?
C. Which is written first—the author's first name or last name? What punctuation is used to separate the first and last name? Is the middle initial of the author always noted?
D. What information is underlined in each entry?
E. How is the name of the article within an encyclopedia or within a magazine or periodical punctuated?
F. In which type of reference is the most recent information recorded?

G. In which entry is the month included as well as the year? Why?

H. In which entry is the page *not* noted? In a textbook, how would a reader find the page?

I. Name three different uses of the *period* in a bibliography.

J. Name two topics you would expect to find discussed in a magazine, but *not* in an encyclopedia.

You are right if you noticed the following:

A. The three sources are a *magazine*, an *encyclopedia*, and a *book*.

B. The author's name is placed *first*.

C. The author's *last name* is written first; a comma separates the first and last name of the author; the middle initial is not always noted.

D. The *name* of the magazine, encyclopedia, and book is underlined.

E. *Quotation marks* enclose an article within an encyclopedia or magazine.

F. The most recent information is recorded in a *magazine*.

G. The month and year are included in a *magazine* because *the magazine is published monthly*.

H. The page is not recorded for the *book*. In a textbook, the *index* would show the page.

I. A period is used (1) *after the complete name of the author,* (2) *after the title of an article in a magazine or encyclopedia,* (3) *after the name of a book,* (4) *after the abbreviation for pages,* and (5) *at the end of the complete entry.*

J. In a magazine, any *recent event, accomplishment, or disaster* would be discussed.

If you have more than one entry under a category, put the entries in alphabetical order. Often there is no author given for an encyclopedia article. In that case, just put the listing without an author, with the name of the article coming first.

★ Choose a topic from a science or social studies textbook. Find information about the topic in an encyclopedia. Use the *Readers' Guide to Periodical Literature* to find a magazine article about it (refer to pages 210 and 211).

Write a bibliography that includes these three kinds of sources. Refer carefully to the bibliography format shown here. Punctuate accurately.

Review of Word Parts

THE STUDENTS SHOULD
—review the prefixes, roots, and
suffixes already presented

ACTIVITY A: The students should
have prefix and suffix definitions
memorized. Many of these affixes
will be used in activity B.

Activity A

Match each prefix or suffix with its meaning.

1.	pre- c	a.	against
2.	-ity e	b.	without
3.	-al f	c.	before
4.	ir- h	d.	full of
5.	anti- a	e.	act of, state of being
6.	mis- i	f.	relating to
7.	sup- j	g.	above, over
8.	-less b	h.	not
9.	super- g	i.	badly, poorly
10.	-ous d	j.	under

ACTIVITY B: Have the students
name the prefix or suffix that is
appropriate for each word. They
should then be able to give the
meaning of each new word.

Activity B

Use a prefix or a suffix to change each word in column A to what is
asked in column B.

Column A	Column B
1. rapid	act of rapidity
2. courage	full of courageous
3. calculate	badly, poorly miscalculate
4. paid	after postpaid
5. perfect	not imperfect
6. explain	act of explanation
7. shape	without shapeless
8. kin	state of being kinship
9. hazard	full of hazardous
10. meditate	before premeditate

Activity C

Tell whether each sentence is *true* or *false*. Pay special attention to the italicized word.

1. If someone *misinterprets* your words, the person understands what you say. F
2. An *indirect* route takes you to your destination as quickly as possible. F
3. If you take the *subway*, you have to go underground. T
4. An *antidote* is a substance that fights poison. T
5. An *aimless* walk is without a definite goal. T
6. Since your computer is *portable*, you won't be able to move it from your bedroom. F
7. When the principal makes an *irrevocable* decision, she may change her mind. F
8. If you have a *legible* handwriting, people can read it easily. T
9. A *prefix* is added at the beginning of a word. T
10. An *extravehicular* walk would be outside of a spaceship. T
11. We had so much food at the picnic that there was a *scarcity*. F
12. Warfare continued between the nations during the *postwar* period. F
13. I enjoyed my *transatlantic* flight over the Pacific Ocean. F
14. Toni received a ticket for *illegal* parking. T
15. Mom had a garage sale to sell our *superfluous* belongings. T

Activity D

Name the root (base) in the italicized word in each sentence. Explain what the italicized word means, using your knowledge of the meaning of the root.

1. Cecilia's *graphic* description of farm life impressed us.
2. The elephant dancing with the lion was quite a *spectacle*.
3. A delicate shell mobile was *suspended* from the ceiling.
4. A *portfolio* containing top-secret information fell from under the agent's arm.
5. No one was pleased with his *dictatorial* attitude.

ACTIVITY C: For every sentence that the students suggest as *false*, have them reread the sentence as *true*. Have them give the meaning of the italicized word.

ACTIVITY D: The students should give the definition of the word using the meaning of the root.

ANSWERS
1. graph—producing a picture through *writing*
2. spect—something fascinating to *see*
3. pend—to *hang* down
4. port—case for papers *carried* by hand
5. dict—pertaining to *saying* or giving orders

Chapter 7

Speaking and Listening Skills

Lesson 1 Oral Presentations

Polished speaking skills improve oral expression.

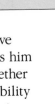

One of the best ways to develop your speaking skills is to observe someone who speaks well. What is it the person does that makes him or her a good speaker? You will find that many factors work together to make a polished speaking presentation: choice of topic (suitability for the audience), preparation of material, use of visual aids, clarity of expression, diction, volume (loudness or softness of voice), eye contact, gestures, poise, and posture.

Steps in Planning and Delivering an Oral Presentation

1. Find a topic of interest and narrow it.
2. Create an attention-grabbing opening statement.
3. Gather sufficient supporting details.
4. Develop an effective ending statement.
5. Write key ideas on 3″ × 5″ index cards.
6. Display some artwork or chalkboard diagrams.

A tapestry is woven with care and skill. What are the skills needed to become an effective speaker and listener?

Activity A

Each topic (below) for oral presentation has been divided into a *beginning idea, details* (the middle), and an *ending idea.* There is a section missing from each topic, however. Fill in the missing part, and then suggest a *visual display* you might use to make each presentation more interesting.

1. **Beginning idea:**

   Dr. Martin Luther King, Jr., stands among the great heroes of the twentieth century.

   Details:

   A. Early career
   B. Civil rights legislation
   C. Nobel Peace Prize

   Ending idea:

   Visual display:

2. **Beginning idea:**

   The study of outer space is a long-standing and never-ending human passion.

   Details:

   A.
   B.
   C.

   Ending idea:

   Moon landings are only one of the more recent episodes in the human quest for knowledge of the universe.

   Visual display:

ANSWERS
1. *Ending idea:* Dr. King encouraged and enabled changes toward justice and equality in the United States.
2. *Details:*
   A. Astronomers
   B. Satellites
   C. Manned spaceships
3. *Beginning idea:* Blue jeans are an American institution, worn by people of all ages in every economic bracket. *or*
   The average American closet may not contain a skeleton, but it probably *does* contain a pair of blue jeans.

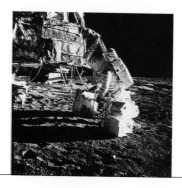

3. __Beginning idea:__

__Details:__

A. American invention
B. First worn as work clothes
C. Popular fashion item worldwide

__Ending idea:__

It seems as if jeans will always be with us, though ever-changing in both design and color.

__Visual display:__

Activity B

Brainstorm for possible topics for your own oral presentation. Use ideas from your science or social studies classes to stimulate your thinking. Then choose a topic and prepare an outline similar to the ones in activity A. Develop the details of your topic, provide a visual display, and give your presentation in class.

Here are some possible topics to help get you started.
1. Changes I would make in school and why
2. Values we learn by watching TV
3. How robots will change our lives
4. Why playing sports is important for everyone
5. How our country has helped its handicapped

More to Explore

Design an evaluation form that could be used to check on the effectiveness of a student's presentation. List the qualities as they are presented in the introduction.

Lesson 2 Poetry Reading

Poetry reading is a special form of speaking that emphasizes rhythm, rhyme, and emotion.

THE STUDENTS SHOULD LEARN

—that reading a poem is different from giving a speech

—that poems are meant to be read aloud

—to be sensitive to rhythm and rhyme when reading a poem

TEACHING THE LESSON

After the students have read the introduction to the lesson, discuss with them the differences between reading poetry and giving an oral presentation. Help them to understand that one type of presentation is not better than the other, but that each requires a different technique and style. Although this lesson presents only a few poems, encourage the students to read a variety of poems for enjoyment. However, before reading poetry to the class, an analysis of the poem should take place (with special emphasis on rhythm and rhyme) so that an understanding of the poem will improve the quality of the reading. When the students prepare an oral reading, suggest that they practice reading before a mirror and record their voices on tape.

Poems are read in different ways depending on their form and content. Some poems rhyme with every line or every other line; other poems do not rhyme at all. Some poems focus on giving a message; other poems seem to express pure emotion. When preparing a poem for oral presentation, a reader should consider the message (if any), the mood (joy, mystery, despair), the tone (serious, humorous, mocking, light), and the poet's use of rhythm and rhyme.

Rhythm

Rhythm is the flow or movement in poetry. It is the arrangement of stressed *(accented)* and unstressed *(unaccented)* syllables within a line. Every line in a poem has a number of *beats*, which are the accented or stressed syllables. Listen to the rhythm in the following lines:

1. Fire, fire, flaming bright
2. There is beauty all around

Count the number of stressed syllables in each line. There are four, which means there are four *beats*. Notice that the accented syllables (ˊ) come before the unaccented syllables (˘).

In the following lines, the rhythm changes. Now the unaccented syllables (˘) are followed by the accented syllables (ˊ).

1. An alligator is quite mean
2. Soft kiss of wavelets on the shore

Count the number of stressed syllables in line 1. There are four, so there are four beats in this line. Now count the stressed syllables in line 2. There are four beats in line 2.

160

Activity A

Mark the meter (rhythm) in each of the following lines, and count the number of beats in each line.

1. The peacock's tail is like a fan. 4 *4*
2. The train is puffing down the track. 4
3. Today I thought of only you. 4
4. Slowly, gently fell the April rain. 5

Activity B

Write a sentence of your own containing

    four beats with accented (´) syllables before unaccented (˘) ones
    four beats with unaccented (˘) syllables before accented (´) ones

Activity C

Read carefully the poem that follows. Read it three or four times until you pick up the rhythm of each line. Discuss in class how many beats you hear in each line of poetry.

The Hippopotamus

Behold the hippopotamus! 4
We laugh at how he looks to us, 4
And yet in moments dark and grim 4
I wonder how we look to him. 4
Peace, peace, thou hippopotamus! 5
We really look all right to us, 4
As you no doubt delight the eye 4
Of other hippopotami. 4

Ogden Nash

ACTIVITIES A, B, and C: Explain to the students that there is a rhythm to all speech, including our everyday speech. In poetry, rhythm is determined by beats. A beat is usually on a stressed or accented syllable. By counting the number of stressed syllables, students can discover the beats per line of poetry. Reciting nursery rhymes is an excellent way of presenting this concept. For activities A and B, have volunteers put their work on the chalkboard. Check for accuracy.

Rhyme

Rhyme has always been an important part of poetry. When an author chooses to use this technique, he or she works out a *rhyme scheme* or *pattern*. The pattern can be seen when each rhyming sound is given a letter. Look at the poem below and notice the letter at the end of each line. Why can you say that this poem has an a-b-c-b rhyming pattern?

Hope Is the Thing with Feathers

Hope is the thing with feathers	a
That perches in the soul,	b
And sings the tune without the words,	c
And never stops at all,	b
And sweetest in the gale is heard;	a
And sore must be the storm	b
That could abash the little bird	c
That kept so many warm.	b
I've heard it in the chillest land,	a
And on the strangest sea;	b
Yet, never, in extremity,	c
It asked a crumb of me.	b

Emily Dickinson

ACTIVITY A: Here again, nursery rhymes can be used to illustrate rhyming patterns. Play poetry records and read other poems aloud to the class. Have students identify the rhyming patterns.

Activity A

Read the poem "Advice to Travelers" three or four times. Listen to the rhyme and then identify it by means of letters.

Advice to Travelers

A burro once, sent by express,	a
His shipping ticket on his bridle,	b
Ate up his name and his address,	a
And in some warehouse, standing idle,	b
He waited until he like to died.	c
The moral hardly needs the showing:	d
Don't keep things locked up deep inside—	c
Say who you are and where you're going.	d

Walker Gibson

Activity B

Read each of the following poems aloud. Try to convey the message you think the poet intended. For each poem, consider the following questions:

1. What is the poet talking about on the surface? Is he or she talking about something else as well?
2. How has the poet used words? Does the poem rhyme (either at the ends of lines or within lines)? Is there a particular rhythm to the poem?
3. What mood has the poet created?

Bam, Bam, Bam

Pickaxes, pickaxes swinging today,
Plaster clouds flying every which way.

Workmen are covered with white dust like snow,
Oh, come see the great demolition show!

Slam, slam, slam,
Goes the steel wrecking-ball;
Bam, bam, bam
Against a stone wall.

It's raining bricks and wood
In my neighborhood.
Down go the houses,
Down go the stores,
Up goes a building
With forty-seven floors.

Crash goes a chimney,
Pow goes a hall,
Zowie goes a doorway,
Zam goes a wall.

Slam, slam, slam,
Goes the steel wrecking-ball;
Bam, bam, bam,
Changing it all.

Eve Merriam

ACTIVITY B: Read each poem to the class at least two or three times before any analysis takes place. Discuss the rhythm, rhyme, and the overall mood or effect on the reader. Do not overdo the analysis, but work for understanding and appreciation. Then ask for volunteers to read the poems aloud. Offer positive criticism about each speaker's presentation. Draw the students' attention to the use of dialect in the poem "Mother to Son" by Langston Hughes. The dialect should not be overemphasized or exaggerated, but when read sensitively should enhance the overall effect of the poem.

Mother to Son

Well, son, I'll tell you:
Life for me ain't been no crystal stair.
It's had tacks in it,
And splinters,
And boards torn up,
And places with no carpet on the floor—
Bare.
But all the time
I'se been a-climbin' on,
And reachin' landin's,
And turnin' corners,
And sometimes goin' in the dark
Where there ain't been no light.
So, boy, don't you turn back.
Don't you set down on the steps
'Cause you finds it kinder hard.
Don't you fall now—
For I'se still goin', honey,
I'se still climbin',
And life for me ain't been no crystal stair.

Langston Hughes

September

The breezes taste
    Of apple peel.
The air is full
    Of smells to feel—

Ripe fruit, old footballs,
    Burning brush,
New books, erasers,
    Chalk, and such.

The bee, his hive
    Well-honeyed, hums,
And Mother cuts
    Chrysanthemums.

Like plates washed clean
    With suds, the days
Are polished with
    A morning haze.

John Updike

Song of the Pop-Bottlers

Pop bottles pop-bottles
    In pop shops;
The pop-bottles Pop bottles
    Poor Pop drops.

When Pop drops pop-bottles,
    Pop-bottles plop!
Pop-bottle-tops topple!
    Pop mops slop!

Stop! Pop'll drop bottle!
    Stop, Pop, stop!
When Pop bottles pop-bottles,
    Pop-bottles pop!

Morris Bishop

Analysis of Baseball

It's about
the ball,
the bat,
and the mitt.
Ball hits
bat, or it
hits mitt.
Bat doesn't
hit ball, bat
meets it.
Ball bounces
off bat, flies
air, or thuds
ground (dud)
or it
fits mitt.

Bat waits
for ball
to mate.
Ball hates
to take bat's
bait. Ball
flirts, bat's
late, don't
keep the date.
Ball goes in
(thwack) to mitt,
and goes out
(thwack) back
to mitt.

Ball fits
mitt, but
not all
the time.
Sometimes
ball gets hit
(pow) when bat
meets it,
and sails
to a place
where mitt
has to quit
in disgrace.
That's about
the bases
loaded,
about 40,000
fans exploded.

It's about
the ball,
the bat,
the mitt,
the bases
and the fans.
It's done
on a diamond,
and for fun.
It's about
home, and it's
about run.

May Swenson

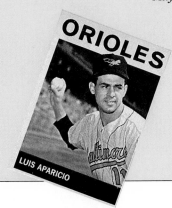

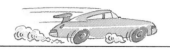

Ambition

I got pocketed behind 7X-3824;
He was making 65, but I can do a little more.
I crowded him on the curves, but I couldn't get past,
And on the straightaways there was always some truck
    coming fast.
Then we got to the top of a mile-long incline
And I edged her out to the left, a little over the white line,
And ahead was a long grade with construction at the bottom,
And I said to the wife, "Now by golly I got'm!"
I bet I did 85 going down the long grade,
And I braked her down hard in front of the barricade,
And I swung in ahead of him and landed fine
Behind 9W-7679.

Morris Bishop

Nonsense!

Nonsense? That's what makes no sense;
a walrus waltzing on a fence,
cats in vats of cheese and chowder,
weasels sniffing sneezing powder,
elephants with bright umbrellas
dancing sprightly tarantellas,
tigers dressed in spotted sweaters
playing chess and writing letters.

Nonsense? Lizards clanging cymbals,
flying eggs and weeping thimbles,
sleeping prunes and crooning poodles,
hopping spoons and creeping noodles,
schools of fish that moo like cattle,
bloomer marching into battle,
pigs with wigs and purple wings.
Nonsense! All these silly things.

Jack Prelutsky

More to Explore

Read the following poem over many times until you feel as the dog might feel having an intruder in the night. Pause where the punctuation indicates; it is not always at the end of a line. Determine the rhythm and rhyming pattern of the poem, and then give an oral presentation to the class.

Dog at Night

At first he stirs uneasily in sleep	a
And, since the moon does not run off, unfolds	b
Protesting paws. Grumbling that he must keep	a
Both eyes awake, he whimpers; then he scolds	b
And, rising to his feet, demands to know	c
The stranger's business. You who break the dark	d
With insolent light, who are you? Where do you go?	c
But nothing answers his indignant bark.	d
The moon ignores him, walking on as though	c
Dogs never were. Stiffened to fury now,	e
His small hairs stand upright, his howls come fast,	f
And terrible to hear is the bow-wow	e
That tears the night. Stirred by this bugle-blast,	f
The farmer's hound grows active; without pause	g
Summons her mastiff and the cur that lies	h
Three fields away to rally to the cause.	g
And the next county wakes. And miles beyond	i
Throats ring themselves and brassy lungs respond	i
With threats, entreaties, bellowings and cries,	h
Chasing the white intruder down the skies.	h

Louis Untermeyer

MORE TO EXPLORE: Read the poem to the students first. Next, have them read it as a group, and then have them read it silently. Give special attention to the end marks of punctuation, reminding the students that thay should read thoughts, not lines. Each line has five beats, and the rhyme is easily determined. Call on volunteers who feel they can convey the feeling and mood of "Dog at Night" to read it to the class.

ENRICHMENT

Provide a number of poetry books for the students to browse through. Have them select one poem that they think is appropriate for oral reading. Explain that a good presentation requires that the speaker know the poem thoroughly; therefore, reading it over ten or more times is almost a necessity. This will help them get a feel for the rhythm and mood of the poem. Have as many students as possible read their selection to the class. Have the class react constructively to each student's presentation.

Lesson 3 Choral Speaking

In choral speaking, a poem is read by a group of people following a specific pattern.

THE STUDENTS SHOULD LEARN

—to appreciate the beauty of choral speaking

—how poems are marked for choral speaking

—the importance of controlled breathing and enunciating clearly

TEACHING THE LESSON

Although this lesson concentrates on the choral reading of poetry, other types of literature can also be expressed through this same medium. In all cases, the key to good choral speaking is to have the voices blend when reading in unison and have distinct differences in voices when solos are required or light, medium, or deep voices are suggested. The poems allow for a variety of different patterns of reading. Ask the class for suggestions about varying the way the poem is read and then experiment with a few of these ideas. Have the students read the introduction and discuss with them the markings for inflection. Practicing the Tuning-Up Exercises will help with breathing and enunciation.

Choral speaking gives people the opportunity to enjoy great poetry by reading it together. As part of a group, they feel the swing of the rhythm, the variations of time and pitch, and the music of the words.

Two simple rules apply to all choral speaking:
1. The thought of the poem must become your own.
2. The feeling you express must fit the thought and must never be exaggerated.

Markings

In this book, certain markings are used to help you phrase poems that will be recited in chorus. The markings are as follows:

> \ for a falling inflection
> / for a rising inflection
> // for a pause

In a falling inflection (\), lower your voice slightly. Statements usually end in a falling inflection.

> He can crawl in your pocket or fit in your locket \

In a rising inflection (/), have your voice rise to a slightly "higher" note. Questions often end with a rising inflection.

> Yes he can, / course he can /

Use rising (/) and falling (\) inflections for words used in pairs and for stressed words used in succession.

> He's the Twistable / Turnable \ Squeezable / Pullable \
> Stretchable / Foldable \ Man. //

Tuning-Up Exercises

Breathing

Breathe deeply. Inhale through your nose, inflating your diaphragm, chest wall, and ribs. Then exhale slowly with the sound of *ah*.

Enunciation

Learn to enunciate—that is, to speak clearly and distinctly—both vowels and consonants. Speak vowels with the mouth round. Speak consonants crisply and accurately.

Exercise for Vowels

Say the vowels, first in a low pitch, then in a high pitch. Use the piano where possible to establish the high and low pitches.

Say these short sounds with a relaxed tongue:

> *a* as in *hat*. Repeat several times: patch, lad, stamp.
> Catch the lad that stamps pads in the pantry.
>
> *e* as in *pet*. Repeat several times: red, wet, tell.
> A wet thread went through the hedge.

Nonsense Poems

Nonsense poems tickle our sense of humor. They amuse by their coined words, strange dialect, ridiculous sayings, or absurd actions.

Activity

Read the following nonsense poem in class. Have the class read all the words that end in *able*. Have one speaker for the other parts. Then read it a second time, experimenting with a different pattern.

Twistable, Turnable Man

He's the Twistable / Turnable \ Squeezable / Pullable \
Stretchable / Foldable Man. //
He can crawl in your pocket / or fit in your locket \
Or screw himself into a twenty-volt socket, \
Or stretch himself up to the steeple or taller, \
Or squeeze himself into a thimble or smaller, \
Yes he can, / course he can, /
He's the Twistable / Turnable \ Squeezable / Pullable \
Stretchable / Shrinkable Man. //
And he lives a passable life \
With his Squeezable / Lovable \ Kissable / Hugable \
Pullable / Tugable Wife. //
And they have two twistable kids \
Who bend up the way that they did. \
And they turn and they stretch \
Just as much as they can \
For this Bendable / Foldable \
Do-what- / you're-toldable \
Easily / moldable \
Buy-what / you're-soldable \
Washable / Mendable \
Highly / dependable \
Buyable / Saleable \
Always / available \
Bounceable / Shakable \
Almost / unbreakable \
Twistable / Turnable Man. //

Shel Silverstein

ACTIVITY: Have the entire class read the poem aloud at least three or four times, and then have a choral reading according to the suggestion in the instructions. Next, ask the students to create a different pattern for recitation.

Lyric Poems

Poems that "sing" are called *lyric* poems. They make the best poems for choral speaking because their rhythm (the beat of the lines) is like the rhythm of music. Lyric poems do not usually tell stories. Instead, they express the emotions of the poet.

Activity

"Daybreak" is a lyric poem, a song sung from the heart of the poet to the hearts of his listeners. The lines are filled with pictures of early morning. All the earth and all the people awake at daybreak; all except the dead lying in the churchyard. The wind from the sea is given a voice through *personification,* a figure of speech in which nonhuman things are imaginatively given human characteristics.

As you prepare the poem for choral speaking, note the time. Use slow time for things that are sad, like the last stanza, and quick time for things that are glad, like the second stanza. Time will help determine pitch. As the time changes with gladness or sadness, so does the pitch of the voice—higher pitch for gladness, lower pitch for sadness.

Once you have worked out time and pitch, and assigned the various parts, read "Daybreak" in class as a choral group.

ACTIVITY: "Daybreak" is divided into light, medium, and deep voices. "Light" does not necessarily mean girls' voices, nor "deep," boys' voices. Experiment with some oral reading in class to determine the students' quality of voice. Try the pattern suggested in the text and then divide into two groups: one being the narrator, and the other, the wind.

Daybreak

MEDIUM VOICES	A wind \ came up out of the sea, / And said, / "O mists, make room for me!" /
LIGHT VOICES	It hailed the ships \ and cried, / "Sail on, / Ye mariners, / the night is gone!" //
DEEP VOICES	And hurried landward \ far away, / Crying, / "Awake! it is the day!" //
MEDIUM VOICES	It said unto the forest, / "Shout! // Hang all your leafy banners out!" //
LIGHT VOICES	It touched the wood-bird's folded wing, \ And said, / "O bird, awake and sing!" //
DEEP VOICES	And o'er the farms, \ "O chanticleer, // Your clarion blow; / the day is near!" //
MEDIUM VOICES	It whispered to the fields of corn, / "Bow down, / and hail the coming morn!" //
LIGHT VOICES	It shouted through the belfry-tower, / "Awake, O bell! \ proclaim the hour." //
ALL	It crossed the churchyard \ with a sigh, / And said, / "Not yet! in quiet lie." /

Henry Wadsworth Longfellow

Narrative Poems

A narrative poem tells a story. In "The Charge of the Light Brigade," for example, the English poet Alfred Tennyson tells of the heroic charge of the British cavalry against the Russian forces during a campaign in the Crimean War (1853-1856).

Activity

As a class, prepare and present a choral reading of "The Charge of the Light Brigade." The poem has a great deal of action and movement. The choral reading should convey this feeling as well as the courage and determination of the British. Remember, if a story is to be told well, it needs to be read and interpreted correctly.

ACTIVITY: Read the poem to the class and discuss the action that is taking place. The students should sense the futility of the attack (less than one-third returned from battle alive) as well as the feeling of the soldiers as they blindly obey orders. The students should read the poem as a group and strive to convey the intensity of the battle. Then have a choral reading according to the suggestions in the text. Choose a group of students to create a new pattern for the poem.

The Charge of the Light Brigade

UNISON	Half a league, / half a league, / Half a league onward, // All in the valley of Death / Rode the six hundred. //
SOLO	"Forward the Light Brigade! // Charge for the guns!" // he said. /
UNISON	Into the valley of Death / Rode the six hundred. //
SOLO	"Forward, / the Light Brigade!" //
LIGHT VOICES	Was there a man dismayed? // Not though the soldier knew \ Some one had blundered. //
DEEP VOICES	Theirs not to make reply, / Theirs not to reason why, / Theirs but to do / and die. //
UNISON	Into the valley of Death \ Rode the six hundred. //

MEDIUM VOICES	Cannon \ to right / of them, /
LIGHT VOICES	Cannon \ to left \ of them, /
DEEP VOICES	Cannon \ in front / of them /
	Volleyed / and thundered; //
UNISON	Stormed at \ with shot and shell, /
(slower)	Boldly they rode / and well, /
	Into the jaws \ of Death, \
	Into the mouth \ of hell \
	Rode the six hundred. //
LIGHT VOICES	Flashed / all their sabres bare, //
	Flashed / as they turned in air //
	Sabring \ the gunners \ there, \
	Charging an army, / while
	All the world \ wondered. //
MEDIUM VOICES	Plunged \ in the battery-smoke /
	Right through the line / they broke; //
DEEP VOICES	Cossack / and Russian /
	Reeled \ from the sabre-stroke
	Shattered \ and sundered. //
UNISON	Then they rode back, \ but not, \
	Not \ the six hunded. //
MEDIUM VOICES	Cannon \ to right of them, /
LIGHT VOICES	Cannon \ to left of them, /
DEEP VOICES	Cannon \ behind them /
	Volleyed \ and thundered; \
UNISON	Stormed at \ with shot and shell,
(slower)	While horse / and hero fell, \
	They that had fought / so well /
	Came through the jaws / of Death, /
	Back from the mouth of hell, //
	All / that was left of them, /
	Left of six hundred. //
MEDIUM VOICES	When can their glory fade? //
LIGHT VOICES	Oh, / the wild charge / they made! //
DEEP VOICES	All the world \ wondered. //
	Honor / the charge they made! //
	Honor / the Light / Brigade, /
	Noble / six hundred! //

Alfred Tennyson

MORE TO EXPLORE: Divide the class into groups of four or five. Have the groups search for appropriate poems in the library, or have some poems already selected for reading (poems should be fairly short). Help each group make decisions about unison and solo readings as well as markings for inflections. After each group has made their presentation, have the poems duplicated for the entire class to do as a choral reading.

More to Explore

Work with a group of students to select a poem that could be used for choral speaking. Decide which lines should be said in unison and which should be read by individuals. Practice your presentation sufficiently before presenting it to the class.

Lesson 4 Listening Skills

Good listening skills allow for accurate understanding of spoken material.

THE STUDENTS SHOULD LEARN
—the difference between hearing and listening
—why it is important to listen carefully
—the keys to effective listening

TEACHING THE LESSON
Have the students identify the various sounds on a sound effects record. Because they are attentive to what they are doing, they are engaged in *listening,* more than *hearing.* Explain to the students that many times a day they hear sounds, but never really listen. Listening is a conscious procedure and a skill that is meant to be practiced and developed. Discuss with the students when listening skills are most needed. Have them also discuss some of the side effects of poor listening skills. The Keys to Effective Listening should be studied and practiced whenever possible.

You *hear* many sounds every day without *listening* to them—street noises, other people talking among themselves, the wind blowing. Sometimes you *hear* things to which you should be *listening* instead (like your parents or teachers talking to you). How do you go about listening to what is really important?

Listening in class is very important. Your teacher gives specific instructions for assignments, and if you are not listening you may do the assignments wrong. Your classmates also make important comments on the material you are studying. Paying attention is the key to understanding what's going on around you. If you're attentive, you have a better chance of hearing and correctly interpreting things that are said—or of asking questions to help clarify your thinking.

Consider each element in the following table when you are in a listening situation.

Keys to Effective Listening

Preparation Know what the speaker's subject will be and think about it before the talk begins.

Position Sit where you can see the speaker and hear everything he or she says.

Attention Watch the speaker and take notes on important points.

Questions Make notes about questions that come to mind while the speaker is talking; ask questions at a time when the speaker will allow them (this may be during the talk or afterward).

Activity A

Following Directions

Listen carefully as your teacher gives you a set of directions. Then ask yourself the following questions:

1. Are the directions clear to me? Do I have any questions about them?
2. Do I need help in doing what I have been told to do?
3. Do I need to collect any materials in order to follow these directions (and, if so, what)?
4. Have I missed anything in the directions?
5. Write down the four steps necessary to change a tire. Make sure they are in the correct order.

ACTIVITY A: Read aloud the following directions. Then lead the students through the questions asked in the text.

This is how you change a flat tire. First, use a prybar or a screwdriver to remove the hubcap. Then use a wrench (preferably the kind with four arms, since it will give you better leverage) to loosen the four bolts holding the wheel on. Next, place the jack under the part of the car that is built to support it, and then use the jack to raise the car. Once the tire is off the ground, finish loosening the bolts until they come off. (Be careful not to lose them!) Now the tire should pull off easily. The spare tire goes on the same way the old tire came off — only backwards.

Other suggestions: give directions from your house to school; give directions to move into certain groups in the classroom; explain how to fold a piece of paper a specific way.

FOLLOW UP: Each student should choose a partner and read to him or her a set of directions for completing an art design. Each direction should be read only once. A correct design would reflect the student's ability to listen carefully and follow directions. (Try to check each student's directions with the completed design first to be certain the directions are precise and accurate.)

ACTIVITY B: Find or create a story that will catch the interest of your particular class. The story should take five minutes or less to read. When finished, ask questions about the story. Have the students write the answers and then check how accurately they listened.

FOLLOW UP: Direct the students to choose an interesting story from their reader or their social studies or science textbook (not too long). They should read this selection to a classroom partner, ask specific questions to see how well their partner has listened, and then check the partner's responses.

ACTIVITY C: Read the following sets of commands:

pull your hair, scratch your leg, walk around — do #1

stamp your feet, open your mouth, blink your eyes — do #2

wiggle your nose, clap your hands, whistle — do #1

write in the air, scream, say your name — do #3

pick up a pencil, close your eyes, bend over — do #3

look at the floor, shake another's hand, smile — do #2

stick out your tongue, pull your ear, touch your nose — do #1

cover your mouth, hold your ankle, stand on one leg — do #2

FOLLOW UP: The students should create lists like the one they just heard. Have volunteers lead the class in this activity.

Activity B

Getting the Facts

Listen carefully as your teacher reads a brief story aloud. When the reading is finished, your teacher will ask you specific questions about the story.

Activity C

Remembering Ideas

Sometimes you need to listen for specific information that you will be required to remember. Suppose, for example, someone names the following three things to do:

Touch your forehead.
Snap your fingers.
Raise your left hand.

You are then told to complete only the second command. You would have to remember that the command was "Snap your fingers."

Listen now as your teacher gives other sets of commands. Listen to remember, because you will then be instructed to do only one of the commands.

Activity D

Tuning Up Your Ears

A speaker's tone of voice affects how you interpret what he or she says. If the speaker stresses one word in a sentence, the sentence may mean one thing. If the speaker stresses a different word in the same sentence, the sentence may mean something totally different. What does each of the following statements mean to you?

You can come to my house.
You can come to my house.
You *can* come to my house.
You can come to *my* house.

Your teacher will read several statements. Discuss as a class their possible interpretations.

Activity E

Listening with Your Eyes

A speaker's facial expressions and body language also affect how you interpret what he or she is saying. For example, if a friend tells you, "I love my father's cooking!" and wrinkles up her nose, you get the message that she probably doesn't care for her father's cooking at all! If she made the same statement while rubbing her stomach and smiling, you would think just the opposite.

Try expressing the following attitudes or feelings with a facial expression, a specific posture, or a combination of both.

1. boredom
2. excitement
3. surprise
4. drowsiness
5. attentiveness
6. disgust
7. anger
8. pity

ACTIVITY D: Study the introductory material to this activity. Stress how tone of voice affects interpretation. Then read the following statements to the class, pausing between each group to allow for student discussion.

I don't want a doughnut.
I don't *want* a doughnut.
I don't want a *doughnut*.

What did you do today?
What did *you* do today?
What did you do *today*?

All students must do this task.
All *students* must do this task.
All students *must* do this task.
All students must do *this* task.

FOLLOW UP: The students should make up a series of three or four statements that can be said with various intonations. Have the class interpret the messages.

ACTIVITY E: Have a class discussion about facial expressions and body language. Have volunteers create the different expressions and body positions suggested in the activity.

FOLLOW UP: Some students will be able to suggest other attitudes or emotions not mentioned in the text. Have volunteers convey the attitudes through facial expression and body language. See if the class can identify the attitude or message conveyed.

ENRICHMENT

Have the students record about thirty seconds' worth of reading on a tape (the content should not identify who they are). Have some students use their natural voice and others a disguised voice. Play the tape for the class and ask them to identify the voices. Check the number of correct responses. What clues revealed the person?

Idea taken from *Listening Instruction by Andrew Wolvin and Carolyn Coakley.* Published 1979 by the ERIC Clearinghouse on Reading and Communication Skills, 1111 Kenyon Road, Urbana, Illinois 61801

Writing Corner 7

Alliteration

Alliteration is the repetition of a consonant sound. Usually the consonant sound comes at the beginning of the word.

Alliteration is often found in poetry. There it enhances the sound of a poem, often adding to the mood the author is trying to create. Note the repetition of the sound *s* in the opening lines of the poem "Silver" by Walter de la Mare. (*Shoon* is an old word for *shoes.*)

> *S*lowly, *s*ilently, now the moon
> Walks the night in her *s*ilver *s*hoon;...

Alliteration is also frequently used in headlines. Check your town's newspaper for examples of alliteration.

Alliteration can be amusing to listen to, especially when it is overused. Look at the following sentences.

> Barbara's beautiful baby blew bubbles.
> Frieda flipped flapjacks frantically.

Sometimes more than one consonant sound is repeated. Can you find an example in the sentence below?

> Several silly sparrows splattered seeds spiritedly.

You are right if you noticed that the blend *sp* is repeated several times at the beginning of words. The sound that *l* stands for is also repeated several times within words in the sentence.

★ Try completing a few silly sentences of your own with alliteration.

Molly munched and munched ...
Nervous Ned ...
Crunchy cookies crumbled ...
Betty, Bobbie, and Bonnie were bored ...

You can also use alliteration for an amusing effect in stories. Here is the beginning of a story in which a student used words beginning with *p* as often as possible.

> The day was perfect for a picnic at the ballpark. I plowed out of bed, plumped up my pillows, and pulled up the pink bedspread. I put on my purple pants and puce pullover. Mom was in the kitchen packing peanut butter sandwiches, pastrami on pumpernickel, pickles, peaches, peanuts, potato chips, and pretzels. Dad picked up the paper ...

Another student wrote

> One sweltering summer Saturday, Sammy skipped to the store. He started in when suddenly he saw Sonny sauntering down the street. Sonny joined Sammy and they both swiftly settled onto a soft stool at the counter. Sammy sipped a soda and Sonny splurged on a super-duper sundae. Suddenly, Sonny spied the clock. Soon Sammy and Sonny swirled around ...

★ Choose your favorite consonant sound, and write a story in which that sound is used at the beginning of many words. Then make an oversize drawing of your letter (about 10 inches high), and write your story in it. Share your creation with the class.

THE STUDENTS SHOULD LEARN
—the meaning of a homophone
—to use homophones correctly in sentences

Word Study 7

Homophones

Homophones are words that sound alike but have different spellings and meanings.

TEACHING THE LESSON

Review the homophones that were presented in grade 6. The students should give oral or written sentences for each pair. Give special attention to the homophones that are contractions. Use the following sentences:

(It's, Its) time for our favorite TV show.
The dog scratched (it's, its) back against the tree.
Will the person (who's, whose) name is called step forward?
The clown (who's, whose) dancing on the tightrope is the funniest.

Make sure that the students read the contraction as *two words* before making a choice.

Review the other homophones that use contractions (presented in grade 6): *your, you're—there, their, they're.* The students should use the homophones in sentences.

Since homophones sound alike, they can often be very confusing when you write. The following homophones were presented in sixth grade. Can you give the meaning of each word and use it in a sentence?

bough—bow	piece—peace
course—coarse	root—route
here—hear	stationery—stationary
knot—not	sum—some
patience—patients	through—threw

Activity A

Answer each question below by giving the correct homophone. Define the remaining homophones. Use your dictionary if necessary.

braid—brayed	maize—maze
cash—cache	nice—gneiss
core—corps	principal—principle
current—currant	taught—taut
key—quay	wet—whet

1. I am a sour berry that grows on a bush. What am I?
2. I am a word that describes the sound a donkey had made. What am I?
3. I am a wharf or dock. What am I?
4. I am a word that means to stimulate your appetite. What am I?
5. I am a type of corn. What am I?
6. I am a place to hide treasure or store food. What am I?
7. I am a type of rock. What am I?
8. I am a specially trained group of people. What am I?
9. I am a basic truth or rule. What am I?
10. I am a word that means something drawn tightly. What am I?

ANSWERS
1. currant
2. brayed
3. quay
4. whet
5. maize
6. cache
7. gneiss
8. corps
9. principle
10. taut

Activity B

Complete each sentence with the correct homophone from activity A.

1. Algernon, the mouse, had to travel through a __maze__ to be rewarded.
2. The students added a piece of __gneiss__ to their rock collection.
3. The hiker had a __cache__ of food stored along the trail.
4. My little sister has a long __braid__.
5. Bruce would not give in. It was a matter of __principle__.
6. After a night in the rain, the newspaper was too __wet__ to read.
7. My mom used a special utensil to __core__ the apples.
8. An old skeleton __key__ finally opened the door.
9. My aunt makes delicious __currant__ jelly.
10. __Maize__ was a common crop of the Indians.
11. Our neighbor __taught__ us gymnastics and aerobics.
12. The donkey __brayed__ when it saw its master.
13. The hospital is staffed by a __corps__ of doctors and nurses.
14. *Lovely* and *gracious* are more precise words than __nice__.
15. The smell of home-baked cookies __whet__ my appetite.
16. Krista paid __cash__ for her new bike.
17. The canoe was carried along by a swift-moving __current__.
18. Hold the end of the string at your nose and pull it __taut__.
19. The ship loaded its cargo at the assigned __quay__.
20. Every student wanted to get a close look at the new __principal__.

Activity C

Sometimes contractions that are homophones cause difficulty. Remember *it's* means "it is" and *who's* means "who is." Select the homophone that correctly completes each sentence.

1. (Who's, <u>Whose</u>) brilliant idea was it to choose a turkey for a class mascot?
2. (<u>It's</u>, its) important for you to proofread your writing.
3. The book was boring, except for (it's <u>its</u>) ending.
4. (<u>Who's</u>, Whose) responsible for leaving handprints on the bathroom wall?
5. Steven Spielberg, (who's, <u>whose</u>) movies are popular, puts many action-filled scenes in them.

Chapter 8
Using the Library

Lesson 1 Finding What You Need

A library contains a wealth of books, articles, and multimedia materials for enjoyment, research, and learning. Before you can make the most effective use of your library, however, you must become familiar with *what* is there and *where* it can be found.

Circulating Books

Some books may be borrowed from the library for a specified period of time, while others must be used in the building. The books that may be checked out are called *circulating books*. There are two main categories of circulating books: *fiction* and *nonfiction*.

Fiction Books

Fiction books are invented stories. The people and events in them have been largely or totally imagined by an author. Novels, science fiction tales, and mysteries are examples of fiction books. These books are shelved in a separate section of the library and often have "F" or "FIC" on their spines, or backs. They are arranged alphabetically according to the author's last name. If you wanted to find the book *Of Mice and Men* by John Steinbeck, for example, you would first have to locate the fiction section in your library and then find the books with authors' names beginning with "S."

In listing fiction books, you write the author's last name followed by a comma, then the author's first name. The title of the book follows the name of the author.

THE STUDENTS SHOULD LEARN
—where fiction and nonfiction materials are located and how they are arranged
—the call numbers for the ten major subject areas of the Dewey Decimal System
—how to locate information through the use of the card catalog

TEACHING THE LESSON
Acquaint yourself beforehand with the floor plan of the school library. Visit the library with the students and point out the card catalog, the fiction section, and the nonfiction section. In nonfiction, show them the ten major classifications of the Dewey Decimal System. In the fiction section, point out the *F* or *Fic* on the spine of a book and show the students where the author's name is located. Have them note that the books are arranged alphabetically by the author's last name.

Allow time for the students to circulate around the library. Then instruct them to list ten books and authors from the fiction section in alphabetical order.

A good book is a treasure. What are some of the book treasures you have discovered in your library?

Activity

On a sheet of paper, alphabetize these fiction books.

Author	Title	
Voigt, Cynthia	*Dick's Song*	9
Adams, Richard	*Watership Down*	1
Lewis, C. S.	*Chronicles of Narnia*	5
Christie, Agatha	*Death in the Air*	2
Hilton, James	*Goodbye, Mr. Chips*	4
Stevenson, Robert Louis	*Treasure Island*	8
Mitchell, Margaret	*Gone with the Wind*	7
London, Jack	*White Fang*	6
Green, Hannah	*I Never Promised You a Rose Garden*	3
Zindel, Paul	*The Undertaker's Gone Bananas*	10

Nonfiction Books

Nonfiction books contain facts and information about real-life events. Since these books cover a wide variety of subjects, some plan of classification is needed so that they can be shelved in a logical order and easily located by library users. One plan that many libraries use is the *Dewey Decimal System.* The system was invented by an American librarian named Melvil Dewey. He arranged all nonfiction material into ten major subject areas. He then assigned each area a range of numbers. Each book in a subject area is assigned a specific number, called a *call number.*

The ten major subject areas and their range of numbers are listed here for your information and use.

Dewey Decimal System

000–099	General reference	Encyclopedias, almanacs, atlases, etc.
100–199	Philosophy	Beliefs, personality, psychology
200–299	Religion	Bible, mythology, theology
300–399	Social sciences	Education, government, law
400–499	Languages	Dictionaries, foreign languages, grammar
500–599	Sciences	Astronomy, biology, chemistry, math
600–699	Useful arts and technology	Aviation, business, cooking, farming, inventions, medicine, sewing, television
700–799	Fine arts	Acting, art, dancing, music, photography, sports
800–899	Literature	Plays, poetry, literary criticism
900–999	Geography and history	Biography, geography, travel

Activity A

Number a sheet of paper from 1 to 10 and write the number range where you would find each of these titles.

1. *Successful Sewing: A Modern Guide* 600-699
2. *Personal Adjustment and Mental Health* 100-199
3. *Modern Tourist* 900-999
4. *School and Library Atlas of the World* 000-099
5. *Essentials of World Literature* 800-899
6. *German for Beginners* 400-499
7. *Famous World Myths* 200-299
8. *History of Mathematics* 500-599
9. *Guide to Folk and Square Dancing* 700-799
10. *Early Childhood Education* 300-399

TEACHING THE LESSON

Have the students locate the nonfiction section of the school library. Show them the classification plan of the Dewey Decimal System. Point out the ten major sections in which books may be classified. Refer to the chart in the textbook. Give the students time to browse in each of these major subject areas. In chart form, have them write down the first line of the call number and the title of one book from each major area.

Explain to the students how each of these major sections can be further divided into smaller subdivisions. For example, the 600s—Useful Arts and Technology—is subdivided into aviation, business, cooking, farming, inventions, medicine, sewing, and television.

ACTIVITIES A AND B: Activity A asks the students to identify the *major area* in which each book title belongs. Activity B asks them to identify the *subdivision* in which each book title belongs. You may have to explain the meaning of terms such as paleontology. For extension, assign each student a major subject area, or let each choose an area of interest. Have the students go to the library and locate the major area they've been assigned. They should then write down the title, number, and subject of one book in each subdivision of that major area (710s, 720s, 730s, etc.). When they return to class, have them write up their findings in chart form.

Within each major subject area, there are ten subdivisions. In the sciences (the 500s), for example, the following subdivisions occur:

500	Pure sciences
510	Mathematics
520	Astronomy
530	Physics
540	Chemistry
550	Sciences of earth and other worlds
560	Paleontology, paleozoology—the study of ancient animals and plants
570	Life sciences
580	Botanical sciences
590	Zoological sciences

Activity B

Number a sheet of paper from 1 to 8. Study the following titles and then use the chart to assign each one a number.

1. *Volcanoes and Earthquakes* 550
2. *Learning about Fossils* 560
3. *Best Environments for Animals* 590
4. *The Abacus—Its Contribution to Math* 510
5. *Origin of Our Solar System* 520
6. *Care of Your House Plants* 580
7. *Handbook of Chemical Terms* 540
8. *Systems of the Human Body* 570

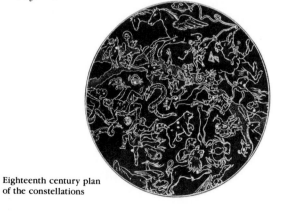

Eighteenth century plan of the constellations

190

The Card Catalog

Every library has a catalog of its books for the public to use. The catalog might be a computer terminal, or it might be a cabinet with small drawers containing 3″ × 5″ cards. Nonfiction books are listed in the catalog in three ways: by author, by title, and by subject. Fiction books usually are listed only by author and title.

Each of the cards for a given book tells the author of the book, the title, the publishing company, the date of publication, and the number of pages, and it provides cross references for further research. It also tells whether the book has illustrations and a bibliography.

The author's name appears *first* on the *author card.* For books with two or more authors, there is an individual author card for each author. If you want to locate some books written by a particular author, you should consult the author card. Here is a sample of an author card for a nonfiction book.

796.019
K661 **Klafs, Carl E**
      The female athlete; conditioning, competition, and culture [by] Carl E. Klafs [and] M. Joan Lyon. Saint Louis, Mosby, 1973.
        x, 216 p.   illus.   24 cm.
      Includes bibliographical references.

      1. Physical education for women.   2. Sports for women.
   3. Athletes, Women.

In the upper left-hand corner is the call number. The first line of the call number is the Dewey Decimal number assigned to that book. This is the number you would use to find the book on the shelf. In the case of the book shown, you would go to the books that are numbered 796.019. Once there, you would use the second line of the call number, K661, to find this particular book. The second number is made up in a special way from the author's last name.

If you know only the title of a book, you need to refer to the *title card* to locate the book. When you search for a title, remember that words such as *a, an,* and *the* are not used in alphabetizing title cards. Here is a sample title card.

           The female athlete

796.019

K661 **Klafs, Carl E**

       The female athlete; conditioning, competition, and culture [by] Carl E. Klafs [and] M. Joan Lyon. Saint Louis, Mosby, 1973.

          x, 216 p.   illus.   24 cm.

       Includes bibliographical references.

       1. Physical education for women.   2. Sports for women.
3. Athletes, Women.

                          ◯

If you are writing a report and want to see what books are available on your topic, you should refer to the *subject card*. There usually will be several cards for a given subject. Here is a sample subject card.

Sports for women
796.019
K661 **Klafs, Carl E**
     The female athlete; conditioning, competition, and culture [by] Carl E. Klafs\[and] M. Joan Lyon. Saint Louis, Mosby, 1973.
       x, 216 p.   illus.   24 cm.
       Includes bibliographical references.

       1. Physical education for women.   2. Sports for women.
     3. Athletes, Women.

After checking all the cards for your subject, you will want to write down the titles and call numbers of the books you think might be most useful to you. Cross references at the bottoms of the cards might provide you with some additional leads. These subjects will be closely related to your topic.

Activity A

Use the sample catalog cards to answer the questions.
1. Who are the authors of *The Female Athlete?*
2. How many cross references are given?
3. How many pages does the body of the book contain?
4. What is the copyright date of this book?
5. What company published this book?

Activity B

Make a visit to your library.
1. List two books written by Charles Dickens.
2. Look up the title card for *The Karate Kid*. Write down the author of this book and the first line of the call number.
3. Look up the subject "hobbies." List two authors and titles in this subject area.

More to Explore

Choose two subject areas in which you are interested. Visit the library, look up four or five books for each subject, and write down the book titles, authors, and call numbers.

Fossil of an ancient fish

A samurai castle in Japan

Vasco da Gama, Portuguese explorer

Lesson 2 Using the Dictionary

There are certain books that may not be borrowed from the library, but instead are kept available on the shelves for library users to consult. These are called *reference* books. The dictionary is probably the most frequently used reference book in the library. This book shows you how to spell words, how to pronounce words, and how to use words correctly in sentences. The mastery of certain basic skills will help you make the most beneficial use of your dictionary.

Alphabetical Order

A dictionary is an alphabetical list of words. In order to locate words quickly, you need to have an accurate working knowledge of *alphabetical order.* Alphabetical order means that all words beginning with *a* come first, then words beginning with *b*, and so forth. If two or more words have the same first letter, they are alphabetized by the second letter. If the second letter is the same, then they are alphabetized by the third letter—and so on.

Activity

Arrange each of these groups of words in alphabetical order.

Group A

plaque	geyser
sincerity	horoscope
nourishment	mosaic
geyser	nourishment
mosaic	plaque
horoscope	sincerity

Group B

amber	abdomen
azalea	agony
awkward	alumni
alumni	amber
agony	awkward
abdomen	azalea

Group C

vapor	vacancy
vault	vagrant
vagrant	validate
vary	vapor
vacancy	vary
validate	vault

Group D

impeach	imp
impose	impartial
imp	impeach
impromptu	implant
implant	impose
impartial	impromptu

THE STUDENTS SHOULD LEARN
—how to alphabetize words to the fourth letter
—how to locate words easily by using the guide words
—what information is available in a dictionary entry
—how to select the correct meaning from the context of the sentence
—that a thesaurus contains words of similar meaning and helps in developing a more accurate writing style

TEACHING THE LESSON
Have the students page through a student dictionary. By seventh grade, students are proficient in alphabetizing by the first and second letters but might still need practice with third and fourth letters. Have them turn to the *ga*...words and list eight *ga*...words with a third letter that is different each time. Next, have them list eight *pan*...words with a fourth letter different each time. Repeat once more with *spr*...words containing a fourth letter different each time.

ACTIVITY: This exercise gives practice in arranging words in alphabetical order by the first, second, third, and fourth letters.

More to Explore

Make up a list of eight words beginning with *br* and having a third letter that is different. Mix up the words and prepare an exercise to be given to another student to alphabetize.

Guide Words

The dictionary has two words at the top of each page called *guide words*. These words are the first and last words on that particular page. If a word can be alphabetically placed between the two guide words, it would then be found on that page.

Study the following example of guide words.

252 Martian * master   **master * mate 253**

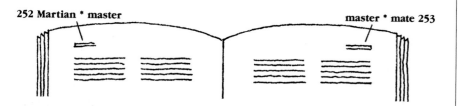

The word *mask* would appear on page 252. Alphabetically it comes after *Martian*, but before *master*. The word *matador* would come on page 253. It comes after *master*, but before *mate*.

Activity A

Check your dictionary and answer the questions.

What are the two guide words that appear on page 37?
What are the two guide words on page 59? Page 104?

Activity B

Look up each of the following words in your dictionary. Write the guide words that appear on the page.

obtuse
prognosis
snorkel
dialect
gesture

Activity C

Copy the following columns of words onto a sheet of paper. Above each column are possible guide words for a dictionary page. If a word in that column would appear on that page, write *on* next to it. If the word would appear before the page, write *before* next to it. If it would appear after the page, write *after*. Give your answers to a partner. Have him or her check your work for correctness.

dash—decide	**pensive—perfection**
decent on	perfume after
debate on	perfect on
darkroom before	penguin before
data on	pentagon on
decimal after	percentage on
decathlon on	peril after

More to Explore

Set up an exercise similar to activity C using *taxi* and *technique* as the guide words on the dictionary page. Make up a list containing two words that would appear before that page, four words that would appear on that page, and two words that would appear after that page. Mix up the words and give the exercise to your partner to complete.

ACTIVITY C: Direct the students to check the second, third, and fourth letters of each word with the guide words to determine whether the word would be before, on, or after a page with those guide words.

MORE TO EXPLORE: Have the students work with partners, exchanging papers and then checking each other's work. To extend the activity, use *fashion* and *fatigue* as the guide words.

Reading Dictionary Entries

A dictionary entry for the word *comfortable* appears below. As you study the various parts of the entry, you can see all the information available to you when you look up a word.

com fort a ble (kum´ fər tə bəl, kumf´ tə bəl), *adj.*
1 giving comfort: *A soft, warm bed is comfortable.* **2** easy; tranquil; undisturbed: *Tony enjoyed a comfortable sleep.*
3 enough for one's needs: *a comfortable income*
[<Latin *comfortis* strong]
—com´ fort a ble ness, *n.* —com´ fort a bly, *adv.*

A. Syllabication   **E.** Meaning
B. Pronunciation   **F.** Sample Phrase or Sentence
C. Accent   **G.** Etymology
D. Part of Speech   **H.** Other Forms of the Word

The *etymology* (g in the example) traces the origin, or history, of a word. It tells from which language the word has originated and what the word meant in that language. The sign < means "taken from." The etymology may appear near the beginning or at the end of an entry, depending on the dictionary. All of the entry information varies slightly with each dictionary. Also, not every dictionary entry will include every item shown in the example. Become familiar with the information in your dictionary in order to profit from its use.

Activity

Refer to the sample dictionary entry to answer the questions.
1. How many pronunciations does *comfortable* have?
2. What is the adverb form for *comfortable*?
3. From which language does *comfortable* originate?
4. What syllable receives the accent?
5. How many syllables does *comfortable* have?
6. How many meanings does *comfortable* have in this entry?
7. Write a sentence for *comfortable* meaning "enough for one's needs."

Choosing the Right Meaning

Many words in the English language have two or more meanings. When you see that a word has several meanings, your challenge is to find the meaning that best fits the sense of your sentence. Study the following entry:

> **laun dry** (lôn´ drē) *n.* **1** room or building where clothes, etc., are washed and ironed **2** clothes, towels, etc., washed or to be washed **3** the washing and ironing of clothes

Each of the sentences matches one of the definitions above.

The *laundry* is done on Monday. 3

Ted took his shirts to the *laundry*. 1

Rosanna's *laundry* remained in the hamper. 2

Activity A

Write the letter of the definition that best fits the meaning of the italicized word.

1. Sheila accomplished the *mammoth* task.
   a. a very large, extinct elephant
   b. huge, gigantic
2. Canada mines a great amount of the world's supply of *nickel*.
   a. a silvery-white metallic element found in igneous rock
   b. coin of U.S. and Canada equal to five cents
3. The boy *shuffled* through the papers on his desk to try to locate his homework.
   a. walk without lifting the feet
   b. mix cards so as to change the order
   c. movement this way and that

TEACHING THE LESSON

Have the students page through their dictionaries to see that most words have two or more meanings. Then direct them to look over the three meanings for *laundry*. Point out how each sentence contains context clues to help decide which definition is best suited to the sentence. If the students need another sample entry, use the word *shell*.

> **shell** (shĕl) n. **1** the hard outside covering of certain animals: *Turtles have a hard shell.* **2** the hard outside covering of an egg: *The eggshell cracked in hot water.* **3** the framework of a house: *The shell of our house is complete.* **4** the cartridge used in a rifle or shotgun: *After target practice, many shells cluttered the ground.*

Have the students identify the meaning that best fits the use of the word *shell* in each of the following sentences: Some pieces of shell got into the dough. (def. 2), Police often use shells as clues in tracking down criminals. (def. 4), My cousin likes to eat oysters in the shell. (def. 1), The shell of skyscrapers is made of beams of iron and steel. (def. 3).

4. The tsunami caused great *tragedy* on the island.
   a. a serious play having an unhappy ending
   b. a very sad or terrible happening
5. Mr. Freeman is a staunch *patron* of the arts.
   a. one who buys regularly at a given store or goes regularly to a certain restaurant
   b. a wealthy or influential supporter of an individual, institution, or cause
   c. a guardian saint or god; protector
6. The new prime rate *inflated* the cost of housing.
   a. force air or gas into a balloon, tire, ball, etc., causing it to swell
   b. swell or puff out
   c. increase prices beyond the normal amount
7. After a year of playing together, a strong bond of *fellowship* developed among the athletes.
   a. companionship, friendliness
   b. group of people having similar tastes or interests
   c. money given by a university or college to a student to enable him or her to continue study
8. My problems were *compounded* when I accidently backed into the principal and spilled her coffee all over.
   a. having more than one point
   b. word made up of two or more words that keep their separate forms
   c. substances formed by chemical combination of two or more elements in definite proportions
   d. add to, increase, multiply
9. The *piers* in many old cathedrals are heavy and massive.
   a. structures that extend into the water
   b. supports for two bridge spans
   c. pillars that support the walls
10. The detective tried to make out the *faint* marks on the paper.
    a. without courage
    b. lacking distinctness
    c. dizzy and likely to faint

Activity B

Look up each italicized word in the dictionary and write the definition that best fits the context of the sentence.

1. The *quack* tried to sell us a quick remedy for arthritis.
2. We used a *balance* to measure the calcium carbonate.
3. One of the *conditions* of the agreement was financial support.
4. The play received excellent *reviews*.
5. San Francisco has a *temperate* climate.
6. Paul gave two weeks' *notice* when he intended to leave his job.
7. The mechanic used a *jack* to lift up our car.
8. An example of an *imperative* sentence is "Do your homework."

ACTIVITY B: This activity gives the students practice in locating a word in the dictionary and finding the correct definition. Have students write their definitions on the chalkboard and explain why they chose them.

More to Explore

Look up each word in the dictionary and write sentences for any two of the definitions.

sunburst	fast
welcome	control
kink	contract

MORE TO EXPLORE: Have students put their sentences on the board and call on members of the class to try defining the word according to the context of the sentence. The student who wrote the sentence can then read the correct dictionary definition.

Using the Thesaurus

A thesaurus is a special type of dictionary that gives synonyms for words. It helps you find the exact word to express your thought and helps you avoid repeating a word. For example, you wrote the following sentence.

> The trapeze artist surprised the audience with a somersault of three turns in midair.

You decide you want to use a more forceful word than *surprised*. You look in a thesaurus and find *astonish* and *amaze* listed as synonyms for *surprise*. Both words suggest a very strong feeling of surprise. Either *astonished* or *amazed* could replace *surprised* in the sentence.

Some thesauruses give the definitions of the synonyms they list. If your thesaurus does not give definitions and you are unsure of the exact meaning of a word, look it up in a dictionary before you use it in your writing.

TEACHING THE LESSON
Have the students examine a thesaurus. Instruct them on the use of the alphabetical index of words in the back. Ask them to look up a word and turn to the entry to see the synonyms that might replace the original word. Suggestions: *difficult, important, inform, result.*

ACTIVITY A: Remind the students that because words are synonyms, it does not mean they are exact substitutes for one another. Synonyms have shades of meaning. Suggest to the students that they read the entire group of four sentences first before choosing a word from the list. Context clues will aid in the selection.

ACTIVITY B: Have students read their sentences, and let the class pick out the synonym and give the original word. If any synonyms are used incorrectly, have the students look them up in the dictionary.

MORE TO EXPLORE: Put as many sentences as possible on the chalkboard. Dictionary skills could be incorporated into the activity by having the student who wrote each sentence read the dictionary definition of the synonym.

ENRICHMENT
1. Refer to activity A on page 199 for "Choosing the Right Meaning." Direct the students to make up five sentences like those in the activity. Have them prepare their activity to be done by another student. For example:
Which definition is most correct for the underlined word? That book is too *juvenile* for junior-high students.
   a. silly, foolish
   b. childish, youthful
   c. a young person
2. Have the students prepare a crossword puzzle using challenging vocabulary words. Some suggestions are *banzai, charlatan, dictatorial, effigy, insatiable, lithe, ostentatious, prodigious, relinquish, solicitous, tapir, venture, zeppelin.* The "Across" and "Down" definitions could be taken from the dictionary, or synonyms taken from a thesaurus could be used as clues.

Activity A

Study the sample entry for the word *look* from a thesaurus. Note that the thesaurus is the type that lists definitions for synonyms. Then find the synonym for *look* that best fits each of the sentences below the entry.

LOOK

The word *look* means "to see or to determine by the use of one's eyes."

SYNONYMS

glance To glance is to look quickly. *The speaker glanced at her watch.*

glare   To glare is to look angrily or fiercely. *The speaker glared at the person whispering in the audience.*

peek   To peek is to look quickly, often so as not to be noticed. *The child peeked out from behind his hiding place.*

stare   To stare is to look fixedly. *The hikers stared in awe at the spectacular sunset.*

1. The hippo just stood and __stared__ at the people.
2. When Alvin saw his brother wearing his best sweater, he __glared__ at him.
3. The students quickly __glanced__ over their homework assignments.
4. Timmy opened the oven and __peeked__ at the cake.

Activity B

Using a thesaurus, write two synonyms for each word below and then use one of the synonyms in a sentence.

1. talk   6. poor
2. money   7. kind
3. nice   8. slow
4. beautiful   9. see
5. annoy   10. impostor

More to Explore

Using the thesaurus, write three synonyms for each of the words below. Choose one synonym for each word and use it in a sentence.

good   power
sign   rough
fair   think
old   request
tale   create

Lesson 3 Using Other Reference Tools

You have learned that there are certain books that are always kept in the library for reference use. Besides books, libraries offer other materials that may be used for reference or research purposes. Pamphlets and audiovisual aids are examples of such materials. Following are some reference sources that you may find in your library.

encyclopedia	a set of books giving general information on many areas of knowledge
almanac	a reference book of current world facts, information, and statistics published each year
atlas	a reference book of maps and geographical data about the world
biographical references	books containing short biographies of important people
media center	contains films, filmstrips, tapes, records, slides, art prints, and miscellaneous audiovisual equipment
vertical file	special reference cabinet that contains pictures, pamphlets, charts, newspaper articles, catalogs, and career information

Sometimes the information you want can be found in a number of sources; however, there is usually one best source. It is important, therefore, to become familiar with all the major reference sources and know what you can expect to find in each. If you have an idea in advance where to look, you will be using your reference tools wisely and your time efficiently.

The following section briefly describes each reference book or area and suggests an exercise that will help you become acquainted with its location and use.

Encyclopedias

An encyclopedia gives you a good, informative overview of people, places, and subjects through articles, pictures, and maps. Encyclopedia articles are arranged in alphabetical order. Guide letters on the spine of each encyclopedia volume inform you that articles beginning with those letters will appear in that particular volume. Therefore, an article on "Thomas Jefferson" would be located in the "J–K" volume of an encyclopedia.

Just as guide words in the dictionary help you locate a word, so the *guide words* on an encyclopedia page assist you in locating the desired article. However, there is only one guide word on each of the facing pages. Articles that can be alphabetized between these two guide words will be found on either of these two pages. Here is an example of encyclopedia guide words.

Thomas Jefferson

Barry, John   baseball

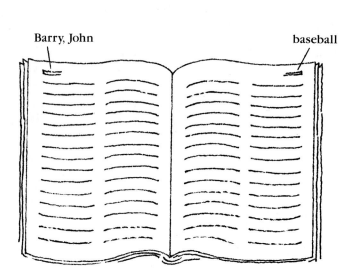

An article on "Clara Barton" would be found on these two pages since "Barton" comes after "Barry" and before "baseball."

Related articles are mentioned at the end of an encyclopedia entry. These are articles to which you can refer for additional information. Encyclopedias also have *index volumes* and *yearbooks*. The index volume helps you locate articles when you aren't sure what word to look under. It has cross references from many words connected with each main subject. Yearbooks help keep an encyclopedia up to date. They contain information about people and events of the past year.

Clara Barton, founder of
the American Red Cross

Activity

Use an encyclopedia to answer the following questions. After your answer, write the letter or letters from the spine of the encyclopedia volume you used and the guide word at the top of the page on which your article began. The first one is done for you.

1. Between what years did James Buchanan serve as president?

    1857–1861   B   Buchanan

2. Where are the safest places to be in a lightning storm?
3. What were the two principal capitals of ancient Egypt?
4. What is O. Henry's real name? What did he do?
5. What is a "yen"?
6. What two countries signed the Webster-Ashburton Treaty?
7. What three religious groups hold Jerusalem sacred?
8. What is the state motto of New Jersey?
9. What are the seven wonders of the ancient world?
10. Who gave us the centigrade scale?

ACTIVITY: This activity is designed to help students gain proficiency in obtaining information from an encyclopedia. It could be completed while the class is visiting the library, by sending small groups to the library afterwards, or by being assigned as a homework activity.

ANSWERS

The volumes and guide words will vary. The answers below were found in *The World Book Encyclopedia* under the headings given in parentheses.

2. car, steel-frame building (Lightning)
3. Memphis, Thebes (Egypt, Ancient)
4. William Sydney Porter; wrote short stories (Henry, O.)
5. chief unit of Japanese money (Yen)
6. United States and Great Britain (Webster-Ashburton Treaty)
7. Christians, Jews, and Moslems (Jerusalem)
8. Liberty and Prosperity (New Jersey)
9. Temple of Diana at Ephesus, Statue of Zeus at Olympia, Pyramids of Egypt, Pharos of Alexandria (lighthouse), Mausoleum at Halicarnassus, Hanging Gardens of Babylon, Colossus of Rhodes (Seven Wonders of the World)
10. Anders Celsius (Centigrade)

Almanacs

An almanac provides you with concise facts and lists. It is published every year and reports data from the year just completed. Therefore, a 1988 almanac would contain facts and information from the 1987 calendar year. An index or table of contents at the front or back of the almanac helps you locate information, since the different subjects are not arranged in alphabetical order. Some topics included in an almanac would be

> associations and societies and their addresses
> awards, medals, and prizes for books, motion pictures, music, efforts towards world peace, science, television, and theater
> economics—national and international
> education
> information on cities, states, and foreign countries
> government officials
> inventions and discoveries
> population statistics
> sports information
> world religions
> world and United States history

Activity

Use a recent almanac to answer the following questions.

1. Draw the flag of Sweden.
2. Who were some of America's most influential women in the year covered by the almanac?
3. Who lost the presidential election to William McKinley in 1896 and 1900?
4. How many representatives does California have in the House of Representatives in Washington, D.C.? New York? Texas? Pennsylvania?
5. Name ten of the largest United States industrial corporations.
6. Who invented the electric battery? The sewing machine? The pendulum?
7. Who won the Rose Bowl in 1985? What was the score?
8. In the 1984 Summer Olympics in Los Angeles, how many gold medals did the United States receive? Silver? Bronze?

Atlases

Atlases provide information about cities, states, countries, continents, bodies of water, mountains, climate, and population around the world. A road atlas gives information about highways, route numbers, distances, and landmarks.

Activity

Consult your library or classroom atlas to answer the following questions.
1. Name the three longest rivers in the world.
2. What is the exact airline distance between Philadelphia and San Francisco?
3. In what state would you find Bryce Canyon National Park?
4. What states border Ohio?
5. What two Central American countries border Mexico?
6. What two South American countries are completely landlocked?
7. What island lies just north of the island of Sardinia?
8. What two countries make up the Malay Peninsula in Asia?

Map of the New World
drawn in 1570

Biographical References

If you wanted to obtain information on what someone had done, invented, written, or won, a biographical reference book would be appropriate. Some of the most common biographical books are

Current Biography
Dictionary of American Biography
Webster's Biographical Dictionary
Who's Who in America
Who's Who among Black Americans

Activity

Look up these people in a biographical reference book and write a brief description of why they are famous.

Space: Sally Ride
Literature: Alice Walker
Medicine: Dr. Christiaan Barnard
Sports: Boris Becker
Government: Thomas O'Neill, Jr.
History: Elizabeth Cady Stanton

Media Center

Most libraries today contain a great deal more than just the written word. For your education and enjoyment, they also have a "media center" or "audiovisual center." Here you will find films, filmstrips, tapes, and records as additional sources of information.

Activity

Visit your library and copy down one item for each category.

	Filmstrip	Tape or Record
Science		
History		
Math		

TEACHING THE LESSON
If possible, have a few biographical reference books from the library available in the classroom so the students can browse through them.

ACTIVITY: This activity helps the students gain competency in handling biographical references. Because of the limited supply of books, the activity could be assigned as a research project over a few days.

TEACHING THE LESSON
Visit the library and show the students the audiovisual materials that are available. Explain how these items can be used to enhance an oral presentation (as discussed in chapter 7), to broaden understanding of a subject (as in hearing a recording of a poet reading his or her own work), or for enjoyment.

ACTIVITY: When time permits, have small groups of students visit the library to complete the activity. Ask the students to describe to the class the filmstrips and tapes or records they chose and explain how these might enhance the teaching of the various subjects. For an extended activity, ask the students to vote on one filmstrip and one tape to be presented in the classroom. After each presentation, discuss the merits of the audiovisual.

Vertical File

When you need more material on a particular subject, facts about your community and local affairs, or information on career and college opportunities, the vertical file in your library is the place to look. It usually has the most current information outside of newspapers and periodicals.

Activity

Check the vertical file in your library. List five recent items, pamphlets, or articles that you found interesting and informative.

More to Explore

Name the reference source to which you would refer if you needed information on each of these topics. Several sources may be possible for some topics.
1. the birthdate of Pablo Picasso
2. a film on volcanoes or earthquakes
3. Greece: a map of its physical features
4. the names and states of our present senators
5. information on Hans Christian Andersen
6. latest developments in cancer research
7. information on astronomy
8. countries that border Czechoslovakia
9. information on careers as a veterinarian
10. address of a major association

A self-portrait by Pablo Picasso

Writing Corner 8

The *Readers' Guide*

This Writing Corner could be used in conjunction with report writing, taught in chapter 5, lesson 2.

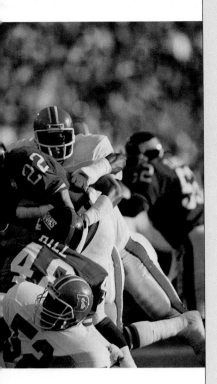

To find a magazine article about a topic you are researching, use a reference book found in the library called the *Readers' Guide to Periodical Literature*. The term periodical refers to publications such as magazines which are published at regular time periods. Some magazines are published every week; some every month. Other magazines may be published every two months (bimonthly) or four times a year (quarterly). The short title for this index of magazines and the articles they contain is the *Readers' Guide*.

The information below, from the *Readers' Guide*, was used by two students. Study the entries and answer the questions below.

Football
Super bowl sunday: sports event or media hype? W. R. Stevens. il *Sports Weekly* 102:66-71 + Ja 10 '88

Aquariums
Tropical fish: livable environments. M. Delaney. il *Petagree Monthly* 49:116-9 + Ag '87

A. Chad was preparing a report on the topic "Super Bowl," a national sports event. The *Readers' Guide* indexes magazine articles under subjects that are broader than topics. For an article on the Super Bowl, under what broad subject did he look?
B. Sue Lin was researching the best way to keep tropical fish as pets. Under what broad subject in the *Readers' Guide* did she look?
C. What is the name of the magazine that contains an article about the Super Bowl? When was this issue published?
D. What is the name of the magazine that contains an article about tropical fish? When was this issue published?
E. The *Readers' Guide* does not use standard punctuation when showing the title of a magazine article. Use capitals and punctuation correctly to copy the names of the two articles.
F. Name the author of each article.
G. How do you know that both articles contain some illustrations?
H. Give the volume and pages where each article is found.

You are right if you noticed the following:

A. The Super Bowl topic is found under the broader subject "football."

B. Researching the topic of how to keep tropical fish, you would look under the broader subject "aquariums."

C. The Super Bowl article is in the magazine *Sports Weekly*, which was published January 10, 1988.

D. The tropical fish article is in the magazine *Petagree Monthly*. The article is in the August 1987 issue.

E. "Super Bowl Sunday: Sports Event or Media Hype?" and "Tropical Fish: Livable Environments" are the titles of the magazine articles.

F. The authors are W. R. Stevens and M. Delaney.

G. The abbreviation *il* in both entries shows that an illustration accompanies the articles.

H. The Super Bowl article is found in volume 102, on pages 66 to 71; the fish article is found in volume 49, on pages 116 to 119.

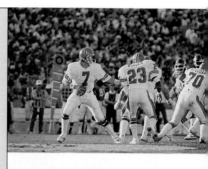

★ At the library, read the *preface* of one of the issues of the *Readers' Guide to Periodical Literature*. Write the meaning of these abbreviations listed in the preface.

My	May	il	illustrated	+	continued on later pages of issue
Mr	March	por	portrait	bi-w	biweekly
Jl	July	pt	part	bi-m	bimonthly

Look carefully at a few pages of the *Readers' Guide*. List five magazine titles. Try to choose five magazines that are familiar to you.

Putting it all together—

1. Choose a topic that interests you. Think of the broader subject under which it would be listed.

2. Find the subject in one of the issues of the *Readers' Guide*.

3. Select an article from a magazine that you can find.

4. On a card, write the information that will help you find the magazine on the shelves. Magazines are arranged alphabetically. *Newsweek*, for example, would be under *N*. Much older issues may be on microfilm rather than on the shelf.

5. Read the article. Take notes on important and interesting parts. Write a report on the article.

Word Study 8

Clichés

A cliché is a phrase that has been overused.

THE STUDENTS SHOULD LEARN
—the definition of a cliché
—to restructure sentences so as to avoid clichés

TEACHING THE LESSON
Put the following sentences on the chalkboard:

Kelly is <u>as cute as a button</u>.
It's <u>raining cats and dogs</u>.
The tire was <u>as flat as a pancake</u>.
This ice cream is <u>as hard as a rock</u>.

Discuss with the class the meaning of a cliché and then have them identify the cliché in each sentence and tell its meaning. Using the introductory material as a guide, elicit ideas from the class as to how the sentences could be written in a more interesting and clever style. Write the new sentences on the chalkboard and discuss the differences.

ACTIVITY: Complete the first two or three examples with the class. If necessary, discuss the meaning of any remaining clichés that pose a problem for the students. Have at least two sentences for each cliché put on the chalkboard and compare the two. Consider the effectiveness of the new images.

Clichés are tired phrases that should be avoided in writing. If you use clichés in your compositions, readers will think you lack imagination. They will see that the thoughts you have put on paper are not really your own. Writing is always much more interesting when the thoughts are fresh and original.

Clichés are sometimes difficult to avoid. Because you've heard them so many times, they seem natural and comfortable. It is always good to look for clichés when you are revising your work. If you find that you have used one, take some time to put the idea into other words. Think about what the cliché means and write something that better expresses what you really want to say. For example, instead of writing, "The directions were as clear as mud," you might write, "The directions were extremely confusing and muddled." Or, instead of writing "The speaker's voice was as loud as thunder," you might write, "The speaker's powerful, deep voice seemed to reach everyone in the audience directly."

Part of the solution is to be as specific as possible. Too many descriptions of a sky, for example, have spoken of "fleecy, white clouds." What do you really see in the sky? A crowd of floating ash-gray clouds? Narrow strips of white smoke? Be original. Think for yourself. If the words you are writing come too easily, read them again. Make sure they are your own.

Activity

The following sentences contain italicized clichés. For each cliché, give its meaning and then write a new, more creative sentence expressing the same idea.

1. The scientist has a memory *like an elephant*.

     meaning: _____good memory_____

     new wording: _____

2. Don't step on those *red hot* coals!

    meaning: _____ very hot coals _____

    new wording: _____

3. The little child huddled in the corner *just as quiet as a mouse*.

    meaning: very quietly, unnaturally quietly

    new wording: _____

4. This farm has cost us a lot of *blood, sweat, and tears*.

    meaning: work, money, emotions, etc.

    new wording: _____

5. Their laughing at my singing was the *last straw*.

    meaning: the final difficulty that could be tolerated

    new wording: _____

6. In Japan, *old meets new* everywhere you look.

    meaning: things from different periods of time are present

    new wording: _____

7. *Counting your chickens before they're hatched* can lead to disappointment.

    meaning: expecting something positive to happen

    new wording: _____

8. Now that my brother is on the wrestling team, he *eats like a horse*.

    meaning: _____ eats a lot _____

    new wording: _____

9. The steady rhythm of the waves was *music to my ears*.

    meaning: _____ sounded good to me _____

    new wording: _____

10. When I climbed out of bed that winter morning, the floorboards were *as cold as ice*.

    meaning: _____ very cold _____

    new wording: _____

ADDITIONAL ACTIVITY

After discussing the meaning of the following clichés, have the students write a short humorous paragraph using any four. The paragraph should then be rewritten using new expressions.

    can't take it with you
    jumping for joy
    sharp as a tack
    as good as gold
    snug as a bug in a rug
    in one ear and out the other

Exploring Our Language

Part II

Grammar, Correct Usage, Mechanics

Chapter 1

Nouns

Lesson 1   Kinds of Nouns

A noun is a name word.

Proper and Common Nouns

There are two main classes of nouns: *proper nouns* and *common nouns*.

> A proper noun names a particular person, place, or thing.
>
> A common noun names any one member of a class of persons, places, or things.

PROPER NOUNS	COMMON NOUNS
Pablo	student
Chicago	city
Brooklyn Bridge	bridge

All proper nouns begin with capital letters.

A bridge helps to bring people and places closer together.
How can language be a bridge?

Exercise 1

Identify the nouns in the following sentences. Tell whether each is *proper* or *common*.

1. Jennifer and her parents visited Washington in the summer.
2. There Jennifer saw many museums and famous historical places.
3. The family was impressed by the Mall, an area surrounded by monuments.
4. The Capitol Building, with its huge dome, is where our laws are made.
5. The Washington Monument, a pillar topped by a pyramid, dominates the skyline.
6. Nearby is the Lincoln Memorial, with its massive statue of the sixteenth president.
7. The Vietnam Memorial, a long black wall, attracts many visitors.
8. On the Mall, the Smithsonian Institution has many buildings and museums.
9. The family enjoyed the museum that has famous airplanes and spacecraft.
10. There Jennifer touched a rock from the moon.
11. Hanging from the ceiling was the plane in which Amelia Earhart flew across the Atlantic Ocean.
12. At another museum, Jennifer saw the Hope Diamond, a famous large gem.
13. The building where money is printed fascinated the tourists.
14. A guide took the family through the White House.
15. Jennifer was disappointed not to see the president!

Amelia Earhart, famous pioneer aviator

218

Collective Nouns

> **A collective noun names a group of persons, animals, or things considered as a unit.**

The words *Congress, committee, group,* and *nation* in the following paragraph name groups of persons as if they were one. These words, therefore, are collective nouns.

> When a bill is introduced in one of the houses of *Congress*, it is studied by a special *committee*. This *group* carefully examines the bill. It weighs the bill's good and bad points to determine whether or not the bill will be of benefit to the *nation*.

The nouns listed below are also examples of collective nouns.

audience   herd
class   public

Exercise 2

Identify the collective nouns in the following sentences.
1. A large group gathered around the fire-eater who was performing on the street.
2. A film on the history of trains was shown to the class.
3. A flock of geese chased my sister around the barnyard.
4. The tryouts for the gymnastics team are next week.
5. Those of us interested in computers should form a club.
6. A swarm of bees hovered around the hive.
7. The committee will appoint someone to be in charge of decorations for the Valentine party.
8. The band entertained the crowd at halftime.
9. At the end of the concert, the audience applauded enthusiastically.
10. The crew of the spaceship lost contact with the station.

Complete each of the following sentences with an appropriate collective noun.
11. The _____ of Scouts is going on a camping trip in June.
12. A _____ of divers explored the sunken ship.
13. All the sheep in the _____ were black!
14. Government officials serve the interests of the _____.
15. The _____ holds meetings every month.

Concrete Nouns

Most nouns are concrete nouns. A concrete noun names something that can be seen or touched.

The nouns listed below are all *concrete* nouns.

governor   uniform
forest   workbench

Proper nouns can be concrete.

Miami   the Gateway Arch

Exercise 3

Identify the concrete nouns in the following sentences.
1. The librarian recommended this book on aquariums.
2. The twins became orange-costumed carrots for the play.
3. Most guitars have six strings.
4. Scientists have obtained rocks from the floor of the ocean.
5. There is a city in Georgia called Athens.
6. Under the couch was my long-lost slipper.
7. A ballad is a story that is sung.
8. The tourists took many photographs of the Grand Canyon.
9. There are more sheep in Australia than there are people.
10. The makeshift raft barely withstood the rapids.

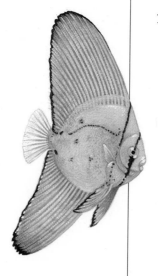

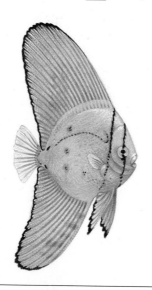

Abstract Nouns

> An abstract noun expresses a quality or a condition, or a mental action. It names something that cannot be seen or touched.

The words *culture, knowledge, appreciation, love*, and *beauty* in the sentences below do not name persons, places, or things. They name qualities and are, therefore, abstract nouns.

> Good books are the gateway to the world of *culture*. They are guides that help to develop *knowledge, appreciation*, and *love* of *beauty*.

The nouns listed below are also examples of abstract nouns.

ability   intelligence
ambition   thought

Exercise 4

Identify the abstract nouns in the following sentences.
1. My idea of sleeping out in a tent in the yard did not appeal to anyone.
2. Joan of Arc was famous for her courage and her strong belief.
3. The fans' enjoyment of the close game was obvious from their cheers.
4. Many experts think that we can all improve our creativity.
5. For many years, the owl has been associated with the quality of wisdom.
6. My uncle Bernardo uses his knowledge of computers daily since he works as a programmer.
7. Most writers of science fiction novels have vivid imaginations.
8. According to Thomas Edison, genius is one percent inspiration and ninety-nine percent perspiration.
9. Kindness and compassion are good qualities for doctors and nurses to have.
10. I enjoy the peacefulness of walking along a deserted beach.

EXERCISE 4: Have the students go back to each sentence and name the proper and common nouns. For another extension of this exercise, direct the students to choose two abstract nouns and write four definitions for each using concrete ideas. For example:

> *Pride* is...getting 100 on a test.
> ...seeing your brother graduate from college.
> ...having a new baby sister.
> ...scoring the winning point in a game.

ANSWERS
The abstract nouns are underlined.

Exercise 5

EXERCISE 5: Instruct the students to give sentences orally for each abstract noun created in this list.

Many abstract nouns may be formed from other words by adding such suffixes as *-ity,* (or *-ty*), *-ness, -hood, -ship, -ment,* or *-ion.* Make an abstract noun from each word listed below by adding the proper suffix. Use a dictionary if you need help.

loyal	loyalty	clever	cleverness
familiar	familiarity	arrange	arrangement
good	goodness	certain	certainty
wicked	wickedness	child	childhood
human	humanity humanness	express	expression
timid	timidity timidness	friend	friendship
agree	agreement	amaze	amazement
content	contentment	leader	leadership
object	objection	enjoy	enjoyment
require	requirement	knight	knighthood

Exercise 6

EXERCISE 6: Create a more thorough review by having the students name common nouns for proper nouns, and vice versa. Make sure that the students understand that collective and abstract nouns can also be considered common nouns.

SHARPENING YOUR SKILLS: The students should try to pick out words that could be used for a specific topic. Have them share their work at the chalkboard or orally.

Tell whether each of the following nouns is *proper* or *common.* Then for the common nouns, tell whether any are *collective* or *abstract.*

club	com., col.	generosity	com., abs.	jury	com., col.
ambition	com., abs.	Aunt Sara	prop.	company	com., col.
dog	com.	band	com., col.	April	prop.
fleet	com., col.	movie	com.	group	com., col.
fair	com.	Paris	prop.	guidance	com., abs.
New York	prop.	leisure	com., abs.	pizza	com.
team	com., col.	gratitude	com., abs.	herd	com., col.
shoe	com.	students	com.	community	com., col.
rocket	com.	poverty	com., abs.	flower	com.
kindness	com., abs.	troupe	com., col.	wisdom	com., abs.

Sharpening Your Skills

Write a five-sentence paragraph using words from the list above. Try to include at least two of every type of noun.

Lesson 2 Qualities of Nouns

Person

> *Person* is the quality of a noun that indicates the speaker, the one spoken to, or the one spoken about.

The *first person* means the speaker.

> I, your *coach*, will send in the plays.

The *second person* means the one spoken to.

> *Players*, prepare for the game.

The *third person* means the one spoken about.

> The *captain* rose and addressed the *team*.

Exercise 7

Give the person of the italicized nouns in the following sentences.
1. Do you know which planets have rings, *Leo*?
2. I, the *expert*, will show you how to change the light bulb, *Edna*.
3. The lead *singer* of the group can also play the guitar.
4. *Margaret*, where did you buy that sequined jacket?
5. Many *lobsters* are caught in the Atlantic Ocean.
6. We, the *members* of the committee, have responsibility for planning the Thanksgiving Day program.
7. The *workers* will complete the new stadium by the start of the football season.
8. *Vicky*, what is the capital of Iceland?
9. *Friends*, give me your attention.
10. I, the *president*, call for a vote on the question.

THE STUDENTS SHOULD LEARN
—to analyze a noun according to its qualities: person, number, and gender

TEACHING THE LESSON
Carefully review the concept of person, number, and gender by focusing on the introduction to each concept. Remind the students that the study of person and number will help them when they study subject/verb agreement in chapter 4.

EXERCISE 7: After they have completed the exercise, have the students answer the following questions:

—What are the most commonly used persons in short stories and novels? (first, third)

—What person do your teachers or parents use when speaking to you? (second)

—If you are representing your organization (team, club, etc.), what person would you most likely use? (first)

ANSWERS
1. second	6. first
2. first, second	7. third
3. third	8. second
4. second	9. second
5. third	10. first

Number

> **Number is the quality of a noun that indicates whether it refers to one person or thing (singular number) or more than one (plural number).**

In the sentence below, *books* is plural, and *book* is singular.

The most important of the three *books* is the *book* on the table.

Methods of Forming the Plural

There are seventeen rules for forming the plural of various types of nouns. If you wish to use the plural of some noun that does not seem to be included in the rules, consult the dictionary. You will find that a choice of plural forms is given for some words. Study the following rules.

1. Most nouns form the plural by adding *s* to the singular.

   SINGULAR: picture   PLURAL: pictures

2. Nouns ending in *s, x, z, ch,* and *sh* form the plural by adding *es* to the singular.

   SINGULAR: box   PLURAL: boxes

3. Nouns ending in *y* preceded by a consonant form the plural by changing the *y* to *i* and adding *es.*

   SINGULAR: lily   PLURAL: lilies

   Nouns ending in *y* preceded by a vowel form the plural by adding *s* to the singular.

   SINGULAR: monkey   PLURAL: monkeys

4. The following nouns form the plural by changing the *f* or *fe* to *ves: calf, elf, half, knife, leaf, life, loaf, self, sheaf, shelf, thief, wife, wolf.*

5. Nouns ending in *o*:

a. All nouns ending in *o* preceded by a vowel form the plural by adding *s* to the singular.

SINGULAR	PLURAL
trio	trios
rodeo	rodeos
studio	studios
patio	patios
radio	radios

b. Nouns ending in *o* preceded by a consonant generally form the plural by adding *es* to the singular.

SINGULAR	PLURAL
tomato	tomatoes
echo	echoes
potato	potatoes

c. Some nouns ending in *o* preceded by a consonant form the plural by adding *s* to the singular.

SINGULAR	PLURAL
piano	pianos
alto	altos
solo	solos
soprano	sopranos
burro	burros

d. Some nouns ending in *o* preceded by a consonant may form the plural by adding *s* or *es* to the singular.

SINGULAR	PLURAL
cargo	cargos or cargoes
zero	zeros or zeroes
buffalo	buffalos or buffaloes
motto	mottos or mottoes
volcano	volcanos or volcanoes

6. A few nouns form the plural by a change within the singular.

SINGULAR	PLURAL
tooth	teeth
foot	feet
goose	geese
man	men
woman	women

7. A few nouns form the plural by the addition of the Old English ending *en*.

SINGULAR: OX   PLURAL: oxen

8. A few nouns have the same form in the plural as in the singular.

SINGULAR	PLURAL	SINGULAR	PLURAL
series	series	sheep	sheep
deer	deer	species	species
swine	swine	salmon	salmon
trout	trout	cod	cod
corps	corps	Chinese	Chinese

9. When a name is preceded by a title, either the name or the title may be made plural.

SINGULAR	PLURAL
Miss Ray	The Misses Ray, The Miss Rays, or The Ms. Rays
Mr. Altman	The Messrs. Altman or The Mr. Altmans

The title *Mrs.* is an exception to this rule, as it cannot be made plural.

SINGULAR: Mrs. Krum   PLURAL: The Mrs. Krums

10. Some nouns taken from foreign languages keep their foreign plurals.

SINGULAR	PLURAL	SINGULAR	PLURAL
alumna	alumnae	alumnus	alumni
radius	radii	basis	bases
datum	data	crisis	crises
oasis	oases	bacterium	bacteria

11. Some nouns taken from foreign languages have both a foreign and an English plural. The English form is preferred.

SINGULAR	ENGLISH PLURAL	FOREIGN PLURAL
index	indexes	indices
tableau	tableaus	tableaux
formula	formulas	formulae
memorandum	memorandums	memoranda
vertex	vertexes	vertices

12. Some nouns are used only in the plural.

slacks	pliers	trousers
clothes	scissors	tweezers

13. Some nouns are plural in form, but usually singular in meaning and use.

news	aeronautics	mathematics
measles	physics	civics

14. Compound nouns usually form the plural by adding *s* to the most important word or words.

SINGULAR	PLURAL
father-in-law	fathers-in-law
proofreader	proofreaders
maid of honor	maids of honor

15. Compound nouns ending in *ful* form the plural by adding *s* to the last syllable.

SINGULAR	PLURAL
cupful	cupfuls
spoonful	spoonfuls

16. Letters form the plural by adding *s* or *'s*. Lowercase letters and capital letters that would be confusing if *s* alone were added form the plural by adding *'s*.

SINGULAR	PLURAL
PTA	PTAs
u	*u*'s
T	*T*'s

17. The plural of numbers is formed by adding *s* without the apostrophe.

SINGULAR	PLURAL
1900	1900s
6	6s

EXERCISES 8 AND 9: Before the students do the exercises, put a singular noun and its plural form on the chalkboard. Elicit from the students the rule that applies. Do this for each rule in order to determine which rules need more reinforcement. Do not spend time on rules that the students have already mastered.

Forming the plural of a noun requires adequate knowledge of spelling rules. Make flash cards containing singular nouns. Have the students spell the plural of each word.

Have the students look up some of the words in the dictionary to see where the plural form is indicated in an entry.

Exercise 8

Write the plural of each item listed below.

chief   chiefs
spoonful   spoonfuls
trout   trout
bicycle   bicycles
valley   valleys
t   t's
point of view   points of view
mousetrap   mousetraps
candy   candies
knife   knives
Portuguese   Portuguese
trumpet   trumpets
gentleman   gentlemen
baby   babies
sheep   sheep
8   8s

fish   fish
chimney   chimneys
potato   potatoes
remedy   remedies
sister-in-law   sisters-in-law
sigh   sighs
cliff   cliffs
portfolio   portfolios
donkey   donkeys
loaf   loaves
1980   1980s
victory   victories
peach   peaches
fox   foxes
sheaf   sheaves
courtesy   courtesies

Exercise 9

Arrange the following nouns in two columns. Put the singular nouns in the first column and the plural nouns in the second column. Some words will go in both columns. Choose any five singular nouns and write sentences using them in the plural form.

roof   S
glasses   P
echoes   P
alumni   P
duo   S
Iroquois   S, P
pulleys   P
mathematics   S in use
goose   S
bucketful   S
series   S, P
Japanese   S, P

shelf   S
houseguest   S
tax   S
tomatoes   P
heiress   S
hoof   S
stepladder   S
drive-ins   P
cuff   S
analyses   P
news   S in use
forget-me-not   S

Gender

> **Gender is that quality of a noun by which sex is distinguished. There are three genders: masculine, feminine, and neuter.**

The masculine gender indicates males.

   father, son

The feminine gender indicates females.

   aunt, mother

The neuter gender indicates objects.

   desk, milk

Some nouns may be considered either masculine or feminine.

   baby, cousin, child, author, director

Many nouns that include both genders are now in common use.

TRADITIONAL	ALTERNATE FORM
fireman	firefighter
policeman	police officer
mailman	mail carrier
chairman	chairperson

How Gender Is Distinguished

Gender may be distinguished in three ways:

1. by using a different word

   MASCULINE: brother   FEMININE: sister

2. by using a different ending

   MASCULINE: actor   FEMININE: actress

3. by changing part of the word

   MASCULINE: salesman   FEMININE: saleswoman

EXERCISE 10: Ask the students to name nouns (other than those in the introduction) that are considered both masculine and feminine.

SHARPENING YOUR SKILLS: This activity will reinforce the use of person, number, and gender. Put on the chalkboard a list of animals in their masculine and feminine forms. Have the students contribute examples. Have the students share their writing with the class.

EXAMPLES

rooster (m)	hen (f)
drake (m)	duck (f)
stallion (m)	mare (f)
fox (m)	vixen (f)
ram (m)	ewe (f)
gander (m)	goose (f)
buck (m)	doe (f)
bull (m)	cow (f)
boar (m)	sow (f)

Exercise 10

Arrange the following nouns in three columns. In one column, write all the masculine nouns; in the next, the feminine nouns; and in the third column, the neuter nouns. For any noun that is masculine, give the feminine form; for any noun that is feminine, give the masculine form.

prince M (princess)	marble N
widower M (widow)	dictionary N
chalkboard N	flag N
gymnast M, F	alumni M (alumnae)
hero M (heroine)	theater N
Bernardine F (Bernard)	hen F (rooster)
heir M (heiress)	student M, F
spectator M, F	emperor M (empress)
uncle M (aunt)	grandson M (granddaughter)
ewe F (ram)	stallion M (mare)
goose F (gander)	nephew M (niece)

Sharpening Your Skills

You have been invited to spend a few days on a farm. In one or two paragraphs, tell about the various animals you encounter. Use as many plural nouns as possible. Make sure you use the correct form of each gender. Tell about your visit, using the third person.

Lesson 3 Nominative Case

Case is the quality of a noun that shows its relation to some other word or words in the sentence. There are three cases: nominative, possessive, and objective.

Before a noun can be classified according to case, its use in a sentence must be determined. You have studied in former years the following uses of the nominative case.

> *Subject.* **A noun used as the subject of a verb is in the nominative case.**

This *book* is a travelogue of adventure.
Books hold many hidden treasures.
What part have *books* played in your life?

> *Subjective Complement.* **A subjective complement is a word that renames or describes the subject. A noun used as a subjective complement is in the nominative case.**

The Himalayas are the highest *mountains* in the world.
The protagonist of this story is an eccentric *character.*
General Lee was *commander in chief* of the Confederate forces.

Subjective complements follow linking verbs such as *be (is, are, was, were).* Since subjective complements rename nouns that are subjects, subjective complements are in the nominative case.

> *Direct Address.* **A noun used in direct address is in the nominative case.**

Paul, you may open the present.
Air is a mixture of gases, *Sue.*

STUDENTS SHOULD LEARN
—to identify nouns in the nominative case
—to use nouns in the nominative case correctly

TEACHING THE LESSON
The study of *case* needs reteaching each year. Elicit from the students the various ways in which a noun is in the nominative case. For those that the students may not know, write a sentence on the chalkboard illustrating the noun in the nominative case and have the students identify it. Use the model diagrams in grammar chapter 9 to help analyze the various uses of nouns in the nominative case.

Extended instruction is needed for teaching restrictive and nonrestrictive appositives. Put other examples on the chalkboard to reinforce the concept.

Tim's dad, *Mr. Johnson*, taught us many survival skills. (nonrestrictive)

Anchored in Long Beach, California, is the British liner *Queen Mary*. (restrictive)

Exercise 11

Give the use of each italicized noun in the following sentences: *subject, subjective complement,* or *direct address.*

1. The *mountains* are the perfect *place* for camping.
2. Our *van* is already packed to the roof for the trip.
3. When will you be ready to leave, *Greg?*
4. The *family* is eager to start off.
5. This *highway* is the quickest *route* to the mountains.
6. Our *campsite* will be a *clearing* next to the lake.
7. *Alice,* help us set up the tent.
8. Be careful, *children,* when you explore the woods.
9. The *woods* are the *home* for some mischievous bears!
10. The little *bubbles* in the lake must mean it is filled with fish.
11. Fresh *fish* cooked over a campfire would make a delicious dinner.
12. *Worms* are a good *bait* for many kinds of fish.
13. *Sandra,* who caught the biggest fish?
14. Please sit with us, *Rick,* and tell us a ghost story.
15. With everyone around the campfire, the perfect *day* of camping ends.

Apposition in the Nominative Case

> **A noun in apposition is in the same case as the noun it explains.**

An appositive is a word or a group of words that follows a noun or a pronoun and explains its meaning. An appositive names the same person, place, or thing as the noun it explains.

Tony, my *brother,* is a teacher in Japan.
A famous teller of fables was the ancient author *Aesop.*

The noun *brother* explains *Tony* and the noun *Aesop* explains *author.* Such nouns that explain are called appositives. Since *Tony* is the subject of the sentence and in the nominative case, the appositive *brother* is also in the nominative case. Why is the noun *Aesop* in the nominative case?

An appositive with its modifiers is separated from the rest of the sentence by commas if the phrase is *nonrestrictive*. This means that it is merely some added information without which the sentence would still be clear. Thus, *my brother* is set off by commas because it is added information about Tony, and the sentence is clear without the phrase.

The noun *Aesop*, however, is not set off by commas because it is *restrictive*. This word is necessary in order to know the exact author the writer of the sentence has in mind.

Exercise 12

Identify the appositives in the following sentences, and name the noun each explains. All the appositives are in the *nominative* case.

1. My sister Michele has a job as a paper carrier.
2. The kiwi, a flightless bird, is native to New Zealand.
3. The Klondike, a region in Alaska, was the scene of a gold rush in the 1890s.
4. The writer of the article on school clubs was Ian Fluher, the editor of the school paper.
5. The well-known poet Ogden Nash was a writer of humorous verse.
6. Jazz, a typically American music, developed from songs sung by black workers.
7. My cousin is a philatelist, a collector of stamps.
8. Our cat Cleo had three calico kittens.
9. The novel *Johnny Tremain* takes place during the American Revolution.
10. Alan, a student at the university, is old enough to vote in this election.
11. Mr. Kimmel, our teacher, will show slides of his trip to Greece.
12. Turtles, the oldest living reptiles, date back to the time of the dinosaurs.
13. One kind of cereal is rice, a basic food in the Orient.
14. By the river stood the mill, a battered ruin.
15. Jake, this is my classmate Frank Rodriguez.

Exercise 13

Give the use of each italicized noun: *subject, subjective complement, direct address*, or *appositive in the nominative case.*

1. *Dom*, did you see the sharks at the aquarium?
2. The scientist *Jocelyn Bell* discovered pulsars, which are rapidly revolving stars.
3. *Al* admitted that he had finally outgrown his well-worn sneakers.
4. *Diego Rivera*, a Mexican *artist*, painted large murals showing life in Mexico.
5. *Sara* and *Marcia* were too tired to enjoy the party after blowing up sixty-five balloons.
6. Elaine was the *winner* of the prize for the largest sweet potato.
7. One kind of phobia is *claustrophobia, fear* of closed-in places.
8. *Steven*, the highest *waterfall* is in South America, not Africa.
9. The circling gaseous layer of light around the sun is its *corona*.
10. Many *persons* enjoy stories of mystery and crime.
11. Young *man*, skateboards are not allowed in the museum.
12. Mrs. Ling, the *director* of the glee club, is planning the assembly.
13. The half eagle was an old five-dollar *coin*.
14. *Tomatoes* are *fruits, Petra*.
15. The *joust*, a *contest* between two knights on horseback, was a *sport* popular in the Middle Ages.

Identify the nouns in the nominative case in the following sentences, and give the use of each.
16. Martin Luther King, Jr., was an ardent advocate of human rights.
17. The toucan, a colorful bird, has a very large bill.
18. Tammy is the best debater on the team.
19. Detroit is the center of the American automobile industry.
20. Did you like the story "The Most Dangerous Game," Craig?
21. The fog blanketed the city for hours.
22. Olympus, an enormous palace, was the home of the Greek gods.
23. Richard, my best friend, is an excellent tuba player.
24. Frieda, Martin cannot go to the beach with us today.
25. A popular resort in the summer is Martha's Vineyard, an island off Massachusetts.

Sharpening Your Skills

Write ten original sentences, illustrating the various uses of the noun in the nominative case. Underline the noun in each sentence.
Exchange papers, give the uses of the nouns, and return for checking.

Lesson 4 Possessive Case

A noun that expresses possession, ownership, or connection is in the possessive case.

Mr. *Dana's* workshop was a busy place.
Mary's hair is black and curly.

The sign of the possessive case is the apostrophe and *s*.

Methods of Forming the Possessive Case

1. To form the possessive singular, add *'s* to the singular form of the noun.

   student, student's   Heather, Heather's

2. To form the possessive plural of nouns ending in *s*, add the apostrophe only.

   teens, teens'   babies, babies'

   If the plural form of the noun does not end in *s*, add *'s*.

   men, men's   children, children's

3. Proper names ending in *s* usually form the possessive case by adding *'s*.

   James, James's   Mrs. Williams, Mrs. Williams's

4. In compound nouns the *'s* is added to the end of the word.

NOUN	SINGULAR POSSESSIVE	PLURAL POSSESSIVE
commander in chief	commander in chief's	commanders in chief's
sister-in-law	sister-in-law's	sisters-in-law's

THE STUDENTS SHOULD LEARN
—to identify nouns in the possessive case
—to use nouns in the possessive case correctly

TEACHING THE LESSON
Put various examples of possessives on the chalkboard: *men's, monkey's, teachers', ladies', trout's*. Have the students identify them as singular possessive or plural possessive. Put a chart on the chalkboard with four headings: Singular, Plural, Singular Possessive, and Plural Possessive. Complete the chart with the words above.

SINGULAR	PLURAL
man	men
monkey	monkeys
teacher	teachers
trout	trout

SING. POSS.	PLURAL POSS.
man's	men's
monkey's	monkeys'
teacher's	teachers'
trout's	trout's

Exercise 14

Write the singular possessive of the words listed below and add an appropriate noun after each possessive. *Example*: clown's hat

child   child's   violinist   violinist's
pony   pony's   wolf   wolf's
lady   lady's   player   player's
Mr. Jones   Mr. Jones's wife   wife's
son-in-law   son-in-law's   Charles   Charles's

Write the plural possessive of the words listed below and add an appropriate noun. *Example*: men's hats

child   children's   fox   foxes'
wife   wives'   chief of police   chiefs of police's
prince   princes'   pony   ponies'
cattle   cattle's   doctor   doctors'
shepherd   shepherds'   senator   senators'

Exercise 15

Identify each noun in the possessive case, and tell whether it is *singular* or *plural* in number.
1. Barbara's report was on pioneer wagon trains.
2. Have you read any of Astrid Lindgren's books about Pippi Longstocking?
3. The campers' tents are near the lake.
4. Is that your brother's or your sister's room?
5. C. S. Lewis's imaginary world is called Narnia.
6. Women's shoes are on sale this week at the shoe store in the mall.
7. The mean stepparent was Allie's least favorite character in the book.
8. The scarecrow's wish was for a brain.
9. Did you see the first-graders' drawings on display?
10. Are a zebra's stripes black or white?

Write the possessive form of the word in parentheses to complete each sentence. Some possessives will be singular, and some, plural.
11. The teacher graded the (students) work.
12. Most of the (baby) rattles were in the crib.
13. My (cousin) cabin is in the woods of Wisconsin.
14. When are your (sisters) birthdays?
15. (King Arthur) knights sat at a round table.

Separate and Joint Possession

If two or more nouns are used together to indicate separate ownership—that is, to show that each person possesses something independently of the other—the *'s* is used after each noun.

Longfellow's and Tennyson's poems were read.

If two or more nouns are used together to indicate joint ownership—that is, to show that one thing is possessed by the group jointly—the *'s* is used after the last noun only.

That is Ann and Peter's boat.

Henry Wadsworth Longfellow

Exercise 16

Indicate possession—separate or joint—in each sentence.
1. Ivan and Jaime ideas about music are very different.
2. Jason and Nicole science project was well done.
3. Fred Martino and Wayne Faber sisters graduated last week.
4. Women and children shoes are sold here.
5. Ed and Vergil uniforms are missing.
6. The secretary and treasurer report was read at the meeting.
7. We just celebrated Mother and Father wedding anniversary.
8. Raphael and Titian paintings are considered masterpieces.
9. Take Margaret and Joan coats to them.
10. Kristen and Libby room was redecorated.

Sharpening Your Skills

Write a newspaper account about a sports event you just attended. Use singular and plural possessives in your writing. Some of these ideas may help.

the team's perseverance
the players' sportsmanship
the crowd's spirit
the cheerleaders' enthusiasm

EXERCISE 16: Put the two examples from the text on the chalkboard. Students should be able to recognize how separate ownership requires that each noun have its own possessive formation, while joint ownership requires that only the last noun show the possession. Discuss the sense of each sentence before making a choice. After completion of this exercise, instruct the students to write three or four sentences illustrating both types of ownership.

ANSWERS
1. Ivan's and Jaime's
2. Jason and Nicole's
3. Fred Martino's and Wayne Faber's
4. Women's, children's
5. Ed's, Vergil's
6. secretary and treasurer's
7. Mother and Father's
8. Raphael's, Titian's
9. Margaret's, Joan's
10. Kristen and Libby's

SHARPENING YOUR SKILLS: Let the students exchange papers and check one another's newspaper accounts for correct use of the possessives. This activity could be extended by using another event, such as a classical or rock concert.

Lesson 5 Objective Case

You have studied in former years the following uses of the objective case.

> *Direct Object.* **A noun used as the direct object of a verb is in the objective case.**

The director took the *tourists* on a tour of the monument.
Melissa carried the bulky *package*.
Cliff washed the mud-splattered *car*.

> *Object of a Preposition.* **A noun used as the object of a preposition is in the objective case.**

Money was found in the old tin *can*.
The spectators gathered around the *clown*.
The skiers went to *Colorado*.

Exercise 17

Give the use of each italicized word in the following sentences: *direct object* or *object of preposition*.
1. Anticipating spring, I eagerly planned my *garden*.
2. I read *articles* about *flowers*.
3. I bought *seed* for my *garden* at a *nursery*.
4. My garden patch was to be located in the *corner* of our *yard*.
5. I got my *rakes* and *shovels*, and I began to dig.
6. My first stroke with the *spade* hit a *rock*.
7. Soon I had accumulated a sizable *pile* of *stones*.
8. Discouraged, I nearly abandoned the entire *project*.
9. Then I looked again at the beautiful *pictures* in my *catalogs*.
10. As I learned, gardening combines *imagination* with hard *work*.

Apposition in the Objective Case

> **A noun in apposition is in the same case as the noun it explains.**

Keith works in the control tower, the *heart* of the airport.

When the noun that an appositive explains is in the objective case, the appositive is also in the objective case. In this sentence, *heart* explains *tower*. Since *tower* is the object of the preposition *in*, both *tower* and *heart* are in the objective case.

Exercise 18

Identify each appositive in the following sentences, and name the noun each explains. All the appositives are in the *objective* case.
  1. People from Indiana have the nickname Hoosiers.
  2. When I was sick, my mother called Dr. Lane, our family physician.
  3. In the Revolutionary War, the colonists were aided by the Polish patriot Count Pulaski.
  4. Victor cooked his favorite dish, spaghetti with clam sauce.
  5. Three billion stars are contained in the Milky Way, our galaxy.
  6. We saw an old movie with Mary Pickford, a star in the 1920s.
  7. The heart-shaped cookies were baked by my sister Ruth.
  8. Johann Strauss wrote the famous waltz "The Blue Danube."
  9. Margaret reported on J. R. R. Tolkien's novel *The Hobbit.*
 10. I gave my last raisin to Esther, my best friend.
 11. My little brother likes Kermit, the frog from the Muppets.
 12. For my art project, I drew a picture of a daddy longlegs, an insect in the same family as the spider.
 13. Cargo is carried in the fuselage, the body of the plane.
 14. Sunlight can cause freckles, small brown marks on the skin.
 15. Our class studied about Williamsburg, a restored colonial town in Virginia.

Use the following words as appositives in sentences of your own. Have each appositive explain a noun in the objective case.

the Rocky Mountains   Herman and Sylvia
the rock star   chocolate

EXERCISE 18: Although appositives were introduced in grade 6, the concept will need to be retaught. Work through each sentence carefully, showing that because an appositive explains a noun in the objective case, the appositive is also in the objective case. Put the sentences from the second part on the chalkboard. Some students will have difficulty making the appositive explain a noun in the objective case; therefore, reconstruct sentences where necessary. Choose some student sentences to diagram.

ANSWERS
The appositives in sentences 1–15 are underlined twice, and the nouns they explain are underlined once.

Indirect Object

> **A noun used as the indirect object of a verb is in the objective case.**

Some sentences contain two objects: the direct object—the receiver of the action—and another object that tells *to whom* or *for whom* the action is done. This object is called the *indirect object*.

> Simon taught *Carol* the song.

The direct object of the verb *taught* is *song*. Carol tells *to whom* the action is directed and is the indirect object. The preposition *to* or *for* can usually be inserted before the indirect object without altering the meaning of the sentence. The indirect object is ordinarily placed between the verb and the direct object.

Among the verbs that may take both direct and indirect objects are *assign, bring, buy, deny, do, forbid, forgive, get, give, grant, hand, lend, offer, owe, pardon, pay, promise, read, refuse, remit, sell, send, show, sing, teach, tell, wish, write.*

Exercise 19

Identify the direct object and the indirect object in each of the following sentences.
1. Cameron, the spelling bee champion, showed the class his trophy.
2. Who taught Wolf that new trick?
3. Will you lend Agnes your camera?
4. The guide showed the group the concealed door in the panel.
5. Janette gave her horse a lump of sugar.
6. The hospital volunteer read the children a story about a friendly dragon.
7. The tired athlete passed the next runner the baton.
8. Joshua sent ten friends handmade invitations to the party.
9. Katy wished her friend a pleasant trip.
10. Alonzo told Ted the latest knock-knock joke.

EXERCISE 19: Present the sentence pattern N–V–N–N to the students. Put the pattern on the chalkboard and write the following underneath the letters:

    N   V
subject   predicate
     N   N
indirect obj.   direct obj.

Explain to the students that there can be no indirect object without a direct object and that the indirect object will precede the direct object. Write three N–V–N sentences using the verbs suggested in the introduction to indirect objects. Show how easy it is to add an indirect object in each sentence. For example:

    N   V   N
The manager assigned the job.

    N   V   N   N
The manager assigned Jan the job.
             (indir. obj.) (dir. obj.)

Add an indirect object to each of the following sentences.
11. Tommy showed his bus pass.
12. The actress read selections from Shakespeare.
13. Will Marty lend his gorilla costume?
14. The mail carrier brought the huge package this morning.
15. Will you do a favor?
16. We offered help.
17. Queen Isabella gave aid.
18. At the entrance, we showed our tickets.
19. Who taught the short way out of the maze?
20. Ray will buy a book on antique cars.

Adverbial Objective

> **A noun used as an adverbial objective is in the objective case.**

We stayed at the lake two *days.*

A noun that is used like an adverb to modify a verb is called an *adverbial objective.* Such nouns are in the objective case. Adverbial objectives usually answer the questions *when, where, how long, how much,* and *how far.*

Exercise 20

Identify the adverbial objective in each of the following sentences.
1. The campers hiked ten miles.
2. My father rides a bicycle to work every morning.
3. Terri worked three months on the portrait of his cat.
4. The smallest armadillo measures six inches long.
5. A special train in France travels 156 miles per hour.
5. We searched an hour for Heather's contact lens.
7. A hippo can eat eighty pounds of food at a time.
8. It can take four years for an oyster to make a pearl.
9. The diamond weighs several carats.
10. My first copy of the skateboarding magazine arrived last week.

Have the students read each sentence in the first part of exercise 19, inserting the preposition *to* or *for* before each indirect object.

As the students complete each sentence in the second part of the exercise, have some sentences placed on the chalkboard to correct any errors. For extension of the activity, choose five verbs from the list given in the introduction and have the students write sentences with indirect objects.

ANSWERS

In sentences 1–10, the direct objects are underlined twice, and the indirect objects are underlined once.

In sentences 11–20, any appropriate noun in the indirect object position is acceptable. Pronouns are also acceptable, but point out they are pronouns, not nouns.

EXERCISE 20: After the students have completed both parts of exercise 20, have them compose four sentences with adverbial objectives. Nouns that function as adverbs are also studied in grammar chapter 5, lesson 2.

ANSWERS

In sentences 1–10, the adverbial objectives are underlined. The answers for sentences 11–20 will vary.

Complete each sentence with an appropriate adverbial objective.

11. Sam jogs _____ every morning.
12. The baby weighs _____.
13. I paid _____ for the cassette.
14. My mother is going on a business trip _____.
15. Ronda takes the bus _____.
16. I saw a funny Marx Brothers movie on TV _____.
17. We spent _____ making the banner to carry in the parade.
18. It usually takes me _____ to get ready in the morning.
19. I clean out my closet _____.
20. The construction crew has been working _____ on the building.

The Marx Brothers: Groucho, Chico, and Harpo

Cognate Object

> **A noun used as a cognate object is in the objective case.**

The rock star sang her latest *song.*

Nouns that repeat the meaning of the verbs of which they are direct objects are called *cognate objects.* Look up the meaning of *cognate* in your dictionary.

Exercise 21

Identify the cognate objects in the following sentences.

1. Olga smiled an ear-to-ear smile.
2. In folklore, a cat lives nine lives.
3. Janice thinks pleasant thoughts of lazy summer days.
4. The kookaburra bird of Australia laughs a humanlike laugh.
5. The Italian folk group will dance a traditional dance with colorful ribbons attached to a maypole.
6. The international children's choir sang songs from around the globe.
7. The suffragettes fought a long fight for the right of women to vote.
8. I dreamed a crazy dream about a ride in a spaceship.
9. Having three wishes from the genie, Muhammed wished his third wish for three more.
10. It rained a steady rain the day I started my paper route.

Exercise 22

Give the use of each italicized noun in the following sentences: *direct object*, *object of a preposition*, *appositive in the objective case*, *indirect object*, *adverbial objective*, or *cognate object*.

1. Carlos taught *Carol* the new dance step.
2. We visited *Warsaw*, the *capital* of Poland.
3. Gorillas often sleep fourteen *hours* in a single day.
4. The troupe rode around the *stage* on *bicycles*.
5. Grandma Moses painted simple *scenes* of *life* in the country.
6. In my *opinion*, my goldfish lives a monotonous *life*.
7. The starfighter defended the *planet* from Xorans, the invading *enemy*.
8. Mr. McCauley gives his *neighbors* the surplus *tomatoes* from his garden.
9. The jungles of *South America* have a tropical *climate*.
10. Jim ran five *miles* every *day* in preparation for the marathon.
11. The cave gave the *hikers shelter.*
12. The fans cheered each *player* with a burst of *applause.*
13. The French restaurant serves *escargots*, *snails* in garlic sauce.
14. The singer sang the *song* "Fame."
15. The trunk of an elephant can easily hold a *gallon* of *water.*

16. family (indir. obj.), headache (dir. obj.)
17. grin (cognate obj.)
18. foundation (dir. obj.), skyscraper (obj. of prep.)
19. hour (adv. obj.), corner (obj. of prep.), Oscar (obj. of prep.)
20. *The Atomic Submarine* (dir. obj.), John Lewellen (obj. of prep.)
21. wood (dir. obj.), glass (dir. obj.)
22. album (dir. obj.), Mahalia Jackson (obj. of prep.), singer (appos.)
23. hacienda (dir. obj.), estate (appos.)
24. fight (cognate obj.), independence (obj. of prep.), India (obj. of prep.)
25. Kathy (indir. obj.), friend (appos.), scarf (dir. obj.)

Identify the nouns in the objective case in the following sentences, and give the use of each.

16. Blake's trumpet noises give the family a headache.
17. Diana grinned a lopsided grin.
18. The workers are building the foundation of the skyscraper.
19. I waited one hour on the corner for Oscar.
20. Have you read *The Atomic Submarine* by John Lewellen?
21. Magnets do not attract wood or glass.
22. Dad has an album by Mahalia Jackson, a powerful black singer.
23. In Mexico, our family visited a hacienda, a large estate.
24. Mahatma Gandhi fought a long fight for the independence of India.
25. I lent Kathy, my best friend, my new scarf.

Exercise 23   Review

Give the person, number, gender, and case of each of the following italicized nouns.

1. As *Matt's* hobby, he collects *autographs* of baseball players.
2. I, the *president*, will supervise the election of the *mascot*.
3. *Allison* spent two *hours* in the library, working on her report.
4. *Emma Lazarus*, a nineteenth century *poet*, wrote the poem on the Statue of Liberty.
5. Did you watch the TV program about *penguins* last *night*, *Martha*?
6. The capital of Hungary is *Budapest*, a *city* divided by the Danube.
7. The trail of flour was noticed immediately by *Hawkeye*, the keen-eyed *detective*.
8. *Gail's car* is ten years old and on its last legs.
9. Mr. Ewald gave the *students* an *explanation* of photosynthesis.
10. William Tell, a *hero* in Swiss legend, shot an *apple* off his son's head.

Sharpening Your Skills

You can design your own robot and make it do whatever you want it to do! Write one or two paragraphs describing your robot. Try to include as many of the various uses of nouns in the objective case as you can.

Chapter Challenge

Read the selection below and then answer the questions that follow.

¹Paris, the capital of France, is regarded by many travelers as the most beautiful city in the world. ²Its tree-lined boulevards and gracious buildings attract many visitors every year. ³Some of the internationally famous monuments of Paris are the Arc de Triomphe, the Cathedral of Notre Dame, and the Eiffel Tower. ⁴The beauty of this capital has enchanted groups of tourists from every continent. ⁵If the opportunity to visit France's most elegant city presents itself to you, readers, be certain to take it.

1. Name the proper nouns in the first sentence.
2. Find an adverbial objective in the second sentence.
3. In the second sentence, which noun is the direct object?
4. Find an abstract noun in the fourth sentence.
5. Name a collective noun in the fourth sentence.
6. Find an appositive in the first sentence. In what case is this appositive?
7. Find a noun that is in direct address.
8. In the fifth sentence, find a noun in the possessive case.
9. What are the subjective complements in the third sentence?
10. What are the objects of the prepositions in the fourth sentence?

A view of the Cathedral of Notre Dame from the Seine River

Creative Space 1

Creative Space is a special section developed to aid the students in the writing of original poetry. The questions are meant to stimulate class discussion about the meaning of the poems and to help the students explore the patterns and word choices that make the poems effective. The poems provide the students with models of structures they might use in creating their own poetry. These structures need not be followed, but for the beginning writer, they will prove helpful in the shaping of ideas. Students who wish to express their thoughts in different structures should be encouraged to do so.

The Coming

In early spring
The frost-painted hills
Soften
Into singing streams.
The silent, shorter
Days
Yawn now,
And stretch,
Awakened finally then
By a loud barrage
Of blossoming.

246

Exploring the Poem...

What season is ending? What season is coming?

Where do you find alliteration in the poem? *Alliteration* is the repetition of the same consonant sound at the beginning of several words. How does the alliteration add to the feeling of the poem?

Poets often use words that describe or appeal to the senses. In several places, the poem uses words that describe sounds. Give some examples. (Look up the meaning of the word *barrage* as used in this poem.)

The poem describes several actions that nature is performing. Give some examples. You may have mentioned that the spring day *yawns* and *stretches* like an awakened sleeper. This is an example of the figure of speech called *personification*. In personification, an object performs humanlike actions. What other meaning of the word *stretch* makes it a good verb to compare spring days with winter days?

★ Think of a calendar picture or a scene you have observed closely. List phrases or sentences that describe the scene. Hint at the actions in nature that could give life to the picture you are describing. After you have finished, arrange the ideas into a poem. Take out any words that do not give life to your poem.

Chapter 2

Pronouns

Lesson 1 Personal Pronouns: Review and Nominative Case

A pronoun is a word used in place of a noun.

The repetition of nouns makes sentences monotonous, and so pronouns are used to take the place of nouns. Which sounds better?

> Ann's mother took *Ann* to the seashore.
> Ann's mother took *her* to the seashore.

The second sentence uses the pronoun *her* to refer to Ann, instead of repeating the name. The word to which a pronoun refers is called its *antecedent*. *Ann* is the antecedent of *her* in the second sentence.

Personal Pronouns: Review

> **A personal pronoun shows by its form the speaker, the person spoken to, or the person or thing spoken of.**

The pronouns of the first person (the speaker) are *I, mine, me, we, ours, us.* The pronouns of the second person (the person spoken to) are *you* and *yours.* Third-person pronouns (the person or the thing spoken of) are *he, she, it, his, hers, its, him, her, they, theirs, them.*

> *I* opened the dusty trunk. (*First person*)
> Will *you* go to the fair? (*Second person*)
> *She* gave *it* to *him.* (*Third person*)

Cars and people are moving every which way in this scene. Does your life often seem hectic and confusing? Discuss some of your experiences.

Pronouns change form to show *number* and *case*. Study the declension below. Number means singular or plural. Case refers to the use of the pronoun in a sentence.

> *We* are going on a field trip. (*Nominative case—for subjects and subjective complements*)
> These drawings are *hers*. (*Possessive case—shows possession*)
> Sal gave the tickets to *him*. (*Objective case—for objects*)

Pronouns in the third person singular change to show *gender*: *he* and *him* are masculine; *she* and *her* are feminine; *it* is neuter.

Declension of the Personal Pronouns

CASE	SINGULAR	PLURAL
	First Person	
Nominative	I	we
Possessive	mine, my*	ours, our*
Objective	me	us
	Second Person	
Nominative	you	you
Possessive	yours, your*	yours, your*
Objective	you	you
	Third Person	
Nominative	he, she, it	they
Possessive	hers, its, his, her*	theirs, their*
Objective	him, her, it	them

*The possessive adjectives are included in this table for the sake of completeness.

Exercise 24

Give the person and number of each italicized personal pronoun.
1. *They* went on a day-long hike.
2. *We* students are forming a camera club.
3. Charley gave *her* and *me* some homemade blueberry muffins.
4. *You* are a very good Ping-Pong player.
5. The juice was divided among *us* players.
6. The messenger actually sang the telegram to *them*.
7. It must have been *he* who called for pizza.
8. *We* do not know what a rutabaga is.
9. The calico cat ran away from *him*.
10. *She* and *I* are studying jazz dance.

Nominative Case

Subject of a Verb

A pronoun used as the subject of a verb is in the
nominative case.

Elizabeth and *I* are loading the van.

The pronoun *I* is in the nominative case. It is the subject of the
sentence, together with the word *Elizabeth*.

Peter and (she, her) have canaries as pets.

The correct form is the nominative pronoun *she*: Peter and *she* have
canaries as pets. The pronoun *she* is the subject of the sentence,
together with *Peter*.

The nominative case personal pronouns are

SINGULAR	PLURAL
I	we
you	you
he, she, it	they

Exercise 25

Select the correct personal pronouns in the following sentences. Give
the reason for your choice.
1. Carol and (I, me) will make the banner together.
2. (She, Her) and Toby can dance the square dance.
3. (He, Him) and (me, I) will get up at five o'clock tomorrow.
4. Did (him, he) or Norman give you a subway token?
5. (Them, They) and (me, I) went sight-seeing on horseback.
6. Kerry and (he, him) picked raspberries.
7. Therese and (me, I) wore colonial costumes to the party.
8. Only (we, us) knew the shortcut to the lake—or so I thought!
9. Did Alex and (he, him) make the team?
10. Margaret and (her, she) are studying ballet.

Write five sentences of your own with pronouns as subjects.

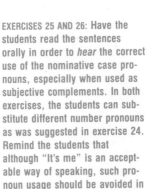

EXERCISES 25 AND 26: Have the
students read the sentences
orally in order to *hear* the correct
use of the nominative case pronouns, especially when used as
subjective complements. In both
exercises, the students can substitute different number pronouns
as was suggested in exercise 24.
Remind the students that
although "It's me" is an acceptable way of speaking, such pronoun usage should be avoided in
writing.

ANSWERS
The correct answers are underlined.
All the pronouns are in the nominative
case because they are subjects. Sentences will vary.

Subjective Complement

> **A pronoun used as a subjective complement is in the nominative case. A subjective complement refers to the same person or thing as the subject.**

The person who found the cat is *he*.

The pronoun *he* is in the nominative case. It is a subjective complement, following the word *is*.

It was (I, me).

The correct form is the nominative *I*: It was *I*. The pronoun *I* is the subjective complement.

Subjective complements follow verbs of being: *is, are, was, were, am, being*, and *been*.

Exercise 26

Select the correct personal pronouns in the following sentences. Give the reason for your choice.
1. It was (he, him) who tracked mud into the house.
2. Was that (her, she) at the door?
3. The person who cleaned the fish tank was (me, I).
4. Was it (them, they) who called?
5. It was (him, he) whom the detective suspected.
6. It was not (they, them) who did it.
7. Was it Elmer or (she, her) who painted the room?
8. The person who sent the blossoming plant was (he, him).
9. Joshua thought it was Elena and (her, she) who had the records.
10. It was (me, I) who absentmindedly put the sugar in the refrigerator.

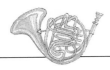

Exercise 27

Select the correct personal pronouns in the following sentences. Tell whether the pronoun is used as the *subject* or *subjective complement*.

1. My friend and (I, me) drew a map for the treasure hunt.
2. Neither Ralph nor (me, I) liked the scary movie.
3. Was it (she, her) hiding behind the rose trellis?
4. Julius and (us, we) are selling tickets at the bazaar.
5. (He, Him) and (I, me) have been friends for many years.
6. The person in the skeleton costume was (he, him).
7. Gina and (them, they) walked up to the twentieth floor.
8. (Us, We) sat in the sunny bleachers at the baseball park.
9. Dwight and (she, her) practice the French horn after school.
10. It is (her, she) and (me, I) who are sisters.

Exercise 28

Complete each sentence with the correct form of a personal pronoun. Give the reason for your choice.

1. It was _____ who made the fudge.
2. Irvin and _he_ have found the hidden passage.
3. Juan and _she_ have seen *Star Wars* five times.
4. Down the street jogged Ernie and _____.
5. It was _they_ who suggested the panda as our team mascot.
6. Sidney and _____ planned a trip to the museum.
7. Was it _he_ who brought in the ant farm?
8. My sister and _____ are taking the subway for the first time.
9. Rob and _we_ are visiting in the neighborhood.
10. In the room were Polly, Justin, and _____.

Sharpening Your Skills

Think of a famous person from history, science, music, sports, or any other area. Write a short paragraph describing this person and his or her accomplishments. Do not use the person's name. Use only personal pronouns. Reveal your mystery person only in the last sentence of the paragraph. Can readers of your paragraph guess who the person is before the last sentence?

EXERCISES 27 AND 28: The students should have no difficulty with either exercise. Make sure that in exercise 28, the students vary their pronoun choice. If review is still needed, instruct the students to write three original sentences using pronouns as subjects and three using pronouns as subjective complements.

ANSWERS
The correct answers are underlined. The use of each pronoun is given below.
1. subj.   6. subj. comp.
2. subj.   7. subj.
3. subj. comp. 8. subj.
4. subj.   9. subj.
5. subjs.   10. subj. comps.

ANSWERS
Any pronoun in the nominative case is correct. Below is listed the reason for each choice of pronoun.
1. subj. comp. 6. subj.
2. subj.   7. subj. comp.
3. subj.   8. subj.
4. subj.   9. subj.
5. subj. comp. 10. subj.

SHARPENING YOUR SKILLS: Discuss with the class some popular personalities from history, science, and so on. Explain that the identity of the person is not to be revealed until the last sentence. Therefore, only the personal pronouns *he*, *she*, or *they* can be used in the other sentences.

Lesson 2 Personal Pronouns: Objective Case

Direct Object

> **A pronoun used as the direct object of a verb is in the objective case.**

My friend from out of town called *me* last night.

The pronoun *me* is in the objective case. It is the direct object of the verb *called*.

Carla took Sandra and (she, her) to the play.

The correct form is the objective pronoun *her*: Carla took Sandra and *her* to the play. *Her* is the direct object, together with *Sandra*.

The objective case personal pronouns are

SINGULAR	PLURAL
me	us
you	you
him, her, it	them

Exercise 29

Select the correct personal pronouns in the following sentences. Give the reason for your choice.
1. We passed Ellen and (she, her) on the road.
2. They didn't recognize (I, me).
3. The team carried (him, he) off the field.
4. Maureen politely thanked Lance and (he, him) for the gift.
5. These shelves will be too long unless we cut (them, they).
6. The receptionist directed Ann and (she, her) to the optometrist's office.
7. Jamie invited (I, me) and (he, him) to go sailing.
8. The changing patterns of the kaleidoscope fascinated (she, her).
9. We have heard the Rollers and (they, them) before.
10. Will you take Thomas and (we, us) to the record store tomorrow?

THE STUDENTS SHOULD LEARN

—to use the personal pronouns in the objective case correctly

—to use the correct pronoun after the conjunctions *than* and *as*

—to make a correct choice between the nominative and objective case personal pronouns

TEACHING THE LESSON

See if the students remember the objective case pronouns that had been grouped on the chalkboard previously. List as many as they can remember and then start to group them beginning with first person singular and plural pronouns, etc.

EXERCISE 29: Most of these objects are compound. Many students use *I* in a phrase such as *Philip and I* regardless of how the phrase is used in the sentence. Suggest that the students choose the main verb in the sentence and then supply the correct objective case pronoun.

ANSWERS

The correct answers are underlined. All the pronouns are in the objective case because they are direct objects.

Indirect Object

> **A pronoun used as the indirect object of a verb is in the objective case.**

Prudence lent *him* her radio.

The pronoun *him* is in the objective case. It is the indirect object of the verb *lent*.

My parents promised my brother and (I, me) new bunk beds.

The correct form is the objective pronoun *me*: My parents promised my brother and *me* new bunk beds. *Me* is the indirect object, together with *brother*.

HINT: To test for an indirect object, insert *to* or *for* before the pronoun. If the pronoun is an indirect object, the meaning of the sentence will not change.

My parents promised *to* my brother and *to* me new bunk beds.

Exercise 30

Select the correct personal pronouns in the following sentences. Give the reason for your choice.

1. Mr. Bonella gave (her, she) his recipe for spaghetti sauce.
2. The store sent (we, us) a replacement set of headphones.
3. Joanne lent (he, him) and (I, me) her Scrabble game.
4. The sailor showed (them, they) his sea chest.
5. The police officer did my father and (I, me) a favor.
6. Vince sent (she, her) a bunch of violets.
7. Mr. Gregoris showed (him, he) and (me, I) his slides of Greece.
8. Don't forget that you promised (we, us) ice-cream sodas this afternoon.
9. The book *Little House on the Prairie* gave (I, me) a picture of pioneer life.
10. The mayor gave (them, they) the good-citizen award.

EXERCISE 30: Review the test for determining an indirect object. Remind the students to use *to* and *for* before the indirect object and to look for the direct object following the indirect object. A review of the sentence pattern N-V-N-N as presented in chapter 1 may be helpful.

ANSWERS
The correct answers are underlined. All the pronouns are in the objective case because they are indirect objects.

Object of a Preposition

> **A pronoun used as the object of a preposition is in the objective case.**

This large gift came from *them*.

The pronoun *them* is in the objective case. It is the object of the preposition *from*.

Clement went roller skating with Fred and (she, her).

The correct form is the objective pronoun *her*: Clement went roller skating with Fred and her. *Her* is the object of the preposition, together with *Fred*.

Exercise 31

Select the correct personal pronouns in the following sentences. Give the reason for your choice.

1. These paintings of the school were done by (she, her).
2. Is there an expert on computers among (we, us)?
3. Debbie has already spoken to (he, him) and (she, her) about joining the camera club.
4. Can anyone explain Newton's law to Isaac and (me, I)?
5. Clement played tennis with (they, them).
6. Soon after writing to her pen pal in India, Nancy received a letter from (she, her).
7. I toured the dairy farm with Betty and (she, her).
8. Marco ran behind (them, they) and (me, I) all around the track.
9. As Richard rode the Ferris wheel, the carnival lights blinked below (he, him).
10. Sit between (she, her) and (I, me).

EXERCISE 31: Insist that the students give the preposition after making their choice of pronoun. If the sentences are written, have the students put a box or circle around the entire phrase. If they have difficulty recognizing prepositions, have them consult the list on page 381 of chapter 6.

ANSWERS
The correct answers are underlined. All the pronouns are objects of prepositions.

Exercise 32

Select the correct personal pronouns in the following sentences. Tell whether each is used as a *direct object*, *indirect object*, or *object of a preposition*.

1. Wendell took a picture of (we, <u>us</u>) at the top of the mountain.
2. Dwayne gave Juanita and (he, <u>him</u>) his hamsters.
3. Ivan impressed (<u>her</u>, she) and (<u>me</u>, I) with his knowledge of music.
4. Sharon has exchanged Christmas presents with (she, <u>her</u>).
5. The babysitter told bedtime stories to (<u>them</u>, they).
6. Marta lent (<u>us</u>, we) her golf clubs.
7. My uncle took Gwen and (<u>me</u>, I) to the television studio where he works.
8. The sudden screeching from the birdhouse scared (they, <u>them</u>).
9. On the roller coaster, Anne always sits between (he, <u>him</u>) and (I, <u>me</u>).
10. Grandmother sent Sara and (she, <u>her</u>) miniature gondolas from Venice.

Exercise 33

Complete the following sentences with the proper form of a personal pronoun. Give the reason for your choice.

1. We saw _____ at the beach.
2. Elvira bought _____ the red balloon.
3. We played soccer with George and _____.
4. Emily Dickinson's poem was read by _____.
5. The story of the pioneers really interests _____.
6. Eugene told _____ and _____ about his dream.
7. Henry rode with _____ in the pickup truck.
8. Beulah picks up a newspaper for _____ every day.
9. Did the mail carrier bring _____ any mail today?
10. The taxi is waiting for Tom and _____.

EXERCISES 32 AND 33: These exercises serve as a review of personal pronouns in the objective case. As a continued review of nominative case, the students could go back to each sentence in exercise 32 and use the nominative case pronoun in a sentence expressing the same idea. For example:

Wendell took a picture of *us* at the top of the mountain.

We suggested that Wendell take our picture on the top of the mountain.

Encourage the students to vary their pronoun choice in exercise 33.

ANSWERS
The correct answers are underlined. The use of each pronoun is given below.
1. obj. of prep.
2. ind. obj.
3. dir. objs.
4. obj. of prep.
5. obj. of prep.
6. ind. obj.
7. dir. obj.
8. dir. obj.
9. objs. of prep.
10. ind. obj.

ANSWERS
Any pronoun in the objective case is correct. Below is given the reason for each choice of pronoun.
1. dir. obj.
2. ind. obj.
3. obj. of prep.
4. obj. of prep.
5. dir. obj.
6. dir. objs.
7. obj. of prep.
8. obj. of prep.
9. ind. obj.
10. obj. of prep.

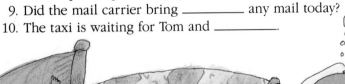

The Case Used after *Than* and *As*

> After the conjunctions *than* and *as*, words often are omitted. The pronoun following these conjunctions must be in the same case as the word with which it is compared.

He is older than (I, me).

The correct form is: He is older than *I* (am old).

I know Anne better than (she, her).

The correct forms are: I know Anne better than (I know) *her*, or I know Anne better than *she* (knows her).

Exercise 34

Select the correct form of the pronoun, and supply the words that were omitted from each sentence. For some sentences, both pronouns may be correct.

1. Sheldon is more friendly than (he, him).
2. Yvette gave me as much as (she, her).
3. We have known Gene longer than (he, him).
4. Andy is as tall as (I, me).
5. Inez dances better than (she, her).
6. I gave him as much help as (they, them).
7. Jake is a better volleyball player than (I, me).
8. They arrived later than (we, us).
9. No one was as surprised as (I, me).
10. Evelyn plays the violin better than (he, him).
11. Rita is as studious as (she, her).
12. No one was more pleased than (I, me).
13. You are younger than (he, him).
14. I know that he is a better speller than (I, me).
15. You are as good a joke teller as (I, me)!

EXERCISE 34: Review the examples in the introduction carefully. Lead the students to understand that a predicate is missing after the words *than* and *as*, and that either a nominative or objective case pronoun may be correct depending upon how the sentence is completed. Make sure a predicate is added after the students have made their choice.

ANSWERS
1. he (is friendly)
2. she (gave me), or (she gave) her
3. he (has known Gene) or (we have known) him
4. I (am tall)
5. she (dances)
6. they (gave him) or (I gave) them
7. I (am)
8. we (arrived)
9. I (was surprised)
10. he (plays)
11. she (is studious)
12. I (was pleased)
13. he (is young)
14. I (am)
15. I (am)

Review of Nominative and Objective Case Pronouns

Exercise 35

Identify the personal pronouns in the following sentences. Tell whether each is in the nominative case or the objective case.

1. You have really improved your backstroke, Beth.
2. Lewis gave me the binoculars.
3. My sister said that she might go with us to the zoo.
4. It is the largest bee that I have ever seen!
5. They picked up Don and her at the airport.
6. Mary Ellen invited them to the picnic.
7. How did you know that was he?
8. Roberto said he would show us some magic tricks.
9. I was surprised that they had not tasted artichokes before.
10. We Americans have the eagle as a national symbol.

Identify the personal pronouns in the following sentences. Give the person, number, gender, and case of each.

11. He is an excellent chess player.
12. I will see you at one o'clock.
13. How did they know about it?
14. She gave me a pair of earrings.
15. We taught them how to walk on stilts.

Exercise 36

Select the correct personal pronouns in the following sentences. Give the reason for your choice.

1. Jack and (I, me) built a snow fort and prepared for the attack.
2. Plants make an interesting hobby for my mother and (she, her).
3. Ricardo and (he, him) changed all the light bulbs.
4. Bernadette drove Jacqueline and (we, us) to the mall.
5. I can't believe the culprit was (he, him).
6. The rug belonged to (they, them) before it belonged to (we, us).
7. Kevin and (she, her) added the numbers accurately.
8. Clare showed (we, us) the picture of her family.
9. Can you believe that Marita and (he, him) won the chess prize?
10. In the afternoon, Ernie and (she, her) cleaned the whole house.

EXERCISE 35: In the first part, besides specifying the case of each pronoun, the students could also give its use (syntax) in the sentence. For the second part, have the students make four columns to give the answers required.

ANSWERS
1. You (nom.)
2. me (obj.)
3. she (nom.), us (obj.)
4. It (nom.), I (nom.)
5. They (nom.), her (obj.)
6. them (obj.)
7. you (nom.), he (nom.)
8. he (nom.), us (obj.)
9. I (nom.), they (nom.)
10. We (nom.)
11. He (third, sing., masc., nom.)
12. I (first, sing., masc. or fem., nom.), you (second, sing. or plural, masc. or fem., obj.)
13. They (third, plural, masc. or fem., nom.), it (third, sing., neuter, obj.)
14. She (third, sing., fem., nom.), me (first, sing., masc. or fem., obj.)
15. We (first, plural, masc. or fem., nom.), them (third, plural, masc. or fem., obj.)

EXERCISE 36: The students should identify the pronoun as in the nominative or objective case. As an added activity, have them choose five sentences that use a compound subject, direct object, or object of the preposition and then create a sentence, with the same information, that uses the other pronoun.
    Jack and *I* built a snow fort.
    A snow fort was built by Jack and *me*.

ANSWERS
The correct pronouns are underlined; the reasons for choices are listed below.
1. subj.
2. obj. of prep.
3. subj.
4. dir. obj.
5. subj. comp.
6. obj. of prep.
   obj. of prep.
7. subj.
8. indir. obj.
9. subj. of *won*
10. subj.

11. Paul, Paula, and (I, me) are in the same carpentry class.
12. The unexpected quiz surprised all of (we, us).
13. Figuring out math problems is challenging to Amanda and (they, them).
14. Yesterday afternoon, Don, Justin, and (he, him) went jogging.
15. The books were arranged in alphabetical order by Tony and (she, her).

Exercise 37

Complete the following sentences with personal pronouns, as indicated.

1. __He__ is going to work on his balsa models this afternoon. (*Third person, singular, masculine, nominative*)
2. Carolyn, will __you__ help __us__ mail these invitations? (*Second person, singular, feminine, nominative; first person, plural, masculine or feminine, objective*)
3. __They__ promised to sing a song at the assembly next week. (*Third person, plural, masculine or feminine, nominative*)
4. When Henry told __her__ a funny story, Kelly couldn't stop laughing. (*Third person, singular, feminine, objective*)
5. __We__ will meet __you__ at the library tonight. (*First person, plural, masculine or feminine, nominative; second person, plural, masculine or feminine, objective*)
6. Lee brought Cecile and __me__ to the street carnival. (*First person, singular, masculine or feminine, objective*)
7. __I__ love to watch the commercials on television. (*First person, singular, masculine or feminine, nominative*)
8. Mary Jane said that __she__ stayed up to see the movie, too. (*Third person, singular, feminine, nominative*)
9. My mother will take __us__ biking in Wisconsin. (*First person, plural, masculine or feminine, objective*)
10. The fish in this tank is making faces at __me__! (*First person, singular, masculine or feminine, objective*)

Sharpening Your Skills

You and your friend have taken a vacation trip to Mars. Write a short narrative about how your Martian tour guide helped you. Use both nominative and objective case pronouns. Underline them when you are finished.

Lesson 3 Possessive and Compound Personal Pronouns

Possessive Pronouns

> **A possessive pronoun takes the place of a noun that shows possession or ownership.**

The possessive pronouns are *mine, ours, yours, his, hers, its,* and *theirs.* They are used to take the place of possessive nouns.

> The skis are *Lila's.* (*Possessive noun*)
> The skis are *hers.* (*Possessive pronoun*)

A possessive pronoun can be used in various ways in a sentence.

> *Mine* is in the oven. (*Subject*)
> Have you seen *his*? (*Direct object*)
> The plants are *theirs.* (*Subjective complement*)

My, our, your, his, her, its, and *their* are possessive adjectives. They modify nouns.

> *Lionel's* paper is on the top. (*Possessive noun*)
> *His* paper is on the top. (*Possessive adjective that modifies the noun* paper)

Both possessive pronouns and possessive adjectives indicate ownership. Do not confuse them, however. Possessive pronouns stand alone. Possessive adjectives always modify nouns.

POSSESSIVE PRONOUNS	POSSESSIVE ADJECTIVES
Mine is new.	*My* bike is new.
Hers is broken.	*Her* skateboard is broken.
That is *his.*	That is *his* car.
Ours is painted gray.	*Our* house is painted gray.
Did you see *theirs*?	Did you see *their* stereo?

THE STUDENTS SHOULD LEARN
—to identify and use possessive pronouns correctly
—to identify and use compound personal pronouns correctly

TEACHING THE LESSON
Although the possessive *adjectives* are mentioned in this lesson, the main area of concentration is the possessive *pronoun*. Spend sufficient time on the introduction so that the students understand the difference between the adjective and the pronoun. Use diagraming to help show the difference, and point out that the spelling between the two parts of speech differs except for *his* and *its*.

When working with the compound personal pronouns, elicit the proper forms from the students by having them add *self* and *selves* to forms of the personal pronouns. Most students have little difficulty with intensive and reflexive pronouns. Show the students that the intensive pronoun can usually be omitted and the sentence will still make sense. This usually cannot happen with reflexive pronouns. For example:

You *yourself* are responsible for this.
You are responsible for this.

EXERCISE 38: After the students have completed the first part, have them go back and substitute a noun for as many of the pronouns as possible. For example:

They traded *theirs* for *ours*.
They traded *Dorothy's* for *Alvin's*.

ANSWERS
The correct answers for the first part are underlined. Sentences for the second part will vary.

Exercise 38

Identify the possessive pronouns in the following sentences.

1. They traded theirs for ours.
2. I think that stuffed kangaroo is his.
3. That card fluttering through the air is not mine.
4. Mine was broken, and so Rosalita gave me hers.
5. When we received the money, Rene put hers in the bank.
6. Theirs glows brighter than ours.
7. Yours has a second hand; mine does not have one.
8. Hers was a great contribution to medical science.
9. Mine came from a garden and yours from a farm, but his came from a supermarket.
10. I think mine is a very smart parrot.

Write five sentences of your own with the possessive pronouns listed below.

mine	ours
yours	theirs
his	hers

Compound Personal Pronouns

Compound personal pronouns are made by adding *self* or *selves* to certain forms of the personal pronouns.

Forms of the Compound Personal Pronouns

	SINGULAR	PLURAL
First Person	myself	ourselves
Second Person	yourself	yourselves
Third Person	himself, herself, itself	themselves

Compound personal pronouns have two uses: they can be *intensive* or *reflexive*.

> **An intensive pronoun is used to emphasize a preceding noun or pronoun.**
>
> **A reflexive pronoun is used as an object referring to and denoting the same person or thing as the subject.**

INTENSIVE PRONOUNS

He *himself* went.
You *yourself* must go.
We will do it *ourselves*.

REFLEXIVE PRONOUNS

Toby hurt *himself*.
You must prepare *yourself* for the speech.
We bought them for *ourselves*.

Exercise 39

Identify the compound personal pronouns in the following sentences. Tell whether each is *intensive* or *reflexive*.

1. You yourself are responsible for this.
2. Sit down and make yourselves comfortable.
3. He completed the crossword puzzle himself.
4. Bernardo taught himself to ride the old unicycle.
5. I myself fixed the handle on my bike.
6. Betty stitched every inch of the quilt herself.
7. Having followed the rabbit, Alice found herself in a strange world.
8. We taught ourselves Spanish by practicing regularly.
9. I want you to tell me the story yourself.
10. I gave myself a reward for studying hard—a piece of strawberry shortcake.

EXERCISE 39: Have the students go back to the sentences with intensive pronouns and see that they can be eliminated.

ANSWERS
The correct answers are underlined. The list below indicates whether the pronouns are intensive or reflexive.

1. I	6. I
2. R	7. R
3. I	8. R
4. R	9. I
5. I	10. R

Agreement of Compound Personal Pronouns

> Compound personal pronouns agree with their antecedents in person, number, and gender. They have two distinct uses, as intensive and as reflexive pronouns.

The coach *herself* trained the team. (*Intensive*)
Jay entertained *himself* by whistling. (*Reflexive*)

Coach is the antecedent of *herself*. Both are third person, singular in number, and feminine in gender. *Jay* is the antecedent of *himself*. Both are third person, singular in number, and masculine in gender.

Exercise 40

Complete the following sentences with the correct compound personal pronouns.

1. We cannot see __ourselves__ as others see us.
2. He __himself__ told me he saw a leprechaun.
3. James bought __himself__ a new basketball.
4. The explorers found __themselves__ in a dense thicket.
5. The carpenter hit __himself/herself__ with the hammer.
6. None but the pilot __himself/herself__ realized the danger.
7. The travelers entertained __themselves__ for hours with the puzzle.
8. The committee disagreed among __themselves__.
9. The climbers __themselves__ prepared their equipment.
10. Charlotte made __herself__ a jewelry box from toothpicks.

Write two sentences of your own with intensive pronouns and two with reflexive pronouns.

Sharpening Your Skills

You and your brother or sister recently lost your bikes. A police officer finds two bikes and asks one of you to identify them. Using possessive and compound personal pronouns, write five or six lines of dialogue between you and the officer explaining why the bikes are not yours.

EXERCISE 40: Direct the students to give the antecedent of each compound personal pronoun. Then have them give the person, number, and gender of both. They should identify the compound personal pronouns as intensive or reflexive.

ANSWERS
The correct answers are in the text. The list below indicates whether the pronouns are intensive or reflexive.
1. R   6. I
2. I   7. R
3. R   8. R
4. R   9. I
5. R   10. R

SHARPENING YOUR SKILLS: The students could work independently or as a class. The sentences need not be complicated, but both possessive and compound personal pronouns should be evident. Some sample sentences might be

Police officer: Are these bikes *yours*?
Randy: Neither bike is *ours*. *Mine* is blue with a black leather seat. *Hers* is green with a wire basket on the back. *Yours* are three-speed bikes, and *ours* are ten-speed.
Police officer: I can certainly see these are not *yours*.
Randy: We'll wait for other bikes to turn up. My sister *herself* will come the next time.

Lesson 4 Interrogative Pronouns

An interrogative pronoun is used in asking a question.

The interrogative pronouns are *who, whom, whose, which,* and *what.* They are used in both direct and indirect questions.

DIRECT QUESTIONS

Who lost the package?
Whom did you see?
Whose is near the door?
Which is yours?
What did you see?

INDIRECT QUESTIONS

He asked *who* lost the package.
They asked us *whom* we saw.
We wonder *whose* is near the door.
Sarah wonders *which* is yours.
They asked us *what* we saw.

Who, whom, and *whose* are used in speaking of persons. *Which* is used in speaking of persons and things and to indicate one of a definite class. *What* is used in speaking of things and in seeking information.

An interrogative pronoun can be in the nominative or objective case. Look at the sentences below and tell why the pronoun is in the nominative or objective case. Are these sentences direct or indirect questions?

1. *Who* lives in that house? (*Nominative case*)
2. From *whom* did you receive the letter? (*Objective case*)
3. *Which* of the stories do you prefer? (*Objective case*)
4. *What* is the matter? (*Nominative case*)
5. *What* did she do? (*Objective case*)

THE STUDENTS SHOULD LEARN
—to identify interrogative pronouns and to determine the case of the pronouns
—the correct use of *who* and *whom* as interrogative pronouns

TEACHING THE LESSON
Before consulting the text, have the students give the interrogative pronouns that they remember from the previous year. Ask them to use each pronoun in a sentence and then show how the pronouns can be in nominative or objective case depending upon their function in the sentence. Explain to the students the difference between the direct and indirect question. The indirect question does not have a question mark at the end of the sentence, and it usually indicates the person speaking. Show the students how to change a direct question into an indirect one. Use the examples in the introduction.

Who lives in that house?
I wonder *who* lives in that house.

ANSWERS
The sentences are all direct questions.
1. subject
2. obj. of prep.
3. obj. of *do prefer*
4. subject
5. obj. of *did do*

Exercise 41

Identify the interrogative pronouns in the following sentences. Give the case of each.

1. What is in the basket?
2. Who is speaking?
3. To whom did Lawrence apply for the position?
4. Who is your favorite TV performer?
5. What was the background of the Battle of Wounded Knee?
6. Which of the songs on the album did you like best?
7. He asked with whom she went.
8. Which of the cats is a Manx?
9. What does the Spanish word *tío* mean?
10. Consuelo asked which we liked best.
11. Who wrote *A Wrinkle in Time*?
12. What is a nautilus?
13. Who were the Vikings?
14. The waitress asked who ordered vanilla ice cream.
15. What are the steppes?

EXERCISE 41: Most students know that *who* is nominative case and *whom* is objective. They will have to determine the use of *which* and *what* in each sentence in order to give the case of those pronouns.

ANSWERS
The interrogative pronouns are underlined. Their case is given below.

1. nom.	9. obj.
2. nom.	10. obj.
3. obj.	11. nom.
4. nom.	12. nom.
5. nom.	13. nom.
6. obj.	14. nom.
7. obj.	15. nom.
8. nom.	

Parts from prows
of Viking ships

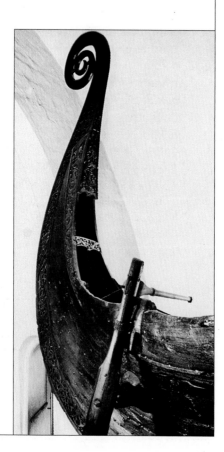

Correct Use of the Interrogative Pronouns *Who* and *Whom*

The interrogative pronoun *who* is used when the sentence requires a pronoun in the nominative case.

The interrogative pronoun *whom* is used when the sentence requires a pronoun in the objective case.

Who won the World Series? (*Subject*)
By *whom* was the *Adventures of Tom Sawyer* written? (*Object of the preposition*)

Exercise 42

Complete each of the following sentences with *who* or *whom*.
1. From __whom__ did the United States get the Statue of Liberty?
2. __Who__ threw out my favorite hairbrush?
3. By __whom__ was baseball invented?
4. With __whom__ did Barb go?
5. __Who__ has the lead role?
6. __Who__ is Neil Armstrong?
7. By __whom__ was Whistler's mother painted?
8. With __whom__ are you speaking?
9. __Who__ bought the house next door?
10. To __whom__ shall I write for the information?
11. __Whom__ have you invited?
12. To __whom__ did you give the toys?
13. __Whom__ does the baby resemble?
14. __Whom__ did you call so late?
15. __Who__ invented the X-ray machine?

Sharpening Your Skills

Write eight questions using material from social studies, science, or current events. In four sentences, use the pronoun *who* and in four, use *whom*. An example might be "*Whom* did the United States support in the Vietnam War?"

EXERCISE 42: Direct the students to tell why they chose *who* or *whom*. It is helpful to have the students rethink the sentence as declarative. For example:

1. _____ does the baby resemble?
2. The baby resembles *his/her dad*. (direct object)
3. The baby resembles *whom*?
4. *Whom* does the baby resemble?

SHARPENING YOUR SKILLS: First, the students should think of a social studies or science fact. Then, they should make it into an interrogative sentence. Let them follow the same procedure (rethinking the sentence as declarative) outlined in the notes for exercise 42. Have as many sentences as possible put on the chalkboard for discussion.

Lesson 5 Relative Pronouns

A relative pronoun joins a subordinate clause to its antecedent in the principal clause.

THE STUDENTS SHOULD LEARN

—to identify the relative pronoun and its antecedent in a sentence

—that a relative pronoun may be used as subject, direct object, object of a preposition, or possessive adjective

—the correct use of *who* and *whom* as relative pronouns

TEACHING THE LESSON

Since relative pronouns introduce adjectival clauses, this lesson could be taught in conjunction with grammar chapter 7 and writing chapter 3. Use the model diagrams in chapter 9 where helpful.

The relative pronouns are *who, whom, whose, which,* and *that.*

Study this complex sentence:

The Lincoln Memorial is a monument *that* was built to honor Abraham Lincoln.

In the above sentence, the subordinate clause is joined to the principal clause by the relative pronoun *that.*

PRINCIPAL CLAUSE: The Lincoln Memorial is a monument
SUBORDINATE CLAUSE: that was built to honor Abraham Lincoln

That is the subject of the verb *was built* in the subordinate clause. Its antecedent is *monument.* The antecedent of a pronoun is the word in the principal clause to which the pronoun refers.

The relative pronouns *who, whom,* and *whose* refer to persons.

Mother Teresa, *who* works among the poor in India, won the Nobel Peace Prize in 1979. (*Who* refers to a person; its antecedent is *Mother Teresa.*)

Mother Teresa, *whom* everyone admires, works among the poor in India. (The antecedent of *whom* is Mother Teresa.)

Mother Teresa, *whose* work among the poor is well known, won the Nobel Peace Prize in 1979. (The antecedent of *whose* is Mother Teresa.)

The relative pronoun *which* refers to animals or things.

A moat surrounds the castle, *which* was built in the Middle Ages. (*Which* refers to a thing; its antecedent is *castle.*)

The relative pronoun *that* refers to persons, animals, or things.

The man *that* left the umbrella soon came back to get it. (*That* refers to a person; its antecedent is *man.*)

Epcot Center is the attraction *that* I want to see most. (*That* refers to a thing; its antecedent is *attraction.*)

Mother Teresa

Exercise 43

Copy each sentence and underline the relative pronoun twice and its antecedent once.

1. Crude oil is obtained from wells that are drilled in the earth.
2. Extra windows, which are called storm windows, reduce the loss of heat.
3. The telescope, which is an instrument for making distant objects appear nearer and larger, was invented by Hans Lippershey.
4. A person who studies butterflies and moths is a lepidopterist.
5. The student who wrote that story is in our class.
6. Zaire, which was once called the Congo, is rich in natural resources.
7. The dog that encountered a porcupine is all healed now.
8. The orange is one fruit that was introduced into the New World from Europe.
9. There are human-powered vehicles that can fly!
10. The Lincoln penny, which was originally issued in 1909, was the first American coin with a portrait.

Exercise 44

Complete each sentence with an appropriate relative pronoun.

1. The skiers were thankful for the snow _that_ had fallen during the night.
2. Gold mines are located near Johannesburg, _which_ is a city in South Africa.
3. Do you know the names of the planets _that_ are in the solar system?
4. The first thing _that_ we did was to visit the Taj Mahal.
5. This football, _which_ we used in the game yesterday, is still too soft.
6. Millions of bats live in the Carlsbad Caverns, _which_ are located in New Mexico.
7. Scientists _who_ study the stars and planets are astronomers.
8. The person to _whom_ you spoke is my cousin.
9. Winslow Homer, _who_ painted *Snap the Whip*, is a famous American artist.
10. The man _whom_ we called Lillipus has traveled to Hollywood.

Agreement of Relative Pronouns

A relative pronoun agrees with its antecedent in person, number, and gender, but its case depends upon its use in the subordinate clause.

We will go with my *uncle, who* is an experienced sailor.

The antecedent of the relative pronoun *who* is *uncle*. To agree with its antecedent, the relative pronoun is in the third person, singular in number, and masculine in gender. The case of the relative pronoun, however, is not determined by its antecedent, but by its use in the subordinate clause. Since *who* is the subject of the verb *is* in the subordinate clause, it is in the nominative case. Even though its antecedent *uncle* is in the objective case (the object of the preposition *with*), the relative pronoun is in the nominative case.

A nineteenth century clipper ship

Study the following uses of the relative pronoun.

1. A relative pronoun may be the subject of the verb in the subordinate clause.

> Niagara Falls, *which* attracts many tourists, is on the border of New York State and Canada.

Since the relative pronoun *which* is the subject of the verb *attracts*, it is in the nominative case.

2. A relative pronoun may be a direct object in the subordinate clause.

> Sara Crewe was the main character in the book *that* I read.

Since the relative pronoun *that* is the direct object of the verb *read*, it is in the objective case.

3. A relative pronoun may be the object of a preposition.

> A greenhouse is a place in *which* plants can be grown throughout the year.

Since the relative pronoun *which* is the object of the preposition *in*, it is in the objective case.

4. The relative pronoun *whose* is used like a possessive adjective. It modifies a noun.

> May Swenson, *whose* poetry we read in class, often shapes her poems into typed pictures.

The relative pronoun *whose* modifies the noun *poetry*. Note that its antecedent, *May Swenson*, is in the principal clause. Therefore, the pronoun is third person, singular, feminine gender to agree with its antecedent.

A nineteenth century painting of Niagara Falls

Exercise 45 Relative Pronouns as Subjects

Identify the relative pronoun in each sentence, and tell its person, number, gender, and case.
1. The building, which has eight stories, has no elevator.
2. Louisa May Alcott, who wrote *Little Women*, wove a classic tale around the lives of four young women.
3. People who put off doing things are procrastinators.
4. Cyrus McCormick, who invented the reaper, was the son of a Virginia farmer.
5. Cynthia has a car that is painted black and red.
6. In Greek mythology, Pegasus was a horse that had wings.
7. The frog, which had gotten loose, hopped around the laboratory.
8. In Pisa, Italy, I climbed all three hundred steps that lead to the top of the Leaning Tower.
9. Lumberjacks who cut down trees are called fellers.
10. Green is a color that signifies hope.

Write three sentences of your own with relative pronouns as subjects.

Exercise 46 Relative Pronouns as Direct Objects

Identify the relative pronoun in each sentence, and tell its person, number, gender, and case.
1. My grandparents live in an old Victorian house, which they bought many years ago.
2. Derek hardly recognized his nephew, whom he had not seen for several years.
3. Monticello, which Thomas Jefferson designed for his home, still stands in Virginia.
4. The actor whom we met on the street gave us his autograph.
5. Some school systems have telephone numbers that students can call for help with homework.
6. Comic strips, which newspapers first published in 1894, quickly became popular.
7. Koala bears, which I saw for the first time last week in the zoo, are really adorable creatures.
8. Minerva, whom the Romans worshiped as the goddess of wisdom, had the owl as her symbol.
9. These tomatoes, which I picked yesterday, are the best of the crop.
10. The audience laughed at the joke that the comedian told.

Write three sentences with relative pronouns as direct objects.

Exercise 47 Relative Pronouns as Objects of Prepositions

Identify the relative pronoun in each sentence, and tell its person, number, gender, and case.

1. The fabric from which this shirt is made came from India.
2. Beatrix Potter, by whom Peter Rabbit was created, made many humorous drawings of animals.
3. A compass is an instrument by which directions are determined.
4. The Roman god of beginnings was called Janus, from whom the month of January takes its name.
5. The supermarket, to which I had hurried, was closed.
6. Is she the person from whom we bought our house?
7. The heart pumps blood into the lungs, from which blood rich in oxygen returns to the heart.
8. The town in which Mighty Casey struck out was Mudville.
9. Isaac Bashevis Singer, to whom the Nobel Prize for literature was given in 1978, has written many simple folktales.
10. The Chinese, about whom we are studying in social studies, have a very ancient culture.

Write three sentences of your own with relative pronouns as objects of prepositions.

Exercise 48 Relative Pronouns as Possessives

Identify the possessive form of the relative pronoun in each sentence, and tell its person, number, and gender.

1. The person whose wallet I found gave me a reward.
2. Annie Oakley, whose real name was Phoebe Anne Oakley Moses, was a famous American frontierswoman.
3. The actors whose voices you now hear are practicing for a play.
4. Anyone whose work is completed may go to the reading center.
5. Gwendolyn Brooks, whose writings deal with the black experience in America, won a Pulitzer Prize for poetry.
6. The Brantleys are the people whose house was just painted.
7. John Philip Sousa, whose rousing marches remain popular, wrote "The Stars and Stripes Forever."
8. Is she the farmer whose cow won the prize at the state fair?
9. Queen Victoria, whose reign extended for sixty-three years, is one of the most famous queens in history.
10. Zookeepers, whose job it is to care for many exotic animals, must be knowledgeable and patient.

Exercise 49

Identify the relative pronouns in the following sentences. Give the case, use, and antecedent of each.

1. It was the ancient Egyptians who first played checkers.
2. Many airliners that are used throughout the world are manufactured in Seattle.
3. Ellis Island, through which many immigrants passed, is now a national monument.
4. In Georgia, I met a man who knew your brother.
5. Pele, who scored 1,000 goals in his career, is considered the greatest soccer player of all time.
6. This headboard, which is made of oak, was carved by my grandfather.
7. The archaeologist examined the rare artifact that he found.
8. The evening meal is a sharing time, during which we relive the joys, pleasures, and experiences of the day.
9. At the camp, the soldiers had only rude huts that offered little protection from the sleet and snow.
10. Most boats that people use for pleasure sailing are constructed of fiberglass.
11. My friend Jana is an adventurer who likes hiking and climbing.
12. Is that the group with whom you study?
13. The clipper ships that were built in the early nineteenth century were then the fastest vessels on the sea.
14. Beside the barn stood a silo in which green corn was stored.
15. This morning I found my homework, which was stamped with five chocolate fingerprints.

Exercise 50

Add clauses that begin with relative pronouns to the following sentences where indicated.

1. The path∧was narrow and dark.
2. The Statue of Liberty∧stands in New York Harbor.
3. That scarf∧was the most beautiful I have ever seen.
4. This book∧was one of the most interesting I have ever read.
5. We wanted to see the movie∧.

Correct Use of the Relative
Pronouns *Who* and *Whom*

> **The relative pronoun *who* is used when the pronoun is the subject of a verb.**
>
> **The relative pronoun *whom* is used when the pronoun is the object of a verb or of a preposition.**

Carlos is the person *who* won the scholarship. (*Subject of* won)
Carlos was the person *whom* the coach nominated for the award.
(*Direct object of* nominated)

HINT: To test whether *who* or *whom* is correct, use these steps.

1. Find the subordinate clause and the antecedent.

   Joan Aiken is the writer _____ Lila recommended.

   SUBORDINATE CLAUSE: Lila recommended
   ANTECEDENT: the writer

2. Put the antecedent into the clause.

   Lila recommended the writer.

3. Determine the use of the antecedent in the clause.

   Writer is the direct object. It is in the objective case.

4. The relative pronoun should be in the case you determined in step 3.

   The relative pronoun should be in the objective case; therefore, *whom* is correct: Joan Aiken is the writer *whom* Lila recommended.

Exercise 51

Select the correct form of the relative pronoun in each sentence. Give the reason for your choice.

1. My cousin, (who, whom) I have not seen in two years, lives in Norway.
2. We were impressed by the musicians (who, whom) performed at Wolf Trap.
3. Terry is one of the gymnasts against (who, whom) I competed in the local meet.
4. The person to (who, whom) the letter is addressed has moved.
5. People (who, whom) live in the Russian city of Moscow are called Muscovites.
6. That was the salesperson to (who, whom) I spoke about the large blue and pink flowers.
7. King Arthur, about (who, whom) stories have been told for more than a thousand years, held his legendary court at Camelot.
8. Is there anyone (who, whom) knows Elaine's telephone number?
9. My mother supports the candidate (who, whom) made the powerful speech.
10. Beth spent last summer with her grandparents, (who, whom) have a home in Arizona.
11. We all need a friend (who, whom) we can trust.
12. Louis Armstrong, (who, whom) was an important jazz musician, was born in New Orleans in 1900.
13. Otto, to (who, whom) I lent some albums, has thanked me several times.
14. Juliette Gordon Low, (who, whom) began a troop of Girl Guides in 1912, is considered the founder of the Girl Scouts of America.
15. The student (who, whom) you just met has won a scholarship to art school.

Sharpening Your Skills

Look in magazines and newspapers for sentences that use relative pronouns. Cut out five sentences and paste them on a piece of paper. Underline the subordinate clause introduced by the relative pronoun, and then circle the antecedent.

Lesson 6 Pronominals

A pronominal is a pronoun that may also be used as an adjective.

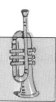

PRONOMINALS AS PRONOUNS

These are mine.
Many were present.

PRONOMINALS AS ADJECTIVES

These keys are mine.
Many people were present.

Some types of pronominals are (1) demonstrative, (2) indefinite, (3) distributive, and (4) possessive.

Demonstrative Pronouns

A demonstrative pronoun points out a definite person, place, or thing.

The demonstrative pronouns are *this*, *that*, *these*, and *those*.

> *This* is my new sleeping bag.
> *That* is the gift for grandmother.

This and *these* are used for objects that are near. *That* and *those* are used for distant objects.

Exercise 52

Identify the demonstrative pronouns in the following sentences. Tell whether each refers to an object *near* or *far*.

1. Is this a homing pigeon?
2. That was a great catch!
3. Are these your glasses?
4. This was an interesting book.
5. These need to be watered; those have had enough water.
6. This is my first attempt at the pole vault.
7. Is that a terrier?
8. I have polished those already.
9. That was a terrible movie.
10. You should practice this every day.

THE STUDENTS SHOULD LEARN
—to identify and use demonstrative, indefinite, distributive, and possessive pronouns correctly

TEACHING THE LESSON
The demonstratives, indefinites, and distributives will again be studied in chapter 3, but as adjectives. Begin to have the students study which indefinite and distributive pronouns are singular and which are plural. The need for a knowledge of "number" arises because pronouns that refer to indefinites and distributives must agree with them and because verbs must agree in number with them. The exercise on "The Correct Use of *Nothing* and *Anything*" is a review of a skill students should already have mastered.

EXERCISES 52–54: Make flash cards with the demonstrative, indefinite, and distributive pronouns on them (possessive pronouns could be included). Use the cards as a drill for the students to be able to identify each type of pronoun. Later on, the students should be able to add the "number" of each pronoun.

ANSWERS
The demonstrative pronouns are underlined. The answers below tell whether the objects they refer to are far or near.

1. near		6. near	
2. far		7. far	
3. near		8. far	
4. near		9. far	
5. near, far		10. near	

Indefinite Pronouns

> An indefinite pronoun points out no particular person, place, or thing.

Somebody left this message.
Has *everybody* prepared her work?
Everything is in order.
Nothing has been broken.
Both of the snakes are poisonous.

The most common indefinite pronouns are

all	both	much	several
another	everybody	nobody	some
any	everyone	none	somebody
anybody	everything	no one	someone
anyone	few	nothing	something
anything	many	one	

Exercise 53

Identify the indefinite pronouns in the following sentences. Tell whether each is used as a *subject* or *object*.

1. Everyone read the same book.
2. Several tried the game, but nobody succeeded in knocking over the bottles.
3. Much of my allowance is spent already.
4. Few seem interested in the new project.
5. I gave some of my peanut-butter sandwich to my friend.
6. No one answered the phone.
7. Both crawled up the wall.
8. Some were destroyed by beetles.
9. I saw someone with a parka on in the middle of summer.
10. He helped many by his charity.
11. Put everything in order before you leave.
12. Has anybody seen my left sock?
13. Something was scratching against the door.
14. All of us enjoyed the folk music.
15. You may invite one of your friends.

Distributive Pronouns

A distributive pronoun refers to each person, place, or thing separately.

The distributive pronouns are *each*, *either*, and *neither*.

> *Each* has his own ticket.
> *Either* may go.
> *Neither* of those jerseys is mine.

Exercise 54

Identify the distributive pronouns in the following sentences. Tell whether each is used as a *subject*, *indirect object*, or *direct object*.

1. Each went for a short run.
2. Neither wanted to give the Saint Bernard a bath.
3. I will take neither of these hats.
4. Either of the vacuum cleaners will do the job.
5. Neither has heard of the red-eyed fugglewhup.
6. Stanley gave each a copy of the music.
7. I do not remember either of these stories.
8. Does either of these sweaters appeal to you?
9. Each gave a different description of the robber.
10. Neither of them was present at the meeting.

The Housekeeper's Revenge

Agreement with Distributive and Indefinite Pronouns

A pronoun or possessive adjective with a distributive or indefinite pronoun as an antecedent must agree with it in person, number, and gender.

The distributive pronouns *each, either, neither* and the indefinite pronouns *one, anyone, no one, anybody, nobody, everyone, everybody, someone, somebody, everything* are always singular. Any pronoun or possessive adjective having one of those pronouns as an antecedent must be singular.

> Each is deciding on *her* topic. (The possessive adjective *her* is singular; its antecedent *each* is singular.)

> Everyone must carry *his* own equipment. (The possessive adjective *his* is singular; its antecedent *everyone* is singular.)

Indefinite pronouns, such as *all, both, few, many, several,* and *some,* are generally plural. Any pronoun or possessive adjective having one of these pronouns as an antecedent will be plural.

> Several of the students have chosen *their* topics. (The possessive adjective *their* is plural; its antecedent *several* is plural.)

When using the masculine and feminine singular possessive adjectives with singular distributive and indefinite pronouns, try to determine the gender of the antecedent. When it is impossible to determine the gender, the masculine possessive adjective or pronoun has traditionally been used. However, the form *his or her* or *he or she* is also acceptable.

> Each worker selected *his* favorite task.
> Each worker selected *his or her* favorite task.

Exercise 55

Identify the number of the indefinite or distributive pronoun in each sentence. Then choose the appropriate form of the pronoun or possessive adjective to complete the sentence.

1. Each of those photographers develops (her, their) own pictures.
2. They found everything in (its, their) place.
3. If anyone wishes to enter the contest, let (him, them) raise (his, their) hand.
4. Several have made (her, their) own travel arrangements.
5. Both have set (his, their) painting easels up on the riverbank.
6. Neither of the patients missed (her, their) appointment.
7. Somebody lost (his, their) ticket.
8. Nobody wrote (his, their) paragraph until (he, they) had made a word map.
9. All may go to (her, their) classrooms since the fire drill is over.
10. One of the books is without (its, their) cover.
11. Not one of them brought (her, their) tennis racket.
12. Each has (his or her, their) own individual style.
13. Many have already purchased (his or her, their) tickets for the game.
14. Has anybody brought (her, their) notebook with her?
15. Everyone can bring a lunch if (he or she, they) would like to.

EXERCISE 55: Have the students first determine whether the pronoun is singular or plural, and then determine which word in parentheses is singular and which is plural. Care is not always given to correct agreement when speaking, but it is essential when writing. Review the instruction in lesson 3, page 261, on the difference between possessive pronouns and possessive adjectives.

ANSWERS
The indefinite or distributive pronouns and the correct form of the pronouns or possessive adjectives are indicated by underlines. The number is given below.

1. S	9. P
2. S	10. S
3. S	11. S
4. P	12. S
5. P	13. P
6. S	14. S
7. S	15. S
8. S	

The Correct Use of *Nothing* and *Anything*

When a sentence contains a negative, such as *not* or *never*, use *anything* to express a negation.

Say "I didn't do anything" to show that you did not do anything. If you say "I didn't do nothing," you really mean that you did do something.

> I should not have said (nothing, anything) about it.

The correct form is: I should not have said *anything* about it.
The following form is also correct: I should have said *nothing* about it.

Exercise 56

EXERCISE 56: Continue to stress that a double negative cancels itself out. Answers are given in the text.

Complete each sentence with *nothing* or *anything*.
1. We never heard __anything__ so interesting before.
2. He did __nothing__ to relieve the situation.
3. There was __nothing__ in the freezer.
4. Harry never said __anything__ about his last trip to the mountains.
5. __Nothing__ will interfere with my going.
6. Hasn't __anything__ been said about the parade?
7. __Nothing__ ventured, __nothing__ gained..
8. You may not take __anything__ from this display.
9. Hasn't that worker __anything__ to do?
10. I don't know __anything__ about the movie.

Sharpening Your Skills

SHARPENING YOUR SKILLS: Let the students share their sentences with the class. Make sure they correctly express the agreement between pronoun and antecedent.

Write a sentence of your own for each combination of words.

everyone. . . his
both . . . . . . their
one . . . . its
each . . . . . . her
many. . . . . . their

Chapter Challenge

Read the selection below and then answer the questions that follow.

[1]Do you know how to make a collage? [2]It is an art that anyone can do! [3]What exactly is a collage? [4]It is a picture made by attaching paper, fabric, or any other material onto a background. [5]The materials are arranged to form a picture or a pleasing pattern. [6]*Collage* comes from the French word for "glue," but that in itself is not enough to produce one—creativity is needed. [7]A material that a new collage artist can use is newspaper. [8]Tear out a page and rub a soft white candle over its back. [9]Once this is done, flip it over and cut out the shapes you want for the collage—triangles, squares, or circles. [10]Arrange the pieces onto a black poster board (waxed side down). [11]Once you learn this technique, experiment with textured fabrics, bright materials, and different glues. [12]When you can plan your collages and get your creativity to come across in each, you may consider yourself a budding collage artist.

1. Give the person, case, and use of the personal pronoun in the first sentence.
2. There is an indefinite pronoun in the first, second, or third sentence. Identify the sentence and the pronoun.
3. Identify the interrogative pronoun in the paragraph and give its case.
4. Name the compound personal pronoun in the sixth sentence.
5. Name the demonstrative pronoun in the ninth sentence.
6. Identify the relative pronoun in the seventh sentence.
7. What kind of pronoun is *it* in the ninth sentence?
8. What kind of pronoun is *each* in the twelfth sentence?
9. Is *its* in the eighth sentence an adjective or a pronoun?
10. In the last sentence, is the pronoun *yourself* intensive or reflexive?
11. What kind of pronoun is *one* in the sixth sentence?
12. Name the relative pronoun in the second sentence and its antecedent.

Creative Space 2

Pete at the Zoo

I wonder if the elephant
Is lonely in his stall
When all the boys and girls are gone
And there's no shout at all,
And there's no one to stamp before,
No one to note his might.
Does he hunch up as I do,
Against the dark of night?

Gwendolyn Brooks

Exploring the Poem...

Why does Pete think the elephant might be lonely? What do the lines "Is lonely in his stall" and "And there's no shout at all" suggest to the reader about Pete's idea of loneliness?

What are Pete's reasons for thinking the elephant enjoys visitors? How does the elephant show off?

What does "hunch up" mean? How could an elephant hunch up against the night? How could Pete?

What is Pete saying about his own feelings toward being in the dark?

Name the sets of words that rhyme in the poem. How would you describe the way the poem rhymes (for example, each pair of lines, every other line)?

★ Write a poem about an animal that you have enjoyed watching. What feelings or thoughts did it suggest to you? End your poem with a question to show what you might be wondering about the animal's feelings or thoughts.

Make your poem rhyme. You might try to make each pair of lines rhyme, or you might use a rhyming pattern similar to the one Gwendolyn Brooks has used in "Pete at the Zoo."

Prendergast

Chapter 3

Adjectives

Lesson 1 Descriptive Adjectives

An adjective describes or limits a noun or a pronoun.

Adjectives are divided into two general classes: *descriptive adjectives* and *limiting adjectives*. Limiting adjectives will be studied in lesson 2.

A descriptive adjective describes a noun or a pronoun.

> The *glossy, black* raven is actually a *large* crow.
> The *powerful* sea engulfed the *deserted* beach.

The two kinds of descriptive adjectives are *proper* and *common* adjectives.

A proper adjective is formed from a proper noun.

A common adjective expresses the ordinary qualities of a noun or a pronoun.

PROPER ADJECTIVES	COMMON ADJECTIVES
Colombian harbor	*deep* harbor
Italian flag	*white* flag

THE STUDENTS SHOULD LEARN
—to identify and use proper and common adjectives
—to use descriptive adjectives in various positions within a sentence

TEACHING THE LESSON
Do not belabor the identification of common and proper adjectives if the students have already mastered the task. Review by putting a few proper nouns on the board from which proper adjectives can be derived: Japan, Japanese; Brazil, Brazilian; England, English, etc. Emphasis should be placed on the position of adjectives so that the students learn to vary their sentences when they are writing.

Only the impressions of people are suggested in this painting. How can adjectives bring vague impressions into sharp focus?

EXERCISE 57: For the first part, have the students make two columns on a piece of paper. In the first column, they should list the common descriptive adjectives, and in the second, the proper descriptive adjectives. For an extension of this exercise, ask the students to supply new adjectives for the ones in the sentences. Have as many sentences as possible from 11–15 put on the chalkboard.

ANSWERS

The descriptive adjectives in sentences 1–10 are underlined. The list below indicates whether they are proper or common. Any appropriate common or proper adjectives are correct for sentences 11–15.

1. C,C   6. C,C,C
2. P,C   7. C,C,C,P
3. P,C   8. C,C
4. C,C,C   9. C,P
5. C,C,C   10. C,C,C

Exercise 57

Identify the descriptive adjectives in the following sentences. Tell whether each is *proper* or *common*.

1. The set of dusty books tumbled from our rickety bookcase.
2. The Korean swimmer won the race by a wide margin.
3. Chopin was a Polish composer who wrote romantic music.
4. The little child is holding a large black hound on a leash.
5. Hot, buttery popcorn scattered everywhere when I tripped in the dark theater.
6. Pelicans have long necks and large, flat beaks.
7. The red, gold, and black colors of the German flag flew over the embassy.
8. Harper Lee's *To Kill a Mockingbird* is a sentimental story about life in a small town in the South.
9. Jupiter was the name of the principal god in Roman mythology.
10. The cold winds of January went right through Ellie's thin red scarf.

Complete the following sentences with common or proper adjectives, as indicated.

11. I like both (*proper*) food and (*proper*) food.
12. We sat on the (*common*) bench near the shore, looking at the (*common*) lake.
13. The (*proper*) gymnastics team gave a (*common*) performance.
14. The (*common*) ship sailed into the (*common*) harbor.
15. Many (*common*) cars are (*proper*).

Exercise 58

1. Use the following adjectives in sentences of your own: ancient, powerful, sincere, historic, Greek, majestic, Italian, energetic, modern, careful, weary, colorful.

2. Use an appropriate adjective with each of these nouns: story, motorcycle, stairs, brook, breeze, leaves, jewels, cherries, squirrel, ocean, lawyer, stage.

3. Write synonyms for the following adjectives: beautiful, rustic, young, violent, short, enthusiastic, delicious, bright, heroic, gentle, immense, sad, delicate.

4. Write antonyms for the following adjectives: easy, regular, prompt, restless, luminous, daring, just, intelligent, progressive, prominent, outgoing, loyal.

Position of Adjectives

1. The usual position of the adjective is before the noun.

   Twinkling stars dotted the *dark* sky.

2. Adjectives can also directly follow nouns. Adjectives after nouns are usually set off by commas.

   The man's face, *wrinkled* and *weathered*, was painted by the artist. Tina marveled at the heron, so *graceful* and *elegant*.

3. An adjective used as a subjective complement follows and completes a linking verb.

   The furniture is *old* and *valuable*.
   The mountains look *majestic*.

EXERCISE 58: The four parts of this exercise could be assigned to different groups of students, or given as a long-term project. Encourage the students to use the dictionary and thesaurus in order to increase word power.

ANSWERS
1. Sentences will vary.
2. Any appropriate adjective is acceptable.
3. Suggested synonyms:
   beautiful (lovely, fair, pretty, comely, handsome)
   rustic (pastoral, rural)
   young (youthful, immature, inexperienced, juvenile)
   violent (fierce, severe, vehement)
   short (brief, concise, terse)
   enthusiastic (ardent, zealous, intense, fervent)
   delicious (delectable, luscious, delightful, appetizing, tasty)
   bright (brilliant, luminous, radiant, sparkling, shining, glittering, glistening)
   heroic (courageous, brave, valiant, gallant, fearless, dauntless)
   gentle (mild, lenient, pleasant, agreeable, calm, serene)
   immense (huge, vast, gigantic, colossal, mammoth)
   sad (unhappy, depressed, blue, miserable)
   delicate (mild, dainty, exquisite, frail, fragile)
4. Suggested antonyms:
   easy (hard, difficult, arduous, exacting)
   regular (irregular)
   prompt (tardy, leisurely)
   restless (composed, unruffled, serene, tranquil)
   luminous (dull, lusterless, opaque)
   daring (fearful, timid, shrinking, cowardly)
   just (unjust, biased, unfair, prejudiced)
   intelligent (unintelligent, stupid, dense, dull)
   progressive (backward, conservative, reactionary)
   prominent (inconspicuous, obscure, unknown)
   outgoing (shy, withdrawn, reserved, introverted)
   loyal (disloyal, faithless, unfaithful, traitorous, fickle)

Exercise 59

Identify what noun each italicized adjective modifies. Then identify the position of the adjective as 1, 2, or 3.

1 = before the noun
2 = after the noun
3 = as a subjective complement

1. Last spring was very *rainy*.
2. This melon tastes *delicious*.
3. The *tired* scientist completed the *complex* experiment at midnight.
4. The store seems very *busy* today.
5. Aisha, *proud* and *ecstatic*, showed her friends her medal.
6. The *entire* block was decorated with *multicolored* lights.
7. My friends are *excited* over the singer's *newest* album.
8. The puzzle remained *incomplete* because of the *missing* piece.
9. A *narrow* and *winding* path led to the top of the volcano.
10. Mark, *baffled* and *annoyed*, tried to figure out the error message on the computer.
11. The Sahara Desert is *larger* than Australia.
12. In *Irish* folklore, the leprechaun is a *mischievous* fairy.
13. The speaker appeared *nervous* and *edgy* as he began to talk.
14. Rome, *fascinating* and *historic*, attracts many visitors.
15. Today's lighthouses have *massive* lanterns that produce *intense* beams.

Sharpening Your Skills

Write interesting sentences describing five objects in your bedroom. Use descriptive adjectives in a variety of positions. To get you started, here is an example:

My guitar, *nicked and scratched*, leans against an *unfinished* bookcase.

Lesson 2 Limiting Adjectives

A limiting adjective either points out an object or denotes number.

Limiting adjectives may be of several types: (1) numeral adjectives, (2) pronominal adjectives, and (3) articles.

The articles *the, an,* and *a* show whether a noun is used definitely or indefinitely.

the icicle   *an* accordion

The is the definite article. *An* and *a* are indefinite articles.

I saw exactly *the* pair of boots I wanted. (Definite: the *specific* pair)
I would like *a* pair of boots with low heels. (Indefinite: *any* such pair)

The following rules apply to articles:

1. The definite article *the* may be used with either singular or plural nouns: *the* island, *the* masks.
2. The indefinite articles *a* and *an* may be used only with singular nouns: *a* diaper, *an* engine.
3. The article *an* is used before a vowel sound: *an* igloo.
4. The article *a* is used before a consonant sound: *a* moth.

A numeral adjective denotes exact number.

five eggs   *third* row

Some numeral adjectives refer to the number of things.

There are *eleven* players on a football team.

Other numeral adjectives refer to the place of an item in a sequence.

God rested on the *seventh* day.

Pronominal adjectives will be studied in the next section.

THE STUDENTS SHOULD LEARN
—to identify types of limiting adjectives: numeral, pronominal, and articles
—when to repeat the article when working with compound elements

TEACHING THE LESSON
The students should have no problem naming numeral adjectives as well as the articles *a, an,* and *the.* If they have already studied the lesson on pronominals (grammar chapter 2, lesson 6), they should be able to recall the types of pronominal adjectives. If flash cards were made when presenting that lesson, use them as a form of review. Explain to the students that the adjectives are the same, but instead of *taking the place of a noun,* they *modify a noun.*

Exercise 60

Identify all the articles and numeral adjectives in the following
sentences.

1. There were forty cars at the starting line.
2. Let Kurt hold the snake.
3. Why is water an important natural resource?
4. Peggy celebrated her thirteenth birthday.
5. A jelly bean has ten calories.
6. Everyone will have two opportunities to try out.
7. The Amazon is a long river in South America.
8. D. W. Griffith made the first full-length movie in 1913.
9. Have you seen the exhibits?
10. A hexagon has six sides.

Complete each of the following sentences with the kind of adjective
indicated.

11. No one is sitting in the (*numeral adjective*) row.
12. The usher guided (*definite article*) patrons to their seats.
13. A short account of an interesting incident is (*indefinite article*)
    anecdote.
14. The expensive jeans cost (*numeral adjective*) dollars.
15. Kevin made (*indefinite article*) photocopy of his report.

D. W. Griffith, a pioneer
director of movies

Like articles and numeral adjectives, pronominal adjectives belong to the class of limiting adjectives.

> **A pronominal adjective may also be used as a pronoun.**

another day   *many* spectators

Words such as *this, his, each, several,* and *what* may be used either as pronouns or adjectives. When they stand alone, they are *pronouns.* When they modify nouns, they are *adjectives.*

Please give me *that.* (*That* is a pronoun.)
Please give me *that* newspaper. (*That* is an adjective that modifies the noun *newspaper.*)

Pronominal adjectives are usually divided into five classes.

> **A demonstrative adjective points out a definite person, place, or thing (*this, that, these, those*).**
>
> **A possessive adjective denotes ownership (*my, our, your, his, her, its, their*).**
>
> **A distributive adjective refers to each person, place, or thing separately (*each, every, either, neither*).**
>
> **An indefinite adjective points out no particular person, place, or thing (*any, all, another, both, few, many, much, several, some, such*, and so forth).**
>
> **An interrogative adjective is used in asking a question (*which, what, whose*).**

Exercise 61

The pronominal adjectives in the following sentences are italicized. Tell whether each is *demonstrative, possessive, distributive, indefinite,* or *interrogative.*

1. *This* bracelet should please Marilyn.
2. Has *your* story been accepted for the newspaper?
3. *What* time is it?
4. The lawn and hedge require *much* care.
5. *Each* task has *its* own difficulties.
6. *Which* galaxy contains the Earth?
7. *Whose* picture is on a ten-dollar bill?
8. The philanthropist contributed *much* money to cancer research.
9. The hurricane changed *its* direction abruptly.
10. Is *every* egg broken?
11. *Both* plans deserve careful consideration.
12. *Their* laughter was heard throughout the building.
13. *Many* varieties of fruit were on display in the street market.
14. *Every* skier should wear goggles to protect *his* or *her* eyes.
15. There are *several* types of human blood.

Exercise 62

Complete the following sentences with pronominal adjectives.

1. _____ number are you trying to reach?
2. We left _____ boots outside the porch door.
3. _____ poems by May Swenson will be read in class.
4. _____ sweater is lying on the ground?
5. Samantha will collect _____ the papers.
6. _____ weather vane is pointing north.
7. _____ knob on this radio is the volume control?
8. I like _____ song on this album.
9. We will have to wait _____ day before we call them.
10. It looks as if _____ apple on that tree is ripe.

Exercise 63

Identify all the limiting adjectives in the following sentences. Tell whether each is an *article*, a *numeral adjective*, or a *pronominal adjective*. For each pronominal adjective, identify its type: *demonstrative, possessive, distributive, indefinite,* or *interrogative.*

1. I enjoyed that astronomy lesson.
2. Which suggestion did you think was best?
3. Gordon is visiting some friends in Montreal.
4. Very few cars pass along this road.
5. Who sent those flowers?
6. The two most primitive kinds of snakes are boas and pythons.
7. Thea's grandparents celebrated their fortieth wedding anniversary.
8. Another train will leave later this afternoon.
9. Every Friday there is a Spanish club meeting.
10. Whose backpack is red?
11. The eyes of all spectators were on the tennis ball.
12. When artists glue several objects onto canvas, they are producing a collage.
13. Many plows will be needed to clear the streets of snow.
14. The first helicopter flight was achieved in 1923.
15. Each audience member was asked to fill out a survey form.
16. In the nineteenth century, many Europeans came to this country.
17. Although we blink our eyes every six seconds, we are hardly aware of doing so.
18. I read both books that I had borrowed from you.
19. That building houses the town library.
20. What topic did you choose for your report?

Repetition of the Article

The repetition of the article changes the meaning of a sentence.

> I know *the* president and manager.
> I know *the* president and *the* manager.

The first sentence, in which the article is used before the first noun only, tells us that the president and manager is one individual. The second sentence, in which the article is repeated before the second noun, tells us that the president and the manager are two distinct individuals.

Exercise 64

Determine whether or not the article in each sentence should be repeated. The number of the verb will help you tell if there are one or two individuals.

1. The principal and (the) superintendent like to meet every new student.
2. The surgeon and (the) neurologist have been called to the hospital.
3. The secretary and (the) assistant manager works in this office.
4. The president and (the) controller were present at the banquet.
5. An author and (a) lecturer was here on Tuesday.
6. The editor and (the) proofreader have not finished their work.
7. The secretary and (the) treasurer have gone home.
8. The class teacher and (the) adviser has taken a trip.
9. The owner and (the) manager is on her vacation.
10. The library and (the) magazine room is on the third floor.
11. The president and (the) dean decide who shall be accepted.
12. The lead singer and (the) guitarist has called another rehearsal.
13. An architect and (a) designer is making the plans for the new city hall.
14. The director and (the) writer of the movie has been deservedly praised.
15. The office and (the) shop were painted yesterday.

EXERCISE 64: Make sure that the students understand the difference between the two sentences in the introduction. Explain that some sentences give clues as to whether to repeat the article or not. When the verb is plural, it shows that the two nouns refer to separate individuals; when it is singular, it indicates the nouns refer to one person. The use of the plural possessive *their* indicates two separate people, while the use of *him* or *her* would indicate one and the same. (See grammar chapter 4, lesson 7, Compound Subjects with *And*.)

ANSWERS
The repetition of the article requires the use of a plural verb in the sentence. The correct answers are given below.

1. Yes	9. No
2. Yes	10. No
3. No	11. Yes
4. Yes	12. No
5. No	13. No
6. Yes	14. No
7. Yes	15. Yes
8. No	

Lesson 3 Comparison of Adjectives

Comparison is the change that adjectives undergo to express different degrees of quality, quantity, or value.

Most adjectives have three degrees of comparison: *positive, comparative,* and *superlative.*

> This is a *tall* tree. (*Positive degree*)
> This is a *taller* tree. (*Comparative degree*)
> This is the *tallest* tree in the forest. (*Superlative degree*)

> This book about lions is *fascinating.* (*Positive degree*)
> This book about lions is *more fascinating* than the one about dinosaurs. (*Comparative degree*)
> This book about lions is the *most fascinating* book I have read this year. (*Superlative degree*)

The positive degree denotes quality.

The comparative degree denotes quality in a greater or a lesser degree.

The superlative degree denotes quality in the greatest or the least degree.

Not all adjectives have comparative and superlative forms. For example, most limiting adjectives cannot be compared.

THE STUDENTS SHOULD LEARN
—to use the comparative and superlative degrees correctly
—to form the comparative and superlative degrees of regular and irregular adjectives

TEACHING THE LESSON
Elicit from the students the degrees of comparison. Put both regular and irregular adjectives in the positive degree and have the students supply the comparative and superlative degrees. Review the use of *more, most, less,* and *least* in the formation of comparative and superlative degrees. Spend sufficient time with the other irregular adjectives as presented in the next section, How Adjectives Form the Comparative and the Superlative Degrees.

The Correct Use of Comparative and Superlative Degrees

The comparative degree of the adjective is used when two things are compared. The superlative degree is used when more than two are compared.

Which of the two cities is *larger*?
Which is the *largest* city in the state?

HINT: Before the word *than*, the comparative form is always used.

The Bears are *stronger* than the Colts this year.

Exercise 65

EXERCISE 65: Have the students tell *why* each degree is used.

ANSWERS
The correct adjectives are underlined, and their degree of comparison is given below.
1. super.   9. pos.
2. pos.   10. super.
3. comp.   11. pos.
4. super.   12. comp.
5. comp.   13. super.
6. super.   14. pos., pos.
7. comp.   15. super.
8. pos., pos.

Identify all the adjectives capable of being compared in the following sentences. Tell whether each is *positive, comparative,* or *superlative.*
1. Angel Falls are the highest falls in the world.
2. An eagle has sharp vision.
3. There are fewer people on the beach now.
4. *Charlotte's Web* is the best book I've read.
5. Microwaves are shorter than radio waves.
6. Which is the quickest way to the mall?
7. A cayenne pepper is hotter than a bell pepper.
8. The pediatrician is gentle with her young patients.
9. The door has a small window near the top.
10. Is the Nile the longest river in Africa?
11. The workers are digging the foundation for the new high-rise.
12. Is the Empire State Building taller than the Eiffel Tower?
13. The French Revolution in 1789 was one of the most important events in the history of Europe.
14. Beethoven's powerful music remains popular.
15. The anthropologist gave one of the most interesting slide lectures that I have ever heard.

How Adjectives Form the Comparative and the Superlative Degrees

1. Most adjectives of one syllable and some adjectives of two syllables (generally those ending in *ow, y* and *e*) form the comparative degree by adding *er* to the positive, and the superlative degree by adding *est* to the positive.

POSITIVE	COMPARATIVE	SUPERLATIVE
narrow	narrower	narrowest
happy	happier	happiest
humble	humbler	humblest

2. Adjectives of three or more syllables, and some of two syllables, form the comparative and the superlative degrees by putting *more* and *most* or *less* and *least* before the positive form of the adjective.

POSITIVE	COMPARATIVE	SUPERLATIVE
studious	*more* studious	*most* studious
beautiful	*less* beautiful	*least* beautiful

3. Certain adjectives are compared irregularly. Those most frequently used are

POSITIVE	COMPARATIVE	SUPERLATIVE
good	better	best
little	less	least
bad, ill, evil	worse	worst
many, much	more	most
late	later, latter	latest, last
far	farther	farthest
old	older, elder	oldest, eldest
_____	*further	furthest

4. Some adjectives cannot be compared: *dead, perpendicular, supreme,* and so on.

---

*The adjective has no positive form.

EXERCISE 66: On a separate piece of paper, have the students make three columns with the headings: Positive, Comparative, and Superlative. Have them copy each word in this exercise under Positive and then complete the two other degrees.

ANSWERS

smooth—smoother, smoothest
neat—neater, neatest
sweet—sweeter, sweetest
eager—more eager, most eager
slow—slower, slowest
timid—more timid, most timid, or timider, timidest
jolly—jollier, jolliest
gentle—gentler, gentlest, or more gentle, most gentle
industrious—more industrious, most industrious
wide—wider, widest
lucky—luckier, luckiest
colorful—more colorful, most colorful
handsome—more handsome, most handsome, or handsomer, handsomest
much—more, most
clever—more clever, most clever, or cleverer, cleverest
worthy—worthier, worthiest
amiable—more amiable, most amiable
stormy—stormier, stormiest
sorry—sorrier, sorriest
expensive—more expensive, most expensive
coherent—more coherent, most coherent

EXERCISES 67 AND 68: After the students have decided upon their answers, have them tell whether *two* or *more than two* things are being compared. Direct the students to go back to exercise 67 and reconstruct each sentence, using the answer not originally chosen.

Exercise 66

Compare the adjectives listed below.

smooth	gentle	clever
neat	industrious	worthy
sweet	wide	amiable
eager	lucky	stormy
slow	colorful	sorry
timid	handsome	expensive
jolly	much	coherent

Exercise 67

Select the correct degree of the adjective in each sentence.
1. This is the (newer, newest) house on our street.
2. This red car with two doors is (less expensive, least expensive) than the blue car with four doors.
3. Joan is the (more industrious, most industrious) student of the three.
4. Is Rhode Island the (smaller, smallest) state in the United States?
5. Sherri has the (more impressive, most impressive) project in the science fair.
6. Is a diamond or a ruby (harder, hardest)?
7. Which continent is (larger, largest), Africa or South America?
8. Anthony Cappello is the (faster, fastest) runner on the track team.
9. Alicia's ant farm is (more active, most active) than Laura's.
10. That is the (riper, ripest) peach of all.

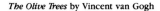
The Olive Trees by Vincent van Gogh

Exercise 68

Complete each of the following sentences with the correct degree of the adjective in parentheses.

1. These stereo speakers have the ___clearest___ (clear) sound of any in the store.
2. This is the ___most difficult___ (difficult) problem in the book so far.
3. Which is the ___longer___ (long) street, Main or Hudson?
4. Do you think van Gogh or Picasso was the ___greater___ (great) painter?
5. Let me tell you about the ___most exciting___ (exciting) vacation I've ever had.
6. The lynx is the ___smaller___ (small) of the two animals.
7. This is the ___busiest___ (busy) intersection in town.
8. Do you think Chris Evert or Martina Navratilova is the ___better___ (good) tennis player?
9. Which of you two lives ___farther___ (far) from school?
10. Yellowstone is the ___oldest___ (old) national park.

Sharpening Your Skills

Choose any five adjectives from the list in exercise 66. Write an original sentence for each one, using the adjective in either the comparative or superlative degree.

Lesson 4 More Work with Adjectives

Correct Use of *Fewer* and *Less*

> Use *fewer* when number is indicated. Use *less* when quantity is indicated.

Our team has *fewer* guards than forwards.
Julia earned *less* money this week.

HINT: *Fewer* is used with nouns in the plural form.

Exercise 69

Complete each of the following sentences with the correct adjective, *fewer* or *less*.

1. Spiders have __fewer__ legs than centipedes.
2. I had __less__ trouble with this problem.
3. This recipe requires __less__ flour than that.
4. There are __fewer__ stairs to my apartment than to yours.
5. Gil ate __less__ ice cream and __fewer__ pretzels than his brother.
6. Our teacher gave us __less__ homework than yours did.
7. __Fewer__ tourists visited Disney World this month than last month.
8. These plants require __less__ attention than those.
9. In our factory we have __less__ time for lunch than in yours.
10. There were __fewer__ guests at the party than I had expected.
11. Are there __fewer__ people living in Boston than in New York?
12. This room gets __less__ fresh air because it has __fewer__ windows.
13. We have __less__ time for practice now because the gym closes earlier.
14. __Fewer__ students qualified for the spelling contest this year.
15. That radio station plays __less__ music than this one.

Correct Use of Demonstrative Adjectives

> The demonstrative adjectives *this* and *that* agree in number with the nouns they modify. The plural of *this* is *these*; the plural of *that* is *those*.

This and *these* refer to objects that are near at hand. *That* and *those* refer to objects that are farther away.

Exercise 70

1. Complete the phrases with the correct demonstrative adjectives for the objects listed below, which are near at hand.

   <u>these</u> houses   <u>this</u> kind of paper

   <u>this</u> sort of pen   <u>this</u> ring

   <u>this</u> news   <u>these</u> tops

   <u>this</u> kind of weather   <u>these</u> kinds of stamps

   <u>these</u> types of sentences   <u>this</u> company

2. Complete the phrases with the correct demonstrative adjectives for the objects listed below, which are far away.

   <u>that</u> kind of candy   <u>those</u> kinds of programs

   <u>those</u> cities   <u>those</u> boxes

   <u>that</u> bar of soap   <u>those</u> plants

   <u>that</u> painting   <u>that</u> toothbrush

   <u>that</u> style of coat   <u>that</u> type of book

Select the correct form of the demonstrative adjective and give the reason for your choice.

1. Rodney does not like (this, these) flavor of ice cream.
2. (This, These) brand of tea is from England.
3. (That, Those) types of lemons are very juicy.
4. (This, These) style of jeans is no longer popular.
5. (This, These) types of plants grow in the tropics.
6. Do (that, those) breeds of dogs make good house pets?
7. (That, Those) kinds of problems are difficult for Cheryl.
8. Shall I buy (this, these) type of radio?
9. (That, Those) kinds of stories always amuse me.
10. I always drink (this, these) kind of juice.

Words Used as Nouns and Adjectives

The use of a word in a sentence determines the part of speech. The same word may frequently be used as a noun or an adjective.

> The *circus* is in town for a week.
> *Circus* animals are well trained.

In the first sentence, *circus* is the name of a traveling show and is therefore a noun. *Circus* in the second sentence describes *animals* and is an adjective.

Exercise 71

EXERCISE 71: A good portion of the words in the English language can be used as more than one part of speech. Lead the students to understand that the part of speech of a word is dependent upon its use in the sentence. Parts of speech are not absolute.

ANSWERS

1. adj.	9. noun
2. noun	10. adj.
3. noun	11. noun
4. adj.	12. adj.
5. noun	13. noun
6. adj.	14. adj.
7. adj.	15. adj.
8. noun	

Decide whether each italicized word is a noun or an adjective.

1. The inexperienced chairperson displayed unusual *executive* ability.
2. The governor is the chief *executive* in the state.
3. Juan Perez owns a large *orchard*.
4. The apple is an *orchard* fruit.
5. Brazil is the largest *country* in South America.
6. How we enjoyed a real *country* breakfast!
7. Some *radio* antennae are collapsible.
8. I have a shortwave *radio* in my room.
9. It is not unusual for a *cucumber* to become a pickle.
10. People in Britain often eat a *cucumber* sandwich or two at tea time.
11. A tapestry with scenes from Aesop's fables covered the *wall*.
12. The principal purchased a new *wall* hanging for the library.
13. The *light* streamed into the room through the large windows.
14. The *light* switch is to the left of the door.
15. A photographer uses a *light* meter to check the level of brightness.

Sharpening Your Skills

SHARPENING YOUR SKILLS: Have the students write their sentences on the chalkboard. See if they are able to use a demonstrative adjective or *fewer* or *less* in some sentences. For example:

> *Less gold* was found in *this* mine than the other.

For each word below, write two sentences—one in which the word is used as an adjective and the other in which the word is used as a noun. In some sentences, also use a demonstrative adjective or the word *fewer* or *less*.

gold	bank
garden	summer

304

Chapter Challenge

Read the selection below and then answer the questions that follow.

¹The humorous writings of Samuel Clemens, who is known to the world as Mark Twain, have entertained countless readers for over a century. ²This great American writer was raised in Hannibal, Missouri, a small town on the west bank of the Mississippi River. ³Here, young Clemens grew enchanted with life on the sprawling Mississippi; in fact, many of his later books would feature the Mississippi and the unusual characters who called it home.

⁴Clemens's most famous books, *The Adventures of Tom Sawyer* and *The Adventures of Huckleberry Finn*, relate the story of two Missouri youths and their lively escapades. ⁵Each boy longs for excitement, and discovers it in the haunted graveyards and dark caves that surround his town. ⁶Although these characters lived in another century, their experiences and adventures amuse today's readers throughout the world.

1. Find a demonstrative adjective in the second sentence.
2. What type of adjective is *humorous* in the first sentence?
3. Name a definite article in the second sentence.
4. Find a demonstrative adjective in the sixth sentence. Is it singular or plural?
5. Find a possessive adjective in the fifth sentence.
6. Compare the adjective *unusual* in the third sentence.
7. What type of adjective is *American* in the second sentence?
8. What is the distributive adjective in the fifth sentence?
9. Find an indefinite adjective in the sixth sentence.
10. Compare the adjective *great* in the second sentence.
11. Find an adjective in the superlative degree in the second paragraph.
12. Find the adjective in the positive degree in the fourth sentence.

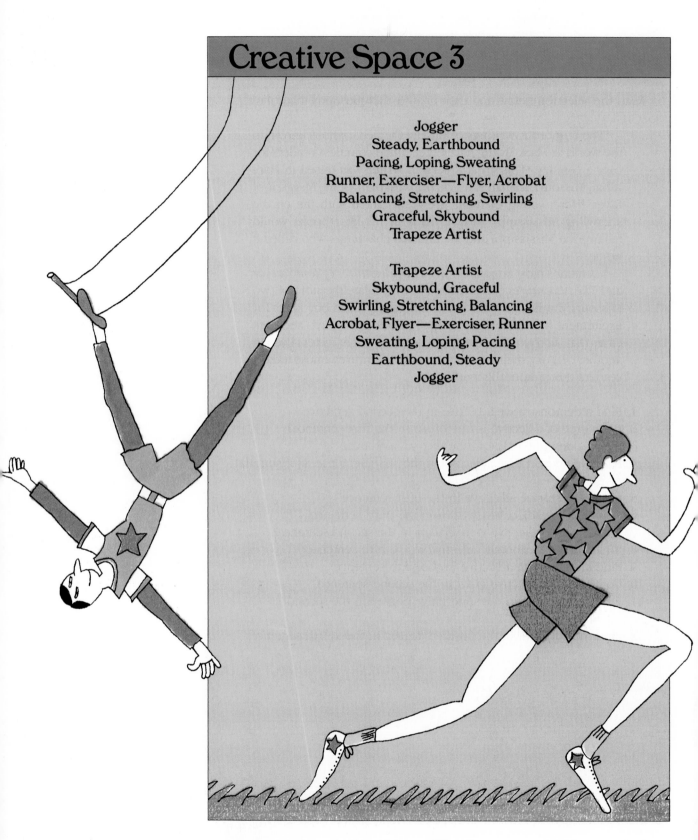

Creative Space 3

Jogger
Steady, Earthbound
Pacing, Loping, Sweating
Runner, Exerciser—Flyer, Acrobat
Balancing, Stretching, Swirling
Graceful, Skybound
Trapeze Artist

Trapeze Artist
Skybound, Graceful
Swirling, Stretching, Balancing
Acrobat, Flyer—Exerciser, Runner
Sweating, Loping, Pacing
Earthbound, Steady
Jogger

Exploring the Poem...

Each of the two parts of the poem is in the shape of a diamond. For each line of the poem, what part of speech is used? Which lines contain nouns? Which lines seem like verbs? Which lines are adjectives? What pattern do you notice within the lines of the poem?

The jogger and the trapeze artist have different styles. What is the essential difference between the jogger and the trapeze artist? Point out the words in the poem that are opposites or that have contrasting meanings. Which line is the turning point in each part of the poem? What idea does the form of the poem help to convey?

★ Can you think of two other people, places, or things that can be compared as opposites? Create a diamond-shaped poem composed of words that describe both. When you have finished, you should be able to create a second diamond from the first by reversing the order of the words.

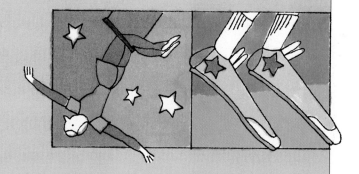

307

Chapter 4

Verbs

Lesson 1 Working with Verbs

A verb is a word that expresses action, being, or state of being.

The street artist *draws* portraits of passersby. (*Action*)
Nylon *is* a human-made fiber. (*Being*)
The cat often *stays* in a basket by the radiator. (*State of being*)

One special kind of verb is an auxiliary verb.

> **Any verb used with another verb is called an auxiliary verb.**

The workers *have painted* the outside of our house.

In the sentence above, the complete verb, or verb phrase, is *have painted*. *Have* is an auxiliary verb. *Painted* is the main verb.

The house *was painted* blue with white trim.

In the sentence above, the verb phrase is *was painted*. The auxiliary verb is *was*. The main verb is *painted*.

Auxiliary verbs come before main verbs. They are used to indicate tense, voice, and mood, which you will study later in this chapter. The common auxiliary verbs are

be	are	have	do	will	would
am	was	has	did	may	might
is	were	had	should	can	could

THE STUDENTS SHOULD LEARN
—the identification, correct forms, and proper use of regular and irregular verbs
—the correct use of troublesome verbs
—to distinguish between a word used both as a noun and as a verb

TEACHING THE LESSON
Students should have already mastered the identification of verbs and verb phrases. When teaching regular and irregular verbs, spend time with the extensive list of irregular verbs, especially the verb *to be*, as well as verbs that have two choices for past and past participle. Have the students give oral sentences for some of the more difficult irregular verbs. Have flash cards printed for easy review of the troublesome verbs.

How do patience and perseverance contribute to the excitement of windsurfing? What other experiences in your life require these qualities?

EXERCISE 72: This exercise reviews identification of verbs. Make sure the students recognize the various auxiliary verbs.

Exercise 72

Identify the verbs and verb phrases in the following sentences. In each verb phrase, identify the auxiliary verb.

1. Silhouette art <u>uses</u> a common, everyday material—paper.
2. Before photographs, silhouette portraits <u>were</u> popular.
3. People <u>wanted</u> silhouette portraits of their family members.
4. Few people <u>could afford</u> the services of a portrait artist.
5. The silhouette portrait <u>became</u> an inexpensive substitute for a painting.
6. The subject of the portrait <u>would sit</u> before a candle.
7. The shadow of that person's face <u>was cast</u> against a paper on the wall.
8. Another person simply <u>traced</u> the outline of the shadow.
9. The area in the outline often <u>was painted</u> a dark color.
10. You <u>can make</u> a silhouette portrait with the same method.
11. You <u>might use</u> a lamp instead of a candle.
12. You simply <u>put</u> a piece of paper on the wall behind your subject's head.
13. Then you <u>can trace</u> the outline.
14. The subject of your portrait <u>should sit</u> absolutely still!
15. Otherwise, the shadow <u>might move</u> out of place.

Regular and Irregular Verbs

The present, past, and past participle are the basic forms of a verb. These forms are called the principal parts of a verb. According to the way in which the principal parts are formed, verbs may be either *regular* or *irregular*.

> **A regular verb forms its past and its past participle by adding *d* or *ed* to the present form.**

PRESENT	PAST	PAST PARTICIPLE
walk	walked	walked
plow	plowed	plowed

> **An irregular verb does not form its past and its past participle by adding *d* or *ed* to the present form.**

PRESENT	PAST	PAST PARTICIPLE
choose	chose	chosen
sing	sang	sung

The past forms of both regular and irregular verbs can stand alone.

The choir *walked* onto the stage.
They *sang* songs from musicals.

The past participles of both regular and irregular verbs are used with auxiliary verbs.

Fields *were* plowed by oxen and horses in the past.
Some people *have* chosen a career at a very early age.

Listed below are the principal parts of the more common irregular verbs. They should be thoroughly mastered.

PRESENT	PAST	PAST PARTICIPLE
am (is, be)	was	been
awake	awoke, awaked	awaked, awoken
beat	beat	beat, beaten
begin	began	begun
bend	bent	bent
bet	bet	bet
bind	bound	bound
bite	bit	bitten
blow	blew	blown
break	broke	broken
bring	brought	brought
build	built	built
burn	burned, burnt	burned, burnt
burst	burst	burst
catch	caught	caught
choose	chose	chosen
come	came	come
do	did	done
draw	drew	drawn
dream	dreamed, dreamt	dreamed, dreamt
drink	drank	drunk
drive	drove	driven
eat	ate	eaten
fall	fell	fallen
find	found	found
fly	flew	flown
forget	forgot	forgotten
freeze	froze	frozen
give	gave	given
go	went	gone
grow	grew	grown
hang	hung	hung
have	had	had
hear	heard	heard
hide	hid	hidden, hid
hold	held	held

PRESENT	PAST	PAST PARTICIPLE
hurt	hurt	hurt
keep	kept	kept
kneel	knelt, kneeled	knelt, kneeled
know	knew	known
lay	laid	laid
leave	left	left
lend	lent	lent
let	let	let
lie (recline)	lay	lain
lose	lost	lost
make	made	made
mean	meant	meant
meet	met	met
read	read	read
ride	rode	ridden
ring	rang	rung
rise	rose	risen
run	ran	run
say	said	said
see	saw	seen
shake	shook	shaken
sing	sang	sung
sink	sank	sunk
sit	sat	sat
speak	spoke	spoken
stand	stood	stood
steal	stole	stolen
stick	stuck	stuck
swim	swam	swum
swing	swung	swung
take	took	taken
teach	taught	taught
tear	tore	torn
throw	threw	thrown
wear	wore	worn
win	won	won
wring	wrung	wrung
write	wrote	written

EXERCISE 73: For extended review, direct the students to read each sentence twice, once using the verb in the past form, and again using the past participle form. When they are using the past participle form, have the students also name the auxiliary verb.

Exercise 73

Complete each of the following sentences with the past tense or the past participle of the irregular verb at the left.

drive
1. In an international auto race in 1895, the driver of the winning car __drove__ at a top speed of fifteen miles an hour.

drink
2. The lady in the fairy tale had __drunk__ a magic potion.

choose
3. Each student __chose__ a book on which to report.

go
4. Frank has __gone__ to see the electronics show.

write
5. The airplane had __written__ a message in the sky above the stadium.

sing
6. Clarissa has __sung__ in the church choir five years.

bite
7. Were you __bitten__ by as many mosquitoes as I was?

say
8. Tim __said__ the tongue twister a total of ten times.

see
9. I had never __seen__ a four-leaf clover before.

give
10. The students have __given__ their old clothes to the needy.

begin
11. The first labor union __began__ in 1868 in England.

swing
12. The batter __swung__; the umpire called a strike.

hang
13. Onalee __hung__ the door on its hinges.

know
14. David has __known__ about his surprise birthday party for some time.

wear
15. Laura __wore__ her grandmother's wedding dress.

speak
16. My parakeet has __spoken__ its first word!

bring
17. Have you __brought__ the game for us to play?

freeze
18. The water in the birdbath has __frozen__.

do
19. I __did__ the dishes every night this week.

eat
20. Have the guests __eaten__ all the popcorn?

fall
21. More than 150 inches of rain __fell__ on Cherrapunji, India, in just five days.

break
22. I was upset because I had __broken__ my favorite mug.

run
23. They have never __run__ in a three-legged bag race.

grow
24. Jack's bean stalk has __grown__ very quickly.

sink
25. The rope __sank__ into the quicksand.

tear
26. Maureen has __torn__ her sister's favorite shirt while wearing it without permission.

shake
27. The windows of the seaside cottage were __shaken__ by the wind.

swim
28. In ancient Greece, soldiers __swam__ as part of their training.

forget
29. I have __forgotten__ where I put the key to my diary.

fly
30. In 1986, a plane __flew__ around the world without refueling.

Troublesome Verbs

The following verbs are often confused. Study these pairs of verbs.

Lie, lay, lain	Lay, laid, laid

The verb *lie* means to *rest* or *recline*. It is always intransitive. (This means it has no direct object to complete its meaning.)

> The dollar *had lain* there all day, unnoticed.

The verb *lay* means to *put* or *place* something in position. It is usually transitive. (This means it has a direct object to complete its meaning.)

> Greta *laid* the ingredients on the table.

Sit, sat, sat	Set, set, set

The verb *sit* means to *have* or *keep* a seat. It is usually intransitive.

> I *sat* in the only empty seat.

The verb *set* means to *place* or *fix* in position. It is usually transitive.

> Please *set* the ladder against the wall.

Rise, rose, risen	Raise, raised, raised

The verb *rise* means to *ascend*. It is always intransitive.

> The diver *rose* to the surface of the water.

The verb *raise* means to *lift*. It is usually transitive.

> I *raised* the picture several inches.

Let, let, let   Leave, left, left

The verb *let* means to *permit* or *allow*.

> *Let* me try to loosen the cap.

The verb *leave* means to *abandon* or *depart from*.

> Ryan *left* his flippers at home.
> The bus will *leave* the terminal in ten minutes.

Teach, taught, taught   Learn, learned, learned

The verb *teach* means to *give* instruction.

> Mom *taught* us how to tie a cat's-paw knot.

The verb *learn* means to *receive* instruction.

> I've already *learned* how to do algebra.

Borrow, borrowed, borrowed   Lend, lent, lent

The verb *borrow* means to *obtain* the use of something *from* another person.

> I *borrowed* a Dracula costume from Bela.

The verb *lend* means to give another person something to use for a time.

> Bela *lent* me his black shoes to go with the costume.

Exercise 74

Select the correct verb form in each of the following sentences.

1. Edna (sat, set) in the beanbag chair.
2. Leaves of many colors (lay, laid) on the ground.
3. Has the hose (lain, laid) there since yesterday?
4. The cat is (laying, lying) on top of the piano.
5. Edgar (set, sat) the fork on the left side of the plate.
6. The spectators let out a gasp as the balloon (rose, raised).
7. He has (laid, lain) the wood in the fireplace.
8. Many Americans follow tradition and (rise, raise) their flags on Flag Day, June 14.
9. Charles, (lie, lay) the present under the Christmas tree.
10. Will you (lend, borrow) me your dictionary?
11. (Leave, Let) me look through the telescope.
12. (Learn, Teach) us how to count to ten in Spanish.
13. Flowers are (raised, risen) in southern France for the perfume industry.
14. The treasure had (laid, lain) on the ocean floor for centuries.
15. The snow that (lay, laid) on the ground served as a good insulator to protect the plants underneath the soil.
16. The worker is (laying, lying) the rug on the newly polished floor.
17. Please do not (rise, raise) your hands from the handlebars!
18. (Let, Leave) Martha sit by the window.
19. Edwin, do not (leave, let) your fencing gear on the floor!
20. Everyone (raised, rose) to take the oath of citizenship.
21. Gary (borrowed, lent) five dollars from Bob to buy a videocassette.
22. Mario, (lend, borrow) me your copy of the skateboard magazine.
23. My cousin (learned, taught) me how to play horseshoes.
24. I have (learned, taught) all four stanzas of the Star-Spangled Banner in less time than I thought possible.
25. Sheila (borrowed, lent) Anne her extra umbrella.

EXERCISE 74: This exercise can be used in conjunction with lesson 2 of the chapter. However, to use the verbs correctly, the students do not necessarily need to master transitive and intransitive verbs. Spend sufficient time distinguishing between the verbs *lie* and *lay*. The verb *lie* rarely takes an object (intransitive) and the verb *lay* usually has an object (transitive). After the students complete the exercise, reinforce the correct use of these verbs by having the students write original sentences for those verbs that cause them the most difficulty.

Words Used as Verbs and Nouns

A verb generally expresses action or being. A noun is a name word. The same word may frequently be used as either a verb or a noun. The use of a word in a sentence determines its part of speech.

Study these examples.

> The youth would *dream* of a future as a singer. (*Verb*)
> I had a *dream* about riding in a roller coaster. (*Noun*)

In the first sentence, *dream* is part of the verb phrase. One clue to its part of speech is that it follows the auxiliary verb *would*. In the second sentence, *dream* is a noun. One clue that it is a noun is that it follows the limiting adjective *a*. Nouns often follow adjectives.

Exercise 75

Tell whether each italicized word is a verb or a noun.
1. All four of us watched the *parade* from Aunt Louise's balcony.
2. The younger children will *parade* in their Halloween costumes.
3. The companies did *ship* many flower bulbs in January.
4. An old sailing *ship* has entered the harbor.
5. Fairy tales usually *end* happily.
6. The *end* of many of O. Henry's stories has a clever twist.
7. The *picture* that Marla bought at the street fair needs a frame.
8. Can you *picture* yourself as a time traveler going back to King Arthur's court?
9. The colors of the Painted Desert *change* with the time of day.
10. There was a *change* in the color of the mixture during the experiment.

Write original sentences using each of the words below, first as a noun and then as a verb.

ride	travels
nail	capture

Sharpening Your Skills

You have just witnessed a fire in a nearby building. In about six sentences, tell what the firefighters were doing. Use regular and irregular verbs, as well as some troublesome verbs.

Lesson 2 Transitive, Intransitive, and Linking Verbs

Transitive Verbs

> A transitive verb expresses an action that passes from a doer to a receiver.

DOER	ACTION	RECEIVER
The president	saw	the visitor.

Saw is a transitive verb because the action passes from the doer, *president*, to the receiver, *visitor*. In the sentence above, the receiver is the *direct object*. If a verb has a direct object, the verb is transitive. To determine if there is a direct object, ask *whom* or *what* after the verb. The president saw *whom*? The answer is *visitor*.

Sometimes the receiver of the action is the *subject*. The action will pass from the doer to the receiver in a different way.

RECEIVER	ACTION	DOER
The visitor	was seen	by the president.

In this sentence, like the one above, *visitor* is the receiver of the action and *president* is the doer. Since the action passes from the doer to the receiver in both sentences, the verb *see*, whether in the form of *saw* or *was seen*, is a transitive verb. It is important to remember that the *receiver* of the action may be in two different positions in the sentence—*subject* or *direct object*.

Sometimes when the verb is transitive, the doer is not expressed.

> The game *was canceled*. (*Doer is not expressed*.)
> The game *was canceled* by the coach. (*Doer is expressed*.)

Exercise 76

Each italicized verb is transitive. Identify the receiver and tell whether it is the *direct object* or the *subject* of the sentence.

1. Rome *ruled* the ancient Western world.
2. The ancient Western world *was ruled* by Rome.
3. The Pantheon *was built* by the Romans in honor of their gods.
4. In honor of their gods, the Romans *built* the Pantheon.
5. Gladiators *fought* wild animals in the Colosseum.
6. Wild animals *were fought* by gladiators in the Colosseum.
7. The many ruins *are* now *surrounded* by trees and gardens.
8. Trees and gardens now *surround* the many ruins.
9. Remains of ancient Rome *can* still *be seen*.
10. Tourists *can* still *see* the remains of ancient Rome.

Each italicized verb is transitive. Identify the receiver and tell whether it is a *direct object* or a *subject*.

11. Fish *are identified* by scientists as vertebrates.
12. Biologists *observe* many different shapes in fish.
13. Some fish *resemble* pancakes in flatness; others *are inflated* like balloons.
14. Some fish *can be compared* to lumpy rocks in appearance; others *can be compared* to wriggly worms.
15. Fish *have* many different colors, too.
16. Marine biologists *have found* scales of rich reds, yellows, blues, and purples.
17. These colors *are combined* in stripes, dots, and intricate lace patterns.
18. Of course, water *is needed* by fish as a habitat.
19. Fish *inhabit* almost all waters.
20. Some fish *prefer* the near-freezing waters of the Arctic; the steaming rivers of the tropical jungles *are preferred* by others.

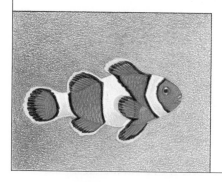

Intransitive Verbs

> **An intransitive verb has no receiver of the action.**

DOER	ACTION	RECEIVER
The president	worked at his desk.	(*none*)

The subject, *president*, is the doer of the action. There is nothing or no one receiving the action; therefore, the verb is intransitive. If you ask *whom* or *what* after the verb, there is no answer: worked *whom* or *what*? Since there is no answer, the verb is intransitive.

It is important to remember that the receiver may *not* be a prepositional phrase or an adverb. Notice that in each sample sentence below, there is no noun as the receiver of the action.

The kangaroo bounced through the forest.
The crowd cheered wildly.

Exercise 77

Identify the verbs and tell why they are intransitive.
1. During the week, temperatures had dropped below freezing.
2. The water on Rose Tree Lake froze solidly.
3. On Saturdays, skaters came from near and far.
4. In warm sweaters and hats, they glided across the surface.
5. On this winter day, experts and amateurs skated happily together.

Identify the italicized verbs as *transitive* or *intransitive*. The verb is transitive if it has a receiver; it is intransitive if it has no receiver.
6. I *walked* into the kitchen, looking for something to eat.
7. The thought of a delicious cheesesteak sandwich *came* to me.
8. In the freezer I *found* thin sandwich steaks.
9. I *sliced* a sweet Bermuda onion.
10. I *fried* the steak and onions.
11. The steak and onions *were* then *placed* on a fresh roll, and melted cheese *was added*.
12. As I *sat* down to enjoy my creation, my little brother *walked* in.
13. Without a word, he *stared* hungrily at me.
14. Yes, I *gave* him the sandwich, and I *made* myself another one.
15. I *ate* that one quickly before anyone else *came*.

TEACHING THE LESSON
An intransitive verb has *no receiver* of the action. In most cases, a doer is expressed, but there is no receiver in the direct object position. Adverbs and prepositional phrases will often follow the intransitive verb.

EXERCISE 77: In the first part of the exercise, lead the students to see that these verbs are intransitive because they have no receivers. Remind them that receivers cannot be prepositional phrases or adverbs. After the students have completed the exercise, have them list the verbs and then read them aloud. This will help give them a sense of the type of verb that is often intransitive. In the second part, remind the students that if the verb is transitive, the receiver may be the direct object or the subject. After they have determined which verbs are transitive and which are intransitive, list examples of both types on the chalkboard.

In sentence 14, *him* and *myself* are indirect objects. The direct objects are *sandwich* and *one*.

ANSWERS
For sentences 1–5, the verbs are underlined. The answers for sentences 6–15 are given below.
6. I   11. T, T
7. I   12. I, I
8. T   13. I
9. T   14. T, T
10. T   15. T, I

Verbs That Can Be Transitive or Intransitive

Sometimes the same verb can be transitive or intransitive depending on how it is used in the sentence.

> DOER   RECEIVER
>
> The team *played* a game of volleyball. (*Transitive*)

> DOER   NO RECEIVER
>
> The team *played* here yesterday. (*Intransitive*)

Exercise 78

The verbs in the following sentences can be used both as transitive and intransitive verbs. Identify the verb in each sentence and tell whether it is *transitive* or *intransitive*.

1. Lee, a dedicated gymnast, practices regularly.
2. Lee practices somersaults in the gym.
3. The drummers beat their drums throughout the ceremony.
4. The rain beat heavily on the roof.
5. My neighbors grow tomatoes in their garden.
6. Tomatoes grow in practically all parts of the United States.
7. James Herriot writes about his work as a country veterinarian.
8. James Herriot wrote the book *All Creatures Great and Small*.
9. We rushed to the window at the sound of the sirens.
10. The television special on the president's visit to China was rushed into production by the station.
11. The hunchback of Notre Dame rang the bell in the cathedral daily.
12. My alarm clock always rings too early.
13. The marathon runner dropped to the ground at the end of the race.
14. Lilian, the winner, dropped all ten clothespins into the bottle.
15. The mail carrier dropped the letters into the mail slot.

Linking Verbs

> A linking verb links a subject to a subjective complement.

The subjective complement describes or renames the subject. It may be a noun, pronoun, or adjective.

SUBJECT	LINKING VERB	COMPLEMENT
Jeff Hansen	was	the *instructor*. (*Noun*)
It	is	*he*. (*Pronoun*)
Velvet	feels	*soft*. (*Adjective*)

The verb *be* in its various forms is the most common linking verb. Other verbs that may be used as linking verbs are *appear, become, continue, feel, grow, look, remain, seem, smell, sound,* and *taste.* When these verbs are used as linking verbs, some part of the verb *be* can be substituted for the original verb: "The velvet *feels* smooth" can be changed to "The velvet *is* smooth."

Exercise 79

Identify the linking verb in each of the following sentences. Tell whether the complement is a *noun*, a *pronoun*, or an *adjective*.

1. Okefenokee Swamp is a sanctuary for many animals.
2. Jackie Robinson was an exciting baseball player.
3. That is she by the pillar.
4. The potato chips from the vending machine tasted stale.
5. The houses seem tiny from the airplane.
6. Joy Adamson is the writer of a famous book about lions.
7. My family became friendly with our new neighbors.
8. The game of marbles remains popular with children.
9. Lee feels unhappy at the thought of a day indoors.
10. In old tales, the fox is sly and cunning.

Complete the following sentences with appropriate complements.

11. The room in the abandoned mansion was _____.
12. The person who designed the bulletin board was _____.
13. The fruit in the bowl on the table looks _____.
14. I am a very talented _____.
15. The month of April is always _____.

Exercise 80

Classify the verbs in the following sentences as *transitive*, *intransitive*, or *linking*.

1. Anita <u>runs</u> around the block every day for exercise.
2. Harry <u>returned</u> all ten books to the library.
3. My sister <u>received</u> a lifesaving certificate.
4. The weather <u>remained</u> hot into October.
5. The Ferris Wheel <u>was</u> the hit of the Columbian Exposition in Chicago in 1893.
6. The snake <u>slithered</u> down the hole.
7. The ice <u>looks</u> thin and unsafe.
8. Every hill <u>has</u> its valley.
9. The overworked carriage horse <u>deserves</u> a long rest.
10. The milers <u>raced</u> through the streets of New York.
11. The directions <u>are</u> long and complicated.
12. In the yard <u>hangs</u> the old swing.
13. Bill Cosby <u>is</u> an actor and a writer.
14. The study of celestial bodies <u>is</u> astronomy.
15. Sandra Day O'Connor <u>was appointed</u> to the Supreme Court in 1981.

Sharpening Your Skills

In the paragraph below, identify each italicized verb (or main verb in a verb phrase) as

1. a regular or an irregular verb
2. an action or a linking verb

Then identify each action verb as *transitive* or *intransitive*.

[1]Have you ever wondered why animals *develop* certain characteristics? [2]Nature *provides* animals, like people, with the qualities necessary for survival. [3]For instance, the whiskers on a catfish *are* really feelers that let it know what is happening around it. [4]The octopus *squirts* a dark, inklike substance, and in this way it *hides* from its enemies. [5]Aside from this, the octopus *uses* another means of protection. [6]It *can move* quickly backward by shooting a stream of water from its back. [7]The brilliant colors of some fish *warn* predators of their poisonous nature. [8]Reptiles with long, sleek bodies *can escape* danger quickly. [9]Even tortoises *are protected* by their thick, hard shells. [10]The various kinds of animal defenses *seem* very clever to us, for they *show* us nature's ingenuity.

Lesson 3 Active and Passive Voice

Voice shows whether the *subject* is the doer or the receiver of the action.

> In the active voice, the subject is the *doer* of the action.
>
> In the passive voice, the subject is the *receiver* of the action.

THE STUDENTS SHOULD LEARN
—to identify verbs in the active and passive voice
—to write sentences using both active and passive voice verbs

Kelly *threw* the ball. (*Active voice: the subject is the doer.*)
The ball *was thrown* by Kelly. (*Passive voice: the subject is the receiver.*)

In the first sentence, *Kelly*, the *subject*, is the *doer* of the action *threw*. The verb, therefore, is in the *active* voice. In the second sentence the subject *ball* is the *receiver* of the action *was thrown*. The verb is, therefore, in the *passive* voice.

Paul painted the fence. (*Active voice*)
The fence was painted by Paul. (*Passive voice*)

TEACHING THE LESSON
Give the students a context for the words *active* and *passive*. Have them imagine that they went to the pet store to buy a kitten. They see two. One kitten is pushing a small ball of string, then chasing it, and pouncing on it. The other kitten is just quietly watching. The first kitten can be described as active; the other described as passive. In grammar, some verbs are called *active voice* verbs, and others are called *passive voice* verbs. Write the following on the chalkboard.

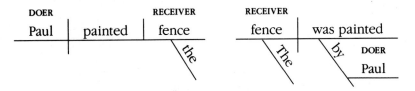

In both sentences, *Paul* performs the action, and the *fence* receives the action. In the first sentence, *Paul* is the subject of the verb *painted*. In the second sentence, *Paul* is the object of the preposition *by*. In the first sentence, *fence*, the receiver of the action, is the direct object of the active verb *painted*. In the second sentence, *fence* becomes the subject of the passive verb *was painted*.

A
The kitten *batted* the string.
The kitten *chased* the string.

B
The kitten *was lifted* gently.
The kitten *was held* carefully.

Ask the students the following:
In which group are the subjects the *doers*?   A
In which group are the subjects the *receivers*?   B

Since Group A subjects are *doers*, the verbs are called *active voice* verbs. Since Group B subjects are *receivers* of the action, these verbs are called *passive voice* verbs. An active voice verb is usually stronger and "more alive" than a.passive voice verb.

Study the following examples of the active and the passive voice.

ACTIVE: Allison *weeds* the garden.
PASSIVE: The garden *is weeded* by Allison.
ACTIVE: Gretchen *will write* the computer program.
PASSIVE: The computer program *will be written* by Gretchen.
ACTIVE: My pig *has won* several blue ribbons.
PASSIVE: Several blue ribbons *have been won* by my pig.

Usually sentences in the active voice are more alive, exciting, and direct. You should use the passive voice sparingly in your writing.

Exercise 81

Rewrite the following sentences. Change the verbs from the passive to the active voice by placing the *doer* in the subject position. The first one has been done for you.

1. PASSIVE VOICE: The fields are covered with daisies.
   ACTIVE VOICE: Daisies cover the fields.
2. The large pink conch shell was found by Margaret.
3. Educational TV programs are watched by millions of children.
4. Captain Hook's hand was bitten off by a crocodile.
5. Nearly three hundred products were made from peanuts by George Washington Carver!
6. The barrel of popcorn will be eaten by the monkeys.
7. The photographers were guided by a native to the zebras' watering hole.
8. The assembly had been planned by the eighth-graders.
9. Tourists are carried from England to France by hydrofoils.
10. The Chinese proverb will be explained by Mr. Ling.
11. This gold bracelet has been lost by a gypsy.
12. Our azalea bushes were trimmed by Chance, the gardener.
13. The Soap Box Derby was begun in 1934 by a newspaper photographer.
14. Firecrackers were invented by whom?
15. The police chief was interviewed by Doris.

Formation of the Passive Voice

Study the following passive voice verb phrases:

are covered   has *been* covered
was found   had *been* decorated
is eaten   will *be* explained

What kind of verb is italicized in each?
What part of the main verb is used?

Use this pattern when you construct passive voice verbs:

> **Passive Voice = form of the verb *be* + past participle of the main verb**

The forms of the verb *be* are *be, am, is, are, was, were, being, been*.

Exercise 82

Change the verbs in these sentences from the active voice to the passive voice. The subject will *not* be the *doer*. The subject will be the *receiver*. The first one has been done for you.

  1. ACTIVE VOICE: DOER
                     Our team *lost* the game.
     PASSIVE VOICE: RECEIVER
                     The game *was lost* by our team.
  2. The chorus recited a silly poem.
  3. Navaho artists make colorful rugs.
  4. Charlene trained the dog to sit.
  5. Charles Dickens wrote *A Christmas Carol* in 1843.
  6. Kyle will invent a new game for the party.
  7. Greek soldiers constructed a huge wooden horse.
  8. The college students had made a bonfire on the hill.
  9. Clark has built the bookcase from old pieces of wood.
 10. Chris places the logs near the kitchen stove.
 11. Alice opened the small, green door carefully.
 12. In legend, Saint George killed the evil dragon.
 13. On Saturday night, my brothers watched the children.
 14. Every student had learned hand signals.
 15. The shaggy dog chased the swirling snowflakes.

TEACHING THE LESSON

To illustrate how the passive voice is formed, write the following passive voice verbs on the chalkboard:

    are learned
    was recited
    is invented
    was constructed
    had been learned
    will be built

Have volunteers underline the part of the verb *be* in each verb phrase. Show them that each of the above verbs contains a part of the verb *be* and the *past participle* of the main verb.

EXERCISE 82: Remind the students that there are two ways of determining a passive voice verb:
1. The *subject* is the *receiver* of the action
2. The verb is formed by some part of the verb *be* plus the *past participle* of the main verb

Work with the students to help them retain tense clues like *will* and *has/had* as they rephrase the sentences.

ANSWERS

The position of the prepositional phrases may vary in the rewritten sentences.
 1. example
 2. A silly poem was recited by the chorus.
 3. Colorful rugs are made by Navaho artists.
 4. The dog was trained by Charlene to sit.
 5. *A Christmas Carol* was written by Charles Dickens in 1843.
 6. A new game for the party will be invented by Kyle.
 7. A huge wooden horse was constructed by Greek soldiers.
 8. On the hill, a bonfire had been made by the college students.
 9. The bookcase has been built by Clark from old pieces of wood.
10. The logs are placed by Chris near the kitchen stove.
11. The small, green door was opened carefully by Alice.
12. In legend, the evil dragon was killed by Saint George.
13. The children were watched by my brothers on Saturday night.
14. Hand signals had been learned by every student.
15. The swirling snowflakes were chased by the shaggy dog.

EXERCISE 83: The students can orally identify the *subject* as *doer* or *receiver*, and then tell if the verb is in the active or passive voice. As the verbs are identified, have them listed on the chalkboard under the headings "Active Voice Verbs" and "Passive Voice Verbs." Review the *formation* of a passive voice verb. Direct the students to go to the chalkboard to underline the part of the verb *be* in each passive voice verb phrase. Caution them not to confuse *have, has,* or *had* with the verb *be.*

ANSWERS
The verbs and the voice are given below.
1. have played (active)
2. was invented (passive)
3. can ride (active)
4. had dropped (active)
5. was aroused (passive)
6. strike (active)
7. have been stenciled (passive)
8. was cleaned (passive)
9. can blow (active)
10. had (active)
11. will weigh (active)
12. can be laid (passive)
13. is covered (passive)
14. may be played (passive)
15. has lowered (active)

EXERCISE 84: The simplest way for the students to determine if a verb is active or passive is to look at the *form* of the verb. If a verb consists of a form of the verb *be* plus a past participle, it is in the passive voice. If the verb is in any other form, it is active. Then it is easier for them to determine if a verb is transitive. If a verb is passive, then it is transitive. For active voice verbs, the students should look to see if the verb has a direct object, or receiver of the action. If it does, then it is transitive. Work with the students for the first seven sentences. Have them use the chart at the top of the right column in determining their answers.

Exercise 83

Identify the verb and tell whether it is in the active or the passive voice.

1. Trisha and Angie have played a quick game of darts.
2. Scuba diving equipment was invented by Jacques Cousteau in the 1940s.
3. They can ride the electric car to the summit of the mountain.
4. I had dropped the rope down from the fire escape.
5. My curiosity was aroused by Detective Zachary's unusual questions.
6. In the hearing process, sound waves strike the eardrum.
7. These hearts have been stenciled on the valentine by Tristan.
8. The garage was cleaned by Henry in time for his club meeting.
9. Lionel Beecher can blow a bubble within a bubble with his bubblegum!
10. Robinson Crusoe had many adventures at sea.
11. Juanita will weigh the spinach at the vegetable stand.
12. Three million eggs can be laid by a queen bee in three years.
13. Most of the earth is covered by water.
14. The game may be played by two or more players.
15. Petra has lowered the new guppy into the aquarium.

Exercise 84

Identify the subject and verb in each sentence. Then tell whether the verb is *active* or *passive* and whether it is *transitive* or *intransitive*.

1. I was greeted by the aroma of fresh bread.
2. We have hiked on the nature trail.
3. That word is misspelled by many people.
4. The outfielder will catch the fly ball.
5. Gila monsters can live for months without food.
6. The guides were asked many questions by the tourists.
7. A tape has been given to Meg by her cousin Allison.
8. Two penguins waddled by the fence.
9. The class watched the final game of the World Series.
10. Money from the dues is deposited by the treasurer.
11. Walter Farley's book about a black stallion was made into a movie.
12. The lighthouse will be painted by expert painters.
13. The rocket soars into space.
14. Nine nations competed in the first modern Olympics in 1896.
15. Books were printed for the first time in the 1300s.

Sharpening Your Skills

Each verb in the following paragraph is written in the passive voice. Rewrite the paragraph using active voice verbs. Decide which paragraph is easier to understand.

The jungle floor is covered with many plants and small trees. This region is inhabited by such animals as armadillos, anteaters, snakes, and wild pigs. The roof of the jungle is formed by the tops of tall trees and vines. The tops of these vines are covered with many beautiful flowers and fruits. This area is inhabited mostly by jungle birds. The roof of the jungle is called the "high jungle" by scientists. Every day, more and more is being learned by scientists about this fascinating world.

Lesson 4 Simple and Compound Tenses

Tense is the form of a verb that expresses the time of the action, the being, or the state of being.

THE STUDENTS SHOULD LEARN
—to identify and use simple and compound tenses correctly

TEACHING THE LESSON
Most students should be familiar with the three simple tenses. Put the verb "prepare" on the chalkboard. Have the students write sentences with that verb in the three simple tenses in the active voice. Review the passive voice as presented in the previous lesson. Using the same sentences, have the students rewrite the verbs in the passive voice. Have them circle the first auxiliary verb in the passive voice because the first auxiliary gives the tense.

Simple Tenses

> **Present tense** signifies action, being, or state of being in present time.
>
> **Past tense** signifies action, being, or state of being in past time.
>
> **Future tense** signifies action, being, or state of being in future time.

Marie *writes* to her sister frequently. (*Present tense*)
Marie *wrote* to her sister yesterday. (*Past tense*)
Marie *will write* to her sister tomorrow. (*Future tense*)

The present tense is formed from the principal part of the verb called *present*. When the subject is in the third person singular, an *s* is added to the end of a present tense verb.

Dolphins *sleep* with one eye open.
The dolphin *delights* the crowd with its tricks. (*Third person singular*)

The past tense is formed from the principal part of the verb called *past*.

The keeper *trained* the dolphin to jump through hoops.

The future tense is formed with the auxiliary verb *will* or *shall*.

The keeper *will reward* the dolphin with food during the show.

> In the passive voice, the tense is shown by the auxiliary verb.

The letter *is written* now. (*Present tense*)
The letter *was written* yesterday. (*Past tense*)
The letter *will be written* tomorrow. (*Future tense*)

Exercise 85

Identify the tense and voice of each verb in the following sentences.
1. Mr. Easton explained the nature of volcanoes in class today.
2. Strange reflections were seen in the lake by the campers.
3. People in some places eat seaweed.
4. A magician will entertain the crowds at the street fair.
5. The practice of numbering houses began in England in the 1700s.
6. They will call you about seven o'clock.
7. The Red River, which flows into the Mississippi, actually appears reddish.
8. The animals' natural habitat is reproduced in the jungle house.
9. Halley's Comet will be seen again about the year 2062.
10. The metal sculpture in the plaza was admired by the art students.
11. The crush of passengers pushed to the front of the bus.
12. Every living cell contains protein.
13. Reggie works as a disc jockey for a local radio station.
14. Karen discovered an abandoned shack by the railroad tracks.
15. Last year the school library was enlarged.

EXERCISE 85: After they have completed the exercise, have the students go back and change the tense of each verb. Make further use of the exercise by suggesting that the students tell whether the verbs are transitive or intransitive.

ANSWERS
The verbs are underlined; their tense and voice are given below.
1. past, act.   8. pres., pass.
2. past, pass.   9. fut., pass.
3. pres., act.   10. past, pass.
4. fut., act.   11. past, act.
5. past, act.   12. pres., act.
6. fut., act.   13. pres., act.
7. pres., act.   14. past, act.
   pres., act.   15. past, pass.

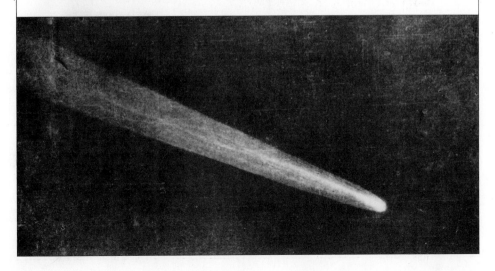

Halley's Comet

Compound Tenses

Present perfect tense signifies action, being, or state of being completed (perfected) in present time.

Past perfect tense signifies action, being, or state of being completed (perfected) before some definite past time.

Future perfect tense signifies action, being, or state of being that will be completed (perfected) before some specified time in the future.

Marie *has written* to her sister today. (*Present perfect tense*)
Marie *had written* to her sister before you called. (*Past perfect tense*)
Marie *will have written* to her sister before night. (*Future perfect tense*)

The present perfect tense is formed by putting the auxiliary *have* or *has* before the past participle of the verb.

The past perfect tense is formed by putting the auxiliary *had* before the past participle of the verb.

The future perfect tense is formed by putting the auxiliary *shall have* or *will have* before the past participle of the verb.

In the passive voice, *been* is inserted between the auxiliary and the past participle in the three tenses.

The letter *has been written* today. (*Present perfect tense*)
The letter *had been written* before you called. (*Past perfect tense*)
The letter *will have been written* before night. (*Future perfect tense*)

Exercise 86

Identify the verbs in the following sentences, and give the tense and voice of each.

1. I never <u>have tasted</u> rhubarb pie.
2. The rose <u>has been named</u> the national flower.
3. Isabel <u>had lived</u> in Mexico for two years as a child.
4. They <u>will have milked</u> the goats before breakfast.
5. The lost hikers <u>had been discovered</u> by a ranger.
6. <u>Have</u> you <u>read</u> the story "The Masque of the Red Death"?
7. The scientist himself <u>had forgotten</u> the formula.
8. The bill <u>will have been paid</u> by the end of the month.
9. Pat already <u>has chosen</u> the color for her bedroom.
10. The sun <u>will have set</u> before we <u>arrive</u> back at the inn.

Exercise 87

Complete each of the following sentences with the tense and voice of the verb as indicated.

1. I _____ all of Humphrey Bogart's films. (*see*, present perfect, active)
2. The snow on our street _____. (*plow*, present perfect, passive)
3. Snails _____ a gourmet delight. (*consider*, present perfect, passive)
4. Our car _____ by the time we take the trip. (*repair*, future perfect, passive)
5. Lori _____ for school before I arrived. (*leave*, past perfect, active)
6. The program nearly _____ by the time I noticed it was on. (*end*, past perfect, active)
7. The field trip already _____ twice when it rained again on the scheduled day. (*postpone*, past perfect, passive)
8. The renovations _____ by the time fall term starts. (*finish*, future perfect, passive)
9. Yolanda _____ a reward for anyone who finds her cat. (*offer*, present perfect, active)
10. That job _____ already. (*do*, present perfect, passive)

Sharpening Your Skills

Write six compound sentences, using a different tense in each sentence. Try to create sentences that contain information from your other classes. Here is a sentence to get you started.

PAST   PAST
The solution *was stirred* constantly, but the experiment *failed*.

Lesson 5 Indicative and Imperative Moods

Mood shows the manner in which the action, the being, or the state of being is expressed.

THE STUDENTS SHOULD LEARN
—to recognize verbs in the indicative and the imperative moods
—to identify and use the potential form of the indicative mood

TEACHING THE LESSON
Explain to the students that a verb can have three moods: *indicative*, *imperative*, and *subjunctive*, but that this year they will only study indicative and imperative moods. Begin by teaching the three ways the indicative mood is expressed. Students can readily see that declarative and interrogative sentences will express this mood. The indicative mood has a special form called *potential*. Put the auxiliaries *may*, *might*, *can*, *could*, *must*, *should*, and *would* on the chalkboard. Use these auxiliaries with a main verb such as *walk*. Have the students give the meaning that each verb suggests. These auxiliaries will express a verb in the potential form of the indicative mood.

Indicative Mood

The indicative mood is used to state a fact, to deny a fact, or to ask a question.

STATES A FACT:	The Golden Gate Bridge *connects* San Francisco to the peninsula north of it.
DENIES A FACT:	The Golden Gate Bridge *is* not the longest suspension bridge in the world.
ASKS A QUESTION:	When *was* the Golden Gate Bridge *built*?

All six tenses are found in the indicative mood. The following sentences use the verb *go* in the six tenses of the indicative:

PRESENT:	I *go* to practice.
PAST:	I *went* to practice yesterday.
FUTURE:	I *will go* to practice tomorrow.
PRESENT PERFECT:	I *have gone* to practice for an entire month.
PAST PERFECT:	I *had gone* to practice before I moved to this neighborhood.
FUTURE PERFECT:	I *will have gone* to practice before the day is over.

334

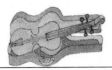

Potential Form of the Indicative Mood

The potential form of the indicative mood is used to express permission, possibility, ability, necessity, and obligation.

PERMISSION: You *may go*, Sonia.
POSSIBILITY: It *could happen*.
ABILITY: I *can do* that work now.
NECESSITY: Some delicate machines *must be oiled* every hour.
OBLIGATION: Everyone *should study* a foreign language.

The potential form is expressed by the use of the following auxiliary verbs:

may	can	must	would
might	could	should	

The potential form can be used with the auxiliary verbs *have* and *be*.

Yul *may have lost* the address.
The phone number *could* not *be found*.
The arrangements *should have been made* yesterday.

Exercise 88

Identify the potential verb phrases in the following sentences. Tell the idea that each expresses.

1. Anyone <u>may take</u> up to eight books out of the library at one time.
2. You <u>should keep</u> the water in the goldfish bowl at sixty-five degrees.
3. Peter <u>might leave</u> early to get the tickets.
4. Some people <u>can throw</u> a boomerang forward one hundred yards before it returns.
5. The antique pocket watch <u>must be wound</u> daily.
6. Where <u>can</u> I <u>buy</u> that kind of pen?
7. Someone <u>should have noticed</u> that the window was left open.
8. Cal <u>could</u> not <u>see</u> the parade from where he stood.
9. Seaweed <u>may be</u> green, brown, or red.
10. To get a patent for an invention, you <u>must show</u> how your invention works.

Exercise 89

Complete each sentence with the potential form of the indicative mood that expresses the idea shown in parentheses.

1. I ___must___ leave now to go to the doctor's office. (necessity)
2. Yes, you ___may___ borrow my tape player. (permission)
3. We ___should___ all work to make the bazaar a success. (obligation)
4. I ___can___ get the information you need. (ability)
5. Alan ___might___ go to pick up the supplies. (possibility)
6. Dad ___can/could___ not find his car keys. (ability)
7. These plants ___must/should___ be watered every day. (necessity)
8. You ___should have___ given him your word. (obligation)
9. ___May___ I buy this on credit? (permission)
10. Scientists ___can___ construct replicas of extinct dinosaurs. (ability)

Imperative Mood

The imperative mood is used to express a command in the second person. A mild command often takes the form of a request.

COMMAND: *Complete* the form immediately.
Do not *pass* on the right.
REQUEST: Please *leave* the room.

The subject of a verb in the imperative mood is always in the second person, either singular or plural, and it is usually not expressed. The subject is understood to be *you*, the person spoken to. There is only one tense in the imperative mood, the present tense.

Exercise 90

Identify the verb in the imperative mood in each sentence. Tell whether it expresses a *command* or a *request*.

1. Help me across the street, please.
2. Keep to the right.
3. John, open the door for Julie.
4. March in a straight line!
5. Take these books to the library, Jack.
6. Don't disappoint the committee.
7. Pretend you are a pirate.
8. Hold that dog.
9. Francine, watch your step.
10. Plan and organize your work well.

EXERCISE 90: Sometimes there is very little difference between a command or a request. Often the difference depends on the inflection of the voice.

ANSWERS
The verbs in the imperative mood are underlined; the idea expressed in each sentence is given below.
1. request   6. request
2. command   7. request
3. request   8. command
4. command   9. command
5. request   10. request

Exercise 91

Identify the verbs in the following sentences. Tell whether each is in the *indicative* or *imperative* mood and in the *active* or *passive* voice. For verbs in the indicative mood, tell if they are in the potential form, or give their tense.

1. Thelma, write your passive voice sentences on the board.
2. They have had a great deal of experience in carpentry.
3. Kangaroos may reach seven feet in height.
4. I was accompanied through the mansion by a well-informed guide.
5. Encyclopedias contain information on almost any topic.
6. Dorothy had lost her contact lens.
7. His plane will have landed before our arrival at the airport.
8. Snow could be seen on the distant mountains.
9. Play "Chopsticks" again, Ludwig.
10. The librarian recommends excellent books, such as winners of the Newbery Medal.
11. Elephants have been hunted for their ivory tusks.
12. May I borrow your calculator?
13. Tepees were made from buffalo hides.
14. Stevie Wonder has received an Academy Award—for best song.
15. For a pound of honey, bees must collect nectar from two million flowers.
16. Remember your sneakers, class.
17. The ranger says that we may go on the cliff walk.
18. I enjoyed the chilling stories by Shirley Jackson.
19. Hundreds of water lilies are found in the pool in the botanical garden.
20. You should perform the experiment with care.

Sharpening Your Skills

Complete each of the following sentences, supplying the verb form indicated.

purchase
1. Louisiana __was purchased__ from France in 1803 for a pricetag of fifteen million dollars. (*Past tense, passive voice, indicative mood*)

plan
2. The actors __had planned__ a one-act play. (*Past perfect tense, active voice, indicative mood*)

scatter
3. The child's toys __are scattered__ about the lawn. (*Present tense, passive voice, indicative mood*)

close
4. __Close__ the door, or the kittens will wander off. (*Present tense, active voice, imperative mood*)

call
5. They __will call__ the airport to check our arrival time. (*Future tense, active voice, indicative mood*)

dress
6. Marita __was dressed__ in a colorful Lithuanian dress for International Day at school. (*Past tense, passive voice, indicative mood*)

freeze
7. The ice cream __is frozen__ in various molds. (*Present tense, passive voice, indicative mood*)

finish
8. Eleanor __will have finished__ the sweater long before Christmas arrives. (*Future perfect tense, active voice, indicative mood*)

admire
9. I __admire__ Susan B. Anthony and other people who fought for women's rights. (*Present tense, active voice, indicative mood*)

prepare
10. Molly __has prepared__ sandwiches for the picnic. (*Present perfect tense, active voice, indicative mood*)

turn
11. The Panama Canal, jointly run by the United States and Panama, __will be turned__ over to the complete control of Panama in 1999. (*Future tense, passive voice, indicative mood*)

raise
12. Jim Mannok __raised__ hybrid corn on his farm last year. (*Past tense, active voice, indicative mood*)

talk
13. At noon tomorrow, Adam __will talk__ about his past year as an exchange student. (*Future tense, active voice, indicative mood*)

value
14. Gold __has been valued__ for thousands of years. (*Present perfect tense, passive voice, indicative mood*)

hold
15. Robyn __held__ on as the raft neared the rapids. (*Past tense, active voice, indicative mood*)

follow
16. __Follow__ the instructions in the cookbook exactly. (*Present tense, active voice, imperative mood*)

Susan B. Anthony, a leader in the movement for women's right to vote

339

clear   17. The snow __had been cleared__ before rush hour. (*Past perfect tense, passive voice, indicative mood*)

stand   18. Pittsburgh ____stands____ where three rivers meet. (*Present tense, active voice, indicative mood*)

build   19. The first phonograph ____was built____ by Thomas Edison in 1877. (*Past tense, passive voice, indicative mood*)

fall   20. The pears __will have fallen__ from the tree by tomorrow. (*Future perfect tense, active voice, indicative mood*)

catch   21. Grandpa claimed he ____had caught____ the biggest fish, but it "got away." (*Past perfect, active voice, indicative mood*)

tell   22. Paul ____told____ me that he was going to Brazil. (*Past tense, active voice, indicative mood*)

lie   23. The tree trunk ____has lain____ across the pond for a long time. (*Present perfect tense, active voice, indicative mood*)

plant   24. They ____will plant____ an herb garden this year. (*Future tense, active voice, indicative mood*)

sell   25. All the tickets ____had been sold____ by the time we reached the window. (*Past perfect tense, passive voice, indicative mood*)

Lesson 6 Agreement of Subject and Verb   Part I

Person and Number

> **The verb must always agree with its subject in person and number.**

A verb may be in the first, the second, or the third person, and either singular or plural in number.

	SINGULAR NUMBER	PLURAL NUMBER
FIRST PERSON:	I eat carrots.	We eat carrots.
SECOND PERSON:	You eat carrots.	You eat carrots.
THIRD PERSON:	He eats carrots.	They eat carrots.

Notice that the only time the verb in the present tense changes spelling is in the *third* person, *singular* number. Here an *s* is added to the verb. In the present tense, there is usually no change in the first and second persons.

Observe the change in the verbs in the following sentences:

SINGULAR	PLURAL
He works hard.	They work hard.
I am cheerful.	We are cheerful.
The rabbit is his.	The rabbits are his.
She has gone.	They have gone.

A singular subject requires a singular verb; a plural subject requires a plural verb.

THE STUDENTS SHOULD LEARN
—that a verb must agree with the subject in person and number
—to identify the subject and choose the correct verb form

TEACHING THE LESSON
Explain to the students that an important proofreading skill is checking subject and verb agreement. Put a series of singular and plural nouns on the chalkboard and then two verbs in parentheses next to each one:

    trains   (*zoom*, zooms)
    Clare   (type, *types*)
    spider crabs   (*measure*, measures)
    papers   (is, *are*)
    the flag   (wave, *waves*)

Point out that plural nouns end in *s* but plural verbs in the present tense do not. Mark the number of each noun and then choose the correct verb form. Next, insert a prepositional phrase between the noun and the verb to show that words or phrases do not affect the number of the verb.

    trains *carrying passengers and freight* zoom
    Clare, *an efficient secretary,* types
    Spider crabs, *which are an unusual species,* measure
    The papers *on the desk* are
    The flag *of the Continental Army* waves

Exercise 92

Identify the verbs in the following sentences. Give the person and number of each.

1. They have returned recently from a trip to Australia.
2. Emma sometimes eats pizza for breakfast.
3. Spiny anteaters roll into balls for protection.
4. Cast, you need more practice on the last scene.
5. Gambia is the smallest independent nation in Africa.
6. I like science fiction, but my sister prefers true-to-life stories.
7. The pond was created by beavers.
8. My shoes need new heels.
9. We take turns on the computer.
10. Snow has fallen in the Sahara Desert!

Exercise 93

Give the person and number of the subject in each sentence. Then select the correct verb form.

1. The seals (seem, seems) happy in their zoo environment.
2. The racing car (speed, speeds) around the curve.
3. Over the hurdle (goes, go) the Arabian horse.
4. Watermelons (is, are) on sale this week.
5. (Is, Are) three scoops sufficient?
6. A gorilla (is, are) very quiet and retiring in nature.
7. In the orchard (was, were) several kinds of fruit trees.
8. We (have, has) visited the Great Pyramid at Giza.
9. The last storm (has, have) severely damaged the orange crop.
10. Roger, here (is, are) your glasses.
11. (Is, Are) these apples sweet or tart?
12. (Has, Have) the invitations been sent?
13. In the center of the boulevard (was, were) a green area with trees.
14. Here (comes, come) the two pumas to get their dinner.
15. Everyone was tense as the votes (was, were) being counted.

Doesn't and *Don't*

If the subject of the sentence is in the third person, *doesn't* is the correct form in the singular; *don't*, the correct form in the plural. In the first and the second persons, the correct form is *don't*, whether the subject is singular or plural.

Cathy (doesn't, don't) like movies with sad endings.

The correct form is *doesn't*: Cathy *doesn't* like movies with sad endings.

The subject, *Cathy*, is in the third person singular.

Exercise 94

Complete each of the following sentences with *doesn't* or *don't*.

1. This train __doesn't__ stop at that station.
2. Nancy __doesn't__ know how to work the cash register.
3. These tourists __don't__ know where the hotel is located.
4. __Doesn't__ Molly have a poodle?
5. __Don't__ the bells ring every half hour?
6. The noises __don't__ annoy me.
7. The river __doesn't__ flow into the bay.
8. It __doesn't__ make any difference to me.
9. Hamsters make good pets because they __don't__ require much care.
10. This part of the puzzle __doesn't__ fit.
11. __Doesn't__ our team have a winning record?
12. Those abstract pictures __don't__ appeal to me.
13. Craig __doesn't__ play in the band.
14. That house __doesn't__ look scary to me—during daylight hours.
15. According to scientists, only one mammal __doesn't__ dream—the echidna, or spiny anteater of Australia.

EXERCISES 94–97: In each exercise, have the students select the subject, read the subject and verb together, and then read the entire sentence. Before the students do an exercise, put examples on the chalkboard to illustrate the concept being taught.

ANSWERS
The correct verbs are underlined; the subjects and their number are given below.
1. lines (plural)
2. pilot (sing.)
3. cars (plural)
4. treasure (sing.)
5. uses (plural)
6. storms (plural)
7. players (plural)
8. musicians (plural)
9. photo (sing.)
10. islands (plural)
11. change (sing.)
12. geese (plural)
13. noises (plural)
14. letters (plural)
15. kings (plural)

There Is and *There Are*

There is (was, has been) should be used when the subject, which usually follows the verb, is singular. *There are (were, have been)* should be used when the subject is plural.

> There (was, were) nine Easter eggs in the basket.

The correct form is *were*: There *were* nine Easter eggs in the basket.

The subject, *eggs*, is plural, and so a plural verb is needed.

Exercise 95

Give the number of the subject in each sentence. Then select the correct verb form. (All subjects are in the third person.)
1. There (is, are) fourteen lines in a sonnet.
2. There (is, are) the pilot of the paddle boat.
3. There (was, were) thirty-three cars on that train.
4. There (were, was) no treasure in the old sea chest.
5. There (is, are) many uses for bamboo—from flutes to food!
6. There (has been, have been) many storms this summer.
7. There (are, is) eleven players on a soccer team.
8. How many musicians (are, is) there in the orchestra?
9. There (were, was) one photo of me in the album.
10. There (are, is) two islands right in the center of Paris.
11. There (has been, have been) a change in plans.
12. There (was, were) ten geese with ribbons round their necks crossing the pedestrian overpass.
13. There (was, were) bumping noises coming from the attic.
14. There (is, are) two letters addressed to me.
15. There (have been, has been) several kings with the name of Charles.

You as Subject

Use the forms *you are* and *you were* whether the subject is singular or plural. Never use *is* or *was* when the subject is in the second person.

> (Was, Were) you invited to the party?

The correct form is *were*: *Were* you invited to the party?

Exercise 96

Select the correct form of the verb in each sentence.
1. You (is, are) an excellent speller!
2. You (was, were) at the rally, (wasn't, weren't) you?
3. (Are, Is) you going by plane or bus?
4. (Was, Were) you in the school play?
5. You (is, are) expected to give the dog a bath.
6. You (wasn't, weren't) going to call Charmaine, (was, were) you?
7. You (are, is) required to go to the gym twice a week.
8. You (weren't, wasn't) at the ice-skating rink!
9. (Was, Were) you tired after trimming all the hedges?
10. (Is, Are) you a fast reader?

Phrases and Parenthetical Expressions

Do not be confused by phrases or parenthetical expressions that may come between the subject and the verb. A verb agrees with its subject. If the subject is singular, the verb must be singular; if plural, the verb must be plural.

> The cost of these plants (has, have) been greatly reduced.

The correct form is the singular verb *has*: The cost of these plants *has* been greatly reduced.

The subject, *cost*, is singular. *Plants* is not the subject: it is the object of the preposition *of*.

Exercise 97

Copy the following sentences. Circle the subject in each and give its number. Then underline the correct verb.

1. One of the members of our group (was, were) chosen to participate in the debate.
2. This kind of movie (doesn't, don't) appeal to me.
3. Bookcases, together with a supply of books, (has, have) been donated to our library.
4. This evergreen, together with several other trees, (was, were) planted yesterday.
5. Her explanation of the charts (was, were) clearly given.
6. Dan Carelli, with his friends, (rent, rents) a canoe for his vacation.
7. The rings on a tree (tells, tell) its age.
8. Millie's choice of words (makes, make) her composition lively.
9. A shipment of records (is, are) expected here today.
10. The first games of the season (was, were) played yesterday.
11. Nora, as well as her friends, (sing, sings) in the youth choir.
12. Guides with parties of ten persons (visit, visits) the monument each day.
13. A selection of baffling problems (was, were) solved by Sherlock Holmes.
14. The colors of the French flag (are, is) red, white, and blue.
15. The director, as well as her cast members, (plan, plans) the school play.

Sharpening Your Skills

Supply a *subject* and a *phrase* before each set of verbs in parentheses; then complete the sentence. Use the example as a model. Have another student complete your exercise by choosing the correct verb forms.

Example: SUBJECT   PHRASE
The suspension bridge in San Francisco (cross, crosses) the San Francisco Bay.

(need, needs)
(invite, invites)
(recommend, recommends)
(worry, worries)
(swim, swims)
(know, knows)

Lesson 7 Agreement of Subject and Verb Part II

Compound Subjects with *And*

Compound subjects connected by *and* usually require a plural verb.

> Jack and José (goes, go) canoeing in the summer.

The correct form is the plural verb *go*: Jack and José *go* canoeing in the summer.

In a few cases, compound subjects refer to the same person or thing, or they express a single idea. Such subjects require a singular verb.

> Waffles and maple syrup (is, are) my favorite breakfast.

The correct form is the singular verb *is*: Waffles and maple syrup *is* my favorite breakfast.

Exercise 98

Identify the compound subjects in each sentence, and then choose the correct verb form.
1. Allison and Janet (collects, collect) foreign stamps.
2. The tug and the ocean liner (was, were) leaving the harbor.
3. Georgia and Alabama (border, borders) Florida.
4. An orangutan and a gibbon (is, are) members of the ape family.
5. A famous actor and director (was, were) Charlie Chaplin.
6. Spaghetti and meatballs (is, are) my favorite dish.
7. Books and papers (covers, cover) the desk.
8. The Cheshire-Cat and the March Hare (appears, appear) in Alice's adventures.
9. The sofa and the rug (was, were) delivered yesterday.
10. Maples and oaks (turns, turn) beautiful shades in the autumn.
11. Queen Elizabeth I and Shakespeare (were, was) contemporaries—that is, people who lived at the same time.
12. Jello and whipped cream (was, were) the dessert that I served.
13. Venice and Amsterdam (have, has) many canals.
14. Isaac Asimov and Ursula Le Guin (write, writes) science fiction.
15. The owner and manager of the store (is, are) helpful to anyone who asks her a question.

THE STUDENTS SHOULD LEARN
—to identify the different types of compound subjects
—to use the correct verb form with each type of compound subject

TEACHING THE LESSON
Review the rules for subject-verb agreement taught in the previous lesson. Then put the sample sentences that precede each exercise (98–100) on the chalkboard to illustrate the correct agreement of the different compound subjects with a verb in the present tense. Model other sentences after these to reinforce the concept.

EXERCISE 98: For most sentences, the plural verb should be chosen. Before choosing the verb, the students should always ask themselves if the subject refers to the same person or thing. Sentence 15 is an example of two nouns referring to only one person since there is no repetition of the article. (See grammar chapter 3, lesson 2, page 296.)

Charlie Chaplin, famous silent film comedian

Compound Subjects Preceded by *Each* and *Every*

Two or more singular subjects connected by *and* but preceded by *each, every,* and *many a* require a singular verb.

> Each student and teacher (was, were) given a book.

The correct form is singular: Each student and teacher *was* given a book.

Exercise 99

Identify the compound subjects in each sentence, and then choose the correct verb form.

1. Every coat and jacket (was, were) on sale.
2. Each joint and muscle (ache, aches) in Brigid's body after her dance class.
3. Many a child and adult (are, is) thrilled by the circus acts.
4. Every light and appliance (are, is) out because of the power cut.
5. Every bone and scrap (were, was) eaten by the hungry dog.
6. Each performer and spectator (enjoys, enjoy) the sing-along.
7. (Are, Is) every dish and glass in the sink?
8. Every bush and tree (need, needs) rain, but last night's downpour was too much!
9. Many a cat and dog (has, have) been cared for by the animal shelter.
10. (Has, Have) each chair and desk been returned to its place?

EXERCISE 99: In every sentence, a singular verb will be chosen. Go back to some of the sentences and read them without the qualifiers. The students should be able to hear the difference.

1. The coat and jacket *were* on sale.

Compound Subjects Connected by *Or* and *Nor*

When compound subjects are connected by *or* and *nor*, the verb agrees with the closer subject.

> Neither he nor *I* (am, is, are) going.
> Neither Leroy nor his *sister* (is, are) sixteen.
> Either my parents or my *grandparents* (give, gives) me money.

The correct forms are these:

> Neither he nor I *am* going.
> Neither Leroy nor his sister *is* sixteen.
> Either my parents or my grandparents *give* me money.

Exercise 100

Identify the compound subjects in each sentence, and then choose the correct verb form.

1. Neither the postcard nor the letter (has, have) reached me.
2. Either Roz or Dorsey (know, knows) how to make a comb kazoo.
3. Neither the encyclopedia nor the magazines (has, have) the information I need.
4. Terry or Sue (is, are) rocking the boat.
5. Neither Switzerland nor Sweden (were, was) involved in World War II.
6. Neither the students nor the teachers (objects, object) to a holiday.
7. Neither the heat nor the lights (were, was) working.
8. Either Art or Alicia (has, have) a yellow jacket.
9. Either you or I (has, have) entirely missed the meaning of the film.
10. Neither the sofa nor the chairs (has, have) been delivered.
11. Either Dallas or you (are, is) wrong about the date.
12. Neither half-dollars nor dollars (contains, contain) silver.
13. Neither Silvia nor Gillian (is, are) going to the aquarium.
14. The Romans or the Greeks (was, were) the inventors of drama.
15. Neither the emu nor the ostrich (are is) able to fly.

EXERCISE 100: Have the students name the subject closer to the verb, read the subject and the correct verb choice, and then read the entire sentence. Stress the combination of *either or*, *neither nor*.

SHARPENING YOUR SKILLS: The first set of five compound subjects relate to exercise 98, the second set to 99, and the third to 100. These sets could be assigned after the appropriate exercise has been completed, or they can be used at the end to check on the students' ability to apply the rules.

Sharpening Your Skills

Write an original sentence for each of the following compound subjects.

1. trucks and tractors
   my partner and friend
   art and music
   the chess board and pieces
   the fishing pole and line

2. every dog and cat
   each clerk and cashier
   each notebook and pad
   many a tourist and passerby
   every idea and comment

3. either the birds or the squirrels
   neither you nor your friend
   Sally or her brothers
   either a book or a magazine
   neither tennis nor golf

Lesson 8 Agreement of Subject and Verb   Part III

Collective Nouns

A collective noun requires a singular verb if the idea expressed by the subject is thought of as a unit. It requires a plural verb if the idea expressed by the subject denotes separate individuals.

> The cast (has, have) prepared a program for Thanksgiving.
> The team (has, have) attended their practices faithfully.

The correct forms are these: The cast *has* prepared a program for Thanksgiving.

The team (members of the team) *have* attended their practices faithfully.

Exercise 101

Identify the collective noun in each sentence, and then choose the correct verb form.

1. The city orchestra (performs, perform) in the band shell in the summer.
2. A troop of scouts (has, have) camped in the valley.
3. A group of geese (are, is) called a gaggle.
4. The council (has, have) disagreed among themselves on the closed campus issue.
5. The audience (appreciates, appreciate) any outstanding performance.
6. The committee (has, have) approved the urban renewal project unanimously.
7. A vast throng (was, were) present at the inauguration.
8. A crowd of joggers (passes, pass) here every day.
9. (Has, Have) the team worn their new uniforms?
10. The choir (was, were) waiting for its cue to begin.

THE STUDENTS SHOULD LEARN
—the correct agreement of plural and singular collective nouns
—the correct agreement of a verb with distributive and indefinite pronouns
—the correct agreement of a verb with special singular and plural nouns

TEACHING THE LESSON
On the chalkboard put sentences that review the rules previously studied. Teach the new rule with each exercise. Put three or four examples of each rule on the chalkboard before the students do the exercise.

EXERCISE 101: Suggest that the students read the entire sentence silently before making a choice. Help them decide whether the collective noun refers to a unit or separate individuals. When the collective noun refers to separate individuals, the word *their* or *themselves* is frequently used. Note the example in the introduction.

ANSWERS
The collective nouns used as subjects are underlined, as are the correct verb forms.

Distributive and Indefinite Pronouns

The distributive pronouns *each, either,* and *neither* are always singular and require singular verbs. Always singular are the indefinite pronouns *anyone, anything, everyone, everybody, everything, no one, nobody, nothing, someone, somebody,* and *something.*

> Each of the dancers (has, have) practiced many hours for the program.

The correct form is the singular verb *has*: Each of the dancers *has* practiced many hours for the program.

Some indefinite pronouns are usually plural and usually require plural verbs. They are *all, both, few, many, several,* and *some.*

> Both of the cats (has, have) brown stripes.

The correct form is the plural form *have*: Both of the cats *have* brown stripes.

Exercise 102

EXERCISE 102: The distributive pronouns are easy to memorize. The indefinite pronouns that are always singular are the compound indefinites. Have the students memorize them in families: *anyone, anybody, anything,* etc. This exercise also incorporates words or phrases between the subject and the verb. Have the students isolate the subject before making a verb choice.

Complete each sentence with the correct form of the verb at the left. Use the present tense form of the verb.

have   1. Each of the skiers __has__ ski poles.

come   2. Nobody __comes__ late to rehearsal.

play   3. Several of the flutists __play__ off key.

wear   4. Everyone __wears__ something green on St. Patrick's Day.

know   5. Neither of them __knows__ how to spell *embarrass.*

live   6. No one __lives__ in the house across the street.

report   7. Many of the volunteers __report__ to campaign headquarters at 7 A.M.

have   8. Somebody __has__ my lunch box.

ride   9. Each of the clowns __rides__ a tricycle.

write   10. Neither of those students __writes__ for the newspaper.

be   11. Either of the answers __is__ correct.

do   12. __Does__ anyone have an extra marker?

plan   13. Few __plan__ to attend the sports banquet.

be   14. No one __is__ permitted on these grounds.

serve   15. Both of the restaurants __serve__ fish cakes.

Special Singular and Plural Nouns

Some nouns are plural in form but usually singular in meaning and require singular verbs. These nouns are *aeronautics, athletics* (training), *civics, mathematics, measles, mumps, news, physics.*

> Civics (is, are) an interesting subject.

The correct form is singular: Civics *is* an interesting subject.

Other nouns that are plural in form do require plural verbs. These nouns are *ashes, clothes, goods, pliers, proceeds, scales, scissors, shears, spectacles, suspenders, thanks, tongs, trousers, tweezers.*

> The electrician's pliers (has, have) been mislaid.

The correct form is plural: The electrician's pliers *have* been mislaid.

Exercise 103

Complete each of the following sentences with the correct form of the verb at the left. Use the present tense of the verbs.

attract   1. Athletics __attracts__ many young people.

spread   2. News __spreads__ rapidly.

be   3. __Are__ those scissors sharp?

need   4. The large pliers __need__ tightening.

be   5. Aeronautics __is__ the science of flight.

cause   6. Measles sometimes __causes__ many absences from school.

be   7. The trousers __are__ big enough for two clowns.

lie   8. Ebenezer's spectacles __lie__ on the mantel.

deal   9. Physics __deals__ with matter and energy.

go   10. The proceeds from the concerts __go__ to charity.

EXERCISE 103: Choosing the correct verb to agree with special singular and plural nouns is usually not difficult for the students. The verb they choose usually *sounds* correct and is correct. The most confusing words are *measles, mumps,* and *thanks.*

EXERCISE 104: This exercise reviews all the rules of subject-verb agreement taught in the chapter. The students should select the subject in each sentence before choosing the verb. As in the other exercises, the students should read the subject and verb separately, and then read the entire sentence.

ANSWERS

1. sound (agrees with *suggestions*)
2. helps (agrees with *Dwayne*)
3. doesn't (agrees with *banana*)
4. were (agrees with *fries*)
5. Were (agrees with *you*)
6. is (agrees with *star*)
7. don't (agrees with *turtles*)
8. go (agrees with *Tom* and *Angelo*)
9. Doesn't (agrees with *anyone*)
10. come (agrees with *coach* and *team*)
11. plans (agrees with *Each*)
12. is (agrees with *One*)
13. are (agrees with *Butter* and *soap*)
14. was (agrees with *bouquet*)
15. is (agrees with *Neither*)
16. are (agrees with *centipedes*)
17. has (agrees with *Marsha*)
18. was (agrees with *crowd*)
19. is (agrees with *Physics*)
20. were (agrees with *coats*)
21. need (agrees with *tongs*)
22. wears (agrees with *Everyone*)
23. are (agrees with *monitor* and *keyboard*)
24. Are (agrees with *tweezers*)
25. was (agrees with *Each*—compound subjects preceded by *each*)

SHARPENING YOUR SKILLS: Each set of words can be assigned after the appropriate exercise, or completed at the end as a review of the three rules. All verbs should be written in the present tense so that there is a distinction between singular and plural.

Exercise 104 Review

Select the correct verb form for each of the following sentences. Give a reason for your choice.

1. Your suggestions (sounds, sound) excellent to me.
2. Dwayne, as well as his brothers, (helps, help) make supper.
3. That banana (doesn't, don't) look ripe.
4. There (was, were) only two french fries left in the bag.
5. (Was, Were) you frightened by the earth tremor?
6. The star, together with the director, (is, are) scheduled to appear.
7. Turtles (doesn't, don't) have a good sense of hearing.
8. There (goes, go) Tom and Angelo, off to the hobby shop.
9. (Doesn't, Don't) anyone feel like shooting baskets?
10. Here (come, comes) the coach and the team onto the field.
11. Each of those students (plan, plans) to audition for the band.
12. One of the driest places in the world (is, are) Death Valley.
13. Butter and soap (is, are) products made from peanuts.
14. A bouquet of flowers (were, was) sent to the graduate.
15. Neither of the pies (are, is) apple.
16. Neither spiders nor centipedes (are, is) insects.
17. Either Rich or Marsha (have, has) the latest copy of *Discover.*
18. A crowd of people (were, was) gathered in the square.
19. Physics (is, are) a subject studied in high school.
20. On the rack (was, were) several down coats.
21. The tongs for the sugar bowl (needs, need) polishing.
22. Everyone in the academy (wears, wear) a uniform.
23. The monitor and the keyboard (are, is) included in the special price on the computer.
24. (Is, Are) there tweezers in the drawer?
25. Each closet and drawer (was, were) searched as I looked for the missing sweater.

Sharpening Your Skills

Write an original sentence for each of the following words. Make sure the subject and verb agree.

COLLECTIVE NOUNS	DISTRIBUTIVE/INDEFINITE PRONOUNS	SPECIAL NOUNS
group	everybody	ashes
crew	someone	scissors
flock	either	measles
band	neither	scales
troop	no one	news

Chapter Challenge

Read this selection and then answer the questions that follow.

¹On that eventful day when the Wright brothers successfully flew their heavier-than-air machine, an age-long ambition of the human race became a reality. ²For hundreds of years, humans had dreamed of flight. ³Long ago the artist Leonardo da Vinci had designed an "artificial bird" and tested wings and propellers. ⁴During the eighteenth and nineteenth centuries, extensive experiments were made with balloons and dirigibles. ⁵Gliders were later developed and improved. ⁶Aviation, however, took a giant step forward when Orville and Wilbur Wright powered their vehicle with a gasoline engine and demonstrated its practicality. ⁷Their ingenuity and perseverance led to the achievement that aeronautics has made and will make in the future.

1. Name a verb phrase in the last sentence.
2. Is the verb *flew* in the first sentence regular or irregular?
3. Find an irregular verb in the sixth sentence.
4. Is *had designed* in the third sentence transitive or intransitive?
5. Find a linking verb in the first sentence.
6. Name the subjective complement in the first sentence. Is it a noun or an adjective?
7. Is the verb in the second sentence in the active or passive voice?
8. The verb in the second sentence is in what tense?
9. What tense is the verb *had designed* in the third sentence?
10. Write the present tense of the verb *flew*.
11. Write the future perfect tense of the verb *took* in the sixth sentence.
12. Find a verb in the future tense.
13. In what mood are the verbs in the selection?
14. The verb *has made* in the last sentence agrees with its subject *aeronautics* in what person and number?
15. Does the verb *powered* in the sixth sentence show action or being?

Conjugation

> Conjugation is the orderly arrangement of a verb according to voice, mood, tense, person, and number. It is a summary of the attributes or qualities of the verb.

Learning to write a conjugation and synopsis of a verb will be a help for students planning to take a foreign language in high school. Do the conjugation and synopsis orally, and then have the students practice writing one of each on their own using the verb *mention* in place of *choose*. Periodic review of this skill is encouraged.

Conjugation of the Verb *choose*

	PRESENT	PAST	PAST PARTICIPLE
PRINCIPAL PARTS:	choose	chose	chosen

Indicative Mood Active Voice

Singular | *Plural*

PRESENT TENSE

I choose	We choose
You choose	You choose
He* chooses	They choose

PAST TENSE

I chose	We chose
You chose	You chose
He chose	They chose

FUTURE TENSE

I will (shall) choose	We will (shall) choose
You will choose	You will choose
He will choose	They will choose

PRESENT PERFECT TENSE

I have chosen	We have chosen
You have chosen	You have chosen
He has chosen	They have chosen

PAST PERFECT TENSE

I had chosen	We had chosen
You had chosen	You had chosen
He had chosen	They had chosen

FUTURE PERFECT TENSE

I will (shall) have chosen	We will (shall) have chosen
You will have chosen	You will have chosen
He will have chosen	They will have chosen

Indicative Mood <u>Passive Voice</u>

Singular   *Plural*

<u>PRESENT TENSE</u>

I am chosen   We are chosen
You are chosen   You are chosen
He is chosen   They are chosen

<u>PAST TENSE</u>

I was chosen   We were chosen
You were chosen   You were chosen
He was chosen   They were chosen

<u>FUTURE TENSE</u>

I will (shall) be chosen   We will (shall) be chosen
You will be chosen   You will be chosen
He will be chosen   They will be chosen

<u>PRESENT PERFECT TENSE</u>

I have been chosen   We have been chosen
You have been chosen   You have been chosen
He has been chosen   They have been chosen

<u>PAST PERFECT TENSE</u>

I had been chosen   We had been chosen
You had been chosen   You had been chosen
He had been chosen   They had been chosen

<u>FUTURE PERFECT TENSE</u>

I will (shall) have been chosen   We will (shall) have been chosen
You will have been chosen   You will have been chosen
He will have been chosen   They will have been chosen

Imperative Mood <u>Active Voice</u>

Choose (you choose)   Choose (you choose)

Imperative Mood <u>Passive Voice</u>

Be chosen (you be chosen)   Be chosen (you be chosen)

*The subject in the third person singular may also be *she* or *it*.

Conjugation of the Verb *be*

	PRESENT	PAST	PAST PARTICIPLE
PRINCIPAL PARTS:	be	was	been

Indicative Mood

Singular *Plural*

PRESENT TENSE

Singular	Plural
I am	We are
You are	You are
He is	They are

PAST TENSE

Singular	Plural
I was	We were
You were	You were
He was	They were

FUTURE TENSE

Singular	Plural
I will (shall) be	We will (shall) be
You will be	You will be
He will be	They will be

PRESENT PERFECT TENSE

Singular	Plural
I have been	We have been
You have been	You have been
He has been	They have been

PAST PERFECT TENSE

Singular	Plural
I had been	We had been
You had been	You had been
He had been	They had been

FUTURE PERFECT TENSE

Singular	Plural
I will (shall) have been	We will (shall) have been
You will have been	You will have been
He will have been	They will have been

Imperative Mood

Singular *Plural*

PRESENT TENSE

Singular	Plural
Be (be you)	Be (be you)

Synopsis of a Verb

A synopsis of a verb is the orderly arrangement of one person and number in all tenses, in both voices, and in a designated mood. It is an abbreviated conjugation.

Synopsis of the Verb *choose*

(Indicative mood, third person, singular number)

	Active Voice	Passive Voice
PRESENT TENSE:	She chooses	She is chosen
PAST TENSE:	She chose	She was chosen
FUTURE TENSE:	She will choose	She will be chosen
PRESENT PERFECT TENSE:	She has chosen	She has been chosen
PAST PERFECT TENSE:	She had chosen	She had been chosen
FUTURE PERFECT TENSE:	She will have chosen	She will have been chosen

Creative Space 4

Battle Won Is Lost

They said, "You are no longer a lad."
    I nodded.
They said, "Enter the council lodge."
    I sat.
They said, "Our lands are at stake."
    I scowled.
They said, "We are at war."
    I hated.
They said, "Prepare red war symbols."
    I painted.
They said, "Count coups."
    I scalped.
They said, "You'll see friends die."
    I cringed.
They said, "Desperate warriors fight best."
    I charged.
They said, "Some will be wounded."
    I bled.
They said, "To die is glorious."
    They lied.

Phil George

Exploring the Poem...

What do you know about the "I" in the poem? Who is it? What words in the poem give clues to the answer?

To whom does the "they" refer?

"I" does not speak. Why? How does each response of "I" fit the words of "they"?

Does the response "I scalped" help you understand the word *coups*? Look up *coup* in the dictionary to check your response.

What is the effect of the repetition of the words "They said"?

How would you express the general meaning of this poem? How could this poem have meaning for anyone asked to go to war?

★ Try writing a poem in which someone speaks to you and you respond in actions, not in words. Use "they," rather than giving the name of a specific person. Have others guess who the "they" might be. Your poem does not have to be serious in tone.

Chapter 5

Adverbs

Lesson 1 The Meaning of Adverbs

An adverb modifies a verb, an adjective, or another adverb.

The band marched *rhythmically* to the music.
(*The adverb* rhythmically *modifies the verb* marched.)

The band played some *very* popular songs.
(*The adverb* very *modifies the adjective* popular.)

The band played *unusually* well.
(*The adverb* unusually *modifies the adverb* well.)

> **Adverbs may indicate time, place, degree, affirmation, negation, or manner.**

Adverbs of time answer the question *when* or *how often*. They include such words as *early, again, usually, now*.

The game started *late* because of the rain.
I *sometimes* walk along the beach to relax.

Adverbs of place answer the question *where*. They include such words as *forward, overhead, above, away*.

The concert was held *outdoors*.
The fans tore the goal post *down*.

THE STUDENTS SHOULD LEARN

—to identify and correctly use adverbs according to time, plac degree, affirmation, negation, and manner

TEACHING THE LESSON

Review by writing *How, When, Where, How Much/How Little* on the chalkboard. Call on the students to list words that would express each one of these ideas. After a suitable list has been given, write the word *Manner* above *How*, *Time* above *When*, *Place* above *Where*, and *Degree* above *How Much/How Little*.

Add the words *Affirmation* and *Negation* to the headings. Begin with *yes* and *no* and then elicit other words that express the same idea.

A marching band has a lively step. What adverbs would you use to tell how these musicians are marching?

Adverbs of degree answer the question *how much* or *how little*. They include such words as *very, quite, almost, merely*.

> My latest sculpture is *nearly* completed.
> Rinaldo's vegetable garden has *barely* begun to sprout.

Adverbs of affirmation and negation tell whether something is true or false. They include such words as *yes, no, undoubtedly, never*.

> Joline is *not* in my class this year.
> *Yes*, you do the backstroke well.

Adverbs of manner answer the question *how* or *in what manner*. They are most common of all adverbs. Adverbs of manner include such words as *rapidly, easily, well, thoughtfully*.

> Therese walked over the ice *cautiously*.
> Jessica dashed toward the station *hurriedly* to catch the train.

Exercise 105

Identify the adverbs in the following sentences. Tell whether they indicate *time, place, degree, affirmation, negation,* or *manner*.

1. The fans cheered <u>noisily</u> at every home basket.
2. Una looked <u>everywhere</u> for her lost lens—and found it in the lens case!
3. The plasterers will start work <u>upstairs</u> <u>soon</u>.
4. Are day and night <u>always</u> of equal length at the equator?
5. At the meet, Vanessa performed <u>flawlessly</u> on the balance beam.
6. <u>No</u>, a dolphin is <u>not</u> a fish—it is a mammal.
7. Snack dips with sour cream are <u>often</u> served with vegetables.
8. Zack's speech was <u>very</u> short—but <u>quite</u> interesting.
9. <u>Yes</u>, the tickets cost <u>nearly</u> twenty dollars.
10. Niagara Falls is moving <u>slowly</u> <u>backward</u>.
11. <u>Excitedly</u>, Ida opened the large brown envelope.
12. Do <u>not</u> talk <u>so</u> <u>fast</u>—take a deep breath and tell me what's wrong.

Complete each sentence with an adverb of the type indicated in parentheses.

13. Danielle looked _____ at the test. (*manner*)
14. I will put the plants _____. (*place*)
15. A rainbow _____ can be seen after a rainfall. (*time*)
16. _____, I have _____ received the ant farm I ordered. (*negation*)
17. After the snowfall, the streets were _____ quiet. (*degree*)
18. _____, Dale will lend us the sled. (*affirmation*)
19. The jeweler cut the gem _____. (*manner*)
20. The seal moved through the water _____. (*manner*)

Exercise 106

1. Use the following adverbs of time in sentences: *already, daily, again, always, late, before, now.*
2. Use the following adverbs of place in sentences: *away, here, above, below, outside, down, overhead.*
3. Use the following adverbs of degree in sentences: *almost, very, enough, too, little, somewhat, rather.*
4. Use the following adverbs of affirmation or negation in sentences: *yes, perhaps, indeed, no, undoubtedly, never, certainly.*
5. Use the following adverbs of manner in sentences: *badly, well, slowly, wisely, sadly, gently, beautifully.*

Exercise 107

1. Select appropriate adverbs to modify the following words:

ripe	runs	happily	laughed
well	brightly	satisfactory	soft
marched	turned	interesting	tripped

2. Write synonyms for the following adverbs:

continually	carefully	lovingly	quickly
bravely	apart	well	quite
almost	seldom	easily	seriously

Sharpening Your Skills

Choose six adverbs from exercise 107, part 2, and write a brief story. Underline your adverbs and tell what kind you used. Share your paragraph with another student.

EXERCISE 106: Depending upon the need for review, the students can give sentences for as few as two adverbs. Some sentences may be written, and others given orally.

ANSWERS
Sentences will vary.

EXERCISE 107: Divide the class into teams. Put the word *ripe* (or any other from the list in part 1) on the chalkboard. See which team can come up with the most adverbs to modify the word. Have the students decide whether the adverbs modify verbs, adjectives, or adverbs.

ANSWERS
1. Answers will vary. Possible answers are given below.
   overly ripe
   quite well
   marched briskly
   runs quickly
   too brightly
   turned suddenly
   so happily
   very satisfactory
   especially interesting
   laughed heartily
   extremely soft
   tripped clumsily

2. Answers will vary. Possible synonyms are given below.
   continually—constantly
   bravely—courageously, valiantly
   almost—nearly, approximately
   carefully—cautiously, warily
   apart—separately, aside
   seldom—rarely, infrequently
   lovingly—fondly, affectionately
   well—favorably, satisfactorily
   easily—effortlessly, smoothly
   quickly—swiftly, rapidly
   quite—rather, very
   seriously—gravely, earnestly

SHARPENING YOUR SKILLS: Put a few student paragraphs on the chalkboard. See if the students can substitute some of the synonyms suggested. Discuss how synonyms may or may not be perfect substitutes.

Lesson 2 The Use of Adverbs

Simple and Interrogative Adverbs

> **A simple adverb is used merely as a modifier.**

We practice free throws *frequently*.

> **An interrogative adverb is used in asking questions. The interrogative adverbs are *how, when, where,* and *why*.**

When did the first Olympics take place?
Why did the Olympics begin again in the modern age?

Exercise 108

Identify the adverbs in the following sentences, and tell whether they are *simple* or *interrogative*.

1. How is the magic of a play created?
2. A playwright works long and hard to write a script.
3. Then a director must carefully read the words of the script and imaginatively translate them to the stage.
4. How are actors chosen to do the roles?
5. At auditions, a number of very talented actors try out, hoping desperately to get a part.
6. The chosen actors rehearse again and again.
7. The actors work to portray the characters well.
8. Working cooperatively with the director, costume designers add their special talents.
9. Why is opening night so exciting?
10. Playwright and director nervously wait backstage for the audience's reaction to their work.
11. The actors hurriedly put the last touches on their makeup.
12. In front of the curtain, the audience talks sociably.
13. Suddenly the house lights go down.
14. The audience enters completely into the action of the play.
15. Where but in the theater are new worlds created so effectively?

Adverbial Nouns

> An adverbial noun performs the function of an adverb: it can modify a verb. An adverbial noun expresses time, distance, measure, weight, value, or direction.

Slowly, gently the snow fell all *night.*

In the sentence above, *night,* a noun, tells how long the snow fell. It indicates time and modifies the verb *fell.* It, therefore, has the characteristics of an adverb. It is called an *adverbial noun.* Adverbial nouns that modify verbs are in the objective case.

Exercise 109

Identify the adverbial nouns in the following sentences. Tell whether each indicates *time, distance, measure, weight, value,* or *direction.*
1. The exhibit of art by Chinese children will last two <u>months.</u>
2. A capybara, a kind of South American rat, can measure four <u>feet.</u>
3. The human heart pumps 2,000 <u>gallons</u> of blood a <u>day.</u>
4. Cynthia rearranges the furniture in her room every <u>month.</u>
5. Look this <u>way</u> and smile.
6. I live only six <u>blocks</u> from the baseball stadium.
7. Windmills were first used in Holland eight hundred <u>years</u> ago.
8. My packed suitcase weighed twenty <u>pounds.</u>
9. Broadway, the world's longest street, extends 150 <u>miles,</u> from New York City to Albany.
10. The rummage sale raised nearly three hundred <u>dollars.</u>

Exercise 110

Complete each sentence below with an appropriate adverbial noun.
You may also add a number before the noun.

1. Presidential elections are held every _____.
2. The veterinarian says my dog weighs _____.
3. The winner of the photo contest will get _____.
4. The committee purchased _____ of potatoes for the potato pancake breakfast.
5. I have been absent _____ this _____.
6. The media of radio and television did not exist _____ ago.
7. It takes me _____ to get to school.
8. The long movie lasted _____.
9. The new super sculpture will stand _____ high.
10. The round-trip ticket to Orlando will cost _____.

Sharpening Your Skills

Write four sentences with the adverbial nouns listed below. In one
sentence, use both an interrogative adverb and an adverbial noun.

each morning	three tons
one thousand feet	every one hundred years

Lesson 3 Comparison of Adverbs

Adverbs, like adjectives, have three degrees of comparison: positive, comparative, and superlative.

Regular Comparison

Some adverbs form the comparative degree by adding *er* to the positive, and the superlative degree by adding *est* to the positive.

POSITIVE	COMPARATIVE	SUPERLATIVE
soon	sooner	soonest
fast	faster	fastest

Other adverbs, particularly those ending in *ly*, form the comparative degree by putting *more* or *less* before the positive form, and the superlative degree by putting *most* or *least* before the positive form.

POSITIVE	COMPARATIVE	SUPERLATIVE
easily	*more* easily	*most* easily
rapidly	*less* rapidly	*least* rapidly

Irregular Comparison

Some adverbs are compared irregularly. In this case, it is necessary to learn the comparative and the superlative degrees.

POSITIVE	COMPARATIVE	SUPERLATIVE
badly	worse	worst
far	farther	farthest
forth	further	furthest
little	less	least
much	more	most
well	better	best

Many adverbs indicating time and place (*here, now, then, when, where, again, always, down, above*) cannot be compared. Adverbs expressing absoluteness or completeness (*round, eternally, universally, never, perfectly, forever*) also cannot be compared.

THE STUDENTS SHOULD LEARN
—to identify and use comparative forms of adverbs correctly

TEACHING THE LESSON
Study the examples in the introduction to the lesson. Have the students note the similarities between the irregular adverbs and irregular adjectives (chapter 3, lesson 3). In many cases only the positive degree differs. Review the use of *er* and *est*, as well as *more/less* and *most/least*.

Exercise 111

Identify the adverbs in the following sentences, and tell their degree of comparison.

1. The carnations lasted longest of all the flowers in the bouquet.
2. Many people say that they write better with a computer than with pencil and paper.
3. The yellow racing car made the turn quickly.
4. Could Superman run faster than a streamline train?
5. The volcano Mauna Loa in Hawaii erupts often.
6. Who ranks highest in the class?
7. The fruit trees had been badly damaged by the frost.
8. This encyclopedia article explains the process of glassmaking more clearly than the textbook does.
9. Despite hours of practice, Leona plays the trombone worse than Alice does.
10. Hilda performed the experiment the most accurately of anyone in class.

John Henry, a legendary American folk hero

11. Which story did you like more—"The Necklace" or "The Lady or the Tiger"?
12. Which was invented earliest—the telegraph, the telephone, or the typewriter?
13. In legend, John Henry worked more powerfully than a steam drill.
14. I study best early in the morning.
15. Allison always solves word problems more quickly than I do.

Exercise 112

In this exercise, only one degree is given for each adverb. Complete the chart by giving the two degrees of the adverb that are missing.

Positive	Comparative	Superlative
badly	worse	worst
slowly	less slowly/more slowly	least slowly/most slowly
earnestly	more earnestly	most earnestly
swiftly	less swiftly	least swiftly
clearly	less clearly/more clearly	least clearly/most clearly
little	less	least
early	earlier	earliest
far	farther	farthest
fervently	more fervently	most fervently
near	nearer	nearest
confidently	less confidently	least confidently
good	better	best
forcefully	more forcefully	most forcefully
sloppily	less sloppily	least sloppily

Sharpening Your Skills

Write eight sentences of your own, using the following adverbs in the degree of comparison indicated.

attentively (comparative)   clearly (superlative)
effectively (superlative)   frequently (comparative)
quickly (comparative)   carelessly (superlative)
little (superlative)   patiently (superlative)

EXERCISE 112: After the students have completed the exercise, direct them to choose five adverbs from part 2 of exercise 107 in this chapter. Have them write the comparative and super-lative degrees of each.

SHARPENING YOUR SKILLS: Put as many sentences as possible on the chalkboard. If more review is needed, have the students orally give sentences with a degree of comparison different from the one in a sentence on the chalkboard.

Lesson 4 The Correct Use of Adverbs

Distinguishing between Adjectives and Adverbs

> **Adjectives modify nouns and pronouns. Adverbs modify verbs, adjectives, and other adverbs.**

You may sometimes be uncertain whether a word following a verb should be an adjective used as a subjective complement or whether it should be an adverb. You should determine whether the word describes the subject or whether it modifies the verb, an adjective, or another adverb.

Subjective complements are used only after linking verbs. The verb *be* in its various forms is the most common linking verb. Other linking verbs are *appear, become, continue, feel, grow, look, remain, seem, smell, sound,* and *taste.* However, some of these may also be used as transitive verbs followed by adverbs, depending on the meaning. If the word following the verb describes the subject, then that word is an adjective. If the word tells more about the verb, then the word is an adverb.

Study each example and ask whether the word following the verb tells something about the subject or the verb.

> Estelle looked *happy*. (*Means Estelle was happy—an adjective*)
> Estelle looked *intently* at the book. (*Tells in what manner she looked—an adverb*)

Words that modify adjectives or adverbs are always adverbs.

> Estelle looked *unusually* cheerful. (*Tells how cheerful—an adverb*)

The word *good* is always an adjective. It can be a subjective complement after linking verbs, but cannot follow other verbs as a complement. The word *well*, on the other hand, is usually an adverb, and it can modify action verbs.

> Geoffrey's special brownies look *good*. (*Good* is an adjective that describes the subject *brownies*. *Look* is a linking verb.)
> Geoffrey makes brownies *well*. (*Well* is an adverb that modifies the action verb *makes*.)

Exercise 113

Select the correct word to complete each sentence, and tell whether it is an *adjective* or an *adverb*.

1. The chicken salad tastes (<u>delicious</u>, deliciously).
2. When my little sister wants something, she smiles (sweet, <u>sweetly</u>).
3. The guard dogs seem (<u>fierce</u>, fiercely).
4. The idea of a trip to the zoo sounds (<u>wonderful</u>, wonderfully).
5. I had answered all the questions (correct, <u>correctly</u>).
6. The price of the catcher's mitt was (considerable, <u>considerably</u>) more than I expected.
7. A rhinoceros sees (poor, <u>poorly</u>), but it hears (good, <u>well</u>).
8. The princess seemed (<u>beautiful</u>, beautifully) when she appeared on the balcony.
9. We looked (close, <u>closely</u>) at the cell under the microscope.
10. The orange package with a black bow looked (<u>strange</u>, strangely) under the Christmas tree.
11. A rose garden in June smells very (<u>sweet</u>, sweetly).
12. The car braked (sudden, <u>suddenly</u>), but no accident resulted.
13. Ick! The medicine tastes (<u>bitter</u>, bitterly).
14. This gerbil will (sure, <u>surely</u>) please my little brother.
15. My clock radio no longer works (good, <u>well</u>).
16. Doesn't the sand feel (<u>rough</u>, roughly) on your toes?
17. From the window, the fog appeared very (<u>dense</u>, densely).
18. I had (scarce, <u>scarcely</u>) arrived at the stadium when the game began.
19. The cat slept (sound, <u>soundly</u>) in the hammock.
20. The detective's methods seemed (<u>amazing</u>, amazingly).

EXERCISE 113: If the students choose an adjective as the correct answer, have them put it in front of the noun that it describes to check that it is indeed an adjective. For example,

The *delicious* chicken salad...

ANSWERS
The correct answers are underlined; whether they are adjectives or adverbs is indicated below.

1. adj.	11. adj.
2. adv.	12. adv.
3. adj.	13. adj.
4. adj.	14. adv.
5. adv.	15. adv.
6. adv.	16. adj.
7. adv., adv.	17. adj.
8. adj.	18. adv.
9. adv.	19. adv.
10. adj.	20. adj.

EXERCISE 114: Have the students select the verbs in each sentence, giving special note to those that can be linking verbs. Remind them that adjectives can follow linking verbs, but not the other verbs. Have a variety of sentences put on the chalkboard. Whether an adverb or adjective is needed is indicated in the text.

Exercise 114

Complete the sentences below with an appropriate adjective or adverb.

1. The car alarm rang ____adv.____ in the still of the night.
2. Michele walked ____adv.____ across the room.
3. The picture looks ____adj.____.
4. Andrea answered the questions in the test ____adv.____.
5. The rabbit's fur felt ____adj.____.
6. A smile came ____adv.____ to his face.
7. The sky looks ____adj.____.
8. He looked ____adv.____ at every detail of the blueprint.
9. John felt ____adj.____ about hurting Morgan's feelings.
10. The dog came ____adv.____ when Brian whistled.

Farther and *Further*

> *Farther* refers to *distance*. *Further* denotes an *addition*.

Both *farther* and *further* may be used either as adjectives or as adverbs.

> Lois lives *farther* from here than Leo. (*Adverb*)
> We camped on the *farther* shore. (*Adjective*)

> The judge explained the decision *further*. (*Adverb*)
> You need *further* proof. (*Adjective*)

Exercise 115

Complete each sentence with the correct word, *farther* or *further*. Tell whether the word indicates *distance* or an *addition*.

1. Atlanta is __farther__ north than Savannah.
2. The teacher said that __further__ revision of my report was necessary.
3. My father was upset because our car needed __further__ repairs.
4. The __farther__ you stay away from a skunk, the better.
5. Upon __further__ search in the library, I found information about terrariums.
6. As the explorers went __farther__ into the jungle, the plants grew denser.
7. There will be __further__ discussion about building a new gym.
8. I walked __farther__ than anyone else without dropping the egg off the spoon.
9. The politician made no __further__ comment.
10. __Farther__ down the road is an old boarded-up cottage.

EXERCISE 115: Before they complete the exercise, have the students give oral sentences illustrating the correct use of *farther* and *further*.

ANSWERS
The correct answers are given in the text. *Farther* indicates *distance*; *further*, an *addition*.

Uses of *There*

> ***There*** **may be an adverb indicating place. It may sometimes be an expletive used to introduce a sentence.**

There is my home. (*Adverb*)

When *there* is used as an adverb, it cannot be omitted from the sentence. In the above example, the sentence would not make sense if the word *there* were omitted. The sentence, however, could be reordered as follows: "My home is *there*."

There is no one at home. (*Expletive*)

The expletive *there* is not a necessary part of the sentence; it merely introduces the sentence and allows the subject to follow the predicate verb. The sentence above can be written without the expletive:

No one is at home.

Do not confuse *there* with *their* or *they're*. *Their* is a possessive adjective: *Their* projects are excellent.

They're is a contraction for *they are*: *They're* coming to the game tonight.

EXERCISE 116: Have the students study the use of the word *there* carefully. *There* as an adverb answers the question *where?* and points out a specific place. Suggest that the students ask the question *where?* if they decide *there* is an adverb. They should read the sentence and omit the word *there* if they decide it is an expletive. When the word *there* is omitted, some sentences may have to be reworded. For example, for sentence 7:

Does the brainteaser have a simple solution?

ANSWERS

1. expl.	9. expl.
2. adv.	10. adv.
3. expl.	11. expl.
4. adv.	12. expl.
5. expl.	13. expl.
6. adv.	14. adv.
7. expl.	15. adv.
8. adv.	

CHAPTER CHALLENGE: Read the paragraph twice with the students, helping them identify all the adverbs in the selection. Once the adverbs are identified, have the students work independently or as a class to answer the questions.

Exercise 116

In each sentence, tell whether *there* is an *adverb* or an *expletive*.

1. There was no notice about the picnic on the bulletin board.
2. There is the latest issue of *National Geographic*.
3. There are cities called Hollywood in California and Florida.
4. There, right in front of my eyes, was the missing rare stamp.
5. There are 206 bones in the human body.
6. There go the members of the band to their practice.
7. Is there a simple solution to the brainteaser?
8. There, in the middle of the park, was the large bandshell.
9. There was no electricity in Erik's apartment during Super Bowl Sunday.
10. There is the good basketball player of whom I spoke.
11. There will be a change in the weather—that's always predictable.
12. There are many interesting old books in that store.
13. There was nothing in my pocket—not even a penny.
14. There, at the bottom of my pocket, was my last penny.
15. There is the house in which my mom lived when she was small.

Chapter Challenge

Read the following selection and then answer the questions.

[1]Candid photography means taking pictures on the spot. [2]Its basic methods can be learned very easily. [3]Here is one rule: you can often photograph people more readily if they are doing something. [4]For example, they may be picnicking in a park or intently watching a game. [5]In such places, you can move almost invisibly among them. [6]Here is another rule: never take pictures wildly. [7]Wait patiently for an interesting gesture or expression. [8]As one last tip, tilt your camera lens up or down. [9]The result may be a surprisingly original portrait. [10]You undoubtedly will get some less-than-perfect shots with candid photography. [11]However, some of the pictures that you take most swiftly can be quite dramatic. [12]This is because you have captured the excitement of a moment in time.

1. Name the adverb of time in the third sentence.
2. Point out two adverbs of place in the eighth sentence.
3. What kind of adverb is *very* in the second sentence?
4. What kind of adverb is *patiently* in the seventh sentence?
5. Find an adverb of negation and indicate in what sentence it is.
6. What kind of adverb is *undoubtedly* in the tenth sentence?
7. Find an adverb in the superlative degree in the paragraph. Write its positive and comparative forms.
8. What degree of comparison is *more readily* in the third sentence?
9. Write the comparative and superlative degrees of the adverb in the ninth sentence.
10. What part of speech does the adverb *invisibly* in the fifth sentence modify?
11. Find an adverb that modifies another adverb in the second sentence.
12. What part of speech does the adverb *quite* in the eleventh sentence modify?

ANSWERS
1. *often*
2. *up, down*
3. degree
4. manner
5. *never* (sixth sentence)
6. affirmation
7. *most swiftly* (eleventh sentence—*swiftly, more swiftly*)
8. comparative
9. *more surprisingly, most surprisingly*
10. verb *(move)*
11. *very* (modifies *easily*)
12. adjective *(dramatic)*

Creative Space 5

Pictures on the Flying Air

A
poem
can play
with the wind
and dart and dance
and fly about in the mind
like a kite in the cloudy white
sky at so dizzy a height it
seems out of reach but
is waiting to be
very gently
pulled
down
to
the
page
below
by a
string
of
musical
words.

Scott Alexander

Exploring the Poem...

In concrete poetry, the shape of the poem suggests something about the poem's meaning. A concrete poem can take the shape of a specific object. Why can "Pictures on the Flying Air" be called a concrete poem?

What is the general meaning of the poem? What comparison is the poet making?

The poet uses a simile in the poem. A *simile* is a comparison with the word *like* or *as*. He says writing a poem is like a kite. Can you think of two ways in which a poem could be like a kite?

★ Writing a concrete poem can be challenging—and entertaining. Think of an idea that you could explain by comparing it to an object. Use the shape of the object for your poem, as Scott Alexander has done, or write about an object in the shape of the object itself. Some possibilities for an object would be a guitar, earphones, a leaf, the traffic on a superhighway, an icicle melting from a roof, and a bat hitting a baseball.

Chapter 6

Prepositions, Conjunctions, Interjections

Lesson 1 Prepositions

A preposition relates a noun, pronoun, phrase, or clause to some other word in the sentence.

Tina waited *at* the window.   Tina waited *beside* the statue.
Tina waited *in* the doorway.   Tina waited *near* the school.

In each sentence, the place where Tina waited is described by a phrase consisting of a preposition and a noun that is the object of the preposition. The preposition connects the noun and the verb *waited*.

The most commonly used prepositions are

about	at	down	near	throughout
above	before	during	of	to
across	behind	except	off	toward
after	beside	for	on	under
against	between	from	over	until
among	beyond	in	past	up
around	by	into	through	with

The following groups of words are considered as one preposition:

according to	for the sake of	instead of
because of	in addition to	on account of
by means of	in place of	outside of

The italicized groups of words are used as one preposition:

Bake the cake *according to* the directions.
Some salespeople receive a commission *instead of* a salary.

THE STUDENTS SHOULD LEARN
—to identify common prepositions
—to use troublesome prepositions correctly
—to distinguish between the same word used as a preposition and as an adverb

TEACHING THE LESSON
Have the students name as many prepositions as they can remember and then tell them to consult the list in the introduction. Direct the students to supply a prepositional phrase for each preposition listed, including the groups of words considered as one preposition. Put at least ten on the chalkboard, circling the preposition and noting the object that follows.

Is the scene outside your window as uncluttered and orderly as this scene? Describe the scene outside your window.

381

The Object of a Preposition

> The object of a preposition is a noun, a pronoun, or a group of words used as a noun. A preposition usually precedes its object.

The horse ambled through the *park*. (*Noun*)
The police officer gave directions to *them*. (*Pronoun*)
We took the stool from *under the desk*. (*Phrase*)
Dorothy was grateful to *whoever assisted her*. (*Clause*)

Exercise 117

EXERCISE 117: Before beginning this exercise, look at the sample sentences that precede it. Take special note of the *phrase* and the *clause* following the preposition. Have the students model other sentences on the examples. When you are working through the exercise, instruct them to tell whether a noun, pronoun, phrase, or clause follows the preposition.

ANSWERS
The prepositions are underlined once and their objects twice.

Identify the prepositions in the following sentences, and name the object of each.

1. Gwen stuffed the souvenirs into her suitcase.
2. A group of frogs is called a knot.
3. Instead of crayons, I used watercolors for my project.
4. One hiking trail extends from Georgia to Maine.
5. A medal was given to whoever had perfect attendance.
6. Athletes from around the world attend the Olympics, which take place every four years.
7. The ball bounced off the backboard and into the basket.
8. The metric system is used by most major countries except the United States.
9. According to her, there are two right answers to question 10.
10. From behind the door came a squeaking sound.
11. On the other side of the mountains lay the mysterious city called Shangri-La.
12. Kyle has spoken about nothing except his new bike for the last two days.
13. The photographer took pictures of whatever captured her interest.
14. Buzzards are a kind of hawk with widespread wings.
15. Because of the noise, I could not hear the song.

The Correct Use of Prepositions

Between and Among

Between is used in speaking of two persons or objects. *Among* is used in speaking of more than two.

> The king divided his fortune *between* his two sons.
> The queen divided her fortune *among* her five children.

Beside and Besides

Beside means *at the side of*. *Besides* means *in addition to*.

> Mario sat *beside* Heather.
> Joan must prepare the speech *besides* her other work.

From

Use *from*, not *off of*, to indicate the person from whom something is obtained.

> We bought the vegetables *from* Joe Arrigio.

Different From

Use *from*, not *than*, after the adjective *different*.

> Your pen is *different from* mine.

Differ From and Differ With

Differ with refers to a disagreement of opinion. *Differ from* refers to differences between persons or things.

> Santiago *differs with* me about the rules of the game.
> The flower beds *differ from* one another in shape.

Within

Use *within*, not *inside of*, to indicate the time within which something will occur.

> You will hear from me *within* a short time.

Angry With and Angry At

Use *angry with* a person; *angry at* a thing.

> Chuck was *angry with* the umpire.
> They were *angry at* the announcement.

At and To

At denotes presence within. *To* denotes motion toward.

> The senator was *at* the president's reception.
> The class went *to* the dance.

Do not confuse these three words—*to, two, too*. They are homonyms. They are pronounced alike and have different meanings and spellings. *To* is a preposition and usually indicates motion toward one place or some person. *Two* is an adjective and refers to the number 2. *Too* is an adverb and means "also," "more than enough," or "besides."

> Throw the ball *to* me, Lois.
> That man has *two* sons.
> It is *too* cold.

In and Into

In denotes position within. *Into* denotes motion or change of position.

> Marie and Jane met *in* the planetarium.
> The visitor came *into* the planetarium.

Exercise 118

EXERCISE 118: Review each of the troublesome prepositions, having the students give other sentences that illustrate correct usage. Then direct the students to write one sentence for each of the prepositions.

ANSWERS
The correct prepositions are underlined.

Select the correct preposition in each of the following sentences.
1. Tess was (to, <u>at</u>) the white elephant sale last Saturday.
2. My answer to question 11 is different (<u>from</u>, than) yours.
3. I found it difficult to choose (between, <u>among</u>) all the flavors of ice cream.
4. My report will be finished (inside of, <u>within</u>) an hour.
5. Katrina borrowed the tent (off of, <u>from</u>) her grandfather.
6. Because I said I didn't like any of the suggestions, everyone is angry (<u>with</u>, at) me.
7. The triplets differ (<u>from</u>, with) one another in personality.
8. Do you want me to wash anything (beside, <u>besides</u>) the socks?
9. The children were swimming (<u>in</u>, into) the pool in the yard.
10. The road runs (<u>beside</u>, besides) the canal for several miles.
11. I threw a penny (in, <u>into</u>) the wishing well.
12. Let this be a secret (<u>between</u>, among) you and me.
13. I differ (from, <u>with</u>) you about who the best shortstop is.
14. Janna put the check (in, <u>into</u>) the envelope but forgot to seal it.
15. Everyone was angry (<u>at</u>, with) the cancellation of the game.

Words Used as Adverbs and Prepositions

An adverb usually tells *how, when,* or *where*. A preposition shows the relation between its object and some other word in the sentence.

Traffic moves swiftly *on* modern superhighways. (*Preposition*)
We must move *on*. (*Adverb*)

HINT: Prepositions must have an object.

Exercise 119

Tell whether each italicized word is a *preposition* or an *adverb*.
1. No one was skating *in* the park.
2. Tomorrow our new neighbors will move *in*.
3. I have never seen a flying plastic bird *before*, have you?
4. We had finished all the popcorn *before* the movie.
5. We will take the decorations *down*, Mr. Ryan.
6. The child slid merrily *down* the slide.
7. The lead marathon runners will be passing *by* soon.
8. The submarine was invented *by* John P. Holland.
9. The carousel went *around* and *around*.
10. From Earth, the ring *around* Jupiter seems fairly faint.
11. *Through* which door did Alice go?
12. Joan will carry the project *through*.
13. *Below* the surface of the pond is a world teeming with life.
14. Look *below* to find the answer to the puzzle.
15. The title of the work and the artist's name were on a card *below* each picture in the exhibit.

Sharpening Your Skills

Use the following prepositional phrases in sentences. Try to tell a story with your sentences.

to whoever was at the door
under the mat
in the mysterious envelope
with whatever she could find

according to him
with excitement
because of that event

EXERCISE 119: Review the questions that the students should ask when looking for an adverb. Lead them to realize that the parts of a prepositional phrase belong together. Adverbs can stand alone, but prepositions cannot. Have the students try omitting the object of the preposition from the sentence. For example:

No one was skating *in the park*.
No one was skating in. (*The park* is needed to complete the thought.)

ANSWERS
1. prep.   9. advs.
2. adv.   10. prep.
3. adv.   11. prep.
4. prep.   12. adv.
5. adv.   13. prep.
6. prep.   14. adv.
7. adv.   15. prep.
8. prep.

SHARPENING YOUR SKILLS: Have the students decide which two examples have a clause used as the object and which prepositions are groups of words. Let them share their stories with the class.

Lesson 2 Conjunctions

A conjunction is used to connect words, phrases, or clauses in a sentence.

THE STUDENTS SHOULD LEARN

—to identify coordinate conjunctions, correlative conjunctions, conjunctive adverbs, and subordinate conjunctions

—to use the conjunctions correctly

TEACHING THE LESSON

Learning to use the different kinds of conjunctions will help the students vary sentence structure when writing. Explain that words, phrases, and clauses connected by coordinate and correlative conjunctions as well as conjunctive adverbs are of *equal value*—meaning that both ideas are equally important and can exist independently of the other. (Conjunctive adverbs are further explained in the teacher's notes below.) Subordinate conjunctions will connect clauses of *unequal value* because one clause is not so important as the other and cannot stand independently.

The day was dark *and* dreary. (*Connects words*)
Oranges grow both in California *and* in Florida. (*Connects phrases*)
I will go with you *if* I can assist you. (*Connects clauses*)

There are three kinds of conjunctions: coordinate conjunctions (including correlative conjunctions), conjunctive adverbs, and subordinate conjunctions.

Coordinate Conjunctions

A coordinate conjunction connects words, phrases, or clauses of equal rank.

The most common coordinate conjunctions are *and, or, nor, but,* and *yet.*

Photography and *calligraphy* are popular hobbies. (*Connects words*)
The graceful jaguar sped *around the bushes* and *into the forest.* (*Connects phrases*)
I brought the catsup, but *Maria forgot the hamburgers.* (*Connects clauses*)

Exercise 120

Identify the coordinate conjunctions in the following sentences. Tell whether they connect words, phrases, or clauses.

1. Scout and Jem are characters in *To Kill a Mockingbird*.
2. People in some parts of Europe boil and eat acorns.
3. I do not know the address, nor can I find it in the directory.
4. The horse on the carousel bobbed up and down.
5. Snakes can live in water, on land, or in trees.
6. I found a rusted key, but I could not find out what it opened.
7. In rodeos, participants rope calves, and they ride wild horses.
8. Where and how did you find the exact book I wanted?
9. The early settlers suffered hardships, but they soon adapted to the new conditions.
10. The photographer took dramatic black and white photos of the skyline.
11. The basketball players were anxious to be on the road, but the bus had not arrived.
12. Peonies and violets grow in our garden and in the greenhouse.
13. Put the sleeping bag in the den or in the living room.
14. The bones of the skeleton support the body, and they provide protection for body organs, such as the heart and lungs.
15. You should take notes or you may forget the directions.

Exercise 121

Complete each sentence below with a coordinate conjunction and an appropriate word, phrase, or clause as indicated.

1. Charlie enjoyed collecting model trains _____. (*word*)
2. The children should not play near the house painter's ladder, _____. (*clause*)
3. Will your grandparents spend the summer in the city _____? (*phrase*)
4. The lights went out, _____. (*clause*)
5. The children waited one hour in the dark, _____. (*clause*)
6. We will plant zucchini, tomatoes, _____. (*word*)
7. The box of old toys is in the basement _____. (*phrase*)
8. The glass vase slipped out of my hand _____. (*word*)
9. Is this yours _____? (*word*)
10. Read the directions carefully, _____. (*clause*)

EXERCISES 120 AND 121: Instruct the students to name the words, phrases, or clauses the coordinate conjunctions connect. In exercise 121, encourage the students to use a variety of coordinate conjunctions.

ANSWERS
The coordinate conjunctions are underlined; the answers below indicate whether the conjunctions connect words, phrases, or clauses.
1. words   9. clauses
2. words   10. words
3. clauses   11. clauses
4. words   12. words, phrases
5. phrases   13. phrases
6. clauses   14. clauses, words
7. clauses   15. clauses
8. words

ANSWERS
Answers will vary.

Correlative Conjunctions

> **Correlative conjunctions are coordinate conjunctions used in pairs.**

The most frequently used correlative conjunctions are

neither…nor	not only…but also
either…or	both…and
whether…or	

Exercise 122

EXERCISE 122: After the students have chosen the correlative conjunction in each sentence, have them substitute other correlatives that will change the meaning of the sentence.

ANSWERS
The correlative conjunctions are underlined.

Identify the correlative conjunctions in the following sentences.
1. The city of Istanbul is in both Europe and Asia.
2. Neither the telephone nor the doorbell rang all day.
3. Both Woodstock and Snoopy are comic-strip characters.
4. Give me either the yellow or the blue chalk.
5. Megan makes both hand-painted T-shirts and baseball caps in her spare time.
6. Not only does the singer play the guitar, but he also writes his own songs.
7. Neither Switzerland nor Luxembourg borders the sea.
8. Many actors appear both in movies and on TV.
9. Sea gulls drink either fresh water or salt water.
10. I cannot decide whether spinach or broccoli is my favorite vegetable.
11. Hawaii produces both pineapples and sugar.
12. The class will schedule either a bake sale or a car wash.
13. Miss Dupond speaks not only French but also Italian.
14. Whether the first-grader in the orange costume was supposed to be a pumpkin or a carrot, I could not tell.
15. Either Linda or Opal can show you how to make a shadow puppet.

Exercise 123

Complete each of the following sentences with an appropriate set of correlative conjunctions.

1. I like pizza with _____ mushrooms _____ sausage.
2. _____ Gil _____ Tony ushered for the Royale Movie Theater.
3. The police officer _____ checked the house _____ the garage.
4. The play had _____ elaborate scenery _____ music.
5. _____ we play checkers _____ Monopoly makes no difference to me.
6. _____ Maine _____ Vermont are New England states.
7. These rugs were woven _____ in Iran _____ Turkey.
8. _____ President Lincoln _____ President Kennedy were assassinated.
9. To find the last article in the scavenger hunt, we did not know _____ to choose the door on the right _____ the one on the left.
10. Brad _____ washed the car _____ waxed it.

Conjunctive Adverbs

> **Adverbs used to connect two *independent* clauses (sentences) are called *conjunctive adverbs*.**

Some of the most common conjunctive adverbs are

consequently	however	besides	finally
therefore	nevertheless	furthermore	later
thus	still	moreover	then

In fact and *indeed* can also be used as conjunctive adverbs.

When a conjunctive adverb links clauses of a compound sentence, a semicolon is used before the conjunction and a comma is usually used after it.

> In colonial days, candles were expensive to make; *consequently*, they were used sparingly.

> Our country needs concerned citizens; *therefore*, let us write more letters to our congressional representatives.

EXERCISE 123: Many of the sentences can take different sets of correlative conjunctions and still make sense. Have the students notice how the meaning changes when different correlatives are used. To reinforce the use of correlatives, have the students write original sentences.

ANSWERS
Answers will vary.

Exercise 124

Identify the conjunctive adverbs in the following sentences. Give special attention to the punctuation.

1. Many animals cannot survive cold weather; therefore, they move southward.
2. Polar bears thrive in the cold; consequently, they stay in northern regions year round.
3. These beautiful animals are a favorite of photographers; moreover, they are studied most closely by scientists.
4. A standing bear appears aggressive; however, biologists say that the posture indicates curiosity.
5. Female bears nurse their cubs from January until April; finally, the mothers lead them to the sea to eat independently.
6. Musk-oxen too, are equipped by nature for cold weather; therefore, they also thrive in Arctic climates.
7. The heavily coated musk-ox is sometimes compared to a sheep; however, it is more closely related to the mountain goat.
8. Because of overhunting by fur traders, musk-oxen almost became extinct; nevertheless, their population is healthy now.
9. Environmentalists succeeded in protecting the musk-ox from excessive hunting; consequently, the species was saved.
10. In parts of Canada and Alaska, there are vast areas for musk-oxen to live; thus, their future looks hopeful.

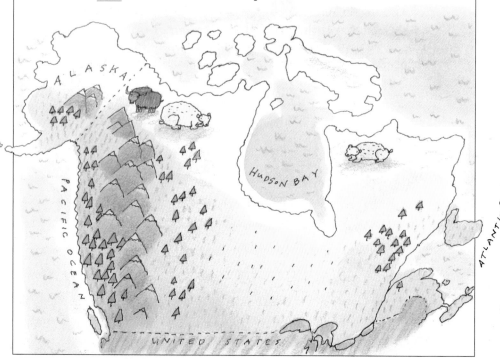

Exercise 125

Rewrite the following sentences, choosing the correct conjunctive adverb. Add semicolons and commas where needed.

1. Manhattan Island is only thirteen miles long and two miles wide (consequently, otherwise) land space is scarce.
2. One solution to the lack of space was to construct buildings high into the air (therefore, nevertheless) land was still scarce.
3. These tall buildings became places to work (still, later) they became places to live.
4. The Empire State Building with its 102 stories was once the tallest building in New York (moreover, however) the World Trade Center now surpasses it.
5. Some space was left for green areas (in fact, nevertheless) there are more than one hundred parks in New York City.
6. Because of its warm climate, Los Angeles attracts many residents (consequently, moreover) the work opportunities in many industries also encourage high population.
7. Before electric lights, bright outdoor light was needed to film early motion pictures (therefore, however) Los Angeles's sunny climate was perfect for the movie industry.
8. At one time, land near Los Angeles was almost desert (in fact, nevertheless) only snakes, lizards, and a few rabbits lived there.
9. Now irrigation pipes divert water to support the large city population (furthermore, consequently) reservoirs save rainwater to be used by the many residents.
10. Once there were many dairy farms near Los Angeles (consequently, later) these farms moved farther out.

EXERCISE 125: Have the students experiment by reading each sentence twice, substituting each of the two conjunctive adverbs. The meaning of the two clauses and their relationship to each other guides the choice of conjunctive adverbs.

ANSWERS
The correct conjunctive adverbs are underlined. Each requires a semicolon before it and a comma after it.

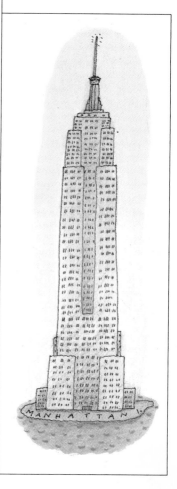

Subordinate Conjunctions

> **A subordinate conjunction connects clauses that are of unequal rank.**

You must work hard *if* you want success.
I will go *because* you ask me.

A subordinate clause is one that depends upon some other part of the sentence. Conjunctions that connect subordinate clauses with principal or independent clauses are called subordinate conjunctions. The most common subordinate conjunctions are

after	because	provided	so that	until
although	before	provided that	than	when
as	if	since	though	wherever
as if	in order that	so	unless	while

Exercise 126

Identify the principal clause, the subordinate clause, and the subordinate conjunction in each sentence.

1. Before individual cakes of soap were manufactured, grocers would cut pieces of soap for customers from a huge block.
2. Melissa looks as if she is about to sneeze.
3. Although skating originated as a fast way of traveling, it has now become a popular sport.
4. Much to everyone's dismay, Margie played the same polka on her accordion until she had memorized it.
5. Potato chips were originally called Saratogas because they were first made in Saratoga Springs, New York.
6. Gerry bent the frame of his bike when he crashed into the fire hydrant.
7. The Great Wall was built so that China would be protected from invaders.
8. I can climb that tree and scoot all the way down before you can get halfway up.
9. Because fish have taste buds all over their bodies, there is a good chance your goldfish uses its fins to taste its meals.
10. When ancient Egyptian kings died, their bodies were mummified.

TEACHING THE LESSON

This section could be taught in conjunction with writing chapter 3, lesson 3, and with grammar chapter 7, lesson 3, where adverbial clauses are covered.

EXERCISE 126: After the students have completed the exercise, have them substitute another subordinate conjunction and subordinate clause for the original one (some changes may be necessary in the subordinate clause).

ANSWERS

The subordinate clauses are underlined, and the remaining part of the sentence is the principal clause. The subordinate conjunctions are given below.

1. Before	9. Because
2. as if	10. When
3. Although	11. while
4. until	12. If
5. because	13. as
6. when	14. than
7. so that	15. After
8. before	

11. My aunt Rosalie knits while she watches television.
12. If I could learn any trick, it would be to pull a rabbit out of a hat.
13. The airplane increased its speed as the air traffic controller directed the pilot to take off.
14. Brown rice contains more nutrients than white rice does.
15. After we put on one coat of paint, we let it dry thoroughly.

Exercise 127

Complete each sentence with an appropriate subordinate clause.

1. Everyone gazed wide-eyed _____.
2. You can stay up to join in the New Year's celebration _____.
3. _____, the engine was checked and rechecked.
4. My parents have looked forward to their Caribbean cruise _____.
5. Priscilla lost the computer programs _____.
6. _____, I will never eat hot chili again!
7. All the graduates tossed their caps in the air _____.
8. The afternoon seemed to pass quickly _____.
9. _____, my grandmother had her first elephant ride.
10. It was very late _____.

EXERCISE 127: Encourage the students to vary the subordinate conjunctions. Suggest that they use the list in the introduction. Remind the students that introductory clauses are followed by a comma. (See grammar chapter 7, page 411.)

ANSWERS
Answers will vary.

The Correct Use of Conjunctions

Unless and *Without*

> *Unless* is a conjunction and introduces a *clause*. *Without* is a preposition and introduces a *phrase*.

SUBJECT PREDICATE
Do not go *unless I accompany you*. (*Clause*)

PRONOUN
Do not go *without me*. (*Phrase*)

Exercise 128

Complete each sentence with the correct word, *unless* or *without*.
1. <u>Unless</u> they come soon, we will leave without them.
2. You must not drive a car <u>without</u> a license.
3. The hinges on my closet door creak <u>unless</u> I oil them now and then.
4. <u>Unless</u> the singers come, the show will not go on.
5. The peculiar plant grew <u>without</u> water.
6. The defending champions won <u>without</u> their star player.
7. <u>Without</u> refrigeration, the food will spoil.
8. We will have no dessert <u>unless</u> you make your special cheesecake.
9. Those apples will decay <u>unless</u> we sort them.
10. Grover will not drink tea <u>unless</u> it has lemon in it.
11. I had to pay postage due because Fred sent the letter <u>without</u> a stamp.
12. We should arrive by noon <u>unless</u> the car breaks down again.
13. The machine is useless <u>without</u> the instructions.
14. Nobody runs that fast <u>unless</u> there is a reason to hurry.
15. <u>Without</u> a word, she slammed the door.

Write five sentences of your own with *unless* and *without*.

EXERCISES 128 AND 129: Put sample sentences on the chalkboard illustrating the difference between the preposition and the conjunction. Remind the students that if they choose to use a conjunction, then a subject and predicate must follow (clause). Typically a noun or pronoun with no verb follows a preposition. Have the students write their own sentences to show the difference between the two parts of speech.

As, As If, and *Like*

> **As** and *as if* are conjunctions and are used to introduce *clauses*. *Like* is a preposition and introduces a *phrase*.

SUBJECT PREDICATE

They performed *as if they were professionals.* (*Clause*)

NOUN

He looks *like his father.* (*Phrase*)

Exercise 129

Complete each sentence with the correct word(s), *like, as,* or *as if.*

1. Walking on the icy sidewalk, I felt _as if_ I were about to fall.
2. Her handwriting is _like_ mine.
3. This car runs _as if_ it were new.
4. Do _as_ I do.
5. You look _as if_ you need a rest.
6. Lace _like_ this comes from Mexico.
7. That is just _like_ you.
8. The walkingstick insect looks _like_ a twig.
9. I put together the model airplane _as_ the directions stated.
10. At dinner, Jason ate _as if_ he had not eaten for days.
11. Children riding on the carousel looked _as if_ they were enjoying themselves.
12. The harsh light from an electric bulb is not _like_ the soft glow from a candle.
13. Somedays it seems _as if_ nothing goes right.
14. _As_ you predicted, the results of the class election were close.
15. Timmy types so fast it seems _as if_ he has three hands.

Write five sentences of your own with *like, as,* and *as if.*

Sharpening Your Skills

Using social studies or science material, write four or five sentences about one topic. Include coordinate and correlative conjunctions, conjunctive adverbs, and subordinate conjunctions in your sentences.

SHARPENING YOUR SKILLS: Have the students brainstorm for possible topics. They could work in pairs to pool information and knowledge about conjunctions.

Lesson 3 Interjections

An interjection expresses some strong or sudden emotion.

Oh! The wind just blew off my hat.

An interjection is grammatically distinct from the rest of the sentence. Interjections may express *delight, disgust, contempt, pain, assent, joy, impatience, surprise, sorrow,* and so forth. An interjection is generally set off from the rest of the sentence by an exclamation point. An entire sentence, however, may be exclamatory. If the sentence is exclamatory, the interjection is followed by a comma, and the exclamation point is put at the end of the sentence.

Ah, how nice and cool the water is!

Common interjections are

Ah!	Good!	Oh!	Ouch!
Alas!	Hello!	Sh!	Well!
Beware!	Hooray!	Oh dear!	What!
Bravo!	Indeed!	Oops!	Whew!

O and *Oh*

The interjection *O* is used only before a noun in direct address. It is not directly followed by an exclamation point. *Oh* is used to express surprise, sorrow, or joy. It is followed by an exclamation point unless the emotion continues throughout the sentence. In this case *Oh* is followed by a comma, and the exclamation point is put at the end of the sentence.

O Marie! I am glad to see you. (*Direct address*)
Oh! Stan has arrived. (*Emotion does not continue.*)
Oh, how exciting the game is! (*Emotion continues.*)

Exercise 130

Identify the interjection and the emotion expressed in each of the following sentences.

1. Hooray, it's stopped raining!
2. What! It can't be time to get up already.
3. Ah, what a delicious pie this is!
4. Ouch! The sand on this beach is hot.
5. Whew! That was a close call.
6. Oh dear! I just missed the bus.
7. Oh, what a nice surprise to see you!
8. Bravo! You did a great job.
9. Sh! I'm thinking.
10. Good! My watch is still working.

Write a sentence expressing each of the following emotions. Use an appropriate interjection.

pain	excitement
contentment	warning
caution	fear
sorrow	surprise

Sharpening Your Skills

You are taking a tour of an ice-cream factory. Hundreds of flavors are being created. Write five sentences about your experience of seeing and tasting so much ice cream. Use interjections, of course!

EXERCISE 130: Have the students put their sentences from the second part of the exercise on the chalkboard. Compare the sentences, noting the different interjections that can be used to express the same emotion.

ANSWERS
Accept appropriate answers such as those that follow.
1. joy, excitement
2. surprise, disappointment
3. pleasure
4. pain, surprise
5. relief
6. disappointment
7. surprise, joy
8. admiration, joy
9. annoyance or entreaty
10. joy, satisfaction
The answers to the second part will vary.

SHARPENING YOUR SKILLS: The overuse of interjections will create humorous stories. Some students may not like ice cream; therefore, their interjections will express dislike. Others may end their paragraph with expressions of discomfort after having tasted so many flavors. Share paragraphs in class.

Chapter Challenge

Read the selection below and then answer the questions.

¹The photographer bent low in the tall grass and watched the lion as it moved gracefully across the plain. ²She could see the smooth muscles ripple as the great beast sauntered along. ³The teeth were large and slightly yellowed, and the tawny mane blew gently in the breeze. ⁴The lion seemed to notice neither the photographer nor her assistant as the pair crept forward. ⁵Suddenly, the beast turned and stopped. ⁶"Oh," the photographer whispered, "it has picked up our scent." ⁷They both slowly retreated until they reached the safety of their vehicle. ⁸There they watched as the lion once again bounded through the tall grass that waved over the plain.

1. Find two prepositions in the first sentence.
2. What is the subordinate conjunction in the second sentence?
3. Does the conjunction in the second sentence connect words, phrases, or clauses?
4. *And* is used twice in the third sentence. Tell what each conjunction connects in this sentence.
5. Find a clause in the fourth sentence connected by a subordinate conjunction.
6. Find a conjunction in the fifth sentence that connects words.
7. Is *along* in the second sentence used as an adverb or preposition? Why?
8. Find an interjection in the paragraph. What emotion does this interjection express?
9. Does *until* in the seventh sentence connect clauses? What part of speech is *until*?
10. What are the objects of the two prepositions in the last sentence?

Review of the Parts of Speech

Test your knowledge by identifying the part of speech of each italicized word.

1. That *parrot* chatters all day.
2. There was no food in the *parrot* cage.
3. With Jana in the race, everyone else seems to fall *behind*.
4. *Behind* the car stood an old-fashioned hitching post.
5. The color of your T-shirt *matches* your eyes.
6. No *matches* were left with which to start a camp fire.
7. *Oops*! I almost cut off too much material from my jeans.
8. *Another* snip and my jeans could have become shorts.
9. Is this yellow jacket *yours*?
10. I think that's *Ralph's* jacket.
11. In the desert, vegetation is *sparse*.
12. Many desert *plants* are very colorful.
13. I will *act* in the class play.
14. My role consists of two lines in the second *act* of the play.
15. My little brother could not *ride* the roller coaster with me.
16. He could *not* ride it because he was too small.
17. Cats need fourteen hours of sleep a day, *but* elephants are able to get by on two.
18. *The* shrew also needs only two hours of sleep.
19. You can go to the beach and have fun *after* you have done the breakfast dishes.
20. There was no one *after* me in the line.
21. *No one* lives on that block.
22. *Those* buildings are empty.
23. Many workers *fish* for lobster off the East Coast.
24. Lobsters belong to the group of *fish* called shellfish.
25. Lobster is an ingredient in many *fish* soups.

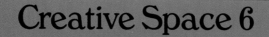

Creative Space 6

Two Famous Limericks

There was a young lady from Niger
Who smiled as she rode on a tiger;
   They returned from the ride
   With the lady inside,
And the smile on the face of the tiger.

Anonymous

An epicure, dining at Crewe,
Found quite a large mouse in his stew.
   Said the waiter, "Don't shout,
   Or wave it about,
Or the rest will be wanting one, too!"

Anonymous

Exploring the Poem...

Most limericks, like those on the opposite page, are humorous. They are meant to make you laugh. The last lines of a limerick are important. Why? If the limericks were jokes told by a comedian, what would you call the last line?

Limericks have a special rhyming pattern and rhythm. Which lines in a limerick rhyme? Which lines have the same rhythm?

★ Write a limerick of your own. You could use one of the following lines to open the limerick, or you might want to use an opening line of your own.

A little boy went to the zoo
There once was a girl from Peru
There was a proud rooster who crowed
A monkey who looked in the mirror

Chapter 7

Phrases, Clauses, Sentences

Lesson 1 Phrases

A phrase is a group of related words that is used as a single part of speech.

Variety in writing is important. You already know you can add variety and interest to your writing by using colorful adjectives and adverbs. You can also obtain variety in writing by learning how to express similar ideas with different structures. Study the following sentences.

> *Canadian* forests cover vast areas.
> The forests *of Canada* cover vast areas.

> Umpires try to give decisions *fairly.*
> Umpires try to give decisions *with fairness.*

In the first set of two sentences, *forests* is described by the adjective *Canadian* and by the phrase *of Canada*. There is no difference in meaning between the two sentences—just a difference in structure. Both sentences in the second set also express a single thought in two ways. The first sentence states that umpires give decisions *fairly*, and the second states that they give decisions *with fairness*. *With fairness* is a phrase taking the place of a single part of speech, the adverb *fairly*.

Clear water provides a mirror image. Can you see something of an author through what he or she writes?

Prepositional Phrases: Adjectival and Adverbial

> A prepositional phrase is a phrase introduced by a preposition. A prepositional phrase may be *adjectival* (modifying a noun) or *adverbial* (modifying a verb).

The plant *with the pink flowers* is an azalea. (*Adjectival*)
The American flag hung *from the window*. (*Adverbial*)

The prepositional phrase *with the pink flowers* modifies *plant*, telling *what kind* of plant. Because the phrase modifies a noun, it is *adjectival*.

The prepositional phrase *from the window* modifies *hung*, answering the question *where*. Because the phrase modifies a verb, it is *adverbial*.

Exercise 131

Identify the prepositional phrases in the following sentences, and tell whether each is *adjectival* or *adverbial*.

1. The nickname of Kansas is the Sunflower State.
2. Three secret ingredients go into my chocolate chip cookies.
3. Do pumpkins grow on vines?
4. Charlie Chaplin, a famous comedian, was the star of many old movies.
5. The rocker with the yellow cushion squeaks.
6. The art class was working with oil paints.
7. Cynthia Voigt's novels about young adults are famous.
8. Many creatures live in the jungle's high canopy of leaves.
9. Did the magician disappear through the panel?
10. The temperature rose during the day, reaching a record high.
11. The members of the camera club are raising money to set up a darkroom.
12. The pictures on the patchwork quilt illustrate family history.
13. In the dusty box were my old stuffed animals.
14. Jim is an enthusiastic fan of old-time rock 'n' roll.
15. The guests at the birthday party each brought a present.

Exercise 132

1. Add adjectival phrases to the following nouns:

boat	star	explorer	lake
flowers	scientist	castle	town
villages	sunshine	people	forest

2. Add adverbial phrases to the following verbs:

speaks	plunged	skipped	were playing
knelt	was carved	lies	clustered
lives	is benefited	have flown	blossom

3. Make phrases your tools and use them in your creative writing as an artist uses brushes to add color, variety, and harmony to the pictures he or she is painting. Practice now by using the colorful groups of words listed below in sentences of your own.

warmth of Indian-summer days	roar of the engine
rainbow balloons on strings	sped down the highway
poured into the room	ring of the hammer
coverlet of snow	flashed in the sunlight

4. Explain how the phrases and other changes improve the expanded sentences, which are by modern short story writers.

The rooms contained a greenish light.

All the rooms were full of greenish light reflected from the maple trees outdoors.   *Elizabeth Enright*

The snow was beginning to stick to the window.

The snow was beginning to form little piles in the corners of the wooden cross of the windowpane.   *Jean Lively*

Satisfied, he regarded the cornfield in the rain.

With a satisfied expression he regarded the field of ripe corn with its kidney bean flowers, draped in a curtain of rain.
   Gregorio Lopez y Fuentes

Sharpening Your Skills

Improve each of the following sentences by adding colorful phrases.
1. She watched the passersby.
2. Their pockets were filled.
3. Trees covered the slopes.
4. They jogged along.
5. The floats moved down the street.

EXERCISE 132: The four parts of this exercise can easily constitute a class project. Give the students an appropriate amount of time to complete the work and hand it in as a booklet.

SHARPENING YOUR SKILLS: This activity could be included with the above project (it relates to part 4). If it is done independently, put examples on the chalkboard both before and after the students have completed the exercise.

Lesson 2 Adjectival Clauses

A clause is a group of words containing a subject and a predicate.

A principal or independent clause expresses a complete thought.

A subordinate clause or dependent clause does not express a complete thought and cannot stand alone.

The coin that we found in the woods is very old.

PRINCIPAL CLAUSE: The coin is very old

SUBORDINATE CLAUSE: that we found in the woods

Adjectival Clauses

> **An adjectival clause is a subordinate clause used as an adjective. An adjectival clause, together with a principal clause, forms a complex sentence.**

The radio announcer told a very *interesting* story.
The radio announcer told a story *of great interest*.
The radio announcer told a story *that was very interesting*.

In the first sentence, *interesting* modifies the noun *story* and is an *adjective*. In the second sentence, the prepositional phrase *of great interest* modifies the noun *story* and is an *adjectival phrase*. The noun *story* in the third sentence is modified by the words *that was very interesting*. This group of words is a *clause* containing the subject *that* and the predicate *was*. Since this clause is used as an adjective, it is an *adjectival clause*.

Adjectival clauses are usually introduced by relative pronouns. The relative pronouns are *who, whom, whose, which,* and *that*. All relative pronouns relate to some word in the principal clause. This word is called the *antecedent*. The arrows in the following sentences point to the antecedents.

The Pueblo, *who live in the Southwest*, have a very old culture.

My little cousin, *whom I took to the zoo*, enjoyed the monkeys' antics.

Odysseus, *whose adventures are told in an epic poem*, was a legendary hero of the ancient Greeks.

The wagon *into which we climbed* was filled with hay.

I finished all the pie *that Carlotta made*.

TEACHING THE LESSON
Have the students study the introduction to the lesson carefully. The students should be able to define clause, principal/independent, and subordinate/dependent. Present the fact that the purpose of a subordinate clause is to subordinate an idea. The idea in the subordinate clause is not so important as the idea set forth in the principal clause. (Refer to writing chapter 3, lesson 2.) Next, list the relative pronouns on the chalkboard. Work with the class creating complex sentences with adjectival clauses. Identify the relative pronoun and the antecedent in each sentence. (Refer to lesson 5, grammar chapter 2, and to lesson 5 of this chapter.) Use the model diagrams in chapter 9 to show the relationship between the clauses. Diagram one or two sentences of the class's sentences on the chalkboard.

EXERCISE 133: After they have completed the exercise, instruct the students to rewrite the sentences keeping the principal/independent clause but adding a new subordinate/adjectival clause. Choose one or two sentences for diagraming.

ANSWERS
The adjectival clauses are underlined. The relative pronouns in the clauses and their antecedents are underlined twice.

Exercise 133

Identify the adjectival clauses in the following sentences. Identify the relative pronoun in each clause and its antecedent.

1. Elizabeth Blackwell, who was the first woman in America to receive a medical degree, was born in England in 1821.
2. The Brooklyn Bridge, which links Manhattan and Brooklyn in New York City, is more than one hundred years old.
3. The mountains that you see in the distance are the Sierras.
4. In Japan, we visited a factory that makes many of the world's toys.
5. Nerve impulses, which send messages to your brain, travel at a speed of about 155 miles per hour.
6. Why are we lost if we are on the same path that we took before?
7. Queen Elizabeth, who lived in the 1500s, was one of the first persons to wear silk stockings.
8. The equator is the line from which latitude is determined.
9. José is visiting Tío Emilio, who lives in San Antonio.
10. These tomatoes, which I picked yesterday, are overripe.
11. In Arlington National Cemetery, the tomb that honors the Unknown Soldier is visited by thousands of people daily.
12. Robin Hood, who robbed from the rich to give to the poor, is a hero in English legend.
13. A prize will be given to the student who can solve the difficult word problem.
14. The rings that surround Saturn are composed of chunks of ice.
15. The child for whom I baby-sat slept the whole evening.

EXERCISE 134: After the students have written a simple adjectival phrase or clause from each adjective, encourage them to expand the phrase or clause to make the sentence more interesting. For example,

A wall *that was made of stone* surrounded the cottage.

A wall *that was solidly built of stone and concrete* surrounded the cottage.

ANSWERS
The following are possible answers.
1. of stone, that was made of stone
2. with spellbound looks, who were spellbound
3. of great accomplishment, who is accomplished
4. with a friendly expression, that was friendly
5. from Switzerland, that came from Switzerland
6. of value, that are valuable
7. of plastic, that is made of plastic
8. with talent, who is talented
9. of glass, that is made of glass
10. with many colors, that is colorful

Exercise 134

Rewrite the following sentences, changing the italicized adjectives to adjectival phrases or adjectival clauses.

1. A *stone* seawall kept the waves from reaching the cottage.
2. The *spellbound* passersby watched the rescue by the firefighters.
3. The *accomplished* musician donates some of his recording profits to charity.
4. The door-to-door salesperson finally encountered a *friendly* face.
5. Aunt Elaine gave me a *Swiss* clock for my graduation.
6. *Valuable* minerals have been discovered in the nearby mountains.
7. My *plastic* umbrella sprang a leak during the last rainstorm.
8. Emma is a *talented* storyteller.
9. A collection of *glass* animals adorns my grandmother's parlor.
10. My little brother made a gadget out of *colorful* Tinkertoys.

Exercise 135

Use the following adjectival clauses in sentences of your own.

1. that I put together
2. that held the treasure
3. whom I met at the concert
4. that has black stripes
5. which was missing
6. which grows best in the shade
7. who is my favorite author
8. that ends sadly
9. that I forgot
10. which takes ten hours

EXERCISE 135: Have as many of these sentences as possible put on the chalkboard. Instruct the students to underline the relative pronoun and circle the antecedent.

Restrictive and Nonrestrictive Clauses

A *restrictive clause* helps to point out or identify a certain person or object and is a necessary part of the sentence.

A *nonrestrictive clause* merely adds to the information about the word it modifies and is not necessary to the sense of the sentence.

A nonrestrictive phrase or clause is separated from the rest of the sentence by commas. No punctuation is required for restrictive clauses.

The man *who lives next door* has a poodle. (*Restrictive clause*)
Coleman Riley, *who lives next door*, has a poodle. (*Nonrestrictive clause*)

Exercise 136

Identify the adjectival clauses in the following sentences, and tell whether each is *restrictive* or *nonrestrictive*. Then identify the antecedent of each adjectival clause.

1. Any student who participated in the bike-a-thon received a special certificate.
2. The largest coral formation in the world is the Great Barrier Reef, which is off the eastern coast of Australia.
3. Kublai Khan, who ruled China in the thirteenth century, established a capital at Peking.
4. The jack-o'-lantern that my brother carved has a silly smile.
5. I saw a movie in which the main character was an invisible rabbit.
6. Mary Shelley, whose best-known work is the horror story *Frankenstein*, was born in England in 1797.
7. Iris, which refers to the colored part of the eye, comes from the Greek word for "rainbow."
8. The boiling point is the temperature at which a substance changes from a liquid to a gas.
9. Joan Aiken's "The Serial Garden," which I read for class, is a fantasy.
10. Mardi Gras, which is the last day before the religious season of Lent, is a time for carnivals in many places.
11. Angela, who is a vegetarian, turned down the option of a steak dinner.
12. The poster that I bought shows the skyline of Manhattan.
13. John Kennedy, who became president in 1961 at the age of forty-three, was the youngest president in United States history.
14. In movies, a shot that shows just a person's face is called a close-up.
15. That is the jockey whose horse won the race.

Sharpening Your Skills

Insert an adjectival clause where indicated. Make sure that each clause begins with a relative pronoun and has a subject and a predicate.

1. Hundreds of people∧ could not believe what they were seeing.
2. A man∧ was scaling a building.
3. From the roof, he hurled down thousands of candy bars∧.
4. Some people∧ grabbed as many as they could.
5. Others∧ just stared in disbelief.

Lesson 3 Adverbial Clauses

An adverbial clause is a subordinate clause used as an adverb. An adverbial clause, together with a principal clause, forms a complex sentence.

Hilda spoke *confidently*.
Hilda spoke *with confidence*.
Hilda spoke *as if she were confident*.

In the first sentence, the adverb *confidently* modifies the verb *spoke*. In the second sentence, the prepositional phrase *with confidence* is used as an adverb and modifies the verb *spoke*. In the third sentence, the verb *spoke* is modified by the words *as if she were confident*. This group of words is a clause containing the subject *she* and the predicate *were*. Since this clause is used as an adverb, it is an *adverbial clause*.

Adverbial clauses are usually introduced by subordinate conjunctions.

after	because	provided	than	until
although	before	provided that	that	when
as	if	since	though	wherever
as if	in order that	so that	unless	while

An adverbial clause, like an adverb, can modify a verb. It may tell time, place, degree (comparison), or manner. It may also express cause and effect or condition.

> *When I removed the top card*, the entire card castle collapsed. (The adverbial clause modifies the verb *collapsed*. It expresses *time*.)

> Keith missed the first act *because he was late*. (The adverbial clause modifies the verb *missed*. It expresses *cause*.)

When an adverbial clause comes at the beginning of the sentence, it is usually followed by a comma. When an adverbial clause comes at the end of a sentence, it is not usually set off by a comma.

> *After the microchip was invented in the 1970s*, computers became smaller. (*Comma used after the introductory clause*)

> Computers became smaller *after the microchip was invented in the 1970s*. (*No comma needed before the clause*)

THE STUDENTS SHOULD LEARN
—to identify the adverbial clause in a complex sentence
—to write adverbial clauses to form complex sentences

TEACHING THE LESSON
Have the students carefully study the three sentences in the introduction, which show the progression from simple adverb to adverbial clause. Remind the students that a clause must contain a *subject* and a *predicate*. Study the subordinate conjunctions and decide which ones tell time, place, cause and effect, manner, degree (comparison), or condition. (Refer to writing chapter 3, lesson 3 for the meaning of subordinate conjunctions.) It is also important to review the meaning of a principal/independent clause, and a subordinate/dependent clause. An adverbial clause expresses an idea of less importance; that is why it, too, is called a subordinate clause. (Refer to grammar chapter 6, lesson 2, and lesson 5 of this chapter for more study of adverbial clauses.) The students should note that a comma is generally used after an *introductory* adverbial clause. Use the model diagrams in chapter 9 to illustrate the relationship of the clauses.

EXERCISE 137: Make sure the students include the helping verbs in determining the verb that the clause modifies. Instruct the students to give the relationship between the clauses: time, place, degree, etc. They should refer to writing chapter 3, lesson 3, if they need help. Have them tell which part of the sentence contains the more important idea (or less important idea). Choose one or two sentences to diagram.

ANSWERS
The adverbial clauses are underlined once, and the word (or words) each clause modifies is underlined twice.

Exercise 137

Identify the adverbial clauses in the following sentences, and tell which word or words each clause modifies.

1. When it is summer in the Northern Hemisphere, it is winter in the Southern Hemisphere.
2. Wherever Johnny Appleseed went, he planted apple trees.
3. We saw "Old Faithful" when we visited Yellowstone National Park.
4. Wasps, very nearsighted insects, will not bother you if you ignore them.
5. Stir the custard mixture constantly until it begins to harden.
6. A national park was established in northern California in 1968 so that the groves of giant redwood trees would be preserved.
7. You can get tickets at half price before the first movie begins.
8. If you want to see the secret message, put the paper under a red light.
9. Until the railroad replaced it, the stagecoach was a basic means of passenger transportation.
10. Whenever I hear the sound of crickets, I think of summers at Aunt Hattie's cottage.
11. Eric probably wrapped this package since he can never get the paper smooth.
12. After refrigerated boats were put into use, bananas could be exported to the United States cheaply.
13. An alloy results when two metals are joined.
14. While you are typing, you do not look at the keys.
15. I will save part of my allowance because I want to buy a ski jacket.
16. The modern circus originated in England in 1768 when Philip Astley launched a horse show with other acts.
17. Because the reference section of the library has valuable sources of information, everyone should become familiar with it.
18. After motorized washing machines appeared in 1907, the old-fashioned washboard became a thing of the past.
19. If you want to teach your parrot to talk, speak to it with its cage covered.
20. Mrs. Pindale tightly clasped her packages as the crush of passengers got onto the bus.

Exercise 138

Complete each sentence with an appropriate adverbial clause. The subordinate conjunction is already given.

1. After _____, the thunder bellowed full force.
2. The baby laughed whenever _____.
3. Rory's father does not let him use the garden hose since

   _____.
4. Dozens of birds flocked toward my balcony when _____.
5. Billie sometimes dots her *i*'s with half circles because _____.
6. As _____, Inez waited and watched nervously.
7. At the sight of the cat, the mouse looked as if _____.
8. The hot pizza had just been delivered when _____.
9. I must get my parents' approval before _____.
10. We first heard that song when _____.

EXERCISE 138: The students should be able to identify the subordinate conjunction and name the word each clause modifies (all modify the verb).

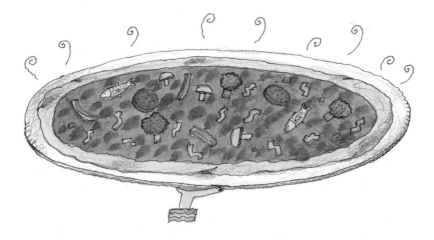

Exercise 139

Use the adverbial clauses listed below in sentences of your own.

1. when the shopping bag broke
2. before you buy a bike
3. unless you are certain
4. after the film crew left my school
5. when the starting gun went off
6. because the TV set was out of order
7. if I could visit any place
8. whenever I am really hungry
9. if you write a letter to the store
10. since computers have become common

EXERCISE 139: Direct the students to write five sentences with an introductory adverbial clause and five sentences with the clause at the end. Students should use a comma after each introductory clause.

EXERCISE 140: Make certain that the students use both adjectival and adverbial clauses in the sentences they write. Instruct them to try to combine some sets with both an adjectival and an adverbial clause.

Milk, which is nutritious, should be part of your daily diet. (adjectival)

Since milk is nutritious, it should be part of your daily diet. (adverbial)

ANSWERS
Answers will vary. Accept any logical sentences with clauses. The following are the relative pronouns and subordinate conjunctions that would most likely be used in the combined sentences.
1. which; because, since
2. which
3. which
4. because, since
5. who; because, since
6. when, after
7. whenever, as
8. that
9. which; since
10. since, because
11. than, although
12. (in) which
13. who; although
14. when, as, while
15. that; because

SHARPENING YOUR SKILLS: After the students have written the sentences, suggest that they vary the position of the adverbial clauses. Two could be introductory and two could follow the principal clause. (For more exercises dealing with complex sentences, see lesson 5 of this chapter.)

Exercise 140

Combine each of the following sets of sentences into a complex sentence with an adjectival or adverbial clause. Be sure to punctuate your sentences correctly. Also tell whether the clause in each sentence is *adjectival* or *adverbial*.

1. Milk is nutritious. It should be part of your daily diet.
2. Buckingham Palace is in the center of London. It has been a residence for British kings and queens since 1837.
3. K2 is the world's second-highest peak. It is in the Asian territory of Kashmir.
4. Jugglers have to be well coordinated. They must keep several objects twirling in the air at the same time.
5. Football fans are devoted. They will go to a game in any kind of weather.
6. You determine the best position for the picture. Hammer in the nail.
7. I watch ice skaters. I want to learn to skate.
8. Modern zoos are setting up new habitats. The habitats re-create animals' natural surroundings.
9. The United States is a big producer of cheese. It makes over one billion pounds annually.
10. Will you lend me your red marker? Mine has run out.
11. A soccer ball is large. A basketball is even larger.
12. Many Spanish towns have plazas. People gather and talk in plazas.
13. Zana is my best friend. I have known her for only six months.
14. The winners of the ribbons for the best pies were being announced. Brenda's heartbeat quickened.
15. We liked the painting. The painting pictured a group of people in the park on a Sunday afternoon.

Sharpening Your Skills

Write six complex sentences about events that have happened in your school. Construct four sentences with adverbial clauses and two with adjectival clauses.

Lesson 4 Sentences and Their Parts

A sentence is a group of words expressing a complete thought.

Study these examples:

INCOMPLETE THOUGHT: The acrobat in the circus
INCOMPLETE THOUGHT: Balancing on one hand

SENTENCE: The acrobat in the circus balances on one hand.
SENTENCE: Can you balance yourself on one hand?
SENTENCE: Try to balance yourself on two hands.

Exercise 141

Identify which of the following groups of words are sentences.

1. Arteries carry blood to the heart.   S
2. Stay there.   S
3. The story of George Washington Carver.
4. Does your state have a song?   S
5. The hurried clerk who wrote down the wrong address.
6. A good computer programmer is always in demand.   S
7. Roller skates in the playground and in the ballroom.
8. Tartan, the checkered fabric of Scotland's native dress.
9. Seeing the fire-eater on the street.
10. Muslims worship in mosques.   S
11. Edith Wharton won a Pulitzer Prize for literature.   S
12. Cranberry, a relish with meats, particularly turkey.
13. Halloween was an ancient Celtic celebration of the new year.   S
14. Gravity, one of the fundamental forces of nature.
15. Having left the pot boiling on the stove.

Sentences Classified according to Use

A *declarative sentence* states a fact.

An *interrogative sentence* asks a question.

An *imperative sentence* expresses a command.

An *exclamatory sentence* expresses strong emotion.

Mount Saint Helens is an active volcano. (*Declarative*)
When did Mount Saint Helens last erupt? (*Interrogative*)
Read the chapter about volcanoes. (*Imperative*)
How powerful volcanoes can be! (*Exclamatory*)

When you are speaking, the inflection of your voice tells the listener whether you are stating a fact, asking a question, giving a command, or expressing surprise. In writing, however, you must use punctuation marks to indicate the various kinds of sentences.

Declarative and *imperative* sentences are followed by periods.

An *interrogative* sentence ends with an interrogation point.

An *exclamatory* sentence is followed by an exclamation point.

Exercise 142

Identify the following sentences as *declarative, interrogative, imperative,* or *exclamatory*. Punctuate each sentence.

1. How many pieces does that jigsaw puzzle have ?
2. Bring me the hair dryer, Denise .
3. Who was the first person in space ?
4. Rangers protect the forests .
5. What a busy restaurant this is !
6. Can you open this locket ?
7. Please pass the pretzels .
8. How clever you are at solving riddles !
9. What is a shamrock ?
10. A seismograph records movements within the earth .
11. The cat seemed to look longingly out the window .
12. Measure and mix the chemicals carefully .
13. What happens during a solar eclipse ?
14. How often do you read the newspaper ?
15. How lifelike the wax figure in the museum seemed !

Exercise 143

Copy the following paragraph, dividing it into sentences. Use a capital letter at the beginning of each sentence and add the correct end punctuation. You should write ten sentences.

a deafening sound broke the silence of the night. every animal in the corral got on its feet almost instantly. at the same time the alarm was given to the hands. what a loud roar it had been! it was like a heavy railroad train passing at no great distance. what was the cause of the sound? everyone guessed that it was a buffalo stampede. the tents quickly emptied of their inmates who went to calm the animals in the corral. how frightened the horses were! everyone and everything in the camp was on the alert for what was coming.

EXERCISES 142 AND 143: Exercise 142 is a review of sentences according to use. Exercise 143 should be completed independently to see if the students can "hear" what groups of words make up a sentence. The students should then read their paragraphs aloud to see if they have conveyed the meaning correctly.

ANSWERS

The end marks are in the text. The kinds of sentences are listed below.

1. inter.   9. inter.
2. imper.   10. declar.
3. inter.   11. declar.
4. declar.   12. imper.
5. exclam.   13. inter.
6. inter.   14. inter.
7. imper.   15. exclam.
8. exclam.

Most students know the essential
elements of a sentence. Carefully
review the concepts of complete
subject and complete predicate by
focusing on the sample sentences
in the introduction. Use diagraming to show that any words to the
left of the subject/predicate line
make up the complete subject;
any words to the right make up
the complete predicate.

The Essential Elements of a Sentence

The essential elements of a sentence are the *subject* and *predicate*.

The subject names a person, place, or thing about which a statement is made.

The predicate tells something about the subject.

SUBJECT	PREDICATE
The *wind*	*filled* the sails of the old sailing ship.

Sometimes the subject of a sentence may not be expressed. The predicate, however, is always expressed.

Give the blueprint to the carpenter.

The subject of the sentence above is not expressed: it is understood to be *you*. The example is an imperative sentence. In imperative sentences, the subject is usually not expressed, but it is understood to be *you*.

The subject with all its modifiers is called the *complete subject*. The predicate with all its modifiers and objects or complements is called the *complete predicate*.

COMPLETE SUBJECT	COMPLETE PREDICATE
Both plants and animals	live in the ocean.
The brilliant sun	beat down on the bathers.
Pencils, pens, and paper	are the basic school tools.

Exercise 144

Identify the subject and complete subject and the predicate and complete predicate in each of the following sentences.

1. Veins | return blood to the heart.
2. My sister | has a pair of slippers in the shape of bear paws.
3. Bring your water wings with you to the beach. (subject: _you_ understood)
4. The savanna | is the name for the tropical grasslands of Africa.
5. The Vikings | were expert shipbuilders and navigators.
6. Tell us about your trip on the blimp. (subject: _you_ understood)
7. We | learned about artificial respiration in health class.
8. Nikki Giovanni | has written many poems about her childhood in Knoxville, Tennessee.
9. Some pigeons | can return to their lofts from great distances.
10. The Colorado River | cuts through the Grand Canyon.

Exercise 145

Add a complete predicate to each of the following complete subjects.

1. The exquisite jewels _____.
2. The floats in the parade _____.
3. A small monkey _____.
4. A bright red sports car _____.
5. The members of the team _____.

Add a complete subject to each of the following complete predicates.

6. _____ zipped the grocery cart down the crowded aisle.
7. _____ made a loud noise during the night.
8. _____ are popular with seventh-graders right now.
9. _____ hung down from the ceiling.
10. _____ left tracks in the newly fallen snow.

EXERCISE 144: Make sure that the students know that the simple predicate includes the main verb and any helping verbs. For imperative sentences, they must indicate that *you* understood is the subject.

ANSWERS
The simple subject is underlined once, and the simple predicate is underlined twice. The complete subject is to the left of the vertical line, and the complete predicate is to the right of the vertical line. For sentences 3 and 6 (imperative sentences), the complete subject is *you*, and the complete predicate is the simple predicate and everything to its right.

EXERCISE 145: Have the students draw a vertical line (|) between the complete subject and the complete predicate. Have sentences read aloud or put on the chalkboard.

Compound Elements of a Sentence

If the subject of a sentence consists of more than one noun or pronoun, it is said to be a *compound subject*.

If the predicate consists of more than one verb, it is said to be a *compound predicate*.

A sentence may have a compound subject, a compound predicate, or a compound subject and a compound predicate.

Sally and *Henry* worked for the prize. (*Compound subject*)
The actress *sang* and *danced*. (*Compound predicate*)

The *wild horses* and *buffalo roamed* and *grazed* freely on the western plains. (*Compound subject and compound predicate*)

Exercise 146

Identify the compound elements in the following sentences. Tell whether each is a *compound subject* or a *compound predicate*. Some sentences may have both.

1. Punch and Judy are famous characters in puppet shows.
2. I peeled and cut a sack of potatoes as a helper for the parents' dinner.
3. We visited the hospital and brought colorful balloons for the children in the pediatric ward.
4. Excellent balance and coordination are required for surfing.
5. Sara and I folded the tent and put it into the van.
6. Red, yellow, and blue are called the primary colors.
7. Last night Marcy wrote and typed her report for social studies.
8. The Navaho artist cut the turquoise stone and set it into the silver bracelet.
9. Solids, liquids, and gases are forms of matter.
10. Spiders spin webs and form cocoons with their silk.

Exercise 147

Complete each of the following subjects below with a compound predicate.

1. The jumping bean _____.
2. The gymnasts _____.
3. A parade of cars _____.
4. The bottle with the note _____.
5. The brightly colored butterfly _____.

Complete each of the following predicates with a compound subject.

6. _____ were on sale at the street market.
7. _____ are my favorite singers.
8. At the circus, _____ performed in the center ring.
9. _____ live in caves.
10. _____ raced down the street.

Natural and Transposed Order in Sentences

A sentence is in the **natural order** whenever the complete subject comes before the complete predicate.

A sentence is in the **transposed order** whenever the complete predicate or part of the predicate comes before the subject.

Study the following examples. The complete subject is underlined once, and the complete predicate is underlined twice.

NATURAL ORDER:
The autumn leaves fluttered down.
Who saw the TV program on lions?
The cheerleaders performed before the game.

TRANSPOSED ORDER:
Down fluttered the autumn leaves.
Did you see the TV program on lions?
Before the game, the cheerleaders performed.

EXERCISE 147: For extended work with compound elements, have the students write original sentences using compound subjects and predicates that apply to social studies: for example, the colonists and the British; plotted and planned; wrote and defended.

TEACHING THE LESSON

Learning to write sentences in the transposed order helps to create variety in sentence structure. To reinforce this skill, put short sentences in natural order on the chalkboard and have the students write transposed sentences. Lead the students to see that adverbs and adverbial phrases usually begin transposed sentences.

Our parrot talked.
Around midnight, our parrot talked incessantly.

A flying squirrel landed.
With outstretched legs, a flying squirrel landed on target.

After the students have completed sentences like those above, suggest that they put a compound element in each sentence.

Exercise 148

Tell whether each sentence is in the *natural order* or the *transposed order*. Identify the subject and predicate in each sentence.

1. Along the streets of New York City are many skyscrapers.
2. The city's streets stretch out like stone and glass canyons.
3. The sight amazes many visitors to the city.
4. On the streets during rush hour are hordes of people.
5. Why do the workers walk so fast, like actors in a speeded-up movie?
6. Down the streets stream cars, cabs, and buses.
7. Frustrated drivers are caught in traffic jams frequently.
8. Messengers on bicycles weave amidst the traffic.
9. On many street corners, pretzels are sold by vendors.
10. In many places, the visitor will find street performers, such as musicians and jugglers.
11. Around the street performers gather large crowds.
12. Police on horses patrol the streets.
13. At every hour of the day and night, cars and people crowd the streets.
14. The city is always on the go.
15. Wouldn't New York be an exhilarating place for a visit?

Sharpening Your Skills

Describe what your perfect room would be like. Include at least four sentences in the transposed order in your description. Use an adverb or an adverbial phrase to introduce the sentences in the transposed order.

Lesson 5 Simple, Compound, and Complex Sentences

Classified according to form, sentences may be simple, compound, or complex.

Simple Sentences

A simple sentence contains one subject and one predicate, either or both of which may be compound.

Canada is rich in natural resources.

This sentence contains one subject, *Canada*, and one predicate, *is*.

Exercise 149

Identify the subject and predicate in each of the following simple sentences.
1. Origami is the ancient Japanese art of paper folding.
2. Crocuses and violets are spring flowers.
3. The Bengal shortstop leaped and caught the ball.
4. Meet me at the bookstore in the mall at noon.   (subject: you)
5. My sister and I work as paper carriers.
6. A junk is a wooden sailing vessel of the Far East.
7. The knife and fork first became popular in England in the 1600s.
8. Deep-sea divers face many dangers.
9. Tom will take his dogs Dick and Harry to obedience school.
10. The ancient Romans used arches in their buildings.

THE STUDENTS SHOULD LEARN
—to identify simple sentences
—to identify and punctuate compound sentences
—to identify and correctly use complex sentences

TEACHING THE LESSON
Most of what is contained in this lesson is review material and can be used for reinforcement, especially of compound and complex sentences. Stress the use of correct punctuation with compound sentences, especially the use of the semicolon. Use the section on complex sentences with lessons 2 and 3 of this chapter.

EXERCISE 149: Make certain that the students can identify the compound elements found in some of the sentences. Also, make sure the students include helping verbs as part of the predicate. For review, direct the students to name the complete subject and complete predicate in each sentence.

ANSWERS
The subjects are underlined once, and the predicates twice.

Compound Sentences

> **A compound sentence contains two or more independent clauses.**

The camel is the ship of the desert, and the reindeer is the camel of the snow land.

The sentence above contains two complete thoughts: *The camel is the ship of the desert. The reindeer is the camel of the snow land.*

Each thought is independent and forms a simple sentence in itself. Any such combination of simple sentences is called a *compound sentence*. Each thought is called an *independent clause*.

The clauses of a compound sentence are connected by *coordinate conjunctions*. The most important coordinate conjunctions are *and, but, or, nor,* and *yet. Conjunctive adverbs* may also link clauses of a compound sentence. Some commonly used conjunctive adverbs are *consequently, however, moreover, nevertheless, thus,* and *therefore.*

Punctuation of Compound Sentences

1. The clauses of a compound sentence connected by the simple conjunctions *and, but,* and *or* are generally separated by a comma.

    Fort Christiana was surrendered to the Dutch in 1655, *and* New Sweden became part of New Netherland.
2. If the clauses are short and closely related, the comma may be omitted.

    The rain descended *and* the floods came.
3. The semicolon is used to separate the clauses of a compound sentence connected by the conjunctive adverbs *consequently, however, moreover, nevertheless, thus,* or *therefore.* A comma is frequently used after these words.

    The coast of Africa is regular; *thus,* it has few natural harbors.
4. Sometimes the clauses of a compound sentence have no connecting word. The connection is then indicated by a semicolon.

    Peaches taste sweet; lemons taste sour.

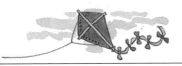

Exercise 150

Indicate what punctuation mark or marks are needed in each of the following compound sentences, and where the marks should be placed.

1. A tornado begins as a whirl of dust, and it soon becomes a funnel of swirling winds.
2. A kite is flying high in the sky; it seems to be racing against the wind.
3. Zoology is the study of animals, and botany is the study of plants.
4. Bald eagles were becoming extinct; therefore, Congress passed a special act for their protection.
5. I smelled smoke in the air, but I could not find its source.
6. Please straighten up the living room; company is coming.
7. Umbrellas are now often used for protection from the rain; however, they were originally used for protection from the sun.
8. Eugenia saw the movie *The Black Stallion*; moreover, she had read the book.
9. The lands near the equator are properly called the evergreen rain forest; nevertheless, they are widely known as the jungle.
10. Dad will prepare the fire, and I will help broil the hamburgers.
11. Like human fingerprints, a tiger's footprints are unique; consequently, experts can identify individual tigers by their footprints.
12. New Year's Day is January 1; however, some people celebrate New Year's Day as late as October.
13. The act of standing still is an amazing feat; over three hundred muscles are used just to keep us balanced.
14. Elaine has painted her ceramic vase, and now she will bake it in a special oven called a kiln.
15. Japanese children attend school six days a week; moreover, many go to special tutoring sessions after regular school.

EXERCISE 150: Wherever a coordinate conjunction has been used to connect the clauses, have the students go back and substitute conjunctive adverbs such as *moreover, therefore, however,* and so on, where possible. (Refer to grammar chapter 6, lesson 3, for the meaning of conjunctive adverbs.) For example:

I smelled smoke in the air, but I could not find its source.
I smelled smoke; however, I could not find its source.

EXERCISE 151: Encourage the students to use a variety of conjunctions, but to make certain the meaning of each new sentence makes sense. Have the students refer to writing chapter 3, lesson 1, and grammar chapter 6, lesson 3, for the meaning of coordinate conjunctions and conjunctive adverbs.

ANSWERS

Accept any appropriate responses. The conjunctions given below are the ones most likely to be used to combine the sentences. Any set can be combined with a semicolon.
1. and; therefore
2. but, yet; however
3. and
4. and; therefore
5. and
6. and, but
7. and
8. but, yet; however
9. and
10. and
11. but, yet; however
12. but; however
13. and; moreover
14. but, yet; however
15. but; however

Exercise 151

Combine each of the following sets of simple sentences into compound sentences. Use conjunctions for some of the sentences, and use the proper punctuation for each.

1. Mrs. Minelli planted her tomatoes late this year. They are still quite small and green on the plant.
2. The anteater has poor eyesight. Its sense of smell is excellent.
3. Rowing gives exercise to the muscles in the upper part of the body. Swimming gives exercise to muscles throughout the body.
4. Trailers are homes on wheels. People often use them on vacations.
5. Many American towns have the same names as places in Europe. Others have Native American names.
6. Magical fairies in Scotland are called brownies. In Hawaii, impish fairies are called menahuni.
7. Kindergarten, school for young children, originated in Germany in the nineteenth century. Its name means "children's garden."
8. Van works in New York City. He lives in New Jersey.
9. My mother led our Scout meeting last week. She taught us how to tie several kinds of knots.
10. Ancient Greek myths tell stories of gods and heroes. These stories still entertain us today.
11. Robyn Lee Patterson has a complete set of Nancy Drew mysteries. She seldom lends them to anyone.
12. Bison were once almost extinct. They are now thriving in places on the Great Plains.
13. Jonathan Swift's *Gulliver's Travels* is a fantasy for children. It is a criticism of society.
14. Pencils are called "lead" pencils. They are made of graphite.
15. Young amphibians are water-dwelling animals without legs. Adult amphibians are air-breathing animals with four legs.

Complex Sentences

> A complex sentence contains one principal clause and one or more subordinate clause.

Orangutans, which are a kind of ape, walk along tree branches.

In the sentence above, the principal idea is *orangutans walk along tree branches.* These words form the principal, or independent, clause. Another clause, of less importance, explains for the reader what orangutans are: *which are a kind of ape.* It is called a subordinate, or dependent, clause. The independent clause forms a complete sentence in itself. A subordinate clause is not complete.

> Subordinate clauses in complex sentences can be adjectival or adverbial.

Li, *who is twelve*, has a paper route. (*Adjectival clause*)
When it was first rung, the Liberty Bell cracked. (*Adverbial clause*)

Exercise 152

Identify the principal and subordinate clauses in the following complex sentences.

1. Because its water is cold and choppy, not many people have successfully swum across the English Channel.
2. Rainbow Bridge, which is the longest natural bridge, is in Utah.
3. Volleyball is a game in which players hit a ball across a net.
4. When Gilda opened the freezer door, the contents slid out.
5. Meteorologists, who study weather, use radar and satellites.
6. Van gets tangled in the telephone cord whenever he talks on the phone and walks around the kitchen.
7. Polaris, which is often called the North Star, is always due north.
8. A pentagon is a figure that has five sides.
9. When reporter Nelly Bly traveled around the world in 1889 in slightly over seventy-two days, she beat the eighty-day mark of Jules Verne's character Phileas Fogg.
10. Langston Hughes wrote short stories and plays although he is best known for his poetry.

EXERCISE 152: Have the students identify the clauses as adjectival or adverbial. For each adjectival clause, they should name the relative pronoun and its antecedent. For each adverbial clause, have them give the relationship (time, manner, comparison, etc.) between the two clauses. (Refer to writing chapter 3, lesson 3, for the meaning of subordinate conjunctions.)

ANSWERS
The subordinate clauses are underlined; the principal clause is the rest of the sentence.

EXERCISE 153: Before they complete sentences 1-10, have the students tell whether the clause will be adjectival or adverbial. In sentences 11-20, have them put the letters *S* and *P* over the subject and predicate of each subordinate clause.

Exercise 153

Complete the subordinate clauses in the following to produce complex sentences.

1. Since _____, the science experiment failed.
2. The bat is an animal that _____.
3. People waited anxiously as _____.
4. Dozens of chickens flew frenziedly out of their cages when _____.
5. She told the story that _____.
6. Edgar visited his sister Peg, who _____.
7. If _____, we may go sledding.
8. Open the envelope that _____.
9. William Shakespeare, who _____, lived in the 1500s.
10. Do not open your eyes until _____.

Use the following groups of words as subordinate clauses in complex sentences.

11. that ran down the stairs
12. as the long-awaited day approached
13. which the Chinese invented
14. that followed me home
15. before the chandelier began to sway
16. when the train left the station
17. which everyone wants to see
18. who can recite the alphabet backwards in almost one breath
19. if I could choose two things to take on a desert island
20. about which we studied in class

Exercise 154

Combine these simple sentences into complex sentences.

1. In winter, some mammals go into a deep sleep. This sleep is called hibernation.
2. My sister visited Venice. She rode in a gondola along the Grand Canal.
3. *The Nutcracker* is a famous ballet. It is often performed during the holiday season.
4. King Arthur was a mythical ruler of England. He has long been a popular subject of fiction and drama.
5. I tried cleaning the spot off my sweater. The spot just grew bigger.
6. Van Gogh painted *Sunflowers*. A copy of the picture hangs in our room.
7. Ocean currents are important to weather. The currents influence the climate of the nearby land.
8. The first working submarine was built in 1620. It was a wooden frame covered with greased leather.
9. The golden hamster is an attractive pet. It is active mostly at night.
10. That clock annoys me. It chimes every fifteen minutes.
11. Vatican City is in Rome. It is the smallest independent state in the world.
12. To the Chinese, the dragon was a positive force. It brought the spring rain.
13. I called the box office. I got a recorded message.
14. *Graffiti* refers to writing on walls. It comes from the Italian word for "scratchings."
15. Grammar is taught in schools throughout the world. It is the study of the structure of a language.

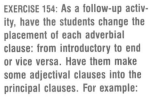

EXERCISE 154: As a follow-up activity, have the students change the placement of each adverbial clause: from introductory to end or vice versa. Have them make some adjectival clauses into the principal clauses. For example:

King Arthur, *who was a mythical ruler of England,* has long been a popular subject of fiction and drama.

King Arthur, *who has long been a popular subject of fiction and drama,* was a mythical ruler of England.

ANSWERS

Answers will vary. Accept any logical sentences with clauses. The following are the relative pronouns and subordinate conjunctions that would most likely be used in the combined sentences.
1. that
2. who; when
3. which
4. who
5. when
6. (of) which
7. which; because
8. which
9. which; although
10. which; because
11. which
12. which; because
13. when
14. which
15. which

Exercise 155

Identify each of the following sentences as *simple, compound,* or *complex.*

1. Thu-Minh came to the United States one year ago.
2. Before Thu-Minh came to America, she played several sports.
3. Thu-Minh was good at sports, but she had never swum.
4. Her country, which was an inland one, had no beaches.
5. In her country, water was scarce; therefore, it was conserved.
6. Although Thu-Minh had never even seen a swimming pool, she signed up for lessons at the local community center.
7. She anxiously awaited the day on which her lessons started.
8. At the center, she surveyed the Olympic-size pool.
9. Many children and adults were enjoying the water.
10. Thu-Minh saw some people who were holding on to the pool's sides.
11. She could easily understand their feelings of nervousness.
12. The instructor gathered the beginners together; then he spoke encouragingly to them.
13. They would start in the part of the pool that was not very deep.
14. With a bit of hesitation, Thu-Minh jumped into the pool.
15. At first, Thu-Minh, who felt cold, clung to the sides of the pool.
16. As she splashed about, the fear of the water gradually left her.
17. At her instructor's directions, she lay back and extended her arms.
18. The instructor demonstrated the basic swimming motions, and the class imitated them.
19. Thu-Minh felt relaxed in the water, but her swimming was jerky.
20. She needed more practice before she would swim smoothly.

Sharpening Your Skills

The paragraph below has only simple sentences. Combine some into compound or complex sentences.

Science fiction books often have extraordinary robots. These robots act like humans. Actual robots are not quite so extraordinary. Most robots in factories are like mechanical arms. They perform the same task over and over. This is not surprising. Even a seemingly simple action such as walking requires coordinating many muscles. Today you can buy a robot. You can put the robot together. The robot can play games. It can move about without bumping into things. Maybe in the future advances in "robotics" will be made. Then you will be able to buy better robots.

Chapter Challenge

Read the two paragraphs below and answer the questions that follow.

¹Jason's ship, which was called the *Argo*, slipped through the narrow channel. ²He and his crew of fifty were now in the waters of the enemy. ³Every hand was prepared for a dangerous mission. ⁴Were these veteran sailors afraid? ⁵No, they were set in their mission, the capture of the Golden Fleece.

⁶What dangers awaited them! ⁷First they had to slip through the Cyanean rocks, two immense boulders that crushed everything between them. ⁸This was accomplished through trickery, and Jason and the Argonauts arrived in the land of the Golden Fleece. ⁹There they subdued a race of skeleton warriors and gave a magic potion to the fire-breathing dragon that never slept. ¹⁰Now out of danger, Jason and his crew seized the Golden Fleece, concealed it aboard the *Argo*, and returned safely home.

1. Name the subordinate clause in the first sentence. Is it used as an adjectival or adverbial clause? Is it restrictive or nonrestrictive?
2. Find a sentence in the first paragraph with a compound element.
3. Is the fourth sentence in the natural or the transposed order?
4. Identify the compound subject of the tenth sentence.
5. Find an adverbial phrase and an adjectival phrase in the second sentence.
6. Is there an exclamatory sentence in the story? If so, identify it.
7. Identify two adverbial phrases in the eighth sentence.
8. Is the eighth sentence compound or complex?
9. How is the phrase *of skeleton warriors* in the ninth sentence used?
10. Is the last sentence simple, compound, or complex?

Creative Space 7

The Presence

Something went crabwise
across the snow this morning.
Something went hard and slow
over our hayfield.
It could have been a raccoon
lugging a knapsack,
it could have been a porcupine
carrying a tennis racket,
it could have been something
supple as a red fox
dragging the squawk and spatter
of a crippled woodcock.
Ten knuckles underground
those bones are seeds now
pure as baby teeth
lined up in the burrow.
I cross on snowshoes
cunningly woven from
the skin and sinews of
something else that went before.

Maxine Kumin

Exploring the Poem...

How does an animal move "crabwise"? Why would the animal in the poem be moving that way? What animals might have crossed the snow that morning?

The poet compares the bones of one animal to another object. To what object does she compare them? Such a direct comparison is called a *metaphor*.

In the last four lines, what observation does the poet make about snowshoes? What connection do the last four lines have with the rest of the poem?

For what reason might the poem be titled "The Presence"?

★ Have you ever seen the tracks of an animal? Were they in the snow, sand, or mud? Tracks give evidence that an animal has been there. Have you wondered where the animal was coming from or where it was going? Might it have run away when it sensed your presence? Write a poem using "The Presence" as a model, but providing your own original observations about the scene and the animal.

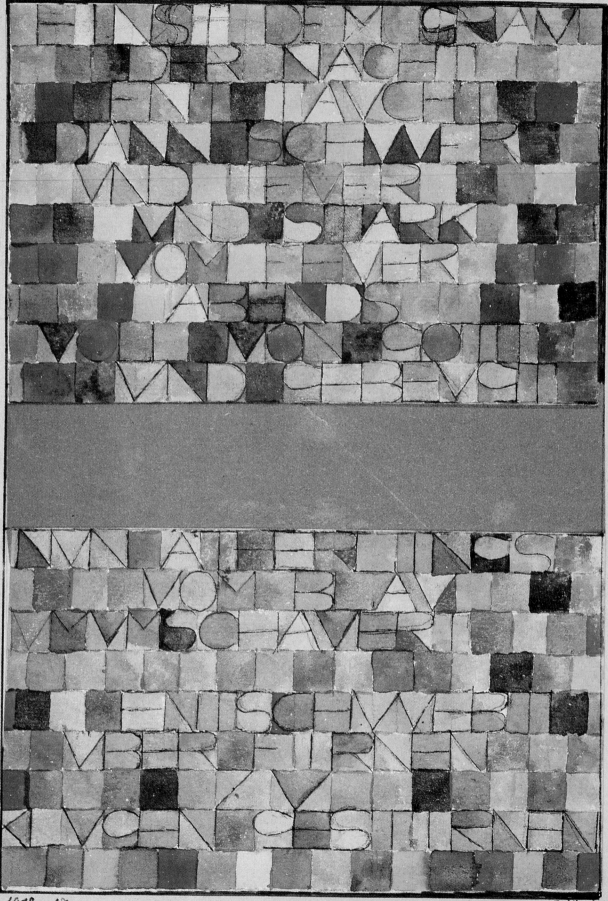

Chapter 8

Punctuation and Capitalization

Lesson 1 Periods and Commas

Punctuation helps make the meaning of written words clear. In speaking, the inflection of a person's voice helps convey the message. In writing, punctuation takes the place of a person's voice and tone. This chapter presents basic rules for punctuation and capitalization.

The Period

Use a period
  1. at the end of a declarative or an imperative sentence

      Labor Day is in September.   Close the door.

  2. after an abbreviation or an initial

      M.D.   Pearl S. Buck

Exercise 156

Add periods where needed in the following items. Note that not all items are sentences.
  1. "One oz.of chocolate" were the words in the recipe.
  2. Several of S.E.Hinton's books have been made into movies.
  3. As we tried to balance ourselves on the slippery log
  4. Open the larger package first, Therese.
  5. What do the letters Ph.D.after a name mean?
  6. The monarch butterflies formed an interesting pattern in flight.
  7. G.K.Chesterton created the fictional detective Father Brown.
  8. Having made it, out of breath, to the finish line
  9. The package was addressed to Mr.and Mrs.Brian J.Davis.
  10. It's not often I can put Feb.29 on the top of my paper.

Sometimes even words in our own language fail to communicate our real feelings. Words can become a wall rather than a bridge. Has this ever happened to you?

The Comma

Use a comma

1. to separate words or groups of words in a series

> Pat, Jason, and Barb were the three students elected.
> Calvin Reed traveled by boat, by train, and by airplane on his trip around the world.

2. to set off a short direct quotation and the parts of a divided quotation, unless an interrogation point or an exclamation point is required

> "Australia is the smallest continent," explained the geographer.
> "I will spend my time," said Will, "preparing for the game."
> "Have you ever read *Percy Wynne*?" asked Janet.
> "What a pretty picture!" exclaimed Marcia.

3. to separate independent elements and words of direct address

> Yes, we will attend the play.
> Team, are we ready?

4. to set off parts of dates, addresses, or geographical names

> We moved to Savannah, Georgia, on December 1, 1986.

5. to separate nonrestrictive phrases and clauses from the rest of the sentence

> The sail, torn by the wind, was mended by the sailors.
> Ernest Hemingway, who wrote *The Old Man and the Sea*, was born near Chicago.

A *nonrestrictive* phrase or clause is one that may be omitted from the sentence without changing its meaning. Some phrases or clauses cannot be omitted without changing the meaning of the sentence. These are called *restrictive* phrases or clauses and are not set off by commas.

> The hospital at which my father works is on Front Street.

A restrictive clause changes the meaning of the sentence by *restricting* or *limiting* the meaning of some word in the sentence, usually the subject or the direct object. If you say, "The students, who are ready, may leave now," you are speaking of *all* students and you mean that they are all ready. If you omitted the commas,

you would not be speaking of *all* students, but of those *only* who are ready. You would imply, therefore, that some students are *not* ready.

Tell why commas are used in this sentence.

> Lead, which is heavier than water, sinks rapidly.

6. after long introductory phrases and introductory clauses and when needed to make the meaning clear

> While the anthem was playing, the fans stood quietly.
> After eating, the horse left the pasture.

7. to set off an appositive that is not part of the name or that is not restrictive

> George Egan, the coach of our team, taught us a new play.
> The emperor Napoleon crowned himself in 1804. (*Napoleon* is restrictive, and so commas are not needed.)

8. to set off a parenthetical expression; that is, a word or a group of words inserted in the sentence as a comment or an explanatory remark, and one that is not necessary to the thought of the sentence

> This is, I tell you, a pleasant task.

Some of the common parenthetical expressions are

of course	I admit	in fact	as you know
indeed	it is true	in truth	no doubt
I assure you	in general	however	notwithstanding

9. to separate the clauses of a compound sentence connected by the conjunctions *and, but, or, nor, yet*

> We waited at the station, yet the train did not come.

If the clauses are short and closely connected, the comma may be omitted.

> Matt called and I answered immediately.

10. after the salutation in a social letter and after the complimentary close in all letters

> Dear Francis,   Sincerely yours,   Very truly yours,

Exercise 157

Explain the use of commas in each of the following sentences.

1. Walt Disney, a pioneer of film cartoons, created Mickey Mouse in the 1920s.
2. Porcupines eat bark, leaves, and twigs all at once!
3. Marian asked, "Where did you put the cat food?"
4. Thomas Jefferson and John Adams both died on July 4, 1826.
5. My friends and I are planning a canoe trip this weekend, and we will sleep outside two nights.
6. I, as you probably know, learned to ski at the age of seven.
7. Eleanor of Aquitaine, who lived in the twelfth century, was queen of both England and France.
8. Although they are called "flying squirrels," the animals actually glide.
9. Yes, my favorite soup is cream of asparagus.
10. Fireworks were first used in warfare, but now they are used for entertainment.

Exercise 158

Copy the following sentences, adding periods and commas where needed.

1. The charter of the United Nations was signed on June 26, 1945.
2. There will be performances of the school play on Thursday, Friday, and Saturday.
3. Pass me the road map, Joan.
4. Cork, which is lighter than water, floats easily.
5. It was, I assure you, the last time I will try the trampoline.
6. I ran to the window, but the truck was already pulling away.
7. Wolves have remarkably keen sight, hearing, and smell.
8. Alice Walker, a black writer, wrote *The Color Purple*.
9. The address on the package was Abracadabra Magic Co., 417 Market St., Norfolk, Va.
10. Linda, I'd like to present my friend B. J. Rago.

11. Pluto, discovered in 1930, is usually the planet farthest from the sun.
12. When athletes in ancient Greece won contests, they received crowns of leaves.
13. Oahu is the third-largest island of Hawaii, and it has most of that state's population.
14. William Shakespeare, who is considered the greatest writer in the English language, died on April 23, 1616.
15. Jamal, no doubt, will order two hamburger platters for himself.
16. No, I have not read *Treasure Island*.
17. The store rented skis, boots, skates, and other winter sporting equipment.
18. After I finished my social studies assignment, I treated myself to a glass of apple juice.
19. Mary Lou Retton, an American gymnast, was a star of the 1984 Summer Olympics.
20. Bronco, which is a cowboy's term for an untamed horse, means "wild" in Spanish.

Sharpening Your Skills

Write a sentence illustrating each of the rules listed below.

Use a comma
1. to set off a nonrestrictive phrase
2. to separate nouns in a series
3. to set off dates
4. to set off a parenthetical expression
5. after an introductory phrase or clause
6. to separate clauses of a compound sentence
7. to set off a brief quotation
8. to illustrate direct address
9. to set off an appositive
10. in a geographical name

SHARPENING YOUR SKILLS: The students may combine as many of these rules as possible. A date, a geographical name, and a name in direct address could be included within a direct quotation. Put sentences on the chalkboard for discussion and clarification.

Lesson 2 Other Types of Punctuation <u>Part I</u>

The Semicolon

Use a semicolon
1. to separate the clauses of a compound sentence when they are not separated by a coordinate conjunction

   The beach was deserted; the swimmers had gone for lunch.

2. to separate the clauses of a compound sentence that are connected by *nevertheless, moreover, therefore, then,* or *thus*

   Roland was here early; nevertheless, I did not see him.

3. before *as* and *namely* when these words introduce an example or an illustration

   The truck lacked one thing; namely, comfort.

Exercise 159

Add semicolons where needed in the following sentences.
1. Richard's watch has three hands; mine has only two.
2. Charlotte Brontë was an English novelist of the nineteenth century; her sister Emily also wrote a famous novel.
3. Plantain is a green fruit; it is a common food in the tropics.
4. The band decided to use some stringed instruments; namely, violins, violas, and cellos.
5. Baseball is an international sport; it is popular in Latin America, Japan, and the United States.
6. Josie washed the car; moreover, she vacuumed the interior.
7. I have not seen the article; therefore, I cannot comment on it.
8. Buttons have been made from many unusual materials; namely, bone, oatmeal, feathers, and hair.
9. James baked three dozen cupcakes for the fund-raiser; all were sold.
10. Rodents spread disease and cause destruction; therefore, they are disliked by many people.

11. My older sister lives in Dallas; my older brother has recently moved to Maine.
12. American children wait for Santa Claus on December 24; Saint Nicholas brings gifts to children of northern Europe on the night of December 5.
13. Yesterday Allison received a camera for her birthday; she has already used two rolls of film.
14. Tim wanted to try the experiment; however, he needed baking soda.
15. Some words have the same form in the singular and in the plural; namely, sheep, trout, and deer.

The Colon

Use a colon
1. after the salutation of a business letter

> Dear Ms. Clarke: Dear Sir or Madam:

2. before a list or enumeration of items

> For this cake, I need the following: butter, eggs, sugar, and flour.

3. before a long direct quotation

> The speaker concluded as follows: "The candidate is trustworthy, honest, and sincere. She is deserving of your vote for the office."

Exercise 160

Copy the following, adding colons as needed. Give the reason for the use of a colon in each case.
1. The following supplies are needed: chalk, eraser, paper, and ink.
2. The parts of speech are as follows: noun, pronoun, verb, adjective, adverb, conjunction, preposition, and interjection.
3. Henry David Thoreau wrote the following: "Why should we be in such desperate haste to succeed, and in such desperate enterprises? If a man does not keep pace with his companions, perhaps it is because he hears a different drummer."
4. Arrange the following words in alphabetical order: *declare, diamond, dream, daring, decide.*
5. Dear Madam:

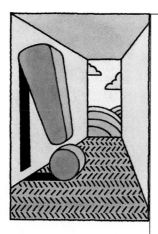

The Exclamation Point

Use an exclamation point
  1. after an exclamatory sentence

     What a beautiful landscape lies before us!

  2. after an exclamatory word, phrase, or clause

     "Order in the court!" shouted the judge.
     Careful! Don't drop the eggs.

The Interrogation Point

Use an interrogation point at the end of a question.

  How many meters are there in a kilometer?

Exercise 161

Add exclamation or interrogation points as needed in the following sentences.
  1. When does the sale end?
  2. Hooray!Your darts have hit the bull's-eye five times in a row.
  3. Do you prefer fiction or nonfiction?
  4. How crowded the pool is!
  5. I don't believe that story!
  6. Where is the Caspian Sea?
  7. Ouch!That pan is hot.
  8. Listen!Is that the ice-cream truck?
  9. How long this shortcut seems!
  10. Oh!The moths ate holes through my favorite wool coat.

Sharpening Your Skills

You are entering a contest entitled "The Perfect Student." Write a letter telling the officials why you are the perfect student. Write sentences that use the marks of punctuation presented in this lesson.

Lesson 3 Other Types of Punctuation <u>Part II</u>

Quotation Marks and Underlining

Use quotation marks

1. before and after every direct quotation and every part of a divided quotation

> Columbus said, "I believe the earth is round."
> "I believe," Columbus said, "the earth is round."

Sometimes a quotation includes another quotation. The included quotation is known as a *quotation within a quotation* and is marked with single quotation marks.

> Clare asked, "Was it Lincoln who said, 'With malice towards none; with charity for all'?"

2. to enclose titles of stories, poems, magazine articles, newspaper articles, television shows, and radio programs

> John Greenleaf Whittier is the author of "Snow-Bound."

Titles of books, magazines, movies, works of art, and newspapers are printed in italics. In typing or handwriting, italics are indicated by underlining.

> *The Oregon Trail* is a story of pioneer days.
> <u>The Oregon Trail</u> is a story of pioneer days.

THE STUDENTS SHOULD LEARN
—the proper use of quotation marks, apostrophe, hyphen, and dash

TEACHING THE LESSON
Spend as much time as needed on quotation marks. Have the students model sentences after ones in the introduction. Find selections of dialogue in novels and short stories and have the students practice placing the speaker at the beginning, in the middle, and at the end of the quotation. These selections should be written on a sheet of paper so that they can practice using the various marks of punctuation. For follow-up material, use the activities on pages 92-93, dealing with writing dialogue.

Encourage the students to think of other examples to illustrate the use of the apostrophe, hyphen, and dash.

EXERCISE 162: Have the students do this exercise on a sheet of paper, and let volunteers put the sentences on the chalkboard. Check for accuracy in the use of quotation marks.

Exercise 162

Copy each of the following sentences, and add the needed punctuation: quotations, underlining, and any of the other punctuation marks studied in this chapter.

1. "The grocery list is on the refrigerator," said Mom.
2. "Have you told anyone else?" asked Amy.
3. "I," bragged Erica, "got one hundred on the English test."
4. Ogden Nash wrote "The Panther" and many other humorous poems about animals.
5. The Phantom Tollbooth is a novel popular with children.
6. "I can't believe I forgot to bring my notes," said the teacher of the class on improving one's memory.
7. Wayne asked, "Are you going anywhere during spring break?"
8. Diane commented, "Many people were deeply moved when Martin Luther King said, 'I have a dream.'"
9. We read Shirley Jackson's short story "The Lottery."
10. My favorite television program is "The Cosby Show."
11. "There was never a good war," wrote Benjamin Franklin, "or a bad peace."
12. "After I threw out the trash, did the dishes, and watered the lawn," Robert explained, "I was too tired to shoot baskets."
13. The movie Friendly Persuasion was based on stories by Jessamyn West about a Quaker family.
14. I read an article about camels in Australia in a recent issue of National Geographic.
15. The teacher said, "Explain the proverb 'A penny saved is a penny earned.'"
16. Emily Dickinson wrote, "Success is counted sweetest by those who ne'er succeed."
17. I titled my short story about baseball "Daffy Demon on the Mound."
18. The Daily Herald had an article about my neighbors' pet skunk.
19. Henry asked, "Did you think it funny when the teacher said, 'Keep it down to a roar'?"
20. Picasso's Three Musicians is one of the most famous paintings of the twentieth century.

The Apostrophe

Use an apostrophe
1. to show possession

   The children's library is open today.

2. with *s* to show the plural of letters

   e's   *a*'s   *s*'s

3. to show the omission of a letter, letters, or numbers

   wouldn't   we'll   spirit of '76

The Hyphen

Use a hyphen
1. to divide a word at the end of a line whenever syllables are carried to the next line

   Many locomotives run on power supplied by electricity from overhead cables.

2. in compound numbers from twenty-one to ninety-nine

   He is thirty-two years old.

3. to separate the parts of some compound words

   self-made   cross-examination   mother-in-law

The Dash

Use a dash to indicate a sudden change of thought.

   Toby came early—an unusual thing for him.

EXERCISE 163: This exercise reviews all marks of punctuation. Encourage the students to explain the reasons for the use of each mark.

Exercise 163

Copy the following sentences, and add the proper punctuation. All forms of punctuation studied in this chapter will be used.

1. Bach, Mozart, and Beethoven are considered the three giants of musical composition.
2. Have you ever traveled in the West, Joan?
3. Our club needs the following office equipment: a typewriter, a filing cabinet, and a calculator.
4. I have just finished reading Dr. Jekyll and Mr. Hyde by Robert Louis Stevenson.
5. The tiger and the lion are members of the cat family; however, they do not purr.
6. The band instruments, uniforms, and banners arrived just in time for the rally.
7. "Who won the game?" Jessica asked.
8. We're having a surprise party for Dad's thirty-ninth birthday.
9. The teacher, it seems, was very busy; he did not correct our compositions.
10. The class of '89 will be going to Springfield for a school trip.
11. There are two c's and two m's in *accommodate*.
12. Texas, the largest state after Alaska, lies north of Mexico.
13. Beverly had the hairdresser cut her hair short—very short.
14. On reaching the North Pole, Robert Peary supposedly said, "This scene my eyes will never see again."
15. Simon Legree was the villain in Harriet Beecher Stowe's famous novel called Uncle Tom's Cabin.
16. Star Wars, The Return of the Jedi, and The Empire Strikes Back form a set of three popular movies.
17. The school cafeteria is a self-service one, and it has a fair selection of sandwiches and hot dishes.
18. When I was in the school play, I was so nervous that I couldn't remember some of my lines.
19. Didn't you know that her nickname of P.J. comes from Patricia Jane?
20. A gust of wind, a loud banging of the doors, and the rattling of the cabin windows foretold the approach of the storm.
21. Instead of sweets, many Europeans eat cheese at the end of a meal.
22. Why did Maya Angelou title her autobiography I Know Why the Caged Bird Sings?
23. "The important thing," wrote Albert Einstein, "is not to stop questioning."

24. "David, watch me go down the slide," his little sister called out.
25. Stevie Wonder, a star of soul music, had a hit at the age of thirteen with the song "Fingertips."
26. While she was rubbing lotion on her rash for poison ivy, Liz said, "This is the last time I'll hike in the woods."
27. "Remember the saying 'All that glitters is not gold,'" warned Carol.
28. Chicago had a light snowfall in June—a very rare occurrence for that city.
29. "How good these brownies taste!" exclaimed Hal.
30. The problem, I think, is with the ignition.

Sharpening Your Skills

Have a conversation with another student about your favorite hobby, sport, or what you have done or plan to do on the weekend. After you talk, write down (transcribe) what you said. Check your punctuation carefully.

Lesson 4 Capitalization

Use a capital letter for
1. the first word in a sentence

> The trees cast inky pools on the silvery lawn.

2. the first word of every line of poetry

> The wind and the wave, the wave and the wind,
> Beat and dazzle me glad and blind…

(Some modern poets do not follow this rule.)

3. the first word of a direct quotation

> Rosemary answered, "My new afghan is made of many colors."

4. proper nouns and proper adjectives

These include particular persons or groups of persons, religious denominations, political parties, institutions, buildings, cities, states, streets, months of the year, days of the week, and holidays.

Michael	St. Valentine's Day	Republican party
Canadian geese	Mormon	American colleges

5. titles of honor and respect when preceding the name

    Queen Victoria   Judge Pawluk   Aunt Ida

Do not capitalize any title not followed by a proper noun unless it is used in direct address as a substitute for the name.

    The coach is in the gymnasium.
    What is the next play, Coach?

6. *north, south, east* and *west* when they refer to sections of a country

    She lived in the South.

7. the abbreviations A.D. (anno Domini—the year of the Lord) and B.C. (before Christ); A.M. (ante meridiem—before noon) and P.M. (post meridiem—after noon)

    The Roman Empire collapsed in A.D. 476.
    The legendary founding of Rome is 753 B.C.
    The work day began at 9 A.M. and ended at 5 P.M.

8. all names referring to the deity, the Bible, parts of the Bible, and other sacred books

    The Talmud consists of commentaries on Jewish law.

9. the principal words in the titles of books, plays, poems, and pictures

    Tennyson wrote "The Charge of the Light Brigade."

10. the pronoun *I* and the interjection *O*

    O John, I do appreciate your kindness.

11. abbreviations when capitals would be used if the words were written in full

    U.S.A.   Dr.   Ave.   Jan.

12. two-letter abbreviations for each state

    KS Kansas PA Pennsylvania OR Oregon

(A complete list of abbreviations is on page 136.)

Do *not* capitalize
1. the seasons of the year

    winter   spring   summer   fall

2. the articles *a, an, the,* conjunctions, or prepositions in titles, unless one of these is the first word

> We dramatized "The Man without a Country."

3. the names of studies, unless they are derived from proper nouns

> history   arithmetic   Spanish

4. the words *high school, college,* and *university,* unless they are parts of the names of particular institutions

> My brother goes to college in Boston.
> My brother goes to Boston College.

Exercise 164

Give the number of the rule that applies to the use of each capital letter in the following sentences.

1. Next summer Alice will go to Texas to visit her grandparents.
2. The headquarters of the United Nations is in New York.
3. The astronaut Neil Armstrong said, "That's one small step for a man, one giant leap for mankind."
4. The peso is the name of Mexican currency.
5. Did you read the poem "The Wind Told Me a Secret"?
6. The person speaking on nutrition is Dr. Clare Pennock from Richardson Hospital.
7. The quality of mercy is not strained;
   It droppeth as the gentle rain from heaven
   Upon the place beneath.
8. The Florentine artist Michelangelo made a famous statue of Moses, a prophet in the Bible.
9. The ancient Greeks regarded Hercules as their most powerful warrior.
10. The writer of *The Mill on the Floss* was Mary Ann Evans, whose pen name was George Eliot.
11. Where are the Apennines located?
12. The Rock of Gibraltar guards the passage from the Atlantic Ocean to the Mediterranean Sea.
13. The largest Egyptian pyramid was built about 2600 B.C.
14. Many British coins have a portrait of Queen Elizabeth II on them.
15. Many pioneers traveled to the West in covered wagons.

EXERCISE 164: The students can give the number of the rule or tell the reason for the use of the capital letter.

ANSWERS
1. Next (rule 1); Alice, Texas (rule 4)
2. The (rule 1); United Nations, New York (rule 4)
3. The (rule 1); Neil Armstrong (rule 4); That (rule 3)
4. The (rule 1); Mexican (rule 4)
5. Did (rule 1); "The Wind Told Me a Secret" (rule 9)
6. The (rule 1); Dr. (rule 11); Clare Pennock, Richardson Hospital (rule 4)
7. The, It, Upon (rule 2)
8. The (rule 1); Florentine, Michelangelo, Moses (rule 4); Bible (rule 8)
9. The (rule 1); Greeks, Hercules (rule 4)
10. The (rule 1); *The Mill on the Floss* (rule 9); Mary Ann Evans, George Eliot (rule 4)
11. Where (rule 1); Apennines (rule 4)
12. The (rule 1); Rock, Gibraltar, Atlantic Ocean, Mediterranean Sea (rule 4)
13. The (rule 1); Egyptian (rule 4); B.C. (rule 7)
14. Many (rule 1); British (rule 4); Queen (rule 5); Elizabeth (rule 4)
15. Many (rule 1); West (rule 6)

EXERCISE 165: Have the students write the sentences on the chalkboard. They should be able to support the use of every capital letter.

ANSWERS
The first letter of each word that requires capitalization is underlined three times

Exercise 165

Copy the following sentences, capitalizing words as necessary.

1. Students can take spanish or french lessons at school before regular classes begin.
2. In recent years, many americans have moved to the south or west.
3. ted and i went to the american museum of natural history to see the dinosaur exhibit last saturday.
4. My sister rhonda is studying mathematics at the university of michigan.
5. Do you think many people have read the entire bible?
6. Hanna asked mr. violeto, "would you please repeat the date?"
7. Apparently the planet venus rotates backwards.
8. In the painting *the song of the lark,* the lark is not visible.
9. Did you see the leaning tower of pisa when you were in italy?
10. My parents are friends of dr. hamid, who is the principal of whitman high school.
11. I have just read *a high wind in jamaica*.
12. The american flag is folded into the shape of a three-cornered hat, as a tribute to soldiers who fought in the american revolution.
13. The colosseum, the huge arena in rome, was completed in a.d. 80.
14. The highest peak in the east is mount mitchell in north carolina.
15. The address of the white house is 1600 pennsylvania avenue, washington, d.c.

Sharpening Your Skills

SHARPENING YOUR SKILLS: The students might like to work in pairs on this project. They will need to use library resources to gather information. (Refer to writing chapter 8, on the use of the library.) Encourage them to make their work attractive and interesting and to proofread their work before the project is handed in.

You are a tour guide taking a group to a foreign country. Create a pamphlet or brochure that tells

the date of departure and return
the airline—departure and arrival times (both ways)
the accommodations included
places to be visited
famous people to be met

Chapter Challenge

All the punctuation marks and capital letters are missing from the selection shown below. Copy the paragraphs onto a sheet of paper and insert the proper punctuation and capitalization.

my cousins olive, helen, oliver, and little dick all stopped eating and looked at one another and then looked at uncle dick and aunt emma. when aunt emma smiled, they smiled, too. everybody seemed happy because uncle dick, who had just come from blakesburg, had found a way to sell the farm. everybody was happy but me. i was sorry uncle dick was going to sell the farm.

"this farm is just as good as sold!" uncle dick talked on. "i've got a real estate man, my old friend melvin spencer, coming here tomorrow to look the place over. he's goin' to sell it for me."

"i'd like to get enough for it to make a big payment on a fine house in blakesburg," aunt emma said. "i've got the one picked out that i want. it's the beautiful coswell house. i understand it's up for sale now and no one's livin' in it!"

"gee, that will be wonderful," cousin olive said. "right on the street and not any mud. we wouldn't have to wear galoshes all winter if we lived there!"

"i'll say it will be wonderful," helen said, with a smile, "daddy, i hope mr. spencer can sell this place."

from "This Farm for Sale" by Jesse Stuart

CHAPTER CHALLENGE: This activity will give substantial practice in punctuation and capitalization. It is best to have the students read the selection three or four times to gain a sense of what is being communicated. Discuss the areas that contain dialogue: who is the speaker and what are the exact words of the speaker. You might wish to tell the students that the author used three exclamation points and a set of dashes. Have them work on the selection independently and then in pairs. If desired, have the selection duplicated for the students so that they can use proofreading symbols to mark the errors. You might also prepare a copy showing the punctuation as actually used in Stuart's story.

ANSWERS
The correct punctuation is included in the text. (Capitals are underlined three times.)

Creative Space 8

Speaking from Experience

Identical twins
are often
alike in
many ways:
same color
of hair
and eyes
(same giggle
some say)
same size
of shoes
and gloves.
Yet in
other ways
each twin
is so
unique—
separate—
different—
alone.
I know.
I am
one.

Exploring the Poem...

Originally the words in the poem on the opposite page were written in ordinary paragraph form.

   Identical twins are often alike in many ways: same color of hair and eyes (same giggle, some say), same size of shoes and gloves. Yet in other ways, each twin is completely unique, separate, different, and alone. I know. I am one.

Think about why the poem is structured as it is. How many words are on most of the lines? How does this structure reflect the meaning of the poem?

Which words are placed by themselves on separate lines? How does the arrangement add to the meaning of the poem?

The words at the end of the poem are "I am one." How does the line sum up the meaning of the last part of the poem? How does the line relate to the first part of the poem?

★ Think of any topic that somehow relates to a *number*. Write a short paragraph on the topic. Choose the best parts to include in a poem. Use the number suggested by the topic to structure the poem. To fit the number of words on a line, you may have to change or leave out some words.

Here are some possible topics:

a pair of parakeets a tricycle
a quartet of singers five basketball players
a six-pointed snowflake a seven-member family

Chapter 9

Model Diagrams

Diagrams show in a graphic manner the relationships that exist among the various words that make up a sentence. As you have seen, there are simple, compound, and complex sentences. Since sentences of all types may contain modifiers, no one form of diagram will serve for every kind of sentence. The diagrams given here are those that should help you in your work. When asked to diagram a sentence, look here for one of the same kind and see how the diagram is made.

The diagraming of sentences serves a double purpose. First, it makes it easier for you to understand the complete meaning of every sentence you read. Secondly, it helps you to write effectively and to avoid the use of faulty sentences. If you keep these purposes in mind, diagraming will improve your English. It should not become merely a mechanical exercise, but instead should help you to read more intelligently and to write more correctly.

Simple Sentences

Nominative Case

Subject: Carl's *birthday* is in September.

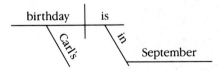

The artist has used lines in a very abstract way. How are lines in a sentence diagram used in a concrete way?

Subjective Complement: Monica is my *sister*.

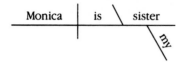

Address: *Team*, remember your signals.

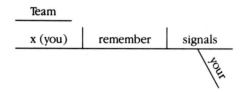

Apposition: Jean, my *friend*, will visit me.

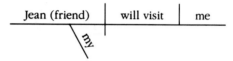

Objective Case

Direct Object: Emma took the *children* to the zoo.

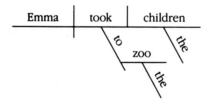

Object of a Preposition: The team ran onto the *field*.

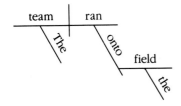

Indirect Object: We gave the *cabdriver* a generous tip.

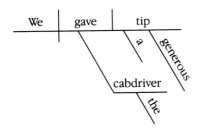

Apposition: We visited Cheyenne, the *capital* of Wyoming.

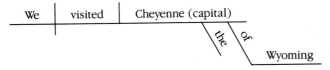

Adverbial Objective: They walked three *kilometers*.

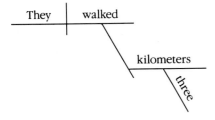

Compound Elements

Compound Subject: *Bridget* and *Helen* worked for the prize.

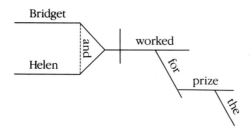

Compound Predicate: The entertainer *sang* and *danced*.

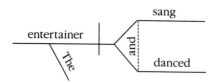

Compound Subject and Compound Predicate: The *cheerleaders* and the *fans applauded* and *shouted* loudly.

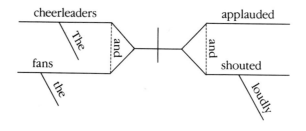

Compound Sentences

The camel is the ship of the desert, and the reindeer is the camel of the snow land.

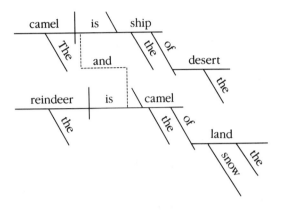

Gorillas may look fierce; however, they are quite timid.

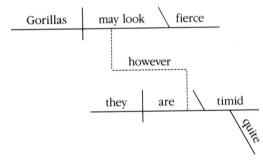

Complex Sentences

Adjectival Clauses

The school presented a play *that was very suspenseful*.

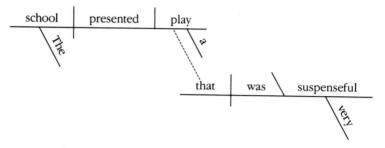

The company *for which my mother works* is having a picnic.

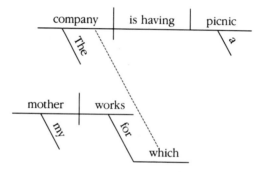

That is the student *whose poem won first prize*.

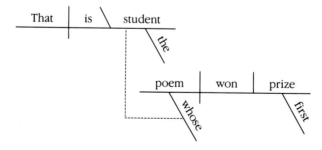

Adverbial Clauses

Because the weather was stormy, the campers postponed the hike.

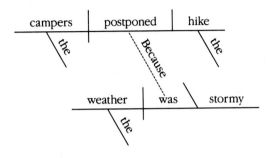

Index

D

Dashes, 445
Dates, use of commas in, 436
"Daybreak" (Longfellow), 174
Declarative sentences, 416
  use of periods to end, 435
Define, writing paragraphs that,
  76–77
Demonstrative adjectives, 294, 303
Demonstrative pronouns, 277
Dependent clauses, 56, 60, 406, 427
Descriptive adjectives, 287
Descriptive paragraphs, 81–82
  proofreading of, 85
  revising, 85
Descriptive writing
  personification in, 24–25
  and use of synonyms, 35–36
Details, in paragraph writing, 14–15
Dewey Decimal System, 189
Diagrams, 455
Dialogue, writing, 90–92
Diamond-shaped poem, 307
Dickinson, Emily, 162
Dictionary
  choosing right meaning, 199
  entries in, 198
  guide words in, 196
  use of alphabetical order in, 195
Dictionary of American Biography,
  208
Different from, 383
Differ from/differ with, 383
Direct address
  commas with, 436
  nouns used in, 231
Direct objects
  nouns used as, 238
  pronouns as, 254
Distributive adjectives, 294
Distributive pronouns, 279
  as antecedents, 280
  verb agreement with, 352
Doesn't, 343
"Dog at Night" (Untermeyer), 169
Don't, 343

E

Each, 279, 348
Editorial
  purpose of, 111
  writing of, 110–11
Either, 279
Encyclopedia, 203, 204–5
Ending sentences, 17–18
Envelope, addressing, 136–37
Etymology, 198
Every, 348
Exclamation points, 416, 442
Exclamatory sentences, 416
Exclamatory words, 442
Expletives, 375
Expository paragraphs, 75–77
  proofreading, 80
  revising, 80
extra-, 50

F

Facts, versus opinions, 110–11
Farther/further, 374
Feminine gender, 229
Fewer, 302
Fiction books, 187
Figures of speech
  metaphors, 433
  personification, 21, 24–25, 173,
    247
  simile, 379
Five Ws, in article writing, 108
Forms, completion of, 147
Friendly letters, 128–29
From, 383
Further/farther, 374
Future perfect tense, 332
Future tense, 331

G

Gender, of nouns, 229
George, Jean Craighead, 116
George, Phil, 360
Gibson, Walker, 162

These, 277, 303
This, 277, 303
Those, 277, 303
Time relationships, words
   expressing, 60
Title card, 192
Titles, personal, 448
Titles of written works
   creating for paragraph, 21
   use of capitalization in, 448
   use of quotation marks with, 443
   use of underlining with, 443
To/at, 384
Topic, selecting and narrowing, 1–2
Topic sentences, 4
   versus beginning sentences, 12
trans-, 50
Transition words, 32
   for adding comparison, 94
   for adding contrast, 95
   in writing how-to paragraphs,
     75–76
   in writing narrative paragraphs,
     86–87
Transitive verbs, 319
"Twistable, Turnable Man"
   (Silverstein), 172

U

Underlining, 443
Unity, 29
Unless/without, 395
Untermeyer, Louis, 169
Updike, John, 165
Usage
   adjectives vs. adverbs, after verbs,
     372
   agreement with distributive and
     indefinite pronouns, 280
   agreement of subject and verb,
     341–54
   comparative vs. superlative
     degree of adjectives, 298
   conjunctions vs. prepositions,
     394–95

demonstrative adjectives in the
   singular and plural, 303
farther vs. *further*, 374
fewer vs. *less*, 302
good vs. *well*, 372
like vs. *as/as if*, 395
nothing vs. *anything*, 282
prepositions, 383–84
pronouns as subjects and objects,
   251–60
repetition of the article, 296
unless vs. *without*, 394
who vs. *whom*, interrogative
  pronouns, 267
who vs. *whom*, relative pronouns,
  275

V

Verbs, 309
   active voice, 325
   agreement of subject and, 341,
     343, 344, 345, 347, 348, 349, 352,
     353
   auxiliary, 309
   compound tenses, 332
   conjugation of, 356–58
   contractions, 343
   imperative mood, 337
   indicative mood, 334–35
   intransitive, 321
   irregular, 311–13, 356–58
   linking, 323
   passive voice, 325, 327
   regular, 311
   simple tense, 330–31
   synopsis of, 359
   transitive, 319
   troublesome, 315–16
   words used as nouns and, 318
Vertical file, 203, 209
Vocabulary skills. *See also* Spelling
   homophones, 184
   synonyms, 16, 35–36
Voice, of verbs
   active, 325
   passive, 325, 327

Acknowledgments

Text

"Advice to Travelers" by Walker Gibson, from *Come As You Are* by Walker Gibson. Copyright (c) 1958. Reprinted by permission of Hastings House Publishers, Kampmann and Company. "Ambition" from *A Bowl of Bishop*. Copyright (c) 1954 by Morris Bishop. Reprinted by permission of Doubleday and Company, Inc. "Analysis of Baseball" by May Swenson is reprinted by permission of the author from *New and Selected Things Taking Place*. Copyright (c) 1971 by May Swenson. *Anchor* activity idea. Copyright (c) 1970. Courtesy of Educational Service, Inc. P.O. Box 219, Stevensville, Michigan 49127. "Bam, Bam, Bam" from *Catch a Little Rhyme* by Eve Merriam. Copyright (c) 1966 by Eve Merriam. All rights reserved. Reprinted by permission of Marian Reiner for the author. "Battle Won Is Lost" by Phil George, from *Voices from Wahkon-Tah*, Robert K. Dodge, Joseph B. McCullough, eds. Copyright (c) 1974, 1976. Reprinted by permission of International Publishers Co., Inc. Dictionary entries on pages 198-99 from *Scott, Foresman Advanced Dictionary*, E. L. Thorndike and Clarence L. Barnhart, authors. Reprinted by permission of Scott, Foresman and Company. "Dog at Night" from *Stars to Steer By* by Louis Untermeyer. Copyright (c) 1941 by Harcourt Brace Jovanovich, Inc. Reprinted by permission of the publisher. "The Hippopotamus" from *Verses from 1929 On* by Ogden Nash. Copyright (c) 1935 by Ogden Nash. First appeared in *The Saturday Evening Post*. "Hope Is the Thing with Feathers" by Emily Dickinson. "Mother to Son," copyright (c) 1926 by Alfred A. Knopf, Inc. and renewed 1954 by Langston Hughes. Reprinted from *Selected Poems of Langston Hughes* by permission of Alfred A. Knopf, Inc. "Nonsense" by Jack Prelutsky, from *The Random House Book of Poetry for Children*, edited by Jack Prelutsky. Copyright (c) 1983 by Random House, Inc. Reprinted by permission of the publisher. "Pete at the Zoo" by Gwendolyn Brooks. Reprinted by permission of the author. Copyright (c) 1960 by Gwendolyn Brooks. "Pictures on the Flying Air" by Scott Alexander. Reprinted from *Instructor*, March, 1966. Copyright (c) 1966 by The Instructor Publications, Inc. Used by permission of the publisher. "The Presence" from *Our Ground Time Here Will Be Brief* by Maxine Kumin. Copyright (c) 1969 by Maxine Kumin. Reprinted by permission of Viking Penguin Inc. Excerpts taken from *The Red Pony* by John Steinbeck. Copyright (c) 1933, 1937, 1938 by John Steinbeck. Copyright renewed (c) 1961, 1965, 1966 by John Steinbeck. Reprinted by permission of Viking Penguin Inc. "September" from *A Child's Calendar* by John Updike. Copyright (c) 1965 by John Updike and Nancy Burkert. Reprinted by permission of Alfred A. Knopf, Inc. "Song of the Pop-Bottlers" by Morris Bishop, from *A Bowl of Bishop*. Copyright (c) 1954 by Morris Bishop. Reprinted by permission of Doubleday and Company, Inc. Excerpt taken from the short story, "This Farm for Sale" by Jesse Stuart. With permission of the Jesse Stuart Foundation/Judy B. Thomas, Chair., P.O. Box 391, Ashland, KY 40001. H.E. Richardson, Editor-in-Chief, Department of English, University of Louisville, Louisville, KY 40292. "Twistable, Turnable Man" from *A Light in the Attic* by Shel Silverstein. Copyright (c) 1981 by Snake Eye Music, Inc. Reprinted by permission of Harper & Row, Publishers, Inc.

Photographs

Cover: Index Stock International, Inc.

James L. Ballard, pages 248, 378; Baseball cards, courtesy A. U. Sports Memorabilia, Skokie, IL/ Photography, James L. Ballard, 2, 167; Fred Bavendam/Peter Arnold, Inc., 289; The Bettman Archive, 121, 158, 242, 268, 292, 331; Dennis Brokaw, 406; Bruce Curtis/Peter Arnold Inc., 288; Brown Brothers, 18, 66, 69, 339, 347; Owen Franken/Stock, Boston, 422; Courtesy: Rod Hanna, The Denver Broncos, 210–11; H. W. Hesselman/The Image Bank, 260; The Image Bank, 9, 38, 165, 192; Index Stock International, Inc., i, xvii–xix, 77, 162, 214–15, 308; Manfred Kage/Peter Arnold, Inc., 45; John Kelly/The Image Bank, 193; P. Edward Kent/Stock, Boston, 379; Robert Madden/Index Stock International, Inc., 160; Magnum Photos, Inc., 18, 377; Arthur Meyerson Photography, Inc., xx, 2, 47, 329, 363; F. S. Mitchell/Tom Stack & Associates, 161; NASA, 3, 158; Obremski/The Image Bank, 194; Brian Parker/Tom Stack & Associates, 9; Bryan F. Peterson Photography, 165, 173, 247, 432; Chuck Place/The Image Bank, 64–65; Jeff Scott/Tom Stack & Associates, 246; Olaf Sööt/Olaf Sööt Photography Associates, 164; Stock, Boston, 102, 367; Larry West, 103.

Fine Art

Illustrations

437, 438, 439, 441, 442, 443, 444, 445, 448, 449, 450, 451, 458, 459, 460, 461;   Joan Landis, 221, 227, 374, 375;   Eileen Mueller Neill, 40, 43, 78, 79, 110, 111, 321(T), 322, 407, 408;   Phil Renaud, 101, 102(M), 128, 129, 197, 429;   William A. Seabright, 17, 60(T), 92(T)(B), 93, 96, 120, 196, 204, 306, 307, 311, 312, 313, 316, 379, 425;   Slug Signorino, 15(T)(B), 16(T)(B), 17(T), 86(T)(B), 87(T)(B), 90(T)(B), 100(T), 108, 109, 297;   Lynn Westphal, 1, 14(B), 103, 118, 119, 124, 129, 131, 133, 134, 135, 138, 142, 143, 152.